COMHAIRLE CHONTAE ÁTHA CLIATH THEAS
SOUTH DUBLIN COUNTY LIBRARIES

LUCAN LIBRARY
TO RENEW ANY ITEM TEL:

Items should be returned on or before the last date below. Fines, as displayed in the Library, will be charged on overdue items.

The School Bag

edited by

SEAMUS HEANEY *and* TED HUGHES

faber and faber

First published in 1997
by Faber and Faber Limited
3 Queen Square London WC IN 3AU

Photoset by Wilmaset Ltd, Wirral
Printed in England by Clays Ltd, St Ives plc

A CIP record for this book
is available from the British Library

ISBN 0–571–17750–6 (cased)
0–571–17751–4 (pbk)

10 9 8 7 6 5 4 3 2 1

CONTENTS

FOREWORD *by* Seamus Heaney

We wanted this anthology to be different from *The Rattle Bag*, less of a carnival, more like a checklist. It would be a school-book in the usual sense – the poems, for example, are grouped in ways that invite different kinds of historical and thematic reading – but it would also resemble 'a school of poetry' gathered on traditional bardic lines, a memory bank, a compendium of examples. And yet there was always going to be a personal element at work in the selections because many of them would represent a homage to poets to whom we ourselves had 'gone to school' in one way or another from the beginning.

The anthology, in other words, is intended to be a kind of listening post, a book where the reader can tune in to the various notes and strains that have gone into the making of the whole score of poetry in English. The further inclusion of poems in translation from the Irish, Welsh and Scottish Gaelic languages was equally a matter of editorial principle and personal taste. It is only in the relatively recent past that there has been any developed awareness of the deep value and high potential of the non-English poetries of Britain and Ireland, so it seemed to us that some account of these basic elements would be both worthwhile and timely.

Considerations of space influenced our decision to take the one-poem-per-poet approach, but once we adopted it, we found a new point and edge to the problem of choosing representative work. Limiting the selection to a single item meant that the very meaning of the term 'representative' came under pressure. Time and again we were forced to decide whether personal affection for something not particularly 'major' could be allowed to outweigh the historical and canonical claims of a more obvious selection. Our decisions are going to be disputed, but these disputes should be another part of the book's contribution to the schooling of its readers. After all, what W. B. Yeats once called the 'singing school' is made up in the end of all of us who value poetry and want to remember it and make sense of it in our lives.

The School Bag

W. B. YEATS

[1939]

Long-legged Fly

That civilisation may not sink,
Its great battle lost,
Quiet the dog, tether the pony
To a distant post;
Our master Caesar is in the tent
Where the maps are spread,
His eyes fixed upon nothing,
A hand under his head.
Like a long-legged fly upon the stream
His mind moves upon silence.

That the topless towers be burnt
And men recall that face,
Move most gently if move you must
In this lonely place.
She thinks, part woman, three parts a child,
That nobody looks; her feet
Practise a tinker shuffle
Picked up on a street.
Like a long-legged fly upon the stream
Her mind moves upon silence.

That girls at puberty may find
The first Adam in their thought,
Shut the door of the Pope's chapel,
Keep those children out.
There on that scaffolding reclines
Michael Angelo.
With no more sound than the mice make
His hand moves to and fro.
Like a long-legged fly upon the stream
His mind moves upon silence.

ANONYMOUS (IRISH)

[6th century] ## Adze-head

Across the sea will come Adze-head,
crazed in the head,
his cloak with hole for the head,
his stick bent in the head.

He will chant impiety
from a table in the front of his house;
all his people will answer:
'Be it thus. Be it thus.'

translated by James Carney

MATTHEW ARNOLD

[1853] ## Dover Beach

The sea is calm to-night,
The tide is full, the moon lies fair
Upon the Straits; – on the French coast, the light
Gleams, and is gone; the cliffs of England stand,
Glimmering and vast, out in the tranquil bay.
Come to the window, sweet is the night air!
Only, from the long line of spray
Where the ebb meets the moon-blanch'd sand,
Listen! you hear the grating roar
Of pebbles which the waves suck back, and fling,
At their return, up the high strand,
Begin, and cease, and then again begin,
With tremulous cadence slow, and bring
The eternal note of sadness in.

Sophocles long ago
Heard it on the Aegaean, and it brought
Into his mind the turbid ebb and flow
Of human misery; we

Find also in the sound a thought,
Hearing it by this distant northern sea.

The sea of faith
Was once, too, at the full, and round earth's
    shore
Lay like the folds of a bright girdle furl'd;
But now I only hear
Its melancholy, long, withdrawing roar,
Retreating to the breath
Of the night-wind down the vast edges drear
And naked shingles of the world.

Ah, love, let us be true
To one another! for the world, which seems
To lie before us like a land of dreams,
So various, so beautiful, so new,
Hath really neither joy, nor love, nor light,
Nor certitude, nor peace, nor help for pain;
And we are here as on a darkling plain
Swept with confused alarms of struggle and
    flight,
Where ignorant armies clash by night.

ELIZABETH BISHOP

[1955]   ## At the Fishhouses

Although it is a cold evening,
down by one of the fishhouses
an old man sits netting,
his net, in the gloaming almost invisible,
a dark purple-brown,
and his shuttle worn and polished.
The air smells so strong of codfish
it makes one's nose run and one's eyes water.
The five fishhouses have steeply peaked roofs
and narrow, cleated gangplanks slant up

5

to storerooms in the gables
for the wheelbarrows to be pushed up and down
    on.
All is silver: the heavy surface of the sea,
swelling slowly as if considering spilling over,
is opaque, but the silver of the benches,
the lobster pots, and masts, scattered
among the wild jagged rocks,
is of an apparent translucence
like the small old buildings with an emerald moss
growing on their shoreward walls.
The big fish tubs are completely lined
with layers of beautiful herring scales
and the wheelbarrows are similarly plastered
with creamy iridescent coats of mail,
with small iridescent flies crawling on them.
Up on the little slope behind the houses,
set in the sparse bright sprinkle of grass,
is an ancient wooden capstan,
cracked, with two long bleached handles
and some melancholy stains, like dried blood,
where the ironwork has rusted.
The old man accepts a Lucky Strike.
He was a friend of my grandfather.
We talk of the decline in the population
and of codfish and herring
while he waits for a herring boat to come in.
There are sequins on his vest and on his thumb.
He has scraped the scales, the principal beauty,
from unnumbered fish with that black old knife,
the blade of which is almost worn away.

Down at the water's edge, at the place
where they haul up the boats, up the long ramp
descending into the water, thin silver
tree trunks are laid horizontally

across the gray stones, down and down
at intervals of four or five feet.

Cold dark deep and absolutely clear,
element bearable to no mortal,
to fish and to seals . . . One seal particularly
I have seen here evening after evening.
He was curious about me. He was interested in
    music;
like me a believer in total immersion,
so I used to sing him Baptist hymns.
I also sang 'A Mighty Fortress Is Our God'.
He stood up in the water and regarded me
steadily, moving his head a little.
Then he would disappear, then suddenly emerge
almost in the same spot, with a sort of shrug
as if it were against his better judgment.
Cold dark deep and absolutely clear,
the clear gray icy water . . . Back, behind us,
the dignified tall firs begin.
Bluish, associating with their shadows,
a million Christmas trees stand
waiting for Christmas. The water seems
    suspended
above the rounded gray and blue-gray stones.
I have seen it over and over, the same sea, the
    same,
slightly, indifferently swinging above the stones,
icily free above the stones,
above the stones and then the world.
If you should dip your hand in,
your wrist would ache immediately,
your bones would begin to ache and your hand
    would burn
as if the water were a transmutation of fire

that feeds on stones and burns with a dark gray
    flame.
If you tasted it, it would first taste bitter,
then briny, then surely burn your tongue.
It is like what we imagine knowledge to be:
dark, salt, clear, moving, utterly free,
drawn from the cold hard mouth
of the world, derived from the rocky breasts
forever, flowing and drawn, and since
our knowledge is historical, flowing, and flown.

MARIANNE MOORE

[1935]   ## A Grave

Man looking into the sea,
taking the view from those who have as much
    right to it as you have to it yourself,
it is human nature to stand in the middle of a
    thing,
but you cannot stand in the middle of this;
the sea has nothing to give but a well excavated
    grave.
The firs stand in a procession, each with an
    emerald turkey-foot at the top,
reserved as their contours, saying nothing;
repression, however, is not the most obvious
    characteristic of the sea;
the sea is a collector, quick to return a rapacious
    look.
There are others besides you who have worn that
    look –
whose expression is no longer a protest; the fish
    no longer investigate them
for their bones have not lasted:
men lower nets, unconscious of the fact that they
    are desecrating a grave,

and row quickly away – the blades of the oars
     moving together like the feet of water-spiders as if
          there were no such thing as death.
The wrinkles progress among themselves in a
     phalanx – beautiful under networks of foam,
and fade breathlessly while the sea rustles in and
     out of the seaweed;
the birds swim through the air at top speed,
     emitting cat-calls as heretofore –
the tortoise-shell scourges about the feet of the
     cliffs, in motion beneath them;
and the ocean, under the pulsation of lighthouses
     and noise of bell-buoys,
advances as usual, looking as if it were not that
     ocean in which dropped things are bound to
     sink –
in which if they turn and twist, it is neither with
     volition nor consciousness.

SAMUEL TAYLOR COLERIDGE

[1798]   ## The Rime of the Ancient Mariner

In Seven Parts

ARGUMENT

How a Ship having passed the Line was driven by storms to the cold Country
towards the South Pole; and how from thence she made her course to the
tropical Latitude of the Great Pacific Ocean; and of the strange things that
befell; and in what manner the Ancyent Marinere came back to his own
Country.

PART I

An ancient Mariner
meeteth three gallants
bidden to a wedding-
feast, and detaineth
one.

It is an ancient Mariner,
And he stoppeth one of three.
'By thy long grey beard and glittering eye,
Now wherefore stopp'st thou me?

9

The Bridegroom's doors are opened wide,
And I am next of kin;
The guests are met, the feast is set:
May'st hear the merry din.'

He holds him with his skinny hand,
'There was a ship,' quoth he.
'Hold off! unhand me, grey-beard loon!'
Eftsoons his hand dropt he.

He holds him with his glittering eye –
The Wedding-Guest stood still,
And listens like a three years' child:
The Mariner hath his will.

The Wedding-Guest sat on a stone:
He cannot choose but hear;
And thus spake on that ancient man,
The bright-eyed Mariner.

'The ship was cheered, the harbour cleared,
Merrily did we drop
Below the kirk, below the hill,
Below the lighthouse top.

The Sun came up upon the left,
Out of the sea came he!
And he shone bright, and on the right
Went down into the sea.

Higher and higher every day,
Till over the mast at noon –'
The Wedding-Guest here beat his breast,
For he heard the loud bassoon.

The bride hath paced into the hall,
Red as a rose is she;
Nodding their heads before her goes
The merry minstrelsy.

The Wedding-Guest he beat his breast,
Yet he cannot choose but hear;
And thus spake on that ancient man,
The bright-eyed Mariner.

The ship drawn by a storm toward the south pole.

'And now the STORM-BLAST came, and he
Was tyrannous and strong:
He struck with his o'ertaking wings,
And chased us south along.

With sloping masts and dipping prow,
As who pursued with yell and blow
Still treads the shadow of his foe,
And forward bends his head,
The ship drove fast, loud roared the blast,
And southward aye we fled.

And now there came both mist and snow,
And it grew wondrous cold:
And ice, mast-high, came floating by,
As green as emerald.

The land of ice, and of fearful sounds where no living thing was to be seen.

And through the drifts the snowy clifts
Did send a dismal sheen:
Nor shapes of men nor beasts we ken –
The ice was all between.

The ice was here, the ice was there,
The ice was all around:
It cracked and growled, and roared and howled,
Like noises in a swound!

Till a great sea-bird, called the Albatross, came through the snow-fog, and was received with great joy and hospitality.

At length did cross an Albatross,
Thorough the fog it came;
As if it had been a Christian soul,
We hailed it in God's name.

It ate the food it ne'er had eat,
And round and round it flew.

The ice did split with a thunder-fit;
The helmsman steered us through!

And lo! the Albatross
proveth a bird of good
omen, and followeth
the ship as it returned
northward through fog
and floating ice.

And a good south wind sprung up behind;
The Albatross did follow,
And every day, for food or play,
Came to the mariner's hollo!

In mist or cloud, on mast or shroud,
It perched for vespers nine;
Whiles all the night, through fog-smoke white,
Glimmered the white Moon-shine.

The ancient Mariner
inhospitably killeth and
the pious bird of good
omen.

'God save thee, ancient Mariner!
From the fiends, that plague thee thus! –
Why look'st thou so?' – With my cross-bow
I shot the Albatross.

PART II

The Sun now rose upon the right:
Out of the sea came he,
still hid in mist, and on the left
Went down into the sea.

And the good south wind still blew behind,
But no sweet bird did follow,
Nor any day for food or play
Came to the mariners' hollo!

The shipmates cry out
against the ancient
Mariner, for killing the
bird of good luck.

And I had done a hellish thing,
And it would work 'em woe:
For all averred, I had killed the bird
That made the breeze to blow.
Ah wretch! said they, the bird to slay,
That made the breeze to blow!

But when the fog cleared off, they justify the same, and thus make themselves accomplices in the crime.

Nor dim nor red, like God's own head,
The glorious Sun uprist:
Then all averred, I had killed the bird
That brought the fog and mist.
'Twas right, said they, such birds to slay,
That bring the fog and mist.

The fair breeze continues; the ship enters the Pacific Ocean, and sails northward, even till it reaches the Line.

The fair breeze blew, the white foam flew,
The furrow followed free;
We were the first that ever burst
Into that silent sea.

The ship hath been suddenly becalmed.

Down dropt the breeze, the sails dropt down,
'Twas sad as sad could be;
And we did speak only to break
The silence of the sea!

All in a hot and copper sky,
The bloody Sun, at noon,
Right up above the mast did stand,
No bigger than the Moon.

Day after day, day after day,
We stuck, nor breath nor motion;
As idle as a painted ship
Upon a painted ocean.

And the Albatross begins to be avenged.

Water, water, every where,
And all the boards did shrink;
Water, water, every where,
Nor any drop to drink.

The very deep did rot: O Christ!
That ever this should be!
Yea, slimy things did crawl with legs
Upon the slimy sea.

About, about, in reel and rout
The death-fires danced at night;

The water, like a witch's oils,
Burnt green, and blue and white.

A Spirit had followed them; one of the invisible inhabitants of this planet, neither departed souls nor angels; concerning whom the learned Jew, Josephus, and the Platonic Constantinopolitan, Michael Psellus, may be consulted. They are very numerous, and there is no climate or element without one or more.

And some in dreams assurèd were
Of the Spirit that plagued us so;
Nine fathom deep he had followed us
From the land of mist and snow.

And every tongue, through utter drought,
Was withered at the root;
We could not speak, no more than if
We had been choked with soot.

The shipmates, in their sore distress, would fain throw the whole guilt on the ancient Mariner: in sign whereof they hang the dead seabird round his neck.

Ah! well a-day! what evil looks
Had I from old and young!
Instead of the cross, the Albatross
About my neck was hung.

PART III

There passed a weary time. Each throat
Was parched, and glazed each eye.
A weary time! a weary time!
How glazed each weary eye,
The ancient Mariner beholdeth a sign in the element afar off.
When looking westward, I beheld
A something in the sky.

At first it seemed a little speck,
And then it seemed a mist;
It moved and moved, and took at last
A certain shape, I wist.

A speck, a mist, a shape, I wist!
And still it neared and neared:
As if it dodged a water-sprite,
It plunged and tacked and veered.

At its nearer approach, it seemeth him to be a ship; and at a dear ransom he freeth his speech from the bonds of thirst.

With throats unslaked, with black lips baked,
We could nor laugh nor wail;
Through utter drought all dumb we stood!
I bit my arm, I sucked the blood,
And cried, A sail! a sail!

With throats unslaked, with black lips baked,
Agape they heard me call:

A flash of joy;

Gramercy! they for joy did grin,
And all at once their breath drew in,
As they were drinking all.

And horror follows. For can it be a ship that comes onward without wind or tide?

See! see! (I cried) she tacks no more!
Hither to work us weal;
Without a breeze, without a tide,
She steadies with upright keel!

The western wave was all a-flame.
The day was well nigh done!
Almost upon the western wave
Rested the broad bright Sun;
When that strange shape drove suddenly
Betwixt us and the Sun.

It seemeth him but the skeleton of a ship.

And straight the Sun was flecked with bars,
(Heaven's Mother send us grace!)
As if through a dungeon-grate he peered
With broad and burning face.

Alas! (thought I, and my heart beat loud)
How fast she nears and nears!

And its ribs are seen as bars on the face of the setting Sun. The spectre-woman and her death-mate, and no other on board the skeleton-ship.

Are those *her* sails that glance in the Sun,
Like restless gossameres?

Are those *her* ribs through which the Sun
Did peer, as through a grate?
And is that Woman all her crew?
Is that a Death? and are there two?
Is Death that woman's mate?

Like vessel, like crew!

Her lips were red, *her* looks were free,
Her locks were yellow as gold:

Death and Life-in-Death have diced for the ship's crew, and she (the latter) winneth the ancient Mariner.

Her skin was as white as leprosy,
The Night-mare Life-in-Death was she,
Who thicks man's blood with cold.

The naked hulk alongside came,
And the twain were casting dice;
'The game is done! I've won! I've won!'
Quoth she, and whistles thrice.

No twilight within the courts of the Sun.

The Sun's rim dips; the stars rush out:
At one stride comes the dark;
With far-heard whisper, o'er the sea,
Off shot the spectre-bark.

At the rising of the Moon.

We listened and looked sideways up!
Fear at my heart, as at a cup,
My life-blood seemed to sip!

The stars were dim, and thick the night,
The steersman's face by his lamp gleamed white;
From the sails the dew did drip –
Till clomb above the eastern bar
The hornèd Moon, with one bright star
Within the nether tip.

One after another,

One after one, by the star-dogged Moon,
Too quick for groan or sigh,
Each turned his face with a ghastly pang,
And cursed me with his eye.

His shipmates drop down dead.

Four times fifty living men,
(And I heard nor sigh nor groan)
With heavy thump, a lifeless lump,
They dropped down one by one.

But Life-in-Death begins her work on the ancient Mariner.

The souls did from their bodies fly, –
They fled to bliss or woe!

And every soul, it passed me by,
Like the whizz of my cross-bow!

PART IV

The wedding guest
feareth that a Spirit is
talking to him.

'I fear thee, ancient Mariner!
I fear thy skinny hand!
And thou art long, and lank, and brown,
As is the ribbed sea-sand.

I fear thee and thy glittering eye,
And thy skinny hand, so brown.' –

But the ancient Mariner
assureth him of his
bodily life, and
proceedeth to relate his
horrible penance.

Fear not, fear not, thou Wedding-Guest!
This body dropt not down.

Alone, alone, all, all alone,
Alone on a wide wide sea!
And never a saint look pity on
My soul in agony.

He despiseth the
creatures of the calm,

The many men, so beautiful!
And they all dead did lie:
And a thousand thousand slimy things
Lived on; and so did I.

And envieth that they
should live, and so
many lie dead.

I looked upon the rotting sea,
And drew my eyes away;
I looked upon the rotting deck,
And there the dead men lay.

I looked to heaven, and tried to pray;
But or ever a prayer had gusht,
A wicked whisper came, and made
My heart as dry as dust.

I closed my lids, and kept them close,
And the balls like pulses beat;
For the sky and the sea, and the sea and the sky

Lay like a load on my weary eye,
And the dead were at my feet.

But the curse liveth for him in the eye of the dead men.

The cold sweat melted from their limbs,
Nor rot nor reek did they:
The look with which they looked on me
Had never passed away.

An orphan's curse would drag to hell
A spirit from on high;
But oh! more horrible than that
Is the curse in a dead man's eye!
Seven days, seven nights, I saw that curse,
And yet I could not die.

In his loneliness and fixedness he yearneth towards the journeying Moon, and the stars that still sojourn, yet still move onward; and every where the blue sky belongs to them, and is their appointed rest, and their native country and their own natural homes, which they enter unannounced as lords that are certainly expected and yet there is a silent joy at their arrival.

The moving Moon went up the sky,
And no where did abide:
Softly she was going up,
And a star or two beside –

Her beams bemocked the sultry main,
Like April hoar-frost spread;
But where the ship's huge shadow lay,
The charmèd water burnt away
A still and awful red.

By the light of the Moon he beholdeth God's creatures of the great calm.

Beyond the shadow of the ship,
I watched the water-snakes:
They moved in tracks of shining white,
And when they reared, the elfish light
Fell off in hoary flakes.

Within the shadow of the ship
I watched their rich attire:
Blue, glossy green, and velvet black,
They coiled and swam; and every track
Was a flash of golden fire.

O happy living things! no tongue
Their beauty might declare:
A spring of love gushed from my heart,

And I blessed them unaware:
Sure my kind saint took pity on me,
And I blessed them unware.

The self-same moment I could pray;
And from my neck so free
The Albatross fell off, and sank
Like lead into the sea.

PART V

Oh sleep! it is a gentle thing,
Beloved from pole to pole!
To Mary Queen the praise be given!
She sent the gentle sleep from Heaven,
That slid into my soul.

The silly buckets on the deck,
That had so long remained,
I dreamt that they were filled with dew;
And when I awoke, it rained.

My lips were wet, my throat was cold,
My garments all were dank;
Sure I had drunken in my dreams,
And still my body drank.

I moved, and could not feel my limbs:
I was so light – almost
I thought that I had died in sleep,
And was a blessed ghost.

And soon I heard a roaring wind;
It did not come anear;
But with its sound it shook the sails,
That were so thin and sere.

The upper air burst into life!
And a hundred fire-flags sheen,
To and fro they were hurried about!
And to and fro, and in and out,
The wan stars danced between.

And the coming wind did roar more loud,
And the sails did sigh like sedge;
And the rain poured down from one black cloud;
The Moon was at its edge.

The thick black cloud was cleft, and still
The Moon was at its side:
Like waters shot from some high crag,
The lightning fell with never a jag,
A river steep and wide.

The bodies of the ship's crew are inspired, and the ship moves on; The loud wind never reached the ship,
Yet now the ship moved on!
Beneath the lightning and the Moon
The dead men gave a groan.

They groaned, they stirred, they all uprose,
Nor spake, nor moved their eyes;
It had been strange, even in a dream,
To have seen those dead men rise.

The helmsman steered, the ship moved on;
Yet never a breeze up-blew;
The mariners all 'gan work the ropes,
Where they were wont to do;
They raised their limbs like lifeless tools –
We were a ghastly crew.

The body of my brother's son
Stood by me, knee to knee:
The body and I pulled at one rope,
But he said nought to me.

'I fear thee, ancient Mariner!'
Be calm, thou Wedding-Guest!
'Twas not those souls that fled in pain,
Which to their corses came again,
But a troop of spirits blest:

For when it dawned – they dropped their arms,
And clustered round the mast;
Sweet sounds rose slowly through their mouths,
And from their bodies passed.

Around, around, flew each sweet sound,
Then darted to the Sun;
Slowly the sounds came back again,
Now mixed, now one by one.

Sometimes a-dropping from the sky
I heard the sky-lark sing;
Sometimes all little birds that are,
How they seemed to fill the sea and air
With their sweet jargoning!

And now 'twas like all instruments,
Now like a lonely flute;
And now it is an angel's song,
That makes the heavens be mute.

It ceased; yet still the sails made on
A pleasant noise till noon,
A noise like of a hidden brook
In the leafy month of June,
That to the sleeping woods all night
Singeth a quiet tune.

Till noon we quietly sailed on,
Yet never a breeze did breathe:
Slowly and smoothly went the ship,
Moved onward from beneath.

The lonesome Spirit from the south pole carries on the ship as far as the Line, in obedience to the angelic troop, but still requireth vengeance.

Under the keel nine fathom deep,
From the land of mist and snow,
The Spirit slid: and it was he
That made the ship to go.
The sails at noon left off their tune,
And the ship stood still also.

The Sun, right up above the mast,
Had fixed her to the ocean:
But in a minute she 'gan stir,
With a short uneasy motion –
Backwards and forwards half her length
With a short uneasy motion.

Then like a pawing horse let go,
She made a sudden bound:
It flung the blood into my head,
And I fell down in a swound.

The Polar Spirit's fellow-daemons, the invisible inhabitants of the element, take part in his wrong; and two of them relate, one to the other, that penance long and heavy for the ancient Mariner hath been accorded to the Polar Spirit, who returneth southward.

How long in that same fit I lay,
I have not to declare;
But ere my living life returned,
I heard, and in my soul discerned
Two voices in the air.

'Is it he?' quoth one, 'Is this the man?
By him who died on cross,
With his cruel bow he laid full low
The harmless Albatross.

The Spirit who bideth by himself
In the land of mist and snow,
He loved the bird that loved the man
Who shot him with his bow.'

The other was a softer voice,
As soft as honey-dew:
Quoth he, 'The man hath penance done,
And penance more will do.'

PART VI

'But tell me, tell me! speak again,
Thy soft response renewing –
What makes that ship drive on so fast?
What is the ocean doing?'

SECOND VOICE
'Still as a slave before his lord,
The ocean hath no blast;
His great bright eye most silently
Up to the Moon is cast –

If he may know which way to go;
For she guides him smooth or grim.
See, brother, see! how graciously
She looketh down on him.'

FIRST VOICE

The Mariner hath been cast into a trance; for the angelic power causeth the vessel to drive northward faster than human life could endure.

'But why drives on that ship so fast,
Without or wave or wind?'

SECOND VOICE
'The air is cut away before,
And closes from behind.

Fly, brother, fly! more high, more high!
Or we shall be belated:
For slow and slow that ship will go,
When the Mariner's trance is abated.'

The supernatural motion is retarded; the Mariner awakes, and his penance begins anew.

I woke, and we were sailing on
As in a gentle weather:
'Twas night, calm night, the moon was high;
The dead men stood together.

All stood together on the deck,
For a charnel-dungeon fitter:

All fixed on me their stony eyes,
That in the Moon did glitter.

The pang, the curse, with which they died,
Had never passed away:
I could not draw my eyes from theirs,
Nor turn them up to pray.

And now this spell was snapt: once more
I viewed the ocean green,
And looked far forth, yet little saw
Of what had else been seen –

Like one, that on a lonesome road
Doth walk in fear and dread,
And having once turned round walks on,
And turns no more his head;
Because he knows, a frightful fiend
Doth close behind him tread.

But soon there breathed a wind on me,
Nor sound nor motion made:
Its path was not upon the sea,
In ripple or in shade.

It raised my hair, it fanned my cheek
Like a meadow-gale of spring –
It mingled strangely with my fears,
Yet it felt like a welcoming.

Swiftly, swiftly flew the ship,
Yet she sailed softly too:
Sweetly, sweetly blew the breeze –
On me alone it blew.

Oh! dream of joy! is this indeed
The light-house top I see?
Is this the hill? is this the kirk?
Is this mine own countree?

We drifted o'er the harbour-bar,
And I with sobs did pray –
O let me be awake, my God!
Or let me sleep alway.

The harbour-bay was clear as glass,
So smoothly it was strewn!
And on the bay the moonlight lay,
And the shadow of the Moon.

The rock shone bright, the kirk no less,
That stands above the rock:
The moonlight steeped in silentness
The steady weathercock.

And the bay was white with silent light,
Till rising from the same,
The angelic spirits leave the dead bodies. Full many shapes, that shadows were,
In crimson colours came.

And appear in their own forms of light. A little distance from the prow
Those crimson shadows were:
I turned my eyes upon the deck –
Oh, Christ! what saw I there!

Each corse lay flat, lifeless and flat,
And, by the holy rood!
A man all light, a seraph-man,
On every corse there stood.

This seraph-band, each waved his hand:
It was a heavenly sight!
They stood as signals to the land,
Each one a lovely light;

This seraph-band, each waved his hand,
No voice did they impart –
No voice; but oh! the silence sank
Like music on my heart.

But soon I heard the dash of oars,
I heard the Pilot's cheer;
My head was turned perforce away
And I saw a boat appear.

The Pilot and the Pilot's boy,
I heard them coming fast:
Dear Lord in Heaven! it was a joy
The dead men could not blast.

I saw a third – I heard his voice:
It is the Hermit good!
He singeth loud his godly hymns
That he makes in the wood.
He'll shrieve my soul, he'll wash away
The Albatross's blood.

PART VII

The Hermit of the wood, This Hermit good lives in that wood
Which slopes down to the sea.
How loudly his sweet voice he rears!
He loves to talk with marineres
That come from a far countree.

He kneels at morn, and noon, and eve –
He hath a cushion plump:
It is the moss that wholly hides
The rotted old oak-stump.

The skiff-boat neared: I heard them talk,
'Why, this is strange, I trow!
Where are those lights so many and fair,
That signal made but now?'

Approacheth the ship with wonder. 'Strange, by my faith!' the Hermit said –
'And they answered not our cheer!
The planks looked warped! and see those sails,
How thin they are and sere!

26

I never saw aught like to them,
Unless perchance it were

Brown skeletons of leaves that lag
My forest-brook along;
When the ivy-tod is heavy with snow,
And the owlet whoops to the wolf below,
That eats the she-wolf's young.'

'Dear Lord! it hath a fiendish look –
(The Pilot made reply)
I am a-feared' – 'Push on, push on!'
Said the Hermit cheerily.

The boat came closer to the ship,
But I nor spake nor stirred;
The boat came close beneath the ship,
And straight a sound was heard.

Under the water it rumbled on,
Still louder and more dread:
It reached the ship, it split the bay;
The ship went down like lead.

Stunned by that loud and dreadful sound,
Which sky and ocean smote,
Like one that hath been seven days drowned
My body lay afloat;
But swift as dreams, myself I found
Within the Pilot's boat.

Upon the whirl, where sank the ship,
The boat spun round and round;
And all was still, save that the hill
Was telling of the sound.

I moved my lips – the Pilot shrieked
And fell down in a fit;

The holy Hermit raised his eyes,
And prayed where he did sit.

I took the oars: the Pilot's boy,
Who now doth crazy go,
Laughed loud and long, and all the while
His eyes went to and fro.
'Ha! ha!' quoth he, 'full plain I see,
The Devil knows how to row.'

And now, all in my own countree,
I stood on the firm land!
The Hermit stepped forth from the boat,
And scarcely he could stand.

'O shrieve me, shrieve me, holy man!'
The Hermit crossed his brow.
'Say quick,' quoth he, 'I bid thee say –
What manner of man art thou?'

Forthwith this frame of mine was wrenched
With a woful agony,
Which forced me to begin my tale;
And then it left me free.

Since then, at an uncertain hour,
That agony returns:
And till my ghastly tale is told,
This heart within me burns.

I pass, like night, from land to land;
I have strange power of speech;
That moment that his face I see,
I know the man that must hear me:
To him my tale I teach.

What loud uproar bursts from that door!
The wedding-guests are there:
But in the garden-bower the bride

And bride-maids singing are:
And hark the little vesper bell,
Which biddeth me to prayer!

O Wedding-Guest! this soul hath been
Alone on a wide wide sea:
So lonely 'twas, that God himself
Scarce seemed there to be.

O sweeter than the marriage-feast,
'Tis sweeter far to me,
To walk together to the kirk
With a goodly company! –

To walk together to the kirk,
And all together pray,
While each to his great Father bends,
Old men, and babes, and loving friends
And youths and maidens gay!

And to teach, by his own example, love and reverence to all things that God made and loveth.

Farewell, farewell! but this I tell
To thee, thou Wedding-Guest!
He prayeth well, who loveth well
Both man and bird and beast.

He prayeth best, who loveth best
All things both great and small;
For the dear God who loveth us,
He made and loveth all.

The Mariner, whose eye is bright,
Whose beard with age is hoar,
Is gone: and now the Wedding-Guest
Turned from the bridegroom's door.

He went like one that hath been stunned,
And is of sense forlorn:
A sadder and a wiser man,
He rose the morrow morn.

[18th century]   *from* Clanranald's Galley

Sun unhusking to gold-yellow
        from its shell,
the sky growing seared and lurid,
        amber bell.

Thick and gloomy and dun-bellied,
        surly curtain,
vibrating with every colour
        in a tartan.

Rainbow in the west appearing
        tempest-born,
speeding clouds by growing breezes
        chewed and torn.

So they raised the speckled sails
        wind-tight, towering.
They stretched the stiff ropes against
        her sudden flowering,
timbers of the resin red
        tapering proudly.

They were knotted with fierce vigour,
        neatly, firmly,
through the eyes of iron hooks
        and round the ring bolts.

Every rope of their equipment
        was adjusted.
Coolly each took his position
        as accustomed.

Windows of the heavens opened
    blue-grey, spotted
with the banging of the tempest
    fierce and haughty.

The sea gathered round about it
    a black cloak,
a rough, ruffled, swarthy mantle
    of ill look.

It swelled to mountains and to valleys
    shaggy-billowed,
the matted lumpy waters rearing
    up to hillocks.

The blue waves were mouthing chasms,
    horned and brutish,
fighting each other in a pouring
    deathly tumult.

It needed courage to be facing
    such tall towerings
phosphorescent flashes sparking
    from each mountain

Grey-headed wave-leaders towering
    with sour roarings,
their followers with smoking trumpets
    blaring, pouring.

When the ship was poised on wave crest
    in proud fashion
it was needful to strike sail
    with quick precision.

When the valleys nearly swallowed us
    by suction
we fed her cloth to take her up to
    resurrection.

The wide-skirted curving waters,
    bellowing, lowing,
before they even had approached you,
    you'd hear roaring,

sweeping before them the small billows,
    onward sheering.
There'd be a massive deathly water
    hard for steering.

When she would plunge from towering summits
    down pell-mell
almost the ship's heel would be bruised
    by the sea-floor's shells,

the ocean churning, mixing, stirring
    its abyss,
seals and huge sea creatures howling
    in distress.

Impetuous tumult of the waters,
    the ship's going,
sparking their white brains about
    an eerie snowing!

And they howling in their horror
    with sad features
pleading by us to be rescued,
    'Save your creatures.'

Every small fish in the ocean
    belly-white
by the rocking violent motion
    killed outright.

Stones and shell fish of the bottom
    on the surface
mown by the relentless threshing
    of the current.

The whole ocean in a porridge
　　foul and muddied,
with filth and gore of the sea-monsters
　　red and bloodied,

the horned splay-footed vast sea-creatures
　　clawed, misshapen,
their many heads in ghastly screaming,
　　mouths jammed open,

the deeps teeming with hobgoblins,
　　ghostly pawing,
monstrous crawling, phantom seething,
　　vague out-clawing.

Loathsome their abhorrent groaning
　　and their raving:
they'd have driven fifty soldiers
　　wholly crazy.

The crew entirely lost their hearing
　　in the maelstrom,
the screaming discord of the demons,
　　beastly wailing.

Crashing of water and its smashing
　　smiting planking,
the prow's rushing as it dashed
　　the ghastly monsters.

Breezes freshening from windward
　　from the west,
torment everywhere from ocean
　　and from beast.

Blinded by the pouring spindrift
　　sky unbrightening,
incredible thunder during nighttime
　　flash of lightning.

Fire balls burning up our tackle
    and our gear
acrid smell and smoke of brimstone
    everywhere.

The elements above below us
    seeking slaughter,
water, earth and fire and air,
    a hostile quartet.

But when the ocean could not beat us
    make us yield
she became a smiling meadow,
    summer field.

Though there was no bolt unbending,
    sail intact,
yard unwrenched or ring unweakened,
    oar uncracked.

There was no stay that had not sprung
    or gear undamaged
no shroud or halyard without ripping.
    Snapping, cracking!

Each bench and gunwale all gave witness
    to the storm.
Every timber, every fitting
    suffered harm.

There was no angle-piece or rib
    which wasn't loosened.
The wale and stern sheets all were damaged,
    smashed, unfastened.

There was no rudder without splitting,
    helm unwounded,
sob and groan from every timber
    sea had pounded.

There was no tree-nail left unpulled,
  or board in use,
every single well-clinched washer
  had been loosed.

There was no nail that was untwisted,
  there was no rivet without bending,
there was no part that still existed
  that wasn't worse at the storm's ending.

The tranquil sea benignly saw us
  in Islay Sound,
the bitter-voiced breezes were appeased
  by God's command.

They left us for the upper regions
  of the heavens
and made for us a noiseless even
  level plain.

We gave thanks to the great Father
  and Creator
that Clanranald came unharmed
  from brutal water.

But we furled then our thin sails
  of linen woven
and we lowered her red masts
  across her floor boards.

We put out melodious oar blades
  finely tinted
of red pine that had been cut
  on Isle of Finnan.

We rowed with smooth and springy motion
  not neglectful
entering harbour at the heights
  of Carrickfergus.

We anchored easily and calmly
    in that roadstead
and we ate and drank, unstinted,
    and abode there.

translated by Iain Crichton Smith

ANONYMOUS (IRISH)

[9th century]   ### The Viking Terror

Bitter is the wind tonight,
It tosses the ocean's white hair:
Tonight I fear not the fierce warriors of Norway
Coursing on the Irish Sea.

translated by Kuno Meyer

GEORGE MACKAY BROWN

[1976]   ### The Stone Cross

At dawn Havard sighted a hill in Ulster.
'A point to west,' said the helmsman. 'There the
    hive is.
There is the barren kingdom of drones.'

We sailed past cave and cormorant and curragh.
We anchored under a stone cross at noon.

Creatures came down to meet us
With stony heads, voices like insects, raised
    hands.

They murmured 'Mother', 'Sancta Maria', 'Our
    Lady'
But that hostess was not to be seen.

Brother Simon drew me from sea to rock.
He made a cross of grey air between us.

It was a household of men only.
A boy offered to wipe salt from our foreheads.

'Havard, it is time to make a start now.'
Havard flashed his axe in the face of a brother.

Then women began to screech from the crag
    above,
Gaelic keenings and cursings.

A dozen eunuchs fell beside the porch.
The boy made a dove of his two hands.

We entered a cave of wax and perfumes.
Mund took a silver cup from a niche.

Cold tinklings like nails
Took us to nothing – a crust, a red splash.

Soon that hive was all smoke and stickiness.

We brought a fair cargo down to the *Skua*.
The abbot had called that treasure 'moth-food'.

Sunset. Sharing of spoils. A harp-stroke.
Soon I drifted into the stone of sleep.

ANONYMOUS

[traditional]

Sir Patrick Spens

The King sits in Dunfermline toun,
    A drinking at the wine.
'O where shall I get a skilly skipper
    To sail this ship o mine?'

fellow

Then up and spake an eldern carle
    Stood by the King's right knee.
'Sir Patrick Spens is the best sailor
    That ever sailed the sea.'

The King has written a lang letter
    And signed it wi his hand,
And sent it to young Patrick Spens
    Was walking on Leith sands.

The first line that Sir Patrick read
    A loud laugh laughèd he.
The next line that Sir Patrick read
    The tear blinded his ee.

'Tae Norrowa, tae Norrowa,
    Tae Norrowa o'er the faem,
The King's daughter frae Norrowa,
    'Tis ye maun brang her hame.'

'O Wha is this done this ill deed,
    And telled the King o me?
Although it were my ain father
    An ill death may he dee.'

They hadna been in Norrowa
    A week but barely three
When all the Lords o Norrowa
    They up and spak sae free.

'These outland Scots waste our King's gold
    And swalla our Queen's fee.'

Wearie fa the tongue that spak
    Sicca mortal lee.

'Tak tent, tak tent, my good men all,
    Our good ship sails the morne.'
'O say na sae, my master dear,
    For I fear a deadly storm.

'Late late yestreen I saw the new moon
    Wi the auld moon in her arm.
I fear, I fear, my dear master
    That we shall come to harm.'

O laith laith were those good Scots Lords
    To wet their cork-heeled shoon,
But long e'er all the play was played
    They wet their hats aboon.

O lang lang may their ladies sit
    Wi their gold fans in their hand
Waiting for Sir Patrick Spens
    Come sailing to the land.

O lang lang may their ladies sit
    Wi the gold combs in their hair
Waiting for their own dear lords,
    They'll see them never mair.

half way over   Haf owre, haf owre, by Aberdour,
    Where the sea's sae wide and deep,
It's there it lies Sir Patrick Spens
    Wi the Scots Lords at his feet.

HERMAN MELVILLE

[1888]

The Berg
A Dream

I saw a ship of martial build
(Her standards set, her brave apparel on)
Directed as by madness mere
Against a stolid iceberg steer,
Nor budge it, though the infatuate ship went
    down.
The impact made huge ice-cubes fall
Sullen, in tons that crashed the deck;
But that one avalanche was all –
No other movement save the foundering wreck.

Along the spurs of ridges pale,
Not any slenderest shaft and frail,
A prism over glass-green gorges lone,

Toppled; nor lace of traceries fine,
Nor pendant drops in grot or mine
Were jarred, when the stunned ship went down.
Nor sole the gulls in cloud that wheeled
Circling one snow-flanked peak afar,
But nearer fowl the floes that skimmed
And crystal beaches, felt no jar.
No thrill transmitted stirred the lock
Of jack-straw needle-ice at base;
Towers undermined by waves – the block
Atilt impending – kept their place.
Seals, dozing sleek on sliddery ledges
Slipt never, when by loftier edges
Through very inertia overthrown,
The impetuous ship in bafflement went down.

Hard Berg (methought), so cold, so vast,
With mortal damps self-overcast;
Exhaling still thy dankish breath –
Adrift dissolving, bound for death;
Though lumpish thou, a lumbering one –
A lumbering lubbard, loitering slow,
Impingers rue thee and go down,
Sounding thy precipice below,
Nor stir the slimy slug that sprawls
Along thy dead indifference of walls.

HART CRANE

[1926]   Repose of Rivers

The willows carried a slow sound,
A sarabande the wind mowed on the mead.
I could never remember
That seething, steady leveling of the marshes
Till age had brought me to the sea.

Flags, weeds. And remembrance of steep alcoves
Where cypresses shared the noon's
Tyranny; they drew me into hades almost.
And mammoth turtles climbing sulphur dreams
Yielded, while sun-silt rippled them
Asunder . . .

How much I would have bartered! the black
    gorge
And all the singular nestings in the hills
Where beavers learn stitch and tooth.
The pond I entered once and quickly fled –
I remember now its singing willow rim.

And finally, in that memory all things nurse;
After the city that I finally passed
With scalding unguents spread and smoking
    darts
The monsoon cut across the delta
At gulf gates . . . There, beyond the dykes

I heard wind flaking sapphire, like this summer,
And willows could not hold more steady sound.

EDWIN MORGAN

[1968] ## The Unspoken

When the troopship was pitching round the Cape
in '41, and there was a lull in the night uproar of
    seas and winds, and a sudden full moon
swung huge out of the darkness like the world it is,
and we all crowded onto the wet deck, leaning on
    the rail, our arms on each other's shoulders,
    gazing at the savage outcrop of great Africa,
and Tommy Cosh started singing 'Mandalay' and
    we joined in with our raucous chorus of the
    unforgettable song,

and the dawn came up like thunder like that
  moon drawing the water of our yearning
though we were going to war, and left us exalted,
that was happiness,
but it is not like that.

When the television newscaster said
the second sputnik was up, not empty
but with a small dog on board,
a half-ton treasury of life orbiting a thousand
  miles above the thin television masts and mists
  of November,
in clear space, heard, observed,
the faint far heartbeat sending back its message
steady and delicate,
and I was stirred by a deep confusion of feelings,
got up, stood with my back to the wall and my
  palms pressed hard against it, my arms held
  wide
as if I could spring from the earth –
not loath myself to go out that very day where
  Laika had shown man, felt
my cheeks burning with old Promethean warmth
rekindled – ready –
covered my face with my hands, seeing only an
  animal
strapped in a doomed capsule, but the future
was still there, cool and whole like the moon,
waiting to be taken, smiling even
as the dog's bones and the elaborate casket of
  aluminium
glow white and fuse in the arc of re-entry,
and I knew what I felt was history,
its thrilling brilliance came down,
came down,

comes down on us all, bringing pride and pity,
but it is not like that.

But Glasgow days and grey weathers, when the
    rain
beat on the bus shelter and you leaned slightly
    against me, and the back of your hand touched
    my hand in the shadows, and nothing was
    said,
when your hair grazed mine accidentally as we
    talked in a café, yet not quite accidentally,
when I stole a glance at your face as we stood in a
    doorway and found I was afraid
of what might happen if I should never see it
    again,
when we met, and met, in spite of such differences
    in our lives,
and did the common things that in our feeling
became extraordinary, so that our first kiss
was like the winter morning moon, and as you
    shifted in my arms
it was the sea changing the shingle that changes
    it
as if for ever (but we are bound by nothing, but
    like smoke
to mist or light in water we move, and mix) –
O then it was a story as old as war or man,
and although we have not said it we know it,
and although we have not claimed it we do it,
and although we have not vowed it we keep it,
without a name to the end

[14th century] ## The Shadow

Yesterday under fine leaves
I stayed for her, my Helen,
Under a green birch mantle
Safe from the rain, foolish lad.
Then I saw a sort of shape
Standing there, all distorted.
It drew back where it stood and
Faced me, like a friendly man,
And I blessed myself and begged
The saints to ward off evil.

'Tell me, and end your silence,
If you're a man, who you are.'

'I am, desist from questions,
The strange shadow of yourself.
Be still, for your benefit,
That I may speak my message.
I am come, a good custom,
Standing naked by your side,
To reveal, gem of complaints,
What you are, by enchantment.'

'O no, misshapen creature,
I'm not like that, goblin form.
The shape of a hunchbacked goat,
You resemble, queer picture,
More a strange apparition
Than the true form of a man.
Bickering herd in motley,
Legs of a hag on black stilts,
Shepherd of grimy goblins,
Bogey like a bald-pate monk,
Herdsman playing at griors,

Heron feeding in the reeds,
Crane stretching his wings full spread,
Goblin walls, by the cornfield,
A dimwitted palmer's face,
A ragged man's black brother,
Form of a coarsely clad corpse,
Where are you from, old yardpost?'

'For days, should I accuse you,
I'd stay, what I know's your bane.'

'What fault of mine do you know,
Other, neck of a pitcher,
Than what all men of judgment
Now know? Devil's shit to you!
I've not disowned my homeland,
Nor struck, I know, a foul blow,
Nor slung a stone at the hens,
Nor said boo to the babies.
I do not twist my talent,
I've not raped a stranger's wife.'

'By my faith, should I tell to
Those who know what I know,
Before the indictment's end,
Faith, you'd be on the gallows.'

'Take care, your snare is cruel,
Not to reveal what you know,
No more, while mine's the secret,
Than lips sewn fast with a stich.'

translated by Joseph P. Clancy

[1807]   # Resolution and Independence

I

There was a roaring in the wind all night;
The rain came heavily and fell in floods;
But now the sun is rising calm and bright;
The birds are singing in the distant woods;
Over his own sweet voice the Stock-dove broods;
The Jay makes answer as the Magpie chatters;
And all the air is filled with pleasant noise of
    waters.

II

All things that love the sun are out of doors;
The sky rejoices in the morning's birth;
The grass is bright with rain-drops; – on the
    moors
The hare is running races in her mirth;
And with her feet she from the plashy earth
Raises a mist; that, glittering in the sun,
Runs with her all the way, wherever she doth run.

III

I was a Traveller then upon the moor;
I saw the hare that raced about with joy;
I heard the woods and distant waters roar;
Or heard them not, as happy as a boy:
The pleasant season did my heart employ:
My old remembrances went from me wholly;
And all the ways of men, so vain and melancholy.

IV

But, as it sometimes chanceth, from the might
Of joy in minds that can no further go,
As high as we have mounted in delight
In our dejection do we sink as low;
To me that morning did it happen so;
And fears and fancies thick upon me came;
Dim sadness – and blind thoughts, I knew not,
    nor could name.

V

I heard the sky-lark warbling in the sky;
And I bethought me of the playful hare:
Even such a happy Child of earth am I;
Even as these blissful creatures do I fare;
Far from the world I walk, and from all care;
But there may come another day to me –
Solitude, pain of heart, distress, and poverty.

VI

My whole life I have lived in pleasant thought,
As if life's business were a summer mood;
As if all needful things would come unsought
To genial faith, still rich in genial good;
But how can He expect that others should
Build for him, sow for him, and at his call
Love him, who for himself will take no heed at all?

VII

I thought of Chatterton, the marvellous Boy,
The sleepless Soul that perished in his pride;
Of Him who walked in glory and in joy
Following his plough, along the mountain-side:
By our own spirits are we deified:

We Poets in our youth begin in gladness;
But thereof come in the end despondency and
   madness.

VIII

Now, whether it were by peculiar grace,
A leading from above, a something given,
Yet it befell, that, in this lonely place,
When I with these untoward thoughts had
   striven,
Beside a pool bare to the eye of heaven
I saw a Man before me unawares:
The oldest man he seemed that ever wore grey
   hairs.

IX

As a huge stone is sometimes seen to lie
Couched on the bald top of an eminence;
Wonder to all who do the same espy,
By what means it could thither come, and
   whence;
So that it seems a thing endued with sense:
Like a sea-beast crawled forth, that on a shelf
Of rock or sand reposeth, there to sun itself;

X

Such seemed this Man, not all alive nor dead,
Nor all asleep – in his extreme old age:
His body was bent double, feet and head
Coming together in life's pilgrimage;
As if some dire constraint of pain, or rage
Of sickness felt by him in times long past,
A more than human weight upon his frame had
   cast.

Himself he propped, limbs, body, and pale face,
Upon a long grey staff of shaven wood:
And, still as I drew near with gentle pace,
Upon the margin of that moorish flood
Motionless as a cloud the old Man stood,
That heareth not the loud winds when they call;
And moveth all together, if it move at all.

XII

At length, himself unsettling, he the pond
Stirred with his staff, and fixedly did look
Upon the muddy water, which he conned,
As if he had been reading in a book:
And now a stranger's privilege I took;
And, drawing to his side, to him did say,
'This morning gives us promise of a glorious day.'

XIII

A gentle answer did the old Man make,
In courteous speech which forth he slowly drew:
And him with further words I thus bespake,
'What occupation do you there pursue?
This is a lonesome place for one like you.'
Ere he replied, a flash of mild surprise
Broke from the sable orbs of his yet-vivid eyes.

XIV

His words came feebly, from a feeble chest,
But each in solemn order followed each,
With something of a lofty utterance drest –
Choice word and measured phrase, above the
    reach
Of ordinary men; a stately speech;

Such as grave Livers do in Scotland use,
Religious men, who give to God and man their
    dues.

XV

He told, that to these waters he had come
To gather leeches, being old and poor:
Employment hazardous and wearisome!
And he had many hardships to endure:
From pond to pond he roamed, from moor to
    moor;
Housing, with God's good help, by choice or
    chance;
And in this way he gained an honest
    maintenance.

XVI

The old Man still stood talking by my side;
But now his voice to me was like a stream
Scarce heard; nor word from word could I divide;
And the whole body of the Man did seem
Like one whom I had met with in a dream;
Or like a man from some far region sent,
To give me human strength, by apt
    admonishment.

XVII

My former thoughts returned: the fear that kills;
And hope that is unwilling to be fed;
Cold, pain, and labour, and all fleshly ills;
And mighty Poets in their misery dead.
– Perplexed, and longing to be comforted,
My question eagerly did I renew,
'How is it that you live, and what is it you do?'

XVIII

He with a smile did then his words repeat;
And said that, gathering leeches, far and wide
He travelled; stirring thus about his feet
The waters of the pools where they abide.
'Once I could meet with them on every side;
But they have dwindled long by slow decay;
Yet still I persevere, and find them where I may.'

XIX

While he was talking thus, the lonely place,
The old Man's shape, and speech – all troubled
    me:
In my mind's eye I seemed to see him pace
About the weary moors continually,
Wandering about alone and silently.
While I these thoughts within myself pursued,
He, having made a pause, the same discourse
    renewed.

XX

And soon with this he other matter blended,
Cheerfully uttered, with demeanour kind,
But stately in the main; and when he ended,
I could have laughed myself to scorn to find
In that decrepit Man so firm a mind.
'God,' said I, 'be my help and stay secure;
I'll think of the Leech-gatherer on the lonely
    moor!'

[1918]   ## Strange Meeting

It seemed that out of battle I escaped
Down some profound dull tunnel, long since
    scooped
Through granites which titanic wars had
    groined.
Yet also there encumbered sleepers groaned,
Too fast in thought or death to be bestirred.
Then, as I probed them, one sprang up, and
    stared
With piteous recognition in fixed eyes,
Lifting distressful hands as if to bless.
And by his smile, I knew that sullen hall,
By his dead smile I knew we stood in Hell.
With a thousand pains that vision's face was
    grained;
Yet no blood reached there from the upper
    ground,
And no guns thumped, or down the flues made
    moan.
'Strange friend,' I said, 'here is no cause to
    mourn.'
'None,' said the other, 'save the undone years,
The hopelessness. Whatever hope is yours,
Was my life also; I went hunting wild
After the wildest beauty in the world,
Which lies not calm in eyes, or braided hair,
But mocks the steady running of the hour,
And if it grieves, grieves richlier than here.
For by my glee might many men have laughed,
And of my weeping something had been left,
Which must die now. I mean the truth untold,
The pity of war, the pity war distilled.
Now men will go content with what we spoiled.

Or, discontent, boil bloody, and be spilled.
They will be swift with swiftness of the tigress,
None will break ranks, though nations trek from
    progress.
Courage was mine, and I had mystery,
Wisdom was mine, and I had mastery;
To miss the march of this retreating world
Into vain citadels that are not walled.
Then, when much blood had clogged their
    chariot-wheels
I would go up and wash them from sweet wells,
Even with truths that lie too deep for taint.
I would have poured my spirit without stint
But not through wounds; not on the cess of war.
Foreheads of men have bled where no wounds
    were.
I am the enemy you killed, my friend.
I knew you in this dark; for so you frowned
Yesterday through me as you jabbed and killed.
I parried; but my hands were loath and cold.
Let us sleep now . . .'

WILLIAM SHAKESPEARE

[1604/5] *from* King Lear (Act III)

SCENE I: *A Heath.*
A storm, with thunder and lightning. Enter Kent and
a Gentleman, meeting.

KENT: Who's there, besides foul weather?
GENTLEMAN: One minded like the weather, most unquietly.
KENT: I know you. Where's the King?
GENTLEMAN: Contending with the fretful elements;
    Bids the wind blow the earth into the sea,
    Or swell the curled waters 'bove the main,

That things might change or cease; tears his
    white hair,
Which the impetuous blasts, with eyeless rage,
Catch in their fury, and make nothing of;
Strives in his little world of man to out-storm
The to-and-fro-conflicting wind and rain.
This night, wherein the cub-drawn bear would
    couch,
The lion and the belly-pinched wolf
Keep their fur dry, unbonneted he runs,
And bids what will take all.

KENT: But who is with him?

GENTLEMAN: None but the Fool, who labours to out-jest
His heart-strook injuries.

KENT: Sir, I do know you;
And dare, upon the warrant of my note,
Commend a dear thing to you. There is division,
Although as yet the face of it is cover'd
With mutual cunning, 'twixt Albany and
    Cornwall;
Who have – as who have not, that their great
    stars
Thron'd and set high? – servants, who seem no
    less,
Which are to France the spies and speculations
Intelligent of our state. What hath been seen,
Either in snuffs and packings of the Dukes,
Or the hard rein which both of them have borne
Against the old kind King; or something deeper,
Whereof perchance these are but furnishings –
But, true it is, from France there comes a power
Into this scatter'd kingdom; who already,
Wise in our negligence, have secret feet
In some of our best ports, and are at point
To show their open banner. Now to you:
If on my credit you dare build so far

quarrels and intrigues

To make your speed to Dover, you shall find
Some that will thank you, making just report
Of how unnatural and bemadding sorrow
The King hath cause to plain.
I am a gentleman of blood and breeding,
And from some knowledge and assurance offer
This office to you.

GENTLEMAN: I will talk further with you.

KENT: No, do not.
For confirmation that I am much more
Than my out-wall, open this purse, and take
What it contains. If you shall see Cordelia, –
As fear not but you shall – show her this ring,
And she will tell you who that fellow is
That yet you do not know. Fie on this storm!
I will go seek the King.

GENTLEMAN: Give me your hand. Have you no more to say?

KENT: Few words, but, to effect, more than all yet;
That, when we have found the King, in which
      your pain
That way, I'll this, he that first lights on him
Holla the other.
(*Exeunt severally.*)

SCENE II: *Another part of the Heath. Storm still.*
Enter Lear and Fool.

LEAR: Blow, winds, and crack your cheeks! rage! blow!
You cataracts and hurricanoes, spout
Till you have drench'd our steeples, drown'd the
      cocks!
You sulph'rous and thought-executing fires,

forerunners Vaunt-couriers of oak-cleaving thunderbolts,
Singe my white head! And thou, all-shaking
      thunder,
Strike flat the thick rotundity o' th' world!

Crack Nature's moulds, all germens spill at once
That makes ingrateful man!

FOOL: O Nuncle, court holy-water in a dry house is better than this rain-water out o' door. Good Nuncle, in, ask thy daughters blessing; here's a night pities neither wise men nor Fools.

LEAR: Rumble thy bellyful! Spit, fire! spout, rain!
Nor rain, wind, thunder, fire, are my daughters:
I tax you not, you elements, with unkindness;
I never gave you kingdom, call'd you children,
You owe me no subscription: then let fall
Your horrible pleasure; here I stand, your slave,
A poor, infirm, weak, and despis'd old man.
But yet I call you servile ministers,
That will with two pernicious daughters join
Your high-engender'd battles 'gainst a head
So old and white as this. O, ho! 'tis foul.

FOOL: He that has a house to put's head in has a good head-piece.

> The cod-piece that will house
> > Before the head has any,
> The head and he shall louse;
> > So beggars marry many.
> The man that makes his toe
> > What he his heart should make,
> Shall of a corn cry woe,
> > And turn his sleep to wake.

For there was never yet fair woman but she made mouths in a glass.

(Enter Kent.)

LEAR: No, I will be the pattern of all patience;
I will say nothing.

KENT: Who's there?

FOOL: Marry, here's grace and a cod-piece; that's a wise man and a Fool.

KENT: Alas! Sir, are you here? things that love night
Love not such nights as these; the wrathful skies

frighten Gallow the very wanderers of the dark,
And make them keep their caves. Since I was man
Such sheets of fire, such bursts of horrid thunder,
Such groans of roaring wind and rain, I never
Remember to have heard; man's nature cannot
carry
Th' affliction nor the fear.

LEAR: Let the great Gods,
That keep this dreadful pudder o'er our heads,
Find out their enemies now. Tremble, thou
wretch,
That hast within thee undivulged crimes,
Unwhipp'd of Justice; hide thee, thou bloody
hand,
Thou perjur'd, and thou simular of virtue
That art incestuous; caitiff, to pieces shake,
That under covert and convenient seeming
Has practis'd on man's life; close pent-up guilts,
Rive your concealing continents, and cry
These dreadful summoners grace. I am a man
More sinn'd against than sinning.

KENT: Alack! bare-headed!
Gracious my Lord, hard by here is a hovel;
Some friendship will it lend you 'gainst the
tempest;
Repose you there while I to this hard house, –
More harder than the stones whereof 'tis rais'd,
Which even but now, demanding after you,
Denied me to come in, – return and force
Their scanted courtesy.

LEAR: My wits begin to turn.
Come on, my boy. How dost, my boy? Art cold?
I am cold myself. Where is this straw, my fellow?
The art of our necessities is strange,

57

And can make vile things precious. Come, your
    hovel.
Poor Fool and knave, I have one part in my heart
That's sorry yet for thee.

FOOL: *He that has and a little tiny wit,*
            With hey, ho, the wind and the rain,
        Must make content with his fortunes fit,
            Though the rain it raineth every day.

LEAR: True, boy. Come, bring us to this hovel.

(*Exeunt Lear and Kent.*)

FOOL: This is a brave night to cool a courtezan.
I'll speak a prophecy ere I go:
When priests are more in word than matter;
When brewers mar their malt with water;
When nobles are their tailors' tutors;
No heretics burn'd, but wenches' suitors;
When every case in law is right;
No squire in debt, nor no poor knight;
When slanders do not live in tongues;
Nor cut-purses come not to throngs;
When usurers tell their gold i' th' field;
And bawds and whores do churches build;
Then shall the realm of Albion
Come to great confusion:
Then comes the time, who lives to see't,
That going shall be us'd with feet.
This prophecy Merlin shall make; for I live before
    his time.

(*Exit.*)

SCENE III. *A Room in Gloucester's Castle.*
Enter Gloucester and Edmund, with lights.

GLOUCESTER: Alack, alack! Edmund, I like not this unnatural
dealing. When I desir'd their leave that I might

pity him, they took from me the use of mine own house; charg'd me, on pain of perpetual displeasure, neither to speak of him, entreat for him, or any way sustain him.

EDMUND: Most savage and unnatural!

GLOUCESTER: Go to; say you nothing. There is division between the Dukes, and a worse matter than that. I have receiv'd a letter this night; 'tis dangerous to be spoken; I have lock'd the letter in my closet. These injuries the King now bears will be revenged home; there is part of a power already footed; we must incline to the King. I will look him and privily relieve him; go you and maintain talk with the Duke, that my charity be not of him perceiv'd. If he ask for me, I am ill and gone to bed. If I die for it, as no less is threatened me, the King, my old master, must be reliev'd. There is strange things toward, Edmund; pray you, be careful. (*Exit.*)

EDMUND: This courtesy, forbid thee, shall the Duke
Instantly know; and of that letter too:
This seems a fair deserving, and must draw me
That much my father loses; no less than all:
The younger rises when the old doth fall.
(*Exit.*)

SCENE IV: *The Heath. Before a Hovel.*
Enter Lear, Kent and Fool.

KENT: Here is the place, my Lord; good my Lord, enter:
The tyranny of the open night's too rough
For nature to endure.
(*Storm still.*)

LEAR: Let me alone.

KENT: Good my Lord, enter here.

LEAR: Wilt break my heart?

59

KENT: I had rather break mine own. Good my Lord,
    enter.
LEAR: Thou think'st 'tis much that this contentious
    storm
Invades us to the skin: so 'tis to thee;
But where the greater malady is fix'd,
The lesser is scarce felt, Thou 'ldst shun a bear;
But if thy flight lay toward the roaring sea,
Thou 'ldst meet the bear i' th' mouth. When the
    mind's free
The body's delicate; this tempest in my mind
Doth from my senses take all feeling else
Save what beats there – filial ingratitude!
Is it not as this mouth should tear this hand
For lifting food to 't? But I will punish home:
No, I will weep no more. In such a night
To shut me out? Pour on; I will endure.
In such a night as this? O Regan, Goneril!
Your old kind father, whose frank heart gave
    all, –
O! that way madness lies; let me shun that;
No more of that.
KENT: Good my Lord, enter here.
LEAR: Prithee, go in thyself; seek thine own ease:
This tempest will not give me leave to ponder
On things would hurt me more. But I'll go in.
(*To the Fool*:) In, boy; go first. You houseless
    poverty, –
Nay, get thee in. I'll pray, and then I'll sleep.
(*Fool goes in.*)
Poor naked wretches, whereso'er you are,
That bide the pelting of this pitiless storm,
How shall your houseless heads and unfed sides,
Your loop'd and window'd raggedness, defend
    you
From seasons such as these? O! I have ta'en

Too little care of this. Take physic, Pomp;
Expose thyself to feel what wretches feel,
That thou mayst shake the superflux to them,
And show the Heavens more just.

EDGAR: (*within*) Fathom and half, fathom and half!
Poor Tom!
(*The Fool runs out from the hovel.*)

FOOL: Come not in here, Nuncle; here's a spirit.
Help me! help me!

KENT: Give me thy hand. Who's there?

FOOL: A spirit: he says his name's poor Tom.

KENT: What art thou that dost grumble there i' th'
straw?
Come forth.
(*Enter Edgar disguised as a madman.*)

EDGAR: Away! the foul fiend follows me! Through the
sharp hawthorn blow the winds. Humh! go to
thy bed and warm thee.

LEAR: Didst thou give all to thy daughters?
And art thou come to this?

EDGAR: Who gives any thing to poor Tom? whom the foul
fiend hath led through fire and through flame,
through ford and whirlpool, o'er bog and quag-
mire; that hath laid knives under his pillow, and
halters in his pew; set ratsbane by his porridge;
made him proud of heart, to ride on a bay trot-
ting-horse over four-inch'd bridges, to course his
own shadow for a traitor. Bless thy five wits!
Tom's a-cold. O! do de, do de, do de. Bless thee
from whirlwinds, star-blasting, and taking! Do
poor Tom some charity, whom the foul fiend
vexes. There could I have him now, and there,
and there again, and there.
(*Storm still.*)

LEAR: What! has his daughters brought him to this
pass?

Couldst thou save nothing? Would'st thou give
  'em all?

FOOL: Nay, he reserv'd a blanket, else we had been all
  sham'd.

LEAR: Now all the plagues that in the pendulous air
  Hang fated o'er men's faults light on thy
    daughters!

KENT: He hath no daughters, Sir.

LEAR: Death, traitor! nothing could have subdu'd
    nature
  To such a lowness but his unkind daughters.
  Is it the fashion that discarded fathers
  Should have thus little mercy on their flesh?
  Judicious punishment! 'twas this flesh begot
  Those pelican daughters.

EDGAR: Pillicock sat on Pillicock hill:
  Alow, alow, loo, loo!

FOOL: This cold night will turn us all to fools and
  madmen.

EDGAR: Take heed o' th' foul fiend. Obey thy parents; keep
  thy word's justice; swear not; commit not with
  man's sworn spouse; set not thy sweet heart on
  proud array. Tom's a-cold.

LEAR: What hast thou been?

EDGAR: A servingman, proud in heart and mind; that
  curl'd my hair, wore gloves in my cap, serv'd the
  lust of my mistress' heart, and did the act of dark-
  ness with her; swore as many oaths as I spake
  words, and broke them in the sweet face of
  Heaven; one that slept in the contriving of lust,
  and wak'd to do it. Wine lov'd I deeply, dice
  dearly, and in woman out-paramour'd the Turk:
  false of heart, light of ear, bloody of hand; hog in
  sloth, fox in stealth, wolf in greediness, dog in
  madness, lion in prey. Let not the creaking of
  shoes nor the rustling of silks betray thy poor

heart to woman: keep thy foot out of brothels, thy hand out of plackets, thy pen from lenders' books, and defy the foul fiend. Still through the hawthorn blows the cold wind; says suum, mun, hey no nonny. Dolphin my boy, boy; sessa! let him trot by.

(*Storm still.*)

LEAR: Thou wert better in a grave than to answer with thy uncover'd body this extremity of the skies. Is man no more than this? Consider him well. Thou ow'st the worm no silk, the beast no hide, the sheep no wool, the cat no perfume. Ha! here's three on 's are sophisticated; thou art the thing itself; unaccommodated man is no more but such a poor, bare, forked animal as thou art. Off, off, you lendings! Come; unbutton here. (*Tearing off his clothes.*)

FOOL: Prithee, Nuncle, be contented; 'tis a naughty night to swim in. Now a little fire in a wild field were like an old lecher's heart; a small spark, all the rest on 's body cold. Look! here comes a walking fire.

(*Enter Gloucester, with a torch.*)

EDGAR: This is the foul Flibbertigibbet: he begins at curfew, and walks till the first cock; he gives the web and the pin, squinies the eye, and makes the hare-lip; mildews the white wheat, and hurts the poor creature of earth.

> Swithold footed thrice the old;
> He met the night-mare, and her nine-fold;
> Bid her alight,
> And her troth plight,
> And aroint thee, witch, aroint thee!

KENT: How fares your Grace?

LEAR: What's he?

KENT: Who's there? What is 't you seek?

cataract

St Withold

63

GLOUCESTER: What are you there? Your names?

EDGAR: Poor Tom; that eats the swimming frog, the toad, the todpole, the wall-newt, and the water; that in the fury of his heart, when the foul fiend rages, eats cow-dung for sallets; swallows the old rat and the ditch-dog; drinks the green mantle of the standing pool; who is whipp'd from tithing to tithing, and stock-punish'd, and imprison'd; who hath had three suits to his back, six shirts to his body,

parish

> Horse to ride, and weapons to wear,
>
> But mice and rats and such small deer,
>
> Have been Tom's food for seven long year.

Beware my follower. Peace, Smulkin! peace, thou fiend!

GLOUCESTER: What! hath your Grace no better company?

EDGAR: The Prince of Darkness is a gentleman; Modo he's called, and Mahu.

GLOUCESTER: Our flesh and blood, my lord, is grown so vile, That it doth hate what gets it.

EDGAR: Poor Tom's a-cold.

GLOUCESTER: Go in with me. My duty cannot suffer T' obey in all your daughters' hard commands: Though their injunction be to bar my doors, And let this tyrannous night take hold upon you, Yet I have ventured to come seek you out And bring you where both fire and food is ready.

LEAR: First let me talk with this philosopher. What is the cause of thunder?

KENT: Good my Lord, take his offer; go into th' house.

LEAR: I'll talk a word with this same learned Theban. What is your study?

EDGAR: How to prevent the fiend, and to kill vermin.

LEAR: Let me ask you one word in private.

KENT: Importune him once more to go, my Lord; His wits begin t' unsettle.

64

GLOUCESTER: Canst thou blame him?
            (*Storm still.*)
            His daughters seek his death. Ah! that good Kent;
            He said it would be thus, poor banish'd man!
            Thou say'st the king grows mad; I'll tell thee,
                friend,
            I am almost mad myself. I had a son,
            Now outlaw'd from my blood; he sought my life,
            But lately, very late; I lov'd him, friend,
            No father his son dearer; true to tell thee,
            The grief hath craz'd my wits. What a night's this
            I do beseech your Grace, –
    LEAR: O! cry you mercy, Sir.
            Noble philosopher, your company.
   EDGAR: Tom's a-cold.
GLOUCESTER: In, fellow, there, into th' hovel: keep thee warm.
    LEAR: Come, let's in all.
    KENT: This way, my Lord.
    LEAR: With him;
            I will keep still with my philosopher.
    KENT: Good my Lord, soothe him; let him take the
                fellow.
GLOUCESTER: Take him you on.
    KENT: Sirrah, come on; go along with us.
    LEAR: Come, good Athenian.
GLOUCESTER: No words, no words: hush.
   EDGAR: *Childe Roland to the dark tower came,*
                His word was still: Fie, foh, and fum,
                I smell the blood of a British man.

[1855]

Childe Roland to the Dark Tower Came

(*See Edgar's song in* Lear)

I

My first thought was, he lied in every word,
   That hoary cripple, with malicious eye
   Askance to watch the working of his lie
On mine, and mouth scarce able to afford
Suppression of the glee, that pursed and scored
   Its edge, at one more victim gained thereby.

II

What else should he be set for, and his staff?
   What, save to waylay with his lies, ensnare
   All travellers who might find him posted
      there,
And ask the road? I guessed what skull-like laugh
Would break, what crutch 'gin write my epitaph
   For pastime in the dusty thoroughfare,

III

If at his counsel I should turn aside
   Into that ominous tract which, all agree,
   Hides the Dark Tower. Yet acquiescingly
I did turn as he pointed: neither pride
Nor hope rekindling at the end descried,
   So much as gladness that some end might be.

IV

For, what with my whole world-wide wandering,
   What with my search drawn out thro' years,
      my hope

Dwindled into a ghost not fit to cope
With that obstreperous joy success would
    bring, –
I hardly tried now to rebuke the spring
  My heart made, finding failure in its scope.

V

As when a sick man very near to death
  Seems dead indeed, and feels begin and end
  The tears and takes the farewell of each friend,
And hears one bid the other go, draw breath
Freelier outside, ('since all is o'er,' he saith,
  'And the blow fallen no grieving can amend;')

VI

While some discuss if near the other graves
  Be room enough for this, and when a day
  Suits best for carrying the corpse away,
With care about the banners, scarves and staves:
And still the man hears all, and only craves
  He may not shame such tender love and stay.

VII

Thus, I had so long suffered in this quest,
  Heard failure prophesied so oft, been writ
  So many times among 'The Band' – to wit,
The knights who to the Dark Tower's search
    addressed
Their steps – that just to fail as they, seemed best,
  And all the doubt was now – should I be fit?

VIII

So, quiet as despair, I turned from him,
    That hateful cripple, out of his highway
    Into the path he pointed. All the day
Had been a dreary one at best, and dim
Was settling to its close, yet shot one grim
     stray animal   Red leer to see the plain catch its estray.

IX

For mark! no sooner was I fairly found
    Pledged to the plain, after a pace or two,
    Than, pausing to throw backward a last view
O'er the safe road, 't was gone; grey plain all
      round:
Nothing but plain to the horizon's bound.
    I might go on; nought else remained to do.

X

So, on I went. I think I never saw
    Such starved ignoble nature; nothing throve:
    For flowers – as well expect a cedar grove!
But cockle, spurge, according to their law
Might propagate their kind, with none to awe,
    You'd think; a burr had been a treasure-trove.

XI

No! penury, inertness and grimace,
    In some strange sort, were the land's portion. 'See
    'Or shut your eyes,' said Nature peevishly,
'It nothing skills: I cannot help my case:
''T is the Last Judgment's fire must cure this
      place,
    'Calcine its clods and set my prisoners free.'

If there pushed any ragged thistle-stalk
 Above its mates, the head was chopped; the
   bents

grasses

 Were jealous else. What made those holes
  and rents
In the dock's harsh swarth leaves, bruised as to
  baulk
All hope of greenness? 't is a brute must walk
 Pashing their life out, with a brute's intents.

XIII

As for the grass, it grew as scant as hair
 In leprosy; thin dry blades pricked the mud
 Which underneath looked kneaded up with
  blood.
One stiff blind horse, his every bone a-stare,
Stood stupefied, however he came there:
 Thrust out past service from the devil's stud!

XIV

Alive? he might be dead for aught I know,
 With that red gaunt and colloped neck
  a-strain,
 And shut eyes underneath the rusty mane;
Seldom went such grotesqueness with such woe;
I never saw a brute I hated so;
 He must be wicked to deserve such pain.

XV

I shut my eyes and turned them on my heart.
 As a man calls for wine before he fights,
 I asked one draught of earlier, happier sights,
Ere fitly I could hope to play my part.

Think first, fight afterwards – the soldier's art:
  One taste of the old time sets all to rights.

XVI

Not it! I fancied Cuthbert's reddening face
  Beneath its garniture of curly gold,
  Dear fellow, till I almost felt him fold
An arm in mine to fix me to the place,
That way he used. Alas, one night's disgrace!
  Out went my heart's new fire and left it cold.

XVII

Giles then, the soul of honour – there he stands
  Frank as ten years ago when knighted first.
  What honest man should dare (he said) he
    durst.
Good – but the scene shifts – faugh! what
    hangman-hands
Pin to his breast a parchment? His own bands
  Read it. Poor traitor, spit upon and curst!

XVIII

Better this present than a past like that;
  Back therefore to my darkening path again!
  No sound, no sight as far as eye could strain.
Will the night send a howlet or a bat?
I asked: when something on the dismal flat
  Came to arrest my thoughts and change their
    train.

XIX

A sudden little river crossed my path
  As unexpected as a serpent comes.
  No sluggish tide congenial to the glooms;

This, as it frothed by, might have been a bath
For the fiend's glowing hoof – to see the wrath
  Of its black eddy bespate with flakes and
    spumes.

XX

So petty yet so spiteful! All along,
  Low scrubby alders kneeled down over it;
  Drenched willows flung them headlong in a fit
Of mute despair, a suicidal throng:
The river which had done them all the wrong,
  What'er that was, rolled by, deterred no whit.

XXI

Which, while I forded, – good saints, how I feared
  To set my foot upon a dead man's cheek,
  Each step, or feel the spear I thrust to seek
For hollows, tangled in his hair or beard!
– It may have been a water-rat I speared,
  But, ugh! it sounded like a baby's shriek.

XXII

Glad was I when I reached the other bank.
  Now for a better country. Vain presage!
  Who were the strugglers, what war did they
    wage,
Whose savage trample thus could pad the dank
Soil to a plash? Toads in a poisoned tank,
  Or wild cats in a red-hot iron cage –

XXIII

The fight must so have seemed in that fell cirque.
  What penned them there, with all the plain to
    choose?

No foot-print leading to that horrid mews,
None out of it. Mad brewage set to work
Their brains, no doubt, like galley-slaves the
    Turk
    Pits for his pastime, Christians against Jews.

XXIV

And more than that – a furlong on – why, there!
    What bad use was that engine for, that wheel,
    Or brake, not wheel – that harrow fit to reel
Men's bodies out like silk? with all the air
Of Tophet's tool, on earth left unaware,
    Or brought to sharpen its rusty teeth of steel.

XXV

Then came a bit of stubbed ground, once a wood,
    Next a marsh, it would seem, and now mere
      earth
Desperate and done with; (so a fool finds mirth,
Makes a thing and then mars it, till his mood
Changes and off he goes!) within a rood –
    Bog, clay and rubble, sand and stark black
      dearth.

XXVI

Now blotches rankling, coloured gay and grim,
    Now patches where some leanness of the soil's
    Broke into moss or substances like boils;
Then came some palsied oak, a cleft in him
Like a distorted mouth that splits its rim
    Gaping at death, and dies while it recoils.

XXVII

And just as far as ever from the end!
    Nought in the distance but the evening,
        nought
    To point my footstep further! At the thought,
A great black bird, Apollyon's bosom-friend,
Sailed past, nor beat his wide wing dragon-
        penned
    That brushed my cap – perchance the guide I
    sought.

XXVIII

For, looking up, aware I somehow grew,
    'Spite of the dusk, the plain had given place
    All round to mountains – with such name to
    grace
Mere ugly heights and heaps now stolen in view.
How thus they had surprised me, – solve it, you!
    How to get from them was no clearer case.

XXIX

Yet half I seemed to recognize some trick
    Of mischief happened to me, God knows
        when –
    In a bad dream perhaps. Here ended, then,
Progress this way. When, in the very nick
Of giving up, one time more, came a click
    As when a trap shuts – you're inside the den!

XXX

Burningly it came on me all at once,
    This was the place! those two hills on the
        right,

Crouched like two bulls locked horn in horn
    in fight;
While to the left, a tall scalped mountain . . .
    Dunce,
Dotard, a-dozing at the very nonce,
    After a life spent training for the sight!

XXXI

What in the midst lay but the Tower itself?
    The round squat turret, blind as the fool's
      heart,
    Built of brown stone, without a counterpart
In the whole world. The tempest's mocking elf
Points to the shipman thus the unseen shelf
    He strikes on, only when the timbers start.

XXXII

Not see? because of night perhaps? – why, day
    Came back again for that! before it left,
    The dying sunset kindled through a cleft:
The hills, like giants at a hunting, lay,
Chin upon hand, to see the game at bay, –
    'Now stab and end the creature – to the heft!'

XXXIII

Not hear? when noise was everywhere! it tolled
    Increasing like a bell. Names in my ears
    Of all the lost adventurers my peers, –
How such a one was strong, and such was bold,
And such was fortunate, yet each of old
    Lost, lost! one moment knelled the woe of
      years.

There they stood, ranged along the hill-sides, met
    To view the last of me, a living frame
    For one more picture! in a sheet of flame
I saw them and I knew them all. And yet
Dauntless the slug-horn to my lips I set,
    And blew. *'Childe Roland to the Dark Tower
    came.'*

ANONYMOUS (IRISH)

[8th century]   ## The Deer's Cry

I arise to-day
Through a mighty strength, the invocation of the
    Trinity,
Through belief in the threeness,
Through confession of the oneness
Of the Creator of Creation.

I arise to-day
Through the strength of Christ's birth with His
    baptism,
Through the strength of His crucifixion with His
    burial,
Through the strength of His resurrection and His
    ascension,
Through the strength of His descent for the
    judgement of Doom.

I arise to-day
Through the strength of the love of Cherubim,
In obdience of angels,
In the service of archangels,
In hope of resurrection to meet with reward,
In prayers of patriarchs,
In predictions of prophets,

In preachings of apostles,
In faiths of confessors,
In innocence of holy virgins,
In deeds of righteous men.

I arise to-day
Through the strength of heaven:
Light of sun,
Radiance of moon,
Splendour of fire,
Speed of lightning,
Swiftness of wind,
Depth of sea,
Stability of earth,
Firmness of rock.

I arise to-day
Through God's strength to pilot me:
God's might to uphold me,
God's wisdom to guide me,
God's eye to look before me,
God's ear to hear me,
God's word to speak for me,
God's hand to guard me,
God's way to lie before me,
God's shield to protect me,
God's host to save me
From snares of devils,
From temptations of vices,
From every one who shall wish me ill,
Afar and anear,
Alone and in multitude.

I summon to-day all these powers between me
    and those evils,
Against every cruel merciless power that may
    oppose my body and soul,

Against incantations of false prophets,
Against black laws of pagandom,
Against false laws of heretics,
Against craft of idolatry,
Against spells of women and smiths and wizards,
Against every knowledge that corrupts man's
  body and soul.

Christ to shield me to-day
Against poison, against burning,
Against drowning, against wounding,
So that there may come to me abundance of
  reward.
Christ with me, Christ before me, Christ behind
  me,
Christ in me, Christ beneath me, Christ above me,
Christ on my right, Christ on my left,
Christ when I lie down, Christ when I sit down,
  Christ when I arise.
Christ in the heart of every man who thinks of me,
Christ in the mouth of every one who speaks of
  me,
Christ in every eye that sees me,
Christ in every ear that hears me.

I arise to-day
Through a mighty strength, the invocation of the
  Trinity,
Through belief in the threeness,
Through confession of the oneness
Of the Creator of Creation.

translated by Whitley Stokes, John Strachan
and Kuno Meyer

JOHN BUNYAN

[1695]

'Who would true valour see'

Who would true valour see,
Let him come hither;
One here will constant be,
Come wind, come weather.
There's no discouragement
Shall make him once relent
His first avow'd intent,
To be a pilgrim.

Whoso beset him round
With dismal stories,
Do but themselves confound,
His strength the more is.
No lion can him fright,
He'll with a giant fight,
But he will have a right
To be a pilgrim.

Hobgoblin, nor foul fiend,
Can daunt his spirit;
He knows he at the end
Shall life inherit.
Then fancies fly away,
He'll fear not what men say,
He'll labour night and day
To be a pilgrim.

P. K. PAGE

[1951]

Photos of a Salt Mine

How innocent their lives look,
how like a child's
dream of caves and winter, both combined;
the steep descent to whiteness

and the stope
with its striated walls
their folds all leaning as if pointing to
the great whiteness still,
that great white bank
with its decisive front,
that seam upon a slope,
salt's lovely ice.

And wonderful underfoot the snow of salt
the fine
particles a broom could sweep,
one thinks
muckers might make angels in its drafts
as children do in snow,
lovers in sheets,
lie down and leave imprinted where they lay
a feathered creature holier than they.

And in the outworked stopes
with lamps and ropes
up miniature matterhorns
the miners climb
probe with their lights
the ancient folds of rock –
syncline and anticline –
and scoop from darkness an Aladdin's cave:
rubies and opals glitter from its walls.

But hoses douse the brilliance of these jewels,
melt fire to brine.
Salt's bitter water trickles thin and forms,
slow fathoms down,
a lake within a cave,
lacquered with jet –
white's opposite.
There grey on black the boating miners float

79

to mend the stays and struts of that old stope
and deeply underground
their words resound,
are multiplied by echo, swell and grow
and make a climate of a miner's voice.

So all the photographs like children's wishes
are filled with caves or winter,
innocence
has acted as a filter,
selected only beauty from the mine.
Except in the last picture,
it is shot
from an acute high angle. In a pit
figures the size of pins are strangely lit
and might be dancing but you know they're not.
Like Dante's vision of the nether hell
men struggle with the bright cold fires of salt,
locked in the black inferno of the rock:
the filter here, not innocence but guilt.

W. S. GRAHAM

[1970]   Malcolm Mooney's Land

I

Today, Tuesday, I decided to move on
Although the wind was veering. Better to move
Than have them at my heels, poor friends
I buried earlier under the printed snow.
From wherever it is I urged these words
To find their subtle vents, the northern dazzle
Of silence craned to watch. Footprint on foot
Print, word on word and each on a fool's errand.
Malcolm Mooney's Land. Elizabeth
Was in my thoughts all morning and the boy.

Wherever I speak from or in what particular
Voice, this is always a record of me in you.
I can record at least out there to the west
The grinding bergs and, listen, further off
Where we are going, the glacier calves
Making its sudden momentary thunder.
This is as good a night, a place as any.

II

From the rimed bag of sleep, Wednesday,
My words crackle in the early air.
Thistles of ice about my chin,
My dreams, my breath a ruff of crystals.
The new ice falls from canvas walls.
O benign creature with the small ear-hole,
Submerger under silence, lead
Me where the unblubbered monster goes
Listening and makes his play.
Make my impediment mean no ill
And be itself a way.

A fox was here last night (Maybe Nansen's,
Reading my instruments.) the prints
All round the tent and not a sound.
Not that I'd have him call my name.
Anyhow how should he know? Enough
Voices are with me here and more
The further I go. Yesterday
I heard the telephone ringing deep
Down in a blue crevasse.
I did not answer it and could
Hardly bear to pass.

Landlice, always my good bedfellows,
Ride with me in my sweaty seams.
Come bonny friendly beasts, brother

To the grammarsow and the word-louse,
Bite me your presence, keep me awake
In the cold with work to do, to remember
To put down something to take back.
I have reached the edge of earshot here
And by the laws of distance
My words go through the smoking air
Changing their tune on silence.

III

My friend who loves owls
Has been with me all day
Walking at my ear
And speaking of old summers
When to speak was easy.
His eyes are almost gone
Which made him hear well.
Under our feet the great
Glacier drove its keel.
What is to read there
Scored out in the dark?

Later the north-west distance
Thickened towards us.
The blizzard grew and proved
Too filled with other voices
High and desperate
For me to hear him more.
I turned to see him go
Becoming shapeless into
The shrill swerving snow.

IV

    Today, Friday, holds the white
    Paper up too close to see
Me here in a white-out in this tent of a place
    And why is it there has to be
Some place to find, however momentarily
To speak from, some distance to listen to?

    Out at the far-off edge I hear
    Colliding voices, drifted, yes
To find me through the slowly opening leads.
    Tomorrow I'll try the rafted ice.
Have I not been trying to use the obstacle
Of language well? It freezes round us all.

V

Why did you choose this place
For us to meet? Sit
With me between this word
And this, my furry queen.
Yet not mistake this
For the real thing. Here
In Malcolm Mooney's Land
I have heard many
Approachers in the distance
Shouting. Early hunters
Skittering across the ice
Full of enthusiasm
And making fly and,
Within the ear, the yelling
Spear steepening to
The real prey, the right
Prey of the moment.
The honking choir in fear
Leave the tilting floe

And enter the sliding water.
Above the bergs the foolish
Voices are lighting lamps
And all their sounds make
This diary of a place
Writing us both in.

Come and sit. Or is
It right to stay here
While, outside the tent
The bearded blinded go
Calming their children
Into the ovens of frost?
And what's the news? What
Brought you here through
The spring leads opening?

Elizabeth, you and the boy
Have been with me often
Especially on those last
Stages. Tell him a story.
Tell him I came across
An old sulphur bear
Sawing his log of sleep
Loud beneath the snow.
He puffed the powdered light
Up on to this page
And here his reek fell
In splinters among
These words. He snored well.
Elizabeth, my furry
Pelted queen of Malcolm
Mooney's Land, I made
You hear beside me
For a moment out
Of the correct fatigue.

I have made myself alone now.
Outside the tent endless
Drifting hummock crests.
Words drifting on words.
The real unabstract snow.

WALTER DE LA MARE

[1912] ## The Listeners

'Is there anybody there?' said the Traveller,
    Knocking on the moonlit door;
And his horse in the silence champed the grasses
    Of the forest's ferny floor:
And a bird flew up out of the turret,
    Above the Traveller's head:
And he smote upon the door again a second time;
    'Is there anybody there?' he said.
But no one descended to the Traveller;
    No head from the leaf-fringed sill
Leaned over and looked into his grey eyes,
    Where he stood perplexed and still.
But only a host of phantom listeners
    That dwelt in the lone house then
Stood listening in the quiet of the moonlight
    To that voice from the world of men:
Stood thronging the faint moonbeams on the
        dark stair,
    That goes down to the empty hall,
Hearkening in an air stirred and shaken
    By the lonely Traveller's call.
And he felt in his heart their strangeness,
    Their stillness answering his cry,
While his horse moved, cropping the dark turf,
    'Neath the starred and leafy sky;
For he suddenly smote on the door, even
    Louder, and lifted his head: –

85

'Tell them I came, and no one answered,
  That I kept my word,' he said.
Never the least stir made the listeners,
  Though every word he spake
Fell echoing through the shadowiness of the still
    house
  From the one man left awake:
Ay, they heard his foot upon the stirrup,
  And the sound of iron on stone,
And how the silence surged softly backward,
  When the plunging hoofs were gone.

RANDALL JARRELL

[1965]   Field and Forest

When you look down from the airplane you see
    lines,
Roads, ruts, braided into a net or web –
Where people go, what people do: the ways of life.

Heaven says to the farmer: 'What's your field?'
And he answers: 'Farming,' with a field,
Or: 'Dairy-farming,' with a herd of cows.
They seem a boy's toy cows, seen from this high.

Seen from this high,
The fields have a terrible monotony.

But between the lighter patches there are dark
    ones.
A farmer is separated from a farmer
By what farmers have in common: forests,
Those dark things – what the fields were to begin
    with.
At night a fox comes out of the forest, eats his
    chickens.

At night the deer come out of the forest, eat his
    crops.

If he could he'd make farm out of all the forest,
But it isn't worth it: some of it's marsh, some
    rocks,
There are things there you couldn't get rid of
With a bulldozer, even – not with dynamite.
Besides, he likes it. He had a cave there, as a boy;
He hunts there now. It's a waste of land,
But it would be a waste of time, a waste of money,
To make it into anything but what it is.

At night, from the airplane, all you see is lights,
A few lights, the lights of houses, headlights,
And darkness. Somewhere below, beside a light,
The farmer, naked, takes out his false teeth:
He doesn't eat now. Takes off his spectacles:
He doesn't see now. Shuts his eyes.
If he were able to he'd shut his ears,
And as it is, he doesn't hear with them.
Plainly, he's taken out his tongue: he doesn't talk.
His arms and legs: at least, he doesn't move them.
They are knotted together, curled up, like a
    child's.
And after he has taken off the thoughts
It has taken him his life to learn,
He takes off, last of all, the world.

When you take off everything what's left? A wish,
A blind wish; and yet the wish isn't blind,
What the wish wants to see, it sees.

There in the middle of the forest is the cave
And there, curled up inside it, is the fox.

He stands looking at it.

Around him the fields are sleeping: the fields
      dream.
At night there are no more farmers, no more
      farms.
At night the fields dream, the fields *are* the forest.
The boy stands looking at the fox
As if, if he looked long enough –
                              he looks at it.
Or is it the fox that's looking at the boy?
The trees can't tell the two of them apart.

W. R. RODGERS

[pub. 1971] ## Field Day

The old farmer, nearing death, asked
To be carried outside and set down
Where he could see a certain field
'And then I will cry my heart out,' he said.

It troubles me, thinking about that man;
What shape was the field of his crying
In Donegal?

I remember a small field in Down, a field
Within fields, shaped like a triangle.
I could have stood there and looked at it
All day long.

And I remember crossing the frontier between
France and Spain at a forbidden point, and seeing
A small triangular field in Spain,
And stopping

Or walking in Ireland down any rutted by-road
To where it hit the highway, there was always
At this turning-point and abuttment
A still centre, a V-shape of grass
Untouched by cornering traffic,

Where country lads larked at night.

I think I know what the shape of the field was
That made the old man weep.

EDWARD THOMAS

[pub. 1918] The Unknown Bird

Three lovely notes he whistled, too soft to be heard
If others sang; but others never sang
In the great beech-wood all that May and June.
No one saw him: I alone could hear him:
Though many listened. Was it but four years
Ago? or five? He never came again.

Oftenest when I heard him I was alone,
Nor could I ever make another hear.
La-la-la! he called, seeming far-off –
As if a cock crowed past the edge of the world,
As if the bird or I were in a dream.
Yet that he travelled through the trees and
      sometimes
Neared me, was plain, though somehow distant
      still
He sounded. All the proof is – I told men
What I had heard.

                              I never knew a voice,
Man, beast, or bird, better than this. I told
The naturalists; but neither had they heard
Anything like the notes that did so haunt me,
I had them clear by heart and have them still.
Four years, or five, have made no difference. Then
As now that La-la-la! was bodiless sweet:
Sad more than joyful it was, if I must say
That it was one or other, but if sad
'Twas sad only with joy too, too far off

For me to taste it. But I cannot tell
If truly never anything but fair
The days were when he sang, as now they seem.
This surely I know, that I who listened then,
Happy sometimes, sometimes suffering
A heavy body and a heavy heart,
Now straightway, if I think of it, become
Light as that bird wandering beyond my shore.

DANTE GABRIEL ROSSETTI

[1861] ## Of the Lady Pietra degli Scrovigni

(from Dante)

To the dim light and the large circle of shade
I have clomb, and to the whitening of the hills,
There where we see no colour in the grass.
Natheless my longing loses not its green,
It has so taken root in the hard stone
Which talks and hears as though it were a lady.

Utterly frozen is this youthful lady,
Even as the snow that lies within the shade;
For she is no more moved than is the stone
By the sweet season which makes warm the hills
And alters them afresh from white to green,
Covering their sides again with flowers and grass.

When on her hair she sets a crown of grass
The thought has no more room for other lady,
Because she weaves the yellow with the green
So well that Love sits down there in the shade,
Love who has shut me in among low hills
Faster than between walls of granite-stone.

She is more bright than is a precious stone;
The wound she gives may not be healed with
    grass:
I therefore have fled far o'er plains and hills
For refuge from so dangerous a lady;
But from her sunshine nothing can give shade,
Not any hill, nor wall, nor summer-green.

A while ago, I saw her dressed in green,
So fair, she might have wakened in a stone
This love which I do feel even for her shade;
And therefore, as one woos a graceful lady,
I wooed her in a field that was all grass
Girdled about with very lofty hills.

Yet shall the streams turn back and climb the hills
Before Love's flame in this damp wood and green
Burn, as it burns within a youthful lady,
For my sake, who would sleep away in stone
My life, or feed like beasts upon the grass,
Only to see her garments cast a shade.

How dark soe'er the hills throw out their shade,
Under her summer-green the beautiful lady,
Covers it, like a stone cover'd in grass.

AUSTIN CLARKE

[1938]   ## The Straying Student

On a holy day when sails were blowing
    southward,
A bishop sang the Mass at Inishmore,
Men took one side, their wives were on the other
But I heard the woman coming from the shore:
And wild in despair my parents cried aloud
For they saw the vision draw me to the doorway.

Long had she lived in Rome when Popes were
    bad,
The wealth of every age she makes her own,
Yet smiled on me in eager admiration,
And for a summer taught me all I know,
Banishing shame with her great laugh that rang
As if a pillar caught it back alone.

I learned the prouder counsel of her throat,
My mind was growing bold as light in Greece;
And when in sleep her stirring limbs were shown,
I blessed the noonday rock that knew no tree:
And for an hour the mountain was her throne,
Although her eyes were bright with mockery.

They say I was sent back from Salamanca
And failed in logic, but I wrote her praise
Nine times upon a college wall in France.
She laid her hand at darkfall on my page
That I might read the heavens in a glance
And I knew every star the Moors have named.

Awake or in my sleep, I have no peace now,
Before the ball is struck, my breath has gone,
And yet I tremble lest she may deceive me
And leave me in this land, where every woman's
    son
Must carry his own coffin and believe,
In dread, all that the clergy teach the young.

GEORGE HERBERT

[1633]   The Collar

I struck the board, and cry'd, No more.
        I will abroad.
    What? shall I ever sigh and pine?
My lines and life are free; free as the road,

Loose as the wind, as large as store.
 Shall I be still in suit?
Have I no harvest but a thorn
To let me bleed, and not restore
 What I have lost with cordial fruit?
  Sure there was wine
Before my sighs did dry it: there was corn
 Before my tears did drown it.
 Is the year only lost to me?
 Have I no bays to crown it?
No flowers, no garlands gay? all blasted?
  All wasted?
 Not so, my heart: but there is fruit,
  And thou hast hands.
Recover all thy sigh-blown age
On double pleasures: leave thy cold dispute
Of what is fit, and not. Forsake thy cage,
  Thy rope of sands,
Which petty thoughts have made, and made to
  thee
 Good cable, to enforce and draw,
  And be thy law,
While thou did wink and would not see.
  Away; take heed:
  I will abroad.
Call in thy deaths head there: tie up thy fears.
  He that forbears
 To suit and serve his need,
  Deserves his load.
But as I rav'd and grew more fierce and wild
  At every word,
 Me thought I heard one calling, *Child!*
  And I reply'd, *My Lord.*

[1979]

Route Six

The city squats on my back.
I am heart-sore, stiff-necked,
exasperated. That's why
I slammed the door,
that's why I tell you now,
in every house of marriage
there's room for an interpreter.
Let's jump into the car, honey,
and head straight for the Cape,
where the cock on our housetop crows
that the weather's fair,
and my garden waits for me
to coax it into bloom.
As for those passions left
that flare past understanding,
like bundles of dead letters
out of our previous lives
that amaze us with their fevers,
we can stow them in the rear
along with ziggurats of luggage
and Celia, our transcendental cat,
past-mistress of all languages,
including Hottentot and silence.
We'll drive non-stop till dawn,
and if I grow sleepy at the wheel,
you'll keep me awake by singing
in your bravura Chicago style
Ruth Etting's smoky song,
'Love Me or Leave Me,'
belting out the choices.

Light glazes the eastern sky
Over Buzzards Bay.

Celia gyrates upward
like a performing seal,
her glistening nostrils aquiver
to sniff the brine-spiked air.
The last stretch toward home!
Twenty summers roll by.

KATHLEEN RAINE

[1943]   Parting

Darling, this is goodbye. The words are
      ordinary
But love is rare. So let it go tenderly
as the sound of violins into silence.

Parting is sad for us, because something is
      over,
But for the thing we have ended, it is a
      beginning –
Let love go like a young bird flying from the
      nest,

Like a new star, airborne into the evening,
Watched out of sight, or let fall gently as a
      tear,
Let our love go out of the world, like the
      prayer for a soul's rest.

Let the roses go, that you fastened in my hair
One summer night in a garden, and the song
That we heard from another house, where a
      piano was playing;
The shadow a street lamp cast through the net of
      a curtain,
The river at night, smooth and silent Thames,
      flowing through London.

For two years Ullswater was silver with my love
    of you,
The golden birch-leaves were holy, the wild
    cherry was sweet
On the fell-sides, scenting the spring for you.
The bees, drunk with the lime-flowers, dropped
    like grapes on the road,
And the silence was yours, over all Westmorland
    at night.

I raised the mountains for you, and set the
    streams
Running down the hills for love. I saw the moss
    grow
And the ferns unroll their croziers for love of you,
The snowdrops, the primrose, the heron, the
    martin, the sheep on the fells.

The snow was yours in winter, and the frost
    crystals
That shone like amethyst and sapphire in the
    starlight,
That grew their geometric beauty on the trees'
    animate branches,
The frozen waterfall, the coral caves of ice,
The noise of water rushing from the thawing
    springs.

The wind on the mountain, the shelter of the
    garden,
The stone seat under the yew-tree, the fire in the
    evening,
Home-baked loaves, and apples, trout from the
    beck
I loved for you, held holy for you, my darling.

That was erotic. That was one with the grass,
One with the night, the animals and the stars,

All that is mortal in us, and must pass,
Creatures whose own death is their unguessed
    secret,
Loving in one another the rose that must fade.

Yours, too, was the anteroom of the angels,
When I could hear a pin drop, or a drop of rain,
Or the creak of a beam, or the butterfly caught in
    the rafters.
I wrestled with angels for you, and in my body
Endured the entire blessing of love's pain.

All this is true. These things, my dear, are a life
Lived for love of you. The fire in the heart, the fire
    on the hearth,
And children's stories in the evening, even hope's
    death
Were precious for you. Precious all things in time
And outside time. The poem I know, and the
    wisdom
That is not mine, the poem that can never be
    written.

To you, one man among all men, I dedicate
The world I have known, my days and nights, my
    flowers,
The angels, the sorrows, the forms of life I
    consecrate
In your name, far beyond ourselves, or any
    selves —
These attributes are God's.

To you, once loved and for ever, from whom I part
Not because fate is blind, or the heart cold,
But because the world is neither yours nor mine,
Not even ourselves, not even what is dearest,
I offer what I can, my living moment,
My human span.

[pub 1633]

A Valediction: Forbidding Mourning

As virtuous men pass mildly away,
   And whisper to their souls, to go,
Whilst some of their sad friends do say,
   The breath goes now, and some say, no:

So let us melt, and make no noise,
   No tear-floods, nor sigh-tempests move,
'Twere profanation of our joys
   To tell the laity our love.

Moving of th'earth brings harms and fears,
   Men reckon what it did and meant,
But trepidation of the spheres,
   Though greater far, is innocent.

Dull sublunary lovers love
   (Whose soul is sense) cannot admit
Absence, because it doth remove
   Those things which elemented it.

But we by a love, so much refin'd,
   That our selves know not what it is,
Inter-assured of the mind,
   Care less, eyes, lips, and hands to miss.

Our two souls therefore, which are one,
   Though I must go, endure not yet
A breach, but an expansion,
   Like gold to airy thinness beat.

If they be two, they are two so
   As stiff twin compasses are two,
Thy soul the fixed foot, makes no show
   To move, but doth, if th'other do.

And though it in the centre sit,
    Yet when the other far doth roam,
It leans, and hearkens after it,
    And grows erect, as it comes home.

Such wilt thou be to me, who must
    Like th'other foot, obliquely run;
Thy firmness makes my circle just,
    And makes me end, where I begun.

PIERCE FERRITER (IRISH)

[17th century]

Lay Your Arms Aside

Gentlest of women, put your weapons by,
Unless you want to ruin all mankind;
Leave the assault or I must make reply,
Proclaiming that you are murderously inclined.
Put by your armour, lay your darts to rest,
Hide your soft hair and all its devious ways:
To see it lie in coils upon your breast
Poisons all hope and mercilessly slays.

Protest you never murdered in your life;
You lie: your hand's smooth touch, your well-
    shaped knee
Destroy as easily as axe or knife.
Your breasts like new spring flowers, your naked
    side
– I cry for aid to heaven – conceal from me;
Let shame for the destruction you have made
Hide your bright eyes, your shining teeth, away;
If all our sighs and trembling and dismay
Can touch your heart or satisfy your pride,
Gentlest of women, lay your arms aside.

translated by Eiléan Ni Chuilleanáin

[pub. 1846]

'Will ye no come back again?'

Will ye no come back again?
Will ye no come back again?
Better lo'ed ye canna be,
Will ye no come back again?

Bonnie Charlie 's now awa,
    Safely owre the friendly main;
Mony a heart will break in twa,
    Should he ne'er come back again.

Ye trusted in your Hieland men,
    They trusted you, dear Charlie;
They kent you hiding in the glen,
clothing   Your cleadin' was but barely.

English bribes were a' in vain;
    An' e'en tho' puirer we may be,
Siller canna buy the heart
    That beats aye for thine and thee.

We watched thee in the gloaming hour,
    We watched thee in the morning grey;
Tho' thirty thousand pounds they'd gie,
    Oh there is nane that wad betray.

lark Sweet's the laverock's note and lang,
    Lilting wildly up the glen;
But aye to me he sings ae sang,
    Will ye no come back again?

The Owl and the Pussy-cat

I

The Owl and the Pussy-cat went to sea
    In a beautiful pea-green boat,
They took some honey, and plenty of money,
    Wrapped up in a five-pound note.
The Owl looked up to the stars above,
    And sang to a small guitar,
'O lovely Pussy! O Pussy, my love,
        What a beautiful Pussy you are,
            You are,
            You are!
    What a beautiful Pussy you are!'

II

Pussy said to the Owl, 'You elegant fowl!
    How charmingly sweet you sing!
O let us be married! too long we have tarried:
    But what shall we do for a ring?'
They sailed away, for a year and a day,
    To the land where the Bong-tree grows
And there in a wood a Piggy-wig stood
    With a ring at the end of his nose,
        His nose,
        His nose,
    With a ring at the end of his nose.

III

'Dear Pig, are you willing to sell for one shilling
    Your ring?' Said the Piggy, 'I will.'
So they took it away, and were married next day
    By the Turkey who lives on the hill.

They dined on mince, and slices of quince,
    Which they ate with a runcible spoon;
And hand in hand, on the edge of the sand,
    They danced by the light of the moon,
        The moon,
        The moon,
They danced by the light of the moon.

JOHN MASEFIELD

[1903] ## Cargoes

Quinquireme of Nineveh from distant Ophir
Rowing home to haven in sunny Palestine,
With a cargo of ivory,
And apes and peacocks,
Sandalwood, cedarwood, and sweet white wine.

Stately Spanish galleon coming from the
    Isthmus,
Dipping through the Tropics by the palm-green
    shores,
With a cargo of diamonds,
Emeralds, amethysts,
Topazes, and cinnamon, and gold moidores.

Dirty British coaster with a salt-caked smoke
    stack
Butting through the Channel in the mad March
    days,
With a cargo of Tyne coal,
Road-rail, pig-lead,
Firewood, iron-ware, and cheap tin trays.

[pre-10th century] ## The Seafarer

May I, for my own self, song's truth reckon,
Journey's jargon, how I in harsh days
Hardship endured oft.
Bitter breast-cares have I abided,
Known on my keel many a care's hold,
And dire sea-surge, and there I oft spent
Narrow nightwatch nigh the ship's head
While she tossed close to cliffs. Coldly afflicted,
My feet were by frost benumbed.
Chill its chains are; chafing sighs
Hew my heart round and hunger begot
Mere-weary mood. Lest man know not
That he on dry land loveliest liveth,
List how I, care-wretched, on ice-cold sea,
Weathered the winter, wretched outcast
Deprived of my kinsmen;
Hung with hard ice-flakes, where hail-scur flew,
There I heard naught save the harsh sea
And ice-cold wave, at whiles the swan cries,
Did for my games, the gannet's clamour,
Sea-fowls' loudness was for me laughter,
The mews' singing all my mead-drink.
Storms, on the stone-cliffs beaten, fell on the
    stern
In icy feathers; full oft the eagle screamed
With spray on his pinion.
                    Not any protector
May make merry man faring needy.
This he little believes, who aye in winsome life
Abides 'mid burghers some heavy business,
Wealthy and wine-flushed, how I weary oft
Must bide above brine.
Neareth nightshade, snoweth from north,

Frost froze the land, hail fell on earth then,

nevertheless Corn of the coldest. Nathless there knocketh now
The heart's thought that I on high streams
The salt-wavy tumult traverse alone.
Moaneth alway my mind's lust
That I fare forth, that I afar hence
Seek out a foreign fastness.
For this there's no mood-lofty man over earth's
   midst,
Not though he be given his good, but will have in
   his youth greed;
Nor his deed to the daring, nor his king to the
   faithful
But shall have his sorrow for sea-fare
Whatever his lord will.
He hath not heart for harping, nor in ring-having
Nor winsomeness to wife, nor world's delight
Nor any whit else save the wave's slash,
Yet longing comes upon him to fare forth on the
   water.

bush Bosque taketh blossom, cometh beauty of berries,
Fields to fairness, land fares brisker,
All this admonisheth man eager of mood,
The heart turns to travel so that he then thinks
On flood-ways to be far departing.
Cuckoo calleth with gloomy crying,
He singeth summerward, bodeth sorrow,
The bitter heart's blood. Burgher knows not –
He the prosperous man – what some perform
Where wandering them widest draweth.
So that but now my heart burst from my
   breastlock,
My mood 'mid the mere-flood,
Over the whale's acre, would wander wide.
On earth's shelter cometh oft to me,
Eager and ready, the crying lone-flyer,

Whets for the whale-path the heart irresistibly,
O'er tracks of ocean; seeing that anyhow
My lord deems to me this dead life
On loan and on land, I believe not
That any earth-weal eternal standeth
Save there be somewhat calamitous
That, ere a man's tide go, turn it to twain.
Disease or oldness or sword-hate
Beats out the breath from doom-gripped body.
And for this, every earl whatever, for those
    speaking after –
Laud of the living, boasteth some last word,
That he will work ere he pass onward,
Frame on the fair earth 'gainst foes his malice,
Daring ado, . . .
So that all men shall honour him after
And his laud beyond them remain 'mid the
    English,
Aye, for ever, a lasting life's-blast,
Delight 'mid the doughty.
                     Days little durable,
And all arrogance of earthen riches,
There come now no kings nor Caesars
Nor gold-giving lords like those gone.
Howe'er in mirth most magnified,
Who'er lived in life most lordliest,
Drear all this excellence, delights undurable!
Waneth the watch, but the world holdeth.
Tomb hideth trouble. The blade is layed low.
Earthy glory ageth and seareth
No man at all going the earth's gait,
But age fares against him, his face paleth,
Grey-haired he groaneth, knows gone
    companions,
Lordly men, are to earth o'ergiven,

Nor may he then the flesh-cover, whose life
   ceaseth,
Nor eat the sweet nor feel the sorry,
Nor stir hand nor think in mid heart,
And though he strew the grave with gold,
His born brothers, their buried bodies
Be an unlikely treasure hoard.

translated by Ezra Pound

EDWARD FITZGERALD

[1859] *from* Rubáiyát of Omar Khayyám

I

Awake! for Morning in the Bowl of Night
Has flung the Stone that puts the Stars to Flight:
   And Lo! the Hunter of the East has caught
The Sultán's Turret in a Noose of Light.

II

Dreaming when Dawn's Left Hand was in the Sky
I heard a Voice within the Tavern cry,
   'Awake, my Little ones, and fill the Cup
'Before Life's Liquor in its Cup be dry.'

III

And, as the Cock crew, those who stood before
The Tavern shouted – 'Open then the Door!
   'You know how little while we have to stay,
'And, once departed, may return no more.'

IV

Now the New Year reviving old Desires,
The thoughtful Soul to Solitude retires,

Where the WHITE HAND OF MOSES on the
     Bough
Puts out, and Jesus from the Ground suspires.

V

Irám indeed is gone with all its Rose,
And Jamshýd's Sev'n-ring'd Cup where no one
     knows;
   But still the Vine her ancient Ruby yields,
And still a Garden by the Water blows.

VI

And David's Lips are lock't; but in divine
High piping Péhlevi, with 'Wine! Wine! Wine!
   '*Red* Wine!' – the Nightingale cries to the Rose
That yellow Cheek of her's to'incarnadine.

VII

Come, fill the Cup, and in the Fire of Spring
The Winter Garment of Repentance fling:
   The Bird of Time has but a little way
To fly – and Lo! the Bird is on the Wing.

VIII

And look – a thousand Blossoms with the Day
Woke – and a thousand scatter'd into Clay;
   And this first Summer Month that brings the
     Rose
Shall take Jamshýd and Kaikobád away.

IX

But come with old Khayyám, and leave the Lot
Of Kaikobád and Kaikhosrú forgot:

Let Rustum lay about him as he will,
Or Hátim Tai cry Supper – heed them not.

X

With me along some Strip of Herbage strown
That just divides the desert from the sown,
    Where name of Slave and Sultán scarce is
        known,
And pity Sultán Máhmúd on his Throne.

XI

Here with a Loaf of Bread beneath the Bough,
A Flask of Wine, a Book of Verse – and Thou
    Beside me singing in the Wilderness –
And Wilderness is Paradise enow.

XII

'How sweet is mortal Sovranty!' – think some:
Others – 'How blest the Paradise to come!'
    Ah, take the Cash in hand and waive the Rest;
Oh, the brave Music of a *distant* Drum!

XIII

Look to the Rose that blows about us – 'Lo,
'Laughing,' she says, 'into the World I blow:
    'At once the silken Tassel of my purse
'Tear, and its Treasure on the Garden throw.'

XIV

The Worldly Hope men set their Hearts upon
Turns Ashes – or it prospers; and anon,
    Like Snow upon the Desert's dusty Face
Lighting a little Hour or two – is gone.

XV

And those who husbanded the Golden Grain,
And those who flung it to the Winds like Rain,
　　Alike to no such aureate Earth are turn'd
As, buried once, Men want dug up again.

XVI

Think, in this batter'd Caravanserai
Whose Doorways are alternate Night and Day,
　　How Sultán after Sultán with his Pomp
Abode his Hour or two, and went his way.

XVII

They say the Lion and the Lizard keep
The Courts where Jamshýd gloried and drank
　　　　deep:
　　And Bahrám, that great Hunter – the Wild Ass
Stamps o'er his Head, and he lies fast asleep.

XVIII

I sometimes think that never blows so red
The Rose as where some buried Cæsar bled;
　　That every Hyacinth the Garden wears
Dropt in its Lap from some once lovely Head.

XIX

And this delightful Herb whose tender Green
Fledges and River's Lip on which we lean –
　　Ah, lean upon it lightly! for who knows
From what once lovely Lip it springs unseen!

XX

Ah, my Belovéd, fill the Cup that clears
To-day of past Regrets and future Fears –
    To-morrow? – Why, To-morrow I may be
Myself with Yesterday's Sev'n Thousand Years.

XXI

Lo! some we loved, the loveliest and best
That Time and Fate of all their Vintage prest,
    Have drunk their Cup a Round or two before,
And one by one crept silently to Rest.

XXII

And we, that now make merry in the Room
They left, and Summer dresses in new Bloom,
    Ourselves must we beneath the Couch of Earth
Descend, ourselves to make a Couch – for whom?

XXIII

Ah, make the most of what we yet may spend,
Before we too into the Dust descend;
    Dust into Dust, and under Dust, to lie,
Sans Wine, sans Song, sans Singer, and – sans
        End!

XXIV

Alike for those who for To-day prepare,
And those that after a To-morrow stare,
    A Muezzin from the Tower of Darkness cries
'Fools! your Reward is neither Here nor There!'

Why, all the Saints and Sages who discuss'd
Of the Two Worlds so learnedly, are thrust
　　Like foolish Prophets forth; their Words to
　　　　Scorn
Are scatter'd, and their Mouths are stopt with
　　Dust.

XXVI

Oh, come with old Khayyám, and leave the Wise
To talk; one thing is certain, that Life flies;
　　One thing is certain, and the Rest is Lies;
The Flower that once has blown for ever dies.

XXVII

Myself when young did eagerly frequent
Doctor and saint, and heard great Argument
　　About it and about: but evermore
Came out by the same Door as in I went.

XXVIII

With them the Seed of Wisdom did I sow,
And with my own hand labour'd it to grow:
　　And this was all the Harvest that I reap'd –
'I came like Water, and like Wind I go.'

SIR WALTER RALEGH

[pub. 1608]　　　## The Lie

Go, Soul, the body's guest,
errand　　Upon a thankless arrant:
Fear not to touch the best;
The truth shall be thy warrant:

Go, since I needs must die,
And give the world the lie.

Say to the court, it glows
And shines like rotten wood;
Say to the church it shows
What's good, and doth no good:
If church and court reply,
Then give them both the lie.

Tell potentates, they live
Acting by others' action;
Not loved unless they give,
Not strong but by affection:
If potentates reply,
Give potentates the lie.

Tell men of high condition
That manage the estate,
Their purpose is ambition,
Their practice only hate:
And if they once reply,
Then give them all the lie.

Tell them that brave it most
They beg for more by spending,
Who, in their greatest cost,
Seek nothing but commending:
And if they make reply,
Then give them all the lie.

Tell zeal it wants devotion,
Tell love it is but lust;
Tell time it metes but motion,
Tell flesh it is but dust:
And wish them not reply,
For thou must give the lie.

Tell age it daily wasteth;
Tell honour how it alters;
Tell beauty how she blasteth;
Tell favour how it falters:
And as they shall reply,
Give every one the lie.

Tell wit how much it wrangles
In tickle points of niceness;
Tell wisdom she entangles
Herself in over-wiseness:
And when they do reply,
Straight give them both the lie.

Tell physic of her boldness;
Tell skill it is pretension;
Tell charity of coldness;
Tell law it is contention:
And as they do reply,
So give them still the lie.

Tell fortune of her blindness;
Tell nature of decay;
Tell friendship of unkindness;
Tell justice of delay:
And if they will reply,
Then give them all the lie.

Tell arts they have no soundness,
But vary by esteeming;
Tell schools they want profoundness,
And stand too much on seeming:
If arts and schools reply,
Give arts and schools the lie.

Tell faith it's fled the city;
Tell how the country erreth;
Tell manhood shakes off pity

And virtue least preferreth:
And if they do reply,
Spare not to give the lie.

So when thou hast, as I
Commanded thee, done blabbing
– Although to give the lie
Deserves no less than stabbing –
Stab at thee he that will,
No stab thy soul can kill.

ANDREW MARVELL

[1650s]   The Garden

How vainly men themselves amaze,
To win the palm, the oak, or bays;
And their incessant labours see
Crowned from some single herb, or tree,
Whose short and narrow-vergèd shade
Does prudently their toils upbraid;
While all the flowers and trees do close,
To weave the garlands of repose!

Fair Quiet, have I found thee here,
And Innocence, thy sister dear?
Mistaken long, I sought you then
In busy companies of men.
Your sacred plants, if here below,
Only among the plants will grow;
Society is all but rude
To this delicious solitude.

No white nor red was ever seen
So amorous as this lovely green.
Fond lovers, cruel as their flame,
Cut in these trees their mistress' name:
Little, alas! they know or heed,

How far these beauties hers exceed!
Fair trees! wheres'e'er your bark I wound,
No name shall but your own be found.

When we have run our passion's heat,
Love hither makes his best retreat.
The gods, that mortal beauty chase,
Still in a tree did end their race;
Apollo hunted Daphne so,
Only that she might laurel grow;
And Pan did after Syrinx speed,
Not as a nymph, but for a reed.

What wondrous life is this I lead!
Ripe apples drop about my head;
The luscious clusters of the vine
Upon my mouth do crush their wine;
The nectarine, and curious peach,
Into my hands themselves do reach;
Stumbling on melons, as I pass,
Insnared with flowers, I fall on grass.

Meanwhile the mind, from pleasure less,
Withdraws into its happiness;
The mind, that ocean where each kind
Does straight its own resemblance find;
Yet it creates, transcending these,
Far other worlds, and other seas,
Annihilating all that's made
To a green thought in a green shade.

Here at the fountain's sliding foot,
Or at some fruit-tree's mossy root,
Casting the body's vest aside,
My soul into the boughs does glide:
There, like a bird, it sits and sings,
Then whets and combs its silver wings,

And, till prepared for longer flight,
Waves in its plumes the various light.

Such was that happy garden-state,
While man there walked without a mate:
After a place so pure and sweet,
What other help could yet be meet!
But 'twas beyond a mortal's share
To wander solitary there:
Two paradises 'twere in one,
To live in paradise alone.

How well the skilful gardener drew
Of flowers, and herbs, this dial new;
Where, from above, the milder sun
Does through a fragrant zodiac run,
And, as it works, the industrious bee
Computes its time as well as we!
How could such sweet and wholesome hours
Be reckoned but with herbs and flowers?

CHARLES COTTON

[c. 1650] ## Evening

The Day's grown old, the fainting Sun
Has but a little way to run,
And yet his Steeds, with all his skill,
Scarce lug the Chariot down the Hill.

With Labour spent, and Thirst opprest,
Whilst they strain hard to gain the West,
From Fetlocks hot drops melted light,
Which turn the Meteors in the Night.

The Shadows now so long do grow,
That Brambles like tall Cedars show,
Mole-hills seem Mountains, and the Ant
Appears a monstrous Elephant.

A very little little Flock
Shades thrice the ground that it would stock;
Whilst the small Stripling following them,
Appears a mighty *Polypheme*.

These being brought into the Fold,
And by the thrifty Master told,
He thinks his Wages are well paid,
Since none are either lost, or stray'd.

Now lowing Herds are each-where heard,
Chains rattle in the Villains Yard,
The Cart's on Tayl set down to rest,
Bearing on high the Cuckolds Crest.

The hedge is stript, the Clothes brought in,
Nought's left without should be within,
The Bees are hiv'd, and hum their Charm,
Whilst every House does seem a Swarm.

The Cock now to the Roost is prest:
For he must call up all the rest;
The Sow's fast pegg'd within the Sty,
To still her squeaking Progeny.

food Each one has had his Supping Mess,
The Cheese is put into the Press,
The Pans and Bowls clean scalded all,
Rear'd up against the Milk-house Wall.

And now on Benches all are sat
In the cool Air to sit and chat,
Till *Phœbus*, dipping in the West,
Shall lead the World the way to Rest.

EARLE BIRNEY

[1952]   ## Bushed

He invented a rainbow but lightning struck it
shattered it into the lake-lap of a mountain
so big his mind slowed when he looked at it

Yet he built a shack on the shore
learned to roast porcupine belly and
wore the quills on his hatband

At first he was out with the dawn
whether it yellowed bright as wood-columbine
or was only a fuzzed moth in a flannel of storm
But he found the mountain was clearly alive
sent messages whizzing down every hot morning
boomed proclamations at noon and spread out
a white guard of goat
before falling asleep on its feet at sundown

When he tried his eyes on the lake   ospreys
would fall like valkyries
choosing the cut-throat
He took then to waiting
till the night smoke rose from the boil of the sunset

But the moon carved unknown totems
out of the lakeshore
owls in the beardusky woods derided him
moosehorned cedars circled his swamps and
    tossed
their antlers up to the stars
then he knew   though the mountain slept   the
    winds
were shaping its peak to an arrowhead
poised

And now he could only
bar himself in and wait
for the great flint to come singing into his heart

ANONYMOUS (OLD ENGLISH)

[10th century] Ice

The wave, over the wave, a weird thing I saw,
through-wrought, and wonderfully ornate:
a wonder on the wave – water became bone.

translated by Michael Alexander

ANONYMOUS (IRISH)

[10th century] A Song of Winter

Cold cold!
Cold to-night is broad Moylurg,
Higher the snow than the mountain-range,
The deer cannot get at their food.

Cold till Doom!
The storm has spread over all:
A river is each furrow upon the slope,
Each ford a full pool.

A great tidal sea is each loch,
A full loch is each pool:
Horses cannot get over the ford of Ross,
No more can two feet get there.

The fish of Ireland are a-roaming,
There is no strand which the wave does not
 pound,
Not a town there is in the land,
Not a bell is heard, no crane talks.

The wolves of Cuan-wood get
Neither rest nor sleep in their lair,

The little wren cannot find
Shelter in her nest on the slope of Lon.

Keen wind and cold ice
Have burst upon the little company of birds,
The blackbird cannot get a lee to her liking,
Shelter for its side in Cuan-wood.

Cosy our pot on its hook,
Crazy the hut on the slope of Lon:
The snow has crushed the wood here,
Toilsome to climb up Ben-bo.

Glen Rye's ancient bird
From the bitter wind gets grief;
Great her misery and her pain,
The ice will get into her mouth.

From flock and from down to rise –
Take it to heart! – were folly for thee:
Ice in heaps on every ford –
That is why I say 'cold'!

translated by Kuno Meyer

JOHN DYER

[1726]   *from* Grongar Hill

　　Now I gain the mountain's brow,
What a landskip lies below!
No clouds, no vapours intervene,
But the gay, the open scene
Does the face of nature show
In all the hues of heaven's bow!
And swelling to embrace the light,
Spreads around beneath the sight.
　　Old castles on the cliff arise,
Proudly tow'ring in the skies!
Rushing from the woods, the spires

Seem from hence ascending fires!
Half his beams Apollo sheds
On the yellow mountain-heads!
Gilds the fleeces of the flocks;
And glitters on the broken rocks!
   Below me trees unnumber'd rise,
Beautiful in various dyes:
The gloomy pine, the poplar blue,
The yellow beech, the sable yew,
The slender fir, that taper grows,
The sturdy oak, with wide-spread boughs,
And beyond the purple grove,
Haunt of Phillis, queen of love!
Gaudy as the op'ning dawn,
Lies a long and level lawn
On which a dark hill, steep and high,
Holds and charms the wand'ring eye!
Deep are his feet in Towy's flood,
His sides are cloath'd with waving wood,
And ancient towers crown his brow,
That cast an awful look below;
Whose ragged walls the ivy creeps,
And with her arms from falling keeps;
So both a safety from the wind
On mutual dependence find.
   'Tis now the raven's bleak abode;
'Tis now th'apartment of the toad;
And there the fox securely feeds;
And there the pois'nous adder breeds,
Conceal'd in ruins, moss, and weeds;
While, ever and anon, there falls
Huge heaps of hoary moulder'd walls.
Yet time has seen, that lifts the low,
And level lays the lofty brow,
Has seen his broken pile compleat,
Big with the vanity of state:

But transient is the smile of fate!
A little rule, a little sway,
A sunbeam in a winter's day,
Is all the proud and mighty have
Between the cradle and the grave.

ANONYMOUS

[traditional]

March

gives birth to

March yeans the lammie
   And buds the thorn,
And blows through the flint
   Of an ox's horn.

HENRY REED

[1946]

Naming of Parts
(from *Lessons of the War*)

To-day we have naming of parts. Yesterday,
We had daily cleaning. And to-morrow morning,
We shall have what to do after firing. But to-day,
To-day we have naming of parts. Japonica
Glistens like coral in all of the neighbouring
   gardens,
     And to-day we have naming of parts.

This is the lower sling swivel. And this
Is the upper sling swivel, whose use you will see,
When you are given your slings. And this is the
   piling swivel,
Which in your case you have not got. The
   branches
Hold in the gardens their silent, eloquent
   gestures,
     Which in our case we have not got.

This is the safety-catch, which is always released
With an easy flick of the thumb. And please do
    not let me
See anyone using his finger. You can do it quite
    easy
If you have any strength in your thumb. The
    blossoms
Are fragile and motionless, never letting anyone
    see
      Any of them using their finger.

And this you can see is the bolt. The purpose of
    this
Is to open the breech, as you see. We can slide it
Rapidly backwards and forwards: we call this
Easing the spring. And rapidly backwards and
    forwards
The early bees are assaulting and fumbling the
    flowers:
      They call it easing the Spring.

They call it easing the Spring: it is perfectly easy
If you have any strength in your thumb: like the
    bolt,
And the breech, and the cocking-piece, and the
    point of balance,
Which in our case we have not got; and the
    almond-blossom
Silent in all of the gardens and the bees going
    backwards and forwards,
      For to-day we have naming of parts.

[13th century]   'Somer is i-comen in'

Somer is i-comen in,
Loude syng cuckow!
meadow   Groweth seed and bloweth meed
wood   And spryngeth the wode now.
Syng cuckow!
Ewe bleteth after lamb,
Loweth after calve cow;
Bullock sterteth, bukke farteth, –
Myrie syng cuckow!
Cuckow! Cuckow!
Wel syngest thou cuckow:
don't ever stop   Ne swik thou nevere now.
    Syng cuckow, now, syng cuckow!
    Syng cuckow, syng cuckow, now!

NORMAN MACCAIG

[1955]   Summer Farm

Straws like tame lightnings lie about the grass
And hang zigzag on hedges. Green as glass
The water in the horse-trough shines.
Nine ducks go wobbling by in two straight lines.

A hen stares at nothing with one eye,
Then picks it up. Out of an empty sky
A swallow falls and, flickering through
The barn, dives up again into the dizzy blue.

I lie, not thinking, in the cool, soft grass,
Afraid of where a thought might take me –
This grasshopper with plated face
Unfolds his legs and finds himself in space.

Self under self, a pile of selves I stand
Threaded on time, and with metaphysic hand
Lift the farm like a lid and see
Farm within farm, and in the centre, me.

ANONYMOUS (IRISH)

[7th or 8th century] ## The Son of the King of Moy

The son of the king of Moy in midsummer
Found a girl in the greenwood.
She gave him black fruit from thornbushes.
She gave an armful of strawberries on rushes.

translated by Myles Dillon

JOHN KEATS

[1819] ## La Belle Dame Sans Merci

O, what can ail thee, knight at arms,
    Alone and palely loitering;
The sedge has withered from the lake,
    And no birds sing.

O, what can ail thee, knight at arms,
    So haggard and so woe-begone?
The squirrel's granary is full,
    And the harvest's done.

I see a lily on thy brow
    With anguish moist and fever-dew,
And on thy cheeks a fading rose
    Fast withereth too.

I met a lady in the meads,
    Full beautiful – a faery's child,
Her hair was long, her foot was light,
    And her eyes were wild.

I made a garland for her head,
    And bracelets too, and fragrant zone,
She looked at me as she did love,
    And made sweet moan.

I set her on my pacing steed
    And nothing else saw all day long;
For sideways would she lean, and sing
    A faery's song.

She found me roots of relish sweet,
    And honey wild and manna dew;
And sure in language strange she said –
    I love thee true.

She took me to her elfin grot,
    And there she gazed and sighed full sore:
And there I shut her wild, wild eyes
    With kisses four.

And there she lullèd me asleep,
    And there I dreamed, ah woe betide,
The latest dream I ever dreamed
    On the cold hill side.

I saw pale kings and princes too,
    Pale warriors, death-pale were they all:
They cry'd – 'La belle Dame sans Merci
    Hath thee in thrall!'

I saw their starved lips in the gloam
    With horrid warning gapèd wide,
And I awoke, and found me here
    On the cold hill side.

And this is why I sojourn here
    Alone and palely loitering,
Though the sedge is withered from the lake,
    And no birds sing.

ANONYMOUS

[16th century]

Tom o' Bedlam's Song

Bedlam: the Hospital of
St Mary of Bethlehem,
London, an asylum for
mad persons

From the hagg and hungrie goblin
That into raggs would rend ye,
And the spirit that stands by the naked man
In the Book of Moones defend yee!
That of your five sounde sences
You never be forsaken,
Nor wander from your selves with Tom
Abroad to begg your bacon.

> *While I doe sing 'any foode, any feeding,*
> *Feedinge, drinke or clothing,'*
> *Come dame or maid, be not afraid,*
> *Poor Tom will injure nothing.*

Of thirty bare years have I
Twice twenty bin enragèd,
And of forty bin three tymes fifteene
In durance soundlie cagèd.
On the lordlie loftes of Bedlam,
With stubble softe and dainty,
Brave braceletts strong, sweet whips ding-dong,
With wholsome hunger plenty.

> *And nowe I sing, etc.*

With a thought I tooke for Maudlin,
bowl   And a cruse of cockle pottage,
With a thing thus tall, skie blesse you all,
I befell into this dotage.
I slept not since the Conquest,
Till then I never wakèd,
Till the rogysh boy of love where I lay
Mee found and strip't mee naked.

> *And nowe I sing, etc.*

When I short have shorne my sowre face
And snigg'd my hairy barrel,
In an oaken inne I pound my skin
As a suite of guilt apparell.
The moon's my constant Mistrisse,
And the lowlie owle my morrowe,
The flaming Drake and the Nightcrowe make
Mee musicke to my sorrowe.

    While I doe sing, etc.

The palsie plagues my pulses
steal / poultry   When I prigg your pigs or pullen,
doves   Your culvers take, or matchles make
goose   Your Chanticleare, or sullen.
go without dinner When I want provant, with Humfrie
I sup, and when benighted,
I repose in Powles with waking soules
Yet nevere am affrighted.

    But I doe sing, etc.

I knowe more then Apollo,
For oft, when hee ly's sleeping,
I see the starres att bloudie warres
In the wounded welkin weeping;
The moone embrace her shepheard,
And the quene of Love her warryor,
While the first doth borne the star of morne,
And the next the heavenly Farrier.

    While I doe sing, etc.

The Gipsie Snap and Pedro
Are none of Tom's comradoes.
prostitute   The punk I skorne and the cut purse sworn
And the roaring boyes bravadoe.
The meeke, the white, the gentle,
Me handle touch and spare not

But those that crosse Tom Rynosseros
Doe what the panther dare not.

Although I sing, etc.

With an host of furious fancies,
Whereof I am commander,
With a burning speare, and a horse of aire,
To the wildernesse I wander.
By a knight of ghostes and shadowes
I summon'd am to tourney
Ten leagues beyond the wide world's end.
Me thinke it is noe journey.

Yet will I sing, etc.

ANONYMOUS

[traditional]   ### Tweed and Till

Says Tweed to Till,
makes / run   What gars ye rin sae still?
Says Till to Tweed,
Though ye rin wi' speed
And I rin slaw,
For ae man that ye droun
I droun twa.

GERARD MANLEY HOPKINS

[1881]   ### Inversnaid

This darksome burn, horseback brown,
His rollrock highroad roaring down,
In coop and in comb the fleece of his foam
Flutes and low to the lake falls home.

A windpuff-bonnet of fáwn-fróth
Turns and twindles over the broth

Of a pool so pitchblack, féll frówning,
It rounds and rounds Despair to drowning.

Degged with dew, dappled with dew
Are the groins of the braes that the brook treads
    through,
Wiry heathpacks, flitches of fern,
And the beadbonny ash that sits over the burn.

What would the world be, once bereft
Of wet and of wildness? Let them be left,
O let them be left, wildness and wet;
Long live the weeds and the wilderness yet.

EDMUND SPENSER

[1596] ## Prothalamion

Calm was the day, and through the trembling air
Sweet-breathing Zephyrus did softly play
A gentle spirit, that lightly did delay
Hot Titan's beams, which then did glister fair;
When I, (whom sullen care,
Through discontent of my long fruitless stay
In princes' court, and expectation vain
Of idle hopes, which still do fly away
Like empty shadows, did afflict my brain,)
Walked forth to ease my pain
Along the shore of silver-streaming Thames;
Whose rutty bank, the which his river hems,
Was painted all with variable flowers,
And all the meads adorned with dainty gems
Fit to deck maidens' bowers,
And crown their paramours
Against the bridal day, which is not long:
    Sweet Thames! run softly, till I end my song.

There in a meadow by the river's side
A flock of nymphs I chanced to espy,
All lovely daughters of the flood thereby,
With goodly greenish locks all loose untied
As each had been a bride;
And each one had a little wicker basket
Made of fine twigs entrailèd curiously,
In which they gathered flowers to fill their flasket,
dexterously   And with fine fingers cropped full feateously
The tender stalks on high.
Of every sort which in that meadow grew
They gathered some; the violet, pallid blue,
The little daisy that at evening closes,
The virgin lily and the primrose true,
With store of vermeil roses,
To deck their bridegrooms' posies
Against the bridal day, which was not long:
    Sweet Thames! run softly, till I end my song.

With that I saw two swans of goodly hue
Come softly swimming down along the Lee;
Two fairer birds I yet did never see;
The snow which doth the top of Pindus strew
Did never whiter shew,
Nor Jove himself, when he a swan would be
For love of Leda, whiter did appear;
Yet Leda was, they say, as white as he,
Yet not so white as these, nor nothing near;
So purely white they were
That even the gentle stream, the which them
    bare,
Seemed foul to them, and bade his billows spare
To wet their silken feathers, lest they might
Soil their fair plumes with water not so fair,
And mar their beauties bright,
That shone as heaven's light,

Against their bridal day, which was not long;
    Sweet Thames! run softly, till I end my song.

Eftsoons the nymphs, which now had flowers
    their fill,
Ran all in haste to see that silver brood
As they came floating on the crystal flood;
Whom when they saw, they stood amazèd still
Their wondering eyes to fill;
Them seemed they never saw a sight so fair,
Of fowls so lovely that they sure did deem
Them heavenly born, or to be that same pair
Which through the sky draw Venus' silver team;
For sure they did not seem
To be begot of any earthly seed,
But rather angels, or of angels' breed;
Yet were they bred of Somers-heat, they say,
In sweetest season, when each flower and weed
The earth did fresh array;
So fresh they seemed as day,
Even as their bridal day, which was not long:
    Sweet Thames! run softly, till I end my song.

Then forth they all out of their baskets drew
Great store of flowers, the honour of the field,
That to the sense did fragrant odours yield,
All which upon those goodly birds they threw,
And all the waves did strew,
That like old Peneus' waters they did seem
When down along by pleasant Tempe's shore,
Scattered with flowers, through Thessally they
    stream,
That they appear, through lilies' plenteous store,
Like a bride's chamber-floor.
Two of those nymphs meanwhile two garlands
    bound

Of freshest flowers which in that mead they
      found,
The which presenting all in trim array,
Their snowy foreheads therewithal they
      crowned,
Whilst one did sing this lay
Prepared against that day,
Against their bridal day, which was not long:
    Sweet Thames! run softly, till I end my song.

'Ye gentle birds! the world's fair ornament,
And heaven's glory, whom this happy hour
Doth lead unto your lovers' blissful bower,
Joy may you have, and gentle heart's content
Of your love's couplement;
And let fair Venus, that is queen of love,
With her heart-quelling son upon you smile,
Whose smile, they say, hath virtue to remove
All love's dislike, and friendship's faulty guile

remove

For ever to assoil.
Let endless peace your steadfast hearts accord,
And blessèd plenty wait upon your board;
And let your bed with pleasures chaste abound,
That fruitful issue may to you afford,
Which may your foes confound,
And make your joys redound
Upon your bridal day, which is not long:
    Sweet Thames! run softly, till I end my song.'

So ended she; and all the rest around
To her redoubled that her undersong,
Which said their bridal day should not be long:
And gentle Echo from the neighbour ground
Their accents did resound.
So forth those joyous birds did pass along,
Adown the Lee that to them murmured low,
As he would speak but that he lacked a tongue,

133

Yet did by signs his glad affection show,
Making his stream run slow.
And all the fowl which in his flood did dwell
Gan flock about these twain, that did excel

put to shame

The rest, so far as Cynthia doth shend
The lesser stars. So they, enragèd well,
Did on those two attend,
And their best service lend
Against their wedding day, which was not long:
  Sweet Thames! run softly, till I end my song.

At length they all to merry London came,
To merry London, my most kindly nurse,
That to me gave this life's first native source,
Though from another place I take my name,
An house of ancient fame:
There when they came whereas those bricky
      towers
The which on Thames' broad agèd back do ride,
Where now the studious lawyers have their
      bowers,

formerly

There whilom wont the Templar knights to bide,
Till they decayed through pride:
Next whereunto there stands a stately place,
Where oft I gainèd gifts and goodly grace
Of that great lord, which therein wont to dwell,
Whose want too well now feels my friendless
      case;
But ah! here fits not well
Old woes, but joys to tell
Against the bridal day, which is not long:
  Sweet Thames! run softly, till I end my song.

Yet therein now doth lodge a noble peer,
Great England's glory and the world's wide
      wonder,

Whose dreadful name late through all Spain did
        thunder,
And Hercules' two pillars standing near
Did make to quake and fear:
Fair branch of honour, flower of chivalry!
That fillest England with thy triumphs' fame,
Joy have thou of thy noble victory,
And endless happiness of thine own name
That promiseth the same;
That through thy prowess and victorious arms
Thy country may be freed from foreign harms,
And great Eliza's glorious name may ring
Through all the world, filled with thy wide
        alarms,
Which some brave Muse may sing
To ages following,
Upon the bridal day, which is not long:
    Sweet Thames! run softly, till I end my song.

From those high towers this noble lord issùing,
Like radiant Hesper when his golden hair
In the ocean billows he hath bathèd fair,
Descending to the river's open viewing,
With a great train ensuing.
Above the rest were goodly to be seen
Two gentle knights of lovely face and feature,
Beseeming well the bower of any queen,
With gifts of wit and ornaments of nature
Fit for so goodly stature,
That like the twins of Jove they seemed in sight
sash worn across chest   Which deck the baldric of the heavens bright;
They two, forth pacing to the river's side,
Received those two fair brides, their love's
        delight;
Which, at the appointed tide,
Each one did make his bride

Against their bridal day, which is not long:
    Sweet Thames! run softly, till I end my song.

STEVIE SMITH

[1957] ## The River God

I may be smelly, and I may be old,
Rough in my pebbles, reedy in my pools,
But where my fish float by I bless their swimming
And I like the people to bathe in me, especially
    women.
But I can drown the fools
Who bathe too close to the weir, contrary to
    rules.
And they take a long time drowning
As I throw them up now and then in a spirit of
    clowning.
Hi yih, yippity-yap, merrily I flow,
O I may be an old foul river but I have plenty of go.
Once there was a lady who was too bold
She bathed in me by the tall black cliff where the
    water runs cold,
So I brought her down here
To be my beautiful dear.
Oh will she stay with me will she stay
This beautiful lady, or will she go away?
She lies in my beautiful deep river bed with many
    a weed
To hold her, and many a waving reed.
Oh who would guess what a beautiful white face
    lies there
Waiting for me to smooth and wash away the fear
She looks at me with. Hi yih, do not let her
Go. There is no one on earth who does not forget
    her
Now. They say I am a foolish old smelly river

But they do not know of my wide original bed
Where the lady waits, with her golden sleepy
    head.
If she wishes to go I will not forgive her.

WILLIAM STAFFORD

[1960] ## At the Bomb Testing Site

At noon in the desert a panting lizard
waited for history, its elbows tense,
watching the curve of a particular road
as if something might happen.

It was looking at something farther off
than people could see, an important scene
acted in stone for little selves
at the flute end of consequences.

There was just a continent without much on it
under a sky that never cared less.
Ready for a change, the elbows waited.
The hands gripped hard on the desert.

TOMOS PRYS (WELSH)

[early 17th century] ## The Porpoise

Fair nimble keen-edged porpoise
Leaping lovely waves at will,
Seacalf, brow strangely shaded,
Smooth the way, strange-sounding lad.
Glad you are to be noticed,
Gay on wavecrests near the shore,
A fierce-looking cold-framed head,
Bear's face in frigid currents.
He skips, he shakes like ague,
And then he waggles away,
Black mushroom, wrestles the sea,

137

Staring at it and snorting.
You are ploughing the breaking
Crests of the waves of the sea;
You split the salty ocean,
Are in the heart of the wave,
Daring shadow, swift and clean,
Skull of the sea, strand's pillion.
He hoes waves, water viper,
His looks give the heart a fright.
You're white-bellied, quite gentle,
Rover of the captive flood.
Boar of the brine, deed of daring,
He roams the sea, long bright trail.
Summers, when weather changes,
You come rocking before storms,
Fierce boar, wild infernal churn,
On wild tides cross and greedy.
Lance with gold-crested breastplate,
Fish in a closely-clasped coat,
Sea's burden, tress on bosom,
He slides, holds on a wave's slope.
Sea's saddle, take your bearing,
Find a path to the fierce brine.
Choose a fathom, go for me,
Steady memory's envoy.
Take a trip, from Menai's bank,
On a sure course for Lisbon,
And then swim in a moment
To Spain's border, the world's breast.
Search along the water's edge,
Great his fame, for a warrior,
Pyrs Gruffudd (are hearts not sad?),
Trust's pearl, heart pure and faithful,
Honour of Penrhyn, sound branch,
Gentle lord, who more manly?

It's six years, O how weary,
Since he went abroad by ship
To seas beyond the inlet,
Cross the bar, across the world.
Is it not high time he left
The salt water, kind hero,
And came, relief of worry,
To his court from that foul place,
And lingered where he's longed for,
And made all his people glad?

When you see him, fine labour,
Very bold aboard his ship,
Call to him, bright his harness,
The petition that you bring,
And greet him, fruitful task,
With much song from his comrade,
Sweetly, a man who once went
Sailing on the same voyage
Till he, cheerful admission,
Purchased wisdom when he waned:
Then truly he discarded
The ocean and all its ways.
Give a groan, and speak to him,
Hope he will change this venture
And abandon the sea at once
To other men hereafter.
Hard to win spoils at twilight
Waiting upon the cold sea,
And, from seafaring, easy
Are evil and ill repute.
Well may a brisk shore-bred man
Range over world and ocean
To win, though clamped by coldness,
A true knowledge of the world,

But it's not good or godly
To follow this path for long.

Show, bitter seed that ripened,
His household's unsated hearts.
If wind blow, sad is the face,
A high gale on the hillside,
The world seems mad and twisted,
There's praying and dreadful wails
For fear the wind, deep trouble,
Endanger his comely head.
Many a one is known to
Lament that he's not ashore,
Losing sleep, their hearts broken,
I hear much talk, from their dreams.
Wastrels go off seafaring,
Men with not a foot of land:
Let him come, now grown mellow,
Out of their midst back to us.
Let him come home, hard gazing,
Lead his men to their fair land.

Of *Grace*, azure ship, captain,
A captain whose hands are clean,
God with grace will reward him,
The grace to part with the sea.

translated by Joseph P. Clancy

ELIZABETH BARRETT BROWNING

[1862]   A Musical Instrument

I

What was he doing, the great god Pan,
    Down in the reeds by the river?
Spreading ruin and scattering ban,
Splashing and paddling with hoofs of a goat,

And breaking the golden lilies afloat
   With the dragon-fly on the river.

II

He tore out a reed, the great god Pan,
   From the deep cool bed of the river:
The limpid water turbidly ran,
And the broken lilies a-dying lay,
And the dragon-fly had fled away,
   Ere he brought it out of the river.

III

High on the shore sate the great god Pan,
   While turbidly flowed the river;
And hacked and hewed as a great god can,
With his hard bleak steel at the patient reed,
Till there was not a sign of a leaf indeed
   To prove it fresh from the river.

IV

He cut it short, did the great god Pan,
   (How tall it stood in the river!)
Then drew the pith, like the heart of a man,
Steadily from the outside ring,
And notched the poor dry empty thing
   In holes, as he sate by the river.

V

'This is the way,' laughed the great god Pan,
   (Laughed while he sate by the river,)
'The only way, since gods began
To make sweet music, they could succeed.'
Then, dropping his mouth to a hole in the reed,
   He blew in power by the river.

[pub. 1933]

Bavarian Gentians

Not every man has gentians in his house
in soft September, at slow, sad Michaelmas.

Bavarian gentians, big and dark, only dark
darkening the day-time torch-like with the
    smoking blueness of Pluto's gloom,
ribbed and torch-like, with their blaze of darkness
    spread blue
down flattening into points, flattened under the
    sweep of white day
torch-flower of the blue-smoking darkness,
    Pluto's dark-blue daze,
black lamps from the halls of Dio, burning dark
    blue,
giving off darkness, blue darkness, as Demeter's
    pale lamps give off light,
lead me then, lead me the way.

Reach me a gentian, give me a torch
let me guide myself with the blue, forked torch of
    this flower
down the darker and darker stairs, where blue is
    darkened on blueness.
even where Persephone goes, just now, from the
    frosted September
to the sightless realm where darkness is awake
    upon the dark
and Persephone herself is but a voice
or a darkness invisible enfolded in the deeper
    dark
of the arms Plutonic, and pierced with the
    passion of dense gloom,

among the splendour of torches of darkness,
    shedding darkness on the lost bride and her
    groom.

A. C. SWINBURNE

[1866] *from* Hymn to Proserpine
(After the Proclamation in Rome of the Christian Faith)

Vicisti, Galilæe

Thou hast conquered, O pale Galilean; the world
    has grown grey from thy breath;
We have drunken of things Lethean, and fed on
    the fulness of death.
Laurel is green for a season, and love is sweet for a
    day;
But love grows bitter with treason, and laurel
    outlives not May.
Sleep, shall we sleep after all? for the world is not
    sweet in the end;
For the old faiths loosen and fall, the new years
    ruin and rend.
Fate is a sea without shore, and the soul is a rock
    that abides;
But her ears are vexed with the roar and her face
    with the foam of the tides.
O lips that the live blood faints in, the leavings of
    racks and rods!
O ghastly glories of saints, dead limbs of gibbeted
    Gods!
Though all men abase them before you in spirit,
    and all knees bend,
I kneel not neither adore you, but standing, look
    to the end.
All delicate days and pleasant, all spirits and
    sorrows are cast

Far out with the foam of the present that sweeps
   to the surf of the past:
Where beyond the extreme sea-wall, and
   between the remote sea-gates,
Waste water washes, and tall ships founder, and
   deep death waits:
Where, mighty with deepening sides, clad about
   with the seas as with wings,
And impelled of invisible tides, and fulfilled of
   unspeakable things,
White-eyed and poisonous-finned, shark-toothed
   and serpentine-curled,
Rolls, under the whitening wind of the future, the
   wave of the world.
The depths stand naked in sunder behind it, the
   storms flee away;
In the hollow before it the thunder is taken and
   snared as a prey;
In its sides is the north-wind bound; and its salt is
   of all men's tears;
With light of ruin, and sound of changes, and
   pulse of years:
With travail of day after day, and with trouble of
   hour upon hour;
And bitter as blood is the spray; and the crests are
   as fangs that devour:
And its vapour and storm of its steam as the
   sighing of spirits to be;
And its noise as the noise in a dream; and its
   depth as the roots of the sea:
And the height of its heads as the height of the
   utmost stars of the air:
And the ends of the earth at the might thereof
   tremble, and time is made bare.
Will ye bridle the deep sea with reins, will ye
   chasten the high sea with rods?

Will ye take her to chain her with chains, who is
  older than all ye Gods?
All ye as a wind shall go by, as a fire shall ye pass
  and be past;
Ye are Gods, and behold, ye shall die, and the
  waves be upon you at last.
In the darkness of time, in the deeps of the years,
  in the changes of things,
Ye shall sleep as a slain man sleeps, and the world
  shall forget you for kings.
Though the feet of thine high priests tread where
  thy lords and our forefathers trod,
Though these that were Gods are dead, and thou
  being dead art a God,
Though before thee the throned Cytherean be
  fallen, and hidden her head,
Yet thy kingdom shall pass, Galilean, thy dead
  shall go down to thee dead.
Of the maiden thy mother men sing as a goddess
  with grace clad around;
Thou art throned where another was king;
  where another was queen she is crowned.
Yea, once we had sight of another: but now she is
  queen, say these.
Not as thine, not as thine was our mother, a
  blossom of flowering seas,
Clothed round with the world's desire as with
  raiment, and fair as the foam,
And fleeter than kindled fire, and a goddess, and
  mother of Rome.
For thine came pale and a maiden, and sister to
  sorrow; but ours,
Her deep hair heavily laden with odour and
  colour of flowers,
White rose of the rose-white water, a silver
  splendour, a flame,

Bent down unto us that besought her, and earth
    grew sweet with her name.
For thine came weeping, a slave among slaves,
    and rejected; but she
Came flushed from the full-flushed wave, and
    imperial, her foot on the sea.
And the wonderful waters knew her, the winds
    and the viewless ways,
And the roses grew rosier, and bluer the sea-blue
    stream of the bays.
Ye are fallen, our lords, by what token? we wist
    that ye should not fall.
Ye were all so fair that are broken; and one more
    fair than ye all.
But I turn to her still, having seen she shall surely
    abide in the end;
Goddess and maiden and queen, be near me now
    and befriend.

CHRISTINA ROSSETTI

[1866]   ## Eve

'While I sit at the door,
Sick to gaze within,
Mine eye weepeth sore
For sorrow and sin:
As a tree my sin stands
To darken all lands;
Death is the fruit it bore.

'How have Eden bowers grown
Without Adams to bend them!
How have Eden flowers blown,
Squandering their sweet breath,
Without me to tend them!
The Tree of Life was ours,

Tree twelvefold-fruited,
Most lofty tree that flowers,
Most deeply rooted:
I chose the Tree of Death.

'Hadst thou but said me nay,
Adam, my brother,
I might have pined away;
I, but none other:
God might have let thee stay
Safe in our garden
By putting me away
Beyond all pardon.

'I, Eve, sad mother
Of all who must live,
I, not another,
Plucked bitterest fruit to give
My friend, husband, lover.
O wanton eyes run over!
Who but I should grieve? –
Cain hath slain his brother:
Of all who must die mother,
Miserable Eve!'

Thus she sat weeping,
Thus Eve, our mother,
Where one lay sleeping
Slain by his brother.
Greatest and least
Each piteous beast
To hear her voice
Forgot his joys
And set aside his feast.

The mouse paused in his walk
And dropped his wheaten stalk;
Grave cattle wagged their heads

In rumination;
The eagle gave a cry
From his cloud station;
Larks on thyme beds
Forbore to mount or sing;
Bees drooped upon the wing;
The raven perched on high
Forgot his ration;
The conies in their rock,
A feeble nation,
Quaked sympathetical;
The mocking-bird left off to mock;
Huge camels knelt as if
In deprecation;
The kind hart's tears were falling;
Chattered the wistful stork;
Dove-voices with a dying fall
Cooed desolation,
Answering grief by grief.

Only the serpent in the dust,
Wriggling and crawling,
Grinned an evil grin, and thrust
His tongue out with its fork.

ROBINSON JEFFERS

[1928]   Fawn's Foster-mother

The old woman sits on a bench before the door
    and quarrels
With her meager pale demoralized daughter.
Once when I passed I found her alone, laughing
    in the sun
And saying that when she was first married
She lived in the old farmhouse up Garapatas
    Canyon.

(It is empty now, the roof has fallen
But the log walls hang on the stone foundation;
     the redwoods
Have all been cut down, the oaks are standing;
The place is now more solitary than ever before.)
'When I was nursing my second baby
My husband found a day-old fawn hid in a fern-
     brake
And brought it; I put its mouth to the breast
Rather than let it starve, I had milk enough for
     three babies.
Hey, how it sucked, the little nuzzler,
Digging its little hoofs like quills into my
     stomach.
I had more joy from that than from the others.'
Her face is deformed with age, furrowed like a bad
     road
With market-wagons, mean cares and decay.
She is thrown up to the surface of things, a cell of
     dry skin
Soon to be shed from the earth's old eyebrows,
I see that once in her spring she lived in the
     streaming arteries,
The stir of the world, the music of the mountain.

EVE LANGLEY

[c. 1940]   Native Born

In a white gully among fungus-red
Where serpent logs lay hissing at the air,
I found a kangaroo. Tall, dewy, dead,
So like a woman, she lay silent there,
Her ivory hands, black-nailed, crossed on her
     breast,
Her skin of sun and moon hues, fallen cold.
Her brown eyes lay like rivers come to rest

And death had made her black mouth harsh and
    old.
Beside her in the ashes I sat deep
And mourned for her, but had no native song
To flatter death, while down the ploughlands
    steep
Dark young Camelli whistled loud and long,
'Love, liberty and Italy are all.'
Broad golden was his breast against the sun.
I saw his wattle whip rise high and fall
Across the slim mare's flanks, and one by one
She drew the furrows after her as he
Flapped like a gull behind her, climbing high,
Chanting his oaths and lashing soundingly,
While from the mare came once a blowing sigh.
The dew upon the kangaroo's white side
Had melted. Time was whirling high around,
Like the thin woomera, and from heaven wide
He, the bull-roarer, made continuous sound.
Incarnate, lay my country by my hand:
Her long hot days, bushfires and speaking rains,
Her mornings of opal and the copper band
Of smoke around the sunlight on the plains.
Globed in fire bodies the meat-ants ran
To taste her flesh and linked us as we lay,
For ever Australian, listening to a man
From careless Italy, swearing at our day.
When, golden-lipped, the eaglehawks came
    down
Hissing and whistling to eat of lovely her,
And the blowflies with their shields of purple
    brown
Plied hatching to and fro across her fur,
I burnt her with the logs, and stood all day
Among the ashes, pressing home the flame

Till woman, logs and dreams were scorched
    away,
And native with night, that land from where they
    came.

ANONYMOUS

[traditional]

The Great Silkie of Sule Skerrie

nursing mother   An eartly nourris sits and sings,
sleep, little one   And aye she sings, 'Ba, lily wean!
    Little ken I my bairnis father,
       Far less the land that he staps in.'

Then ane arose at her bed-fit,
    An' a grumly guest I'm sure was he:
'Here am I, thy bairnis father,
    Although that I be not comelie.

'I am a man, upo the lan,
seal   An' I am a silkie in the sea;
    And when I'm far and far frae lan,
       My dwelling is in Sule Skerrie.'

'It was na weel,' quo the maiden fair,
    'It was na weel, indeed,' quo she,
    'That the Great Silkie of Sule Skerrie
given   Suld hae come and aught a bairn to me.'

Now he has taen a purse of goud,
    And he has pat it upo her knee,
Sayin, 'Gie to me my little young son,
    An' tak thee up thy nourris-fee.

'An' it sall come to pass on a simmer's day,
    When the sin shines het on evera stane,
That I will tak my little young son,
    An' teach him for to swim the faem.

'An' thu sall marry a proud gunner,
    An' a proud gunner I'm sure he'll be,
An' the very first schot that ere he schoots,
    He'll schoot baith my young son and me.'

EZRA POUND

[1925]

Canto I

And then went down to the ship,
Set keel to breakers, forth on the godly sea, and
dark   We set up mast and sail on that swart ship,
Bore sheep aboard her, and our bodies also
Heavy with weeping, and winds from sternward
Bore us out onward with bellying canvas,
Circe's this craft, the trim-coifed goddess.
Then sat we amidships, wind jamming the tiller,
Thus with stretched sail, we went over sea till
        day's end.
Sun to his slumber, shadows o'er all the ocean,
Came we then to the bounds of deepest water,
To the Kimmerian lands, and peopled cities
Covered with close-webbed mist, unpierced ever
With glitter of sun-rays
Nor with stars stretched, nor looking back from
        heaven
Swartest night stretched over wretched men
        there.
The ocean flowing backward, came we then to
        the place
Aforesaid by Circe.
Here did they rites, Perimedes and Eurylochus,
And drawing sword from my hip
arm's length / small pit I dug the ell-square pitkin;
Poured we libations unto each the dead,
First mead and then sweet wine, water mixed
        with white flour.

152

Then prayed I many a prayer to the sickly
    death's-heads;
As set in Ithaca, sterile bulls of the best
For sacrifice, heaping the pyre with goods,
A sheep to Tiresias only, black and a bell-sheep.
Dark blood flowed in the fosse,
Souls out of Erebus, cadaverous dead, of brides
Of youths and of the old who had borne much;
Souls stained with recent tears, girls tender,
Men many, mauled with bronze lance heads,

bloodstained   Battle spoil, bearing yet dreory arms,
These many crowded about me; with shouting,
Pallor upon me, cried to my men for more beasts;
Slaughtered the herds, sheep slain of bronze;
Poured ointment, cried to the gods,
To Pluto the strong, and praised Proserpine;
Unsheathed the narrow sword,
I sat to keep off the impetuous impotent dead,
Till I should hear Tiresias.
But first Elpenor came, our friend Elpenor,
Unburied, cast on the wide earth,
Limbs that we left in the house of Circe,
Unwept, unwrapped in sepulchre, since toils
    urged other.
Pitiful spirit. And I cried in hurried speech:
'Elpenor, how art thou come to this dark coast?
'Cam'st thou afoot, outstripping seamen?'
        And he in heavy speech:
'Ill fate and abundant wine. I slept in Circe's
    ingle.
'Going down the long ladder unguarded,
'I fell against the buttress,
'Shattered the nape-nerve, the soul sought
    Avernus.
'But thou, O King, I bid remember me, unwept,
    unburied,

'Heap up mine arms, be tomb by sea-bord, and
    inscribed:
'*A man of no fortune, and with a name to come.*
'And set my oar up, that I swung mid fellows.'

And Anticlea came, whom I beat off, and then
    Tiresias Theban,
Holding his golden wand, knew me, and spoke
    first:
'A second time? why? man of ill star,
'Facing the sunless dead and this joyless region?
'Stand from the fosse, leave me my bloody bever
'For soothsay.'
                And I stepped back,
And he strong with the blood, said then:
    'Odysseus
'Shalt return through spiteful Neptune, over dark
    seas,
'Lose all companions.' And then Anticlea came.
Lie quiet Divus. I mean, that is Andreas Divus,
In officina Wecheli, 1538, out of Homer.
And he sailed, by Sirens and thence outward and
    away
And unto Circe.
                Venerandam,
In the Cretan's phrase, with the golden crown,
    Aphrodite,
Cypri munimenta sortita est, mirthful,
    orichalchi, with golden
Girdles and breast bands, thou with dark eyelids
Bearing the golden bough of Argicida. So that:

drink

*'in the workshop of
Wechelus'*

'adorable'

*'she decided the fate of
Cyprus' defences'*
'bronze'

154

[1565–7]   *from* Ovid's *Metamorphoses* (Book III)

thicket   There was a valley thicke
With Pinaple and Cipresse trees that armed be
    with pricke.
Gargaphie hight this shadie plot, it was a sacred
    place
To chast Diana and the Nymphes that wayted on
    hir grace.
Within the furthest end thereof there was a
    pleasant Bowre
So vaulted with the leavie trees the Sunne had
    there no powre:
Not made by hand nor mans devise: and yet no
    man alive,
A trimmer piece of worke than that could for his
    life contrive.
pumice   With flint and Pommy was it wallde by nature
    halfe about,
And on the right side of the same full freshly
    flowed out
A lively spring with Christall streame: whereof
    the upper brim
Was greene with grasse and matted herbes that
    smelled verie trim.
When Phebe felt hir selfe waxe faint, of following
    of hir game,
It was hir custome for to come and bath hir in the
    same.
That day she, having timely left hir hunting in
    the chace,
Was entred with hir troupe of Nymphes within
    this pleasant place.
She tooke hir quiver and hir bow the which she
    had unbent,

And eke hir Javelin to a Nymph that served that
    intent.
Another Nymph to take hir clothes among hir
    traine she chose,
boots   Two losde hir buskins from hir legges and pulled
    off hir hose.
The Thebane Ladie Crocale more cunning than
    the rest
Did trusse hir tresses handsomly which hung
    behind undrest.
And yet hir owne hung waving still. Then Niphe
    nete and cleene
With Hiale glistring like the grass in beautie fresh
    and sheene,
And Rhanis clearer of hir skin than are the rainie
    drops,
chattering   And little bibling Phyale, and Pseke that pretie
moppet   Mops
Powrde water into vessels large to washe their
    Ladie with.
custom   Now while she keepes this wont, behold, by
wood   wandring in the frith
He wist not whither (having staid his pastime till
    the morrow)
Comes Cadmus Nephew to this thicke: and
    entring in with sorrow
(Such was his cursed cruell fate) saw Phebe
    where she washt.
The Damsels at the sight of man quite out of
    countnance dasht,
(Bicause they everichone were bare and naked to
    the quicke)
Did beate their handes against their breasts, and
    cast out such a shricke,
That all the wood did ring thereof: and clinging to
    their dame

Did all they could to hide both hir and eke
    themselves fro shame.
But Phebe was of personage so comly and so tall,
That by the middle of hir necke she overpeerd
    them all.
Such colour as appeares in Heaven by Phebus
    broken rayes
Directly shining on the Cloudes, or such as is
    alwayes
The colour of the Morning Cloudes before the
    Sunne doth show,
Such sanguine colour in the face of Phoebe gan to
    glowe
There standing naked in his sight. Who though
    she had hir gard
Of Nymphes about hir: yet she turnde hir bodie

away from him   from him ward.

And casting back an angrie looke, like as she
    would have sent
An arrow at him had she had hir bow there readie
    bent,
So raught she water in hir hande and for to

revenge the injury   wreake the spight

Besprinckled all the heade and face of this
    unluckie knight,
And thus forespake the heavie lot that should
    upon him light:
Now make thy vaunt among thy Mates, thou
    sawste Diana bare.
Tell if thou can: I give thee leave: tell hardily: doe
    not spare.
This done she makes no further threates, but by
    and by doth spread
A payre of lively olde Harts hornes upon his
    sprinckled head.

She sharpes his ears, she makes his necke both
    slender, long and lanke.
She turns his fingers into feete, his armes to
    spindle shanke.
She wrappes him in a hairie hyde beset with
    speckled spottes,
And planteth in him fearefulnesse. And so away
    he trottes,
Full greatly wondring to him selfe what made
    him in that cace

strong   To be so wight and swift of foote. But when he
    saw his face
And horned temples in the brooke, he would
    have cryde Alas,
But as for then no kinde of speach out of his lippes
    could passe.
He sighde and brayde: for that was then the
    speach that did remaine,
And downe the eyes that were not his, his bitter
    teares did raine.
No part remayned (save his minde) of that he
    earst had beene.
What should he doe? turne home againe to
    Cadmus and the Queene?
Or hyde himselfe among the Woods? Of this he
    was afrayd,
And of the tother ill ashamde. While doubting
    thus he stayd.
His houndes espyde him where he was, and
    Blackfoote first of all
And Stalker speciall good of scent began aloud to
    call.
This latter was a hounde of Crete, the other was
    of Spart.
Then all the kenell fell in round, and everie for his
    part,

Dyd follow freshly in the chase more swifter than
    the winde,
Spy, Eateal, Scalecliffe, three good houndes
Arcadian   comne all of Arcas kinde,
Strong Bilbucke, currish Savage, Spring, and
    Hunter fresh of smell,
And Lightfoote who to lead a chase did beare
take the prize   away the bell,
Fierce Woodman hurte not long ago in hunting
    of a Bore,
cattle And Shepheird woont to follow sheepe and neate
    to field afore.
And Laund, a fell and eger bitch that had a Wolfe
    to Syre:
bitch Another brach callde Greedigut with two hir
    Puppies by her.
greyhound And Ladon gant as any Greewnd, a hownd in
    Sycion bred,
Blab, Fleetewood, Patch whose flecked skin with
    sundrie spots was spred:
Wight, Bowman, Royster, Beautie faire and
    white as winters snow,
And Tawnie full of duskie haires that over all did
    grow,
With lustie Ruffler passing all the resdue there in
    strength,
And Tempest best of footemanshipe in holding
    out at length.
And Cole and Swift, and little Woolfe, as wight as
    any other,
Accompanide with a Ciprian hound that was his
    native brother,
And Snatch amid whose forehead stoode a starre
    as white as snowe,
The resdue being all as blacke and slicke as any
    Crowe.

And shaggie Rugge with other twaine that had a
    Syre of Crete,
And Dam of Sparta: T' one of them callde
    Jollyboy, a great
And large flewd hound: the tother Chorle who

snarling

    ever gnoorring went,
And Kingwood with a shyrle loude mouth the
    which he freely spent,
With divers mo whose names to tell it were but
    losse of tyme.
This fellowes over hill and dale in hope of pray
    doe clyme.
Through thicke and thin and craggie cliffes
    where was no way to go,
He flyes through groundes where oftentymes he

then

    chased had ere tho.
Even from his owne folke is he faine (alas) to flee
    away.
He strayned oftentymes to speake, and was about
    to say:
I am Acteon: know your Lorde and Mayster, sirs,
    I pray.
But use of wordes and speach did want to utter
    forth his minde.
Their crie did ring through all the Wood
    redoubled with the winde,
First Slo did pinch him by the haunch, and next
    came Kildeere in,
And Hylbred fastned on his shoulder, bote him
    through the skinne.
These cam forth later than the rest, but coasting
    thwart a hill,

catch up with, encounter

They did gainecope him as he came, and helde
    their Master still
Untill that all the rest came in, and fastned on
    him too.

No part of him was free from wound. He could
    none other do
But sigh, and in the shape of Hart with voyce as
    Hartes are woont,
(For voyce of man was none now left to helpe him
    at the brunt)
By braying shew his secret grief among the
    Mountaynes hie,
And kneeling sadly on his knees with dreerie
    tears in eye,
As one by humbling of himself that mercy seemde
    to crave,
With piteous looke in stead of handes his head
    about to wave.
Not knowing that it was their Lord, the
    huntsmen cheere their hounds
With wonted noyse and for Acteon looke about
    the grounds.
They hallow who could lowdest crie still calling
    him by name,
As though he were not there, and much his
    absence they do blame
In that he came not to the fall, but slackt to see
    the game.
As often as they named him he sadly shooke his
    head,
And faine he would have beene away thence in
place   some other stead.
But there he was. And well he could have found
    in heart to see
His dogges fell deedes, so that to feele in place he
    had not bee.
They hem him in on everie side, and in the shape
    of Stagge,
With greedie teeth and griping pawes their Lord
    in peeces dragge.

So fierce was cruell Phoebes wrath, it could not
   be alayde,
Till of his fault by bitter death the raunsome he
   had payde.

ANONYMOUS

[traditional]   # Thomas Rymer

True Thomas lay on Huntlie bank,
marvel   A ferlie he spied wi' his ee,
And there he saw a lady bright,
            Come riding down by the Eildon Tree.

Her shirt was o the grass-green silk,
            Her mantle o the velvet fyne,
every   At ilka tett of her horse's mane
            Hang fifty siller bells and nine.

True Thomas, he pulld aff his cap,
bowed   And louted low down to his knee:
'All hail, thou mighty Queen of Heaven!
            For thy peer on earth I never did see.'

'O no, O no, Thomas,' she said,
            'That name does not belang to me;
I am but the queen of fair Elfland,
            That am hither come to visit thee.

'Harp and carp, Thomas,' she said,
            'Harp and carp along wi me,
And if ye dare to kiss my lips,
            Sure of your bodie I will be.'

'Betide me weal, betide me woe,
fate / intimidate   That weird shall never daunton me;'
then   Syne he has kissed her rosy lips,
            All underneath the Eildon Tree.

'Now, ye maun go wi me,' she said,
　'True Thomas, ye maun go wi me,
And ye maun serve me seven years,
　Thro weal or woe, as may chance to be.'

She mounted on her milk-white steed,
　She's taen True Thomas up behind,
And aye wheneer her bridle rung,
　The steed flew swifter than the wind.

O they rade on, and farther on –
　The steed gaed swifter than the wind –
Until they reached a desart wide,
　And living land was left behind.

'Light down, light down, now, True Thomas,
　And lean your head upon my knee;
Abide and rest a little space,
　And I will show you ferlies three.

'O see ye not yon narrow road,
　So thick beset with thorns and briers?
That is the path of righteousness,
　Tho after it but few enquires.

lovely greensward

'And see not ye that braid braid road,
　That lies across that lily leven?
That is the path of wickedness,
　Tho some call it the road to heaven.

'And see not ye that bonny road,
　That winds about the fernie brae?
That is the road to fair Elfland,
　Where thou and I this night maun gae.

'But, Thomas, ye maun hold your tongue,
　Whatever ye may hear or see,
For, if you speak word in Elflyn land,
　'Ye'll neer get back to your ain countrie.'

O they rade on and farther on,

above   And they waded thro rivers aboon the knee,
And they saw neither sun nor moon,
But they heard the roaring of the sea.

star   It was mirk mirk night, and there was nae stern
light,
And they waded thro red blude to the knee;
For a' the blude that's shed on earth
Rins thro the springs o that countrie.

Syne they came on to a garden green,
And she pu'd an apple frae a tree:
'Take this for they wages, True Thomas,
It will give the tongue that can never lie.'

'My tongue is mine ain,' True Thomas said;
'A gudely gift ye wad gie to me!
fear   I neither dought to buy nor sell,
meeting   At fair or tryst where I may be.

'I dought neither speak to prince or peer,
Nor ask of grace from fair ladye:'
'Now hold they peace,' the lady said,
'For as I say, so must it be.'

He has gotten a coat of the even cloth,
And a pair of shoes of velvet green,
And till seven years were gane and past
True Thomas on earth was never seen.

LOUIS SIMPSON

[1949]   ## Carentan O Carentan

Trees in the old days used to stand
And shape a shady lane
Where lovers wandered hand in hand
Who came from Carentan.

164

This was the shining green canal
Where we came two by two
Walking at combat-interval.
Such trees we never knew.

The day was early June, the ground
Was soft and bright with dew.
Far away the guns did sound,
But here the sky was blue.

The sky was blue, but there a smoke
Hung still above the sea
Where the ships together spoke
To towns we could not see.

Could you have seen us through a glass
You would have said a walk
Of farmers out to turn the grass,
Each with his own hay-fork.

The watchers in their leopard suits
Waited till it was time,
And aimed between the belt and boot
And let the barrel climb.

I must lie down at once, there is
A hammer at my knee.
And call it death or cowardice,
Don't count again on me.

Everything's all right, Mother,
Everyone gets the same
At one time or another.
It's all in the game.

I never strolled, nor ever shall,
Down such a leafy lane.
I never drank in a canal,
Nor ever shall again.

There is a whistling in the leaves
And it is not the wind,
The twigs are falling from the knives
That cut men to the ground.

Tell me, Master-Sergeant,
The way to turn and shoot.
But the Sergeant's silent
That taught me how to do it.

O Captain, show us quickly
Our place upon the map.
But the Captain's sickly
And taking a long nap.

Lieutenant, what's my duty,
My place in the platoon?
He too's a sleeping beauty,
Charmed by that strange tune.

Carentan O Carentan
Before we met with you
We never yet had lost a man
Or known what death could do.

ANONYMOUS

[traditional]   ## Lord Randal

'O where hae ye been, Lord Randal, my son?
O where hae ye been, my handsome young man?'
'I have been to the wild wood; mother, make my
     bed soon,
For I'm weary wi hunting, and fain wald lie
     down.'

'Where gat ye your dinner, Lord Randal, my son?
Where gat ye your dinner, my handsome young
     man?'

'I dined wi my true-love; mother, make my bed
    soon,
For I'm weary wi hunting, and fain wald lie
    down.'

'What gat ye to your dinner, Lord Randal, my
    son?
What gat ye to your dinner, my handsome young
    man?'
'I gat a dish o' wee fishes; mother, make my bed
    soon,
For I'm weary wi hunting, and fain wald lie
    down.'

'What like were the fishes, Lord Randal, my son?
What like were the fishes, my handsome young
    man?'
'Black-backs and spreckle bellies; mother, make
    my bed soon,
For I'm weary wi hunting, and fain wald lie
    down.'

'What became of your bloodhounds, Lord
    Randal, my son?
What became of your bloodhounds, my
    handsome young man?'
'O they swelld and they died; mother, make my
    bed soon,
For I'm weary wi hunting, an fain wald lie down.'

'O I fear ye are poisond, Lord Randal, my son!
O I fear ye are poisond, my handsome young
    man!'
'O yes! I am poisond; mother, make my bed soon,
For I'm sick at the heart and I fain wald lie down.'

[14th century]   # The Pardoner's Tale

once
were accustomed to
game of dice / brothels

In Flaundres whylom was a companye
Of yonge folk, that haunteden folye,
As ryot, hasard, stewes, and tavernes,
Wher-as, with harpes, lutes, and giternes,
They daunce and pleye at dees bothe day and
    night,
And ete also and drinken over hir might,
Thurgh which they doon the devel sacrifyse
With-in that develes temple, in cursed wyse,
By superfluitee abhominable;
Hir othes been so grete and so dampnable,
That it is grisly for to here hem swere;

tear in pieces   Our blissed lordes body they to-tere;
Hem thoughte Jewes rente him noght y-nough;

laughed   And ech of hem at otheres sinne lough.

dancing girls   And right anon than comen tombesteres
graceful / fruit-sellers   Fetys and smale, and yonge fruytesteres,
confectioners   Singers with harpes, baudes, wafereres,
Whiche been the verray develes officeres
To kindle and blowe the fyr of lecherye,
That is annexed un-to glotonye;
The holy writ take I to my witnesse,
That luxurie is in wyn and dronkenesse.

Lot / unnaturally   Lo, how that dronken Loth, unkindely,
Lay by his doghtres two, unwitingly;
did not know   So dronke he was, he niste what he wroghte.
Herodes, (who-so wel the stories soghte),
Whan he of wyn was replet at his feste,
Right at his owene table he yaf his heste
To sleen the Baptist John ful giltelees.
Senek seith eek a good word doutelees;
He seith, he can no difference finde
Bitwix a man that is out of his minde

addicted to drink

madness affecting a scoundrel

paid for

doubt

forbidden

if a man knew

work hard

belly

privy

And a man which that is dronkelewe,
But that woodnesse, y-fallen in a shrewe,
Persevereth lenger than doth dronkenesse.
O glotonye, ful of cursednesse,
O cause first of our confusioun,
O original of our dampnacioun,
Til Crist had boght us with his blood agayn!
Lo, how dere, shortly for to sayn,
Aboght was thilke cursed vileinye;
Corrupt was all this world for glotonye!

    Adam our fader, and his wyf also,
Fro Paradys to labour and to wo
Were driven for that vyce, it is no drede;
For whyl that Adam fasted, as I rede,
He was in Paradys; and whan that he
Eet of the fruyt defended on the tree,
Anon he was out-cast to wo and peyne.
O glotonye, on thee wel oghte us pleyne!
O, wiste a man how many maladyes
Folwen of excesse and of glotonyes,
He wolde been the more mesurable
Of his diete, sitinge at his table.
Allas! the shorte throte, the tendre mouth,
Maketh that, Est and West, and North and South,
In erthe, in eir, in water men to-swinke
To gete a glotoun deyntee mete and drinke!
Of this matere, o Paul, wel canstow trete,
'Mete un-to-wombe, and wombe eek un-to mete,
Shal god destroyen bothe,' as Paulus seith.
Allas! a foul thing is it, by my feith,
To seye this word, and fouler is the dede,
Whan man so drinketh of the whyte and rede,
That of his throte he maketh his privee,
Thurgh thilke cursed superfluitee.

    The apostel weping seith ful pitously,
'Ther walken many of whiche yow told have I,

169

I seye it now weping with pitous voys,
[That] they been enemys of Cristes croys,
Of whiche the ende is deeth, wombe is her god.'

stomach O wombe! O bely! O stinking cod,
Fulfild of donge and of corrupcioun!
At either ende of thee foul is the soun.
How greet labour and cost is thee to finde!
Thise cokes, how they stampe, and streyne, and
　　grinde,
And turnen substaunce in-to accident,

gluttonous desire To fulfille all thy likerous talent!
Out of the harde bones knokke they

marrow The mary, for they caste noght a-way

gullet That may go thurgh the golet softe and swote;
Of spicerye, of leef, and bark, and rote
Shal been his sauce y-maked by delyt,
To make him yet a newer appetyt,
But certes, he that haunteth swich delyces
Is deed, whyl that he liveth in tho vyces.

　　A lecherous thing is wyn, and dronkenesse
Is full of stryving and of wrecchednesse.
O dronke man, disfigured is thy face,
Sour is thy breeth, foul artow to embrace,
And thurgh thy dronke nose semeth the soun
As though thou seydest ay 'Sampsoun,
　　Sampsoun';
And yet, god wot, Sampsoun drank never no wyn.

slaughtered pig Thou fallest, as it were a stiked swyn;
Thy tonge is lost, and al thyn honest cure;
For dronkenesse is verray sepulture
Of mannes wit and his discrecioun.
In whom that drinke hath dominacioun,
He can no conseil kepe, it is no drede.
Now kepe yow fro the whyte and fro the rede,
And namely fro the whyte wyn of Lepe,
That is to selle in Fish-strete or in Chepe.

This wyn of Spayne crepeth subtilly
In othere wynes, growing faste by,
Of which ther ryseth swich fumositee,
That whan a man hath dronken draughtes three,
And weneth that he be at hoom in Chepe,
He is in Spayne, right at the toune of Lepe,
Nat at the Rochel, ne at Burdeux toun;
And thanne wol he seye, 'Sampsoun, Sampsoun.'

But herkneth, lordings, o word, I yow preye,
That alle the sovereyn actes, dar I seye,
Of victories in th'olde testament,
Thurgh verray god, that is omnipotent,
Were doon in abstinence and in preyere;

learn Loketh the Bible, and ther ye may it lere.

Loke, Atilla, the grete conquerour,
Deyde in his sleep, with shame and dishonour,
Bledinge ay at his nose in dronkenesse;
A capitayn shoulde live in sobrenesse.

consider And over al this avyseth yow right wel
What was comaunded un-to Lamuel –
Nat Samuel, but Lamuel, seye I –
Redeth the Bible, and finde it expresly

wine-giving Of wyn-yeving to hem that han justyse.
Na-more of this, for it may wel suffyse.

And now that I have spoke of glotonye,

gambling Now wol I yow defenden hasardrye.

mother / losses Hasard is verray moder of lesinges,
And of deceite, and cursed forsweringes,
Blaspheme of Christ, manslaughtre, and wast
        also

property Of catel and of tyme; and forthermo,
It is repreve and contrarie of honour

considered For to ben holde a commune hasardour.
And ever the hyèr he is of estaat,
The more is he holden desolaat.
If that a prince useth hasardrye,

In alle governaunce and policye
He is, as by commune opinoun,
Y-holde the lasse in reputacioun.
　　Stilbon, that was a wys embassadour,
Was sent to Corinthe, in ful greet honour,
Fro Lacidomie, to make hir alliaunce.
And whan he cam, him happede, par chaunce,
That alle the grettest that were of that lond,
Pleyinge atte hasard he hem fond.
For which, as sone as it mighte be,
He stal him hoom agayn to his contree,
And seyde, 'ther wol I nat lese my name;
N' I wol nat take on me so greet defame,
Yow for to allye un-to none hasardours.
Sendeth othere wyse embassadours;
For, by my trouthe, me were lever dye,
Than I yow sholde to hasardours allye.
For ye that been so glorious in honours
Shul nat allyen yow with hasardours
As by my wil, ne as by my tretee.'
This wyse philosophre thus seyde he.
　　Loke eek that, to the king Demetrius
The king of Parthes, as the book seith us,
Sente him a paire of dees of gold in scorn,
For he hadde used hasard ther-biforn;
For which he heeld his glorie or his renoun
At no value or reputacioun.
Lordes may finden other manere pley
Honeste y-nough to dryve the day awey.
　　Now wol I speke of othes false and grete
A word or two, as olde bokes trete.
Gret swering is a thing abhominable,
And false swering is yet more reprevable.
The heighe god forbad swering at al,
Witnesse on Mathew; but in special
Of swering seith the holy Jeremye,

would rather die

172

'Thou shalt seye sooth thyn othes, and nat lye,

And swere in dome, and eek in rightwisnesse;'
But ydel swering is a cursednesse.
Bihold and see, that in the firste table

Of heighe goddes hestes honurable,
How that the seconde heste of him is this –
'Tak nat my name in ydel or amis.'
Lo, rather he forbedeth swich swering
Than homicyde or many a cursed thing;
I seye that, as by ordre, thus it stondeth;
This knowen, that his hests understondeth,
How that the second heste of god is that.
And forther over, I wol thee telle al plat,
That vengeance shal nat parten from his hous,
That of his othes is to outrageous.
'By goddes precious herte, and by his nayles,
And by the blode of Crist, that it is in Hayles,

Seven is my chaunce, and thyn is cink and treye;
By goddess armes, if thou falsly pleye,
This dagger shal thurgh-out thyn herte go' –

This fruyt cometh of the bicched bones two,
Forswering, ire, falsnesse, homicyde.
Now, for the love of Crist that for us dyde,
Leveth your othes, bothe grete and smale;
But, sirs, now wol I telle forth my tale.

Thise ryotoures three, of whiche I telle,
Longe erst er pryme rong of any belle,
Were set hem in a taverne for to drinke;
And as they satte, they herde a belle clinke

Biforn a cors, was caried to his grave;
That oon of hem gan callen to his knave,
'Go bet,' quod he, 'and axe redily,
What cors is this that passeth heer forby;
And look that thou reporte his name wel.'

'Sir,' quod this boy, 'it nedeth never-a-del.

It was me told, er ye cam heer, two houres;
He was, pardee, an old felawe of youres;
And sodeynly he was y-slayn to-night,
For-dronke, as he sat on his bench upright;
secret   Ther cam a privee theef, men clepeth Deeth,
That in this contree al the people sleeth,
And with his spere he smoot his herte a-two,
And wente his wey with-outen wordes mo.
He hath a thousand slayn this pestilence:
And, maister, er ye come in his presence,
Me thinketh that it were necessarie
For to be war of swich on adversarie:
Beth redy for to mete him evermore.
Thus taughte me my dame, I sey na-more.'
'By seinte Marie,' seyde this taverner,
'The child seith sooth, for he hath slayn this yeer,
hence   Henne over a myle, with-in a greet village,
servant   Both man and womman, child and hyne, and
           page.
I trowe his habitacioun be there;
forewarned   To been avysed greet wisdom it were,
Er that he dide a man a dishonour.'
'Ye, goddes armes,' quod this ryotour.
'Is it swich peril with him for to mete?
I shal him seke by wey and eek by strete,
I make avow to goddes digne bones!
Herkneth, felawes, we three been al ones;
Lat ech of us holde up his hond til other,
And ech of us bicomen otheres brother,
And we wol sleen this false traytour Deeth;
He shal be slayn, which that so many sleeth,
By goddes dignitee, er it be night.'
together   Togidres han thise three her trouthes plight,
To live and dyen ech of hem for other,
As though he were his owene y-boren brother.
And up they sterte al dronken, in this rage,

And forth they goon towardes that village,
Of which the taverner had spoke biforn,
And many a grisly ooth than han they sworn,
And Cristes blessed body they to-rente –

seize 'Deeth shal be deed, if that they may him hente.'

Whan they han goon nat fully half a myle,
Right as they wolde han troden over a style,
An old man and a povre with hem mette.
This olde man ful mekely hem grette,
And seyde thus, 'now, lordes, god yow see!'

The proudest of thise ryotoures three

fellow Answerde agayn, 'what? carl, with sory grace,

covered up Why artow al forwrapped save thy face?
Why livestow so longe in so greet age?'

This olde man gan loke in his visage,
And seyde thus, 'for I ne can nat finde
A man, though that I walked in-to Inde,
Neither in citee nor in no village,
That wolde chaunge his youthe for myn age;
And therfore moot I han myn age stille,
As longe time as it is goddes wille.

Ne deeth, allas! ne wol nat han my lyf;

captive Thus walke I, lyk a restelees caityf,
And on the ground, which is my modres gate,
I knokke with my staf, bothe erly and late,
And seye, "leve moder, leet me in!
Lo, how I vanish, flesh, and blood, and skin!
Allas! whan shul my bones been at reste?

clothes-chest Moder, with yow wolde I chaunge my cheste,
That in my chambre longe tyme hath be,

hair cloth Ye! for an heyre clout to wrappe me!"
But yet to me she wol nat do that grace,
For which ful pale and welked is my face.

But, sirs, to yow it is no curteisye
To speken to an old man vileinye,
But he trespasse in worde, or elles in dede.

175

In holy writ ye may your-self wel rede,

in the presence of / white hair 'Agayns an old man, hoor upon his heed,
Ye sholde aryse;' wherfor I yeve yow reed,
Ne dooth un-to an old man noon harm now,
Na-more than ye wolde men dide to yow
In age, if that ye so longe abyde;
And god be with yow, wher ye go or ryde.
I moot go thider as I have to go.'
   'Nay, olde cherl, by god, thou shalt nat so,'
Seyde this other hasardour anon;
'Thou partest nat so lightly, by seint John!
Thou spak right now of thilke traitour Deeth,
That in this contree alle our frendes sleeth.

spy Have heer my trouthe, as thou art his aspye,
pay dearly for Tel wher he is, or thou shalt it abye,
By god, and by the holy sacrament!
opinion For soothly thou art oon of his assent,
To sleen us yonge folk, thou false theef!'
keen   'Now, sirs,' quod he, 'if that yow be so leef
To finde Deeth, turne up his croked wey,
faith For in that grove I lafte him, by my fey,
Under a tree, and ther he wol abyde;
Nat for your boost he wold him no-thing hyde,
See ye that ook? right ther ye shul him finde.
God save yow, that boghte agayn mankinde,
And yow amende!' – thus seyde this olde man.
And everich of thise ryotoures ran,
Til he cam to that tree, and ther they founde
Of florins fyne of golde y-coyned rounde
Wel ny an eighte busshels, as hem thoughte.
No lenger thanne after Deeth they soughte,
But ech of hem so glad was of that sighte,
For that the florins been so faire and brighte,
That doun they sette hem by this precious hord.
The worste of hem he spake the firste word.
   'Brethren,' quod he, 'tak kepe what I seye;

My wit is greet, though that I bourde and pleye. *jest*
This tresor hath fortune un-to us yiven,
In mirthe and jolitee our lyf to liven,
And lightly as it comth, so wol we spende.
Ey! goddes precious dignitee! who wende
To-day, that we sholde han so fair a grace?
But mighte this gold be caried fro this place
Hoom to myn hous, or elles un-to youres –
For wel ye woot that al this gold is oures –
Than were we in heigh felicitee.
But trewely, by daye it may nat be;
Men wolde seyn that we were theves stronge,
And for our owene tresor doon us honge. *have us hanged*
This tresor moste y-caried be by nighte
As wysly and as slyly as it mighte.
Wherfore I rede that cut among us alle *lot*
Be drawe, and lat see wher the cut wol falle;
And he that hath the cut with herte blythe
Shal renne to the toune, and that ful swythe, *quickly*
And bringe us breed and wyn ful prively.
And two of us shul kepen subtilly
This tresor wel; and, if he wol nat tarie,
Whan it is night, we wol this tresor carie
By oon assent, wher-as us thinketh best.'
That oon of hem the cut broughte in his fest, *fist*
And bad hem draw, and loke wher it wol falle;
And it fil on the yongeste of hem alle;
And forth toward the toun he wente anon.
And al-so sone as that he was gon,
That oon of hem spak thus un-to that other,
'Thou knowest wel thou art my sworne brother,
Thy profit wol I telle thee anon.
Thou woost wel that our felawe is agon;
And heer is gold, and that ful greet plentee,
That shal departed been among us three.
But natheles, if I can shape it so

That it departed were among us two,
Hadde I nat doon a freendes torn to thee?'
That other answerde, 'I noot how that may be;
He woot how that the gold is with us tweye,
What shal we doon, what shal we to him seye?'

secret   'Shal it be conseil?' seyde the firste shrewe,
'And I shal tellen thee, in wordes fewe,
What we shal doon, and bringe it wel aboute.'
'I graunte,' quod that other, 'out of doute,

betray   That, by my trouthe, I wol thee nat biwreye.'
'Now,' quod the firste, 'thou woost wel we be
    tweye,
And two of us shul strenger be than oon.
Look whan that he is set, and right anoon
Arys, as though thou woldest with him pleye;

pierce   And I shal ryve him thurge the sydes tweye
Whyl that thou strogelest with him as in game,
And with thy dagger look thou do the same;
And than shal al this gold departed be,
My dere freend, bitwixen me and thee;

desires   Than may we bothe our lustes al fulfille,
And pleye at dees right at our owene wille.'
And thus acorded been thise shrewes tweye
To sleen the thridde, as ye han herd me seye.

This yongest, which that wente un-to the
    toun,
Ful ofte in herte he rolleth up and doun
The beautee of thise florins newe and brighte.
'O lord!' quod he, 'if so were that I mighte
Have al this tresor to my-self allone,
Ther is no man that liveth under the trone
Of god, that sholde live so mery as I!'
And atte laste the feend, our enemy,
Putte in his thought that he shold poyson beye,
With which he mighte sleen his felawes tweye;
For-why the feend fond him in swich lyvinge,

That he had leve him to sorwe bringe,

absolutely For this was outrely his fulle entente

To sleen hem bothe, and never to repente.

And forth he gooth, no lenger wolde he tarie,

Into the toun, un-to a pothecarie,

And preyed him, that he him wolde selle

kill Som poyson, that he mighte his rattes quelle;

yard And eek ther was a polcat in his hawe,

slain That, as he seyde, his capouns hadde y-slawe,

avenge himself And fayn he wolde wreke him, if he mighte,

On vermin, that destroyed him by nighte.

The pothecarie answerde, 'and thou shalt have

A thing that, al-so god my soule save,

In al this world ther nis no creature,

mixture That ete or drinke hath of this confiture

quantity Noght but the mountance of a corn of whete,

given up That he ne shal his lyf anon forlete;

Ye, sterve he shal, and that in lasse whyle

Than thou wolt goon a paas nat but a myle;

This poyson is so strong and violent.'

This cursed man hath in his hond y-hent

thereupon This poyson in a box, and sith he ran

In-to the nexte strete, un-to a man,

And borwed [of] him large botels three;

And in the two his poyson poured he;

The thridde he kepte clene for his drinke.

intended For al the night he shoop him for to swinke

In caryinge of the gold out of that place.

And whan this ryotour, with sory grace,

Had filled with wyn his grete botels three,

To his felawes agayn repaireth he.

What nedeth it to sermone of it more?

For right as they had cast his deeth bifore,

Right so they han him slayn, and that anon.

And whan that this was doon, thus spak that oon,

'Now lat us sitte and drinke, and make us merie,

And afterward we wol his body berie.'
And with that word it happed him, par cas,
To take the botel ther the poyson was,
And drank, and yaf his felawe drinke also,
For which anon they storven bothe two.

But, certes, I suppose that Avicen
Wroot never in no canon, ne in no fen,
Mo wonder signes of empoisoning
Than hadde thise wrecches two, er hir ending.
Thus ended been thise homicydes two,
And eek the false empoysoner also.

O cursed sinne, ful of cursednesse!
O traytours homicyde, o wikkednesse!
O glotonye, luxurie, and hasardrye!
Thou blasphemour of Crist with vileinye
And othes grete, of usage and of pryde!
Allas! mankinde, how may it bityde,
That to thy creatour which that thee wroghte,
And with his precious herte-blood thee boghte,
Thou art so fals and so unkinde, allas!
Now, goode men, god forgeve yow your
trespas,
And ware yow fro the sinne of avaryce.
Myn holy pardoun may yow alle waryce,
So that ye offre nobles or sterlinges,
Or elles silver broches, spones, ringes.
Boweth your heed under this holy bulle!
Cometh up, ye wyves, offreth of your wolle!
Your name I entre heer in my rolle anon;
In-to the blisse of hevene shul ye gon;
I yow assoile, by myn heigh power,
Yow that wol offre, as clene and eek as cleer
As ye were born; and, lo, sirs, thus I preche.
And Jesu Crist, that is our soules leche,
So graunte yow his pardon to receyve;

chapter (gloss for "fen")

avoid (gloss for "ware")

cure (gloss for "waryce")

nobles or sterling, i.e. money (gloss for "nobles or sterlinges")

wool (gloss for "wolle")

absolve (gloss for "assoile")

doctor (gloss for "leche")

For that is best; I wol yow nat deceyve.
But sirs, o word forgat I in my tale,
bag I have relikes and pardon in my male,
As faire as any man in Engelond,
Whiche were me yeven by the popes hond.
If any of yow wol, of devocioun,
Offren, and han myn absolucioun,
Cometh forth anon, and kneleth heer adoun,
And mekely receyveth my pardoun:
Or elles, taketh pardon as ye wende,
Al newe and fresh, at every tounes ende,
So that ye offren alwey newe and newe
pence Nobles and pens, which that be gode and trewe.
It is an honour to everich that is heer,
That ye mowe have a suffisant pardoneer
T'assouille yow, in contree as ye ryde,
accidents For aventures which that may bityde.
Peraventure ther may falle oon or two
Doun of his hors, and breke his nekke atwo.
Look which a seuretee is it to yow alle
That I am in your felaweship y-falle,
That may assoille yow, bothe more and lasse,
Whan that the soule shal fro the body passe.
I rede that our hoste heer shal biginne,
For he is most envoluped in sinne.
Com forth, sir hoste, and offre first anon,
And thou shalt kisse the reliks everichon,
Ye, for a grote! unbokel anon thy purs.'
'Nay, nay,' quod he, 'than have I Cristes curs!
as I hope to prosper Lat be,' quod he, 'it shal nat be, so thee'ch!
Thou woldest make me kisse thyn old breech,
And swere it were a relik of a seint,
stained Thogh it were with thy fundement depeint!
But by the croys which that seint Eleyne fond,
testicles I wolde I hadde thy coillons in myn hond
holy objects In stede of relikes or of seintuarie;

Lat cutte hem of, I wol thee helpe hem carie;
They shul be shryned in an hogges tord.'
   This pardoner answerde nat a word;
So wrooth he was, no word ne wolde he seye,
   'Now,' quod our host, 'I wold no lenger pleye
With thee, ne with noon other angry man.'
But right anon the worthy Knight bigan,
Whan that he saugh that al the peple lough,
'Na-more of this, for it is right y-nough;
Sir Pardoner, be glad and mery of chere;
And ye, sir host, that been to me so dere,
I prey yow that ye kisse the Pardoner.
And Pardoner, I prey thee, drawe thee neer,
And, as we diden, lat us laughe and pleye.'
Anon they kiste, and riden forth hir weye.

GEORGE MEREDITH

[1883] ## Lucifer in Starlight

On a starred night Prince Lucifer uprose.
Tired of his dark dominion swung the fiend
Above the rolling ball in cloud part screened,
Where sinners hugged their spectre of repose.
Poor prey to his hot fit of pride were those.
And now upon his western wing he leaned,
Now his huge bulk o'er Afric's sands careened,
Now the black planet shadowed Arctic snows.
Soaring through wider zones that pricked his
    scars
With memory of the old revolt from Awe,
He reached a middle height, and at the stars,
Which are the brain of heaven, he looked, and
    sank.
Around the ancient track marched, rank on
    rank,
The army of unalterable law.

[1967]

Behold the Lilies of the Field

For Leonard Baskin

And now. An attempt.
Don't tense yourself; take it easy.
Look at the flowers there in the glass bowl.
Yes, they are lovely and fresh. I remember
Giving my mother flowers once, rather like those
(Are they narcissus or jonquils?)
And I hoped she would show some pleasure in
    them
But got that mechanical enthusiastic show
She used on the telephone once in praising some
    friend
For thoughtfulness or good taste or whatever it
    was,
And when she hung up, turned to us all and said,
'God, what a bore she is!'
I think she was trying to show us how honest she
    was,
At least with us. But the effect
Was just the opposite, and now I don't think
She knows what honesty is. 'Your mother's a
    whore,'
Someone said, not meaning she slept around,
Though perhaps this was part of it, but
Meaning she had lost all sense of honor,
And I think this is true.

But that's not what I wanted to say.
What was it I wanted to say?
When he said that about Mother, I had to laugh,
I really did, it was so amazingly true.
Where was I?
Lie back. Relax.

Oh yes. I remember now what it was.
It was what I saw them do to the emperor.
They captured him, you know. Eagles and all.
They stripped him, and made an iron collar for
    his neck,
And they made a cage out of our captured spears,
And they put him inside, naked and collared,
And exposed to the view of the whole enemy
    camp.
And I was tied to a post and made to watch
When he was taken out and flogged by one of
    their generals
And then forced to offer his ripped back
As a mounting block for the barbarian king
To get on his horse;
And one time to get down on all fours to be the
    royal throne
When the king received our ambassadors
To discuss the question of ransom.
Of course, he didn't want ransom.
And I was tied to a post and made to watch.
That's enough for now. Lie back. Try to relax.
No, that's not all.
They kept it up for two months.
We were taken to their outmost provinces.
It was always the same, and we were always
    made to watch,
The others and I. How he stood it, I don't know.
And then suddenly
There were no more floggings or humiliations,
The king's personal doctor saw to his back,
He was given decent clothing, and the collar was
    taken off,
And they treated us all with a special courtesy.
By the time we reached their capital city
His back was completely healed.

They had taken the cage apart –
But of course they didn't give us back our spears.
Then later that month, it was a warm afternoon
    in May,
The rest of us were marched out to the central
    square.
The crowds were there already, and the posts
    were set up,
To which we were tied in the old watching
    positions.
And he was brought out in the old way, and
    stripped,
And then tied flat on a big rectangular table
So that only his head could move.
Then the king made a short speech to the crowds,
To which they responded with gasps of wild
    excitement,
And which was then translated for the rest of us.
It was the sentence. He was to be flayed alive,
As slowly as possible, to drag out the pain.
And we were made to watch. The king's personal
    doctor,
The one who had tended his back,
Came forward with a tray of surgical knives.
They began at the feet.
And we were not allowed to close our eyes
Or to look away. When they were done, hours
    later,
The skin was turned over to one of their saddle-
    makers
To be tanned and stuffed and sewn. And for
    what?
A hideous life-sized doll, filled out with straw,
In the skin of the Roman Emperor, Valerian,
With blanks of mother-of-pearl under the eyelids,

And painted shells that had been prepared
    beforehand
For the fingernails and toenails,
Roughly cross-stitched on the inseam of the legs
And up the back to the center of the head,
Swung in the wind on a rope from the palace flag-
    pole;
And young girls were brought there by their
    mothers
To be told about the male anatomy.
His death had taken hours.
They were very patient.
And with him passed away the honor of Rome.

In the end, I was ransomed. Mother paid for me.
You must rest now. You must. Lean back.
Look at the flowers.
Yes. I am looking. I wish I could be like them.

JOHN CROWE RANSOM

[1927]

Captain Carpenter

Captain Carpenter rose up in his prime
Put on his pistols and went riding out
But had got wellnigh nowhere at that time
Till he fell in with ladies in a rout.

It was a pretty lady and all her train
That played with him so sweetly but before
An hour she'd taken a sword with all her main
And twined him of his nose for evermore.

Captain Carpenter mounted up one day
And rode straightway into a stranger rogue
That looked unchristian but be that as may
The Captain did not wait upon prologue.

186

But drew upon him out of his great heart
The other swung against him with a club
And cracked his two legs at the shinny part
And let him roll and stick like any tub.

Captain Carpenter rode many a time
From male and female took he sundry harms
He met the wife of Satan crying 'I'm
The she-wolf bids you shall bear no more arms.'

Their strokes and counters whistled in the wind
I wished he had delivered half his blows
But where he should have made off like a hind
The bitch bit off his arms at the elbows.

And Captain Carpenter parted with his ears
To a black devil that used him in this wise
O Jesus ere his threescore and ten years
Another had plucked out his sweet blue eyes.

Captain Carpenter got up on his roan
And sallied from the gate in hell's despite
I heard him asking in the grimmest tone
If any enemy yet there was to fight?

'To any adversary it is fame
If he risk to be wounded by my tongue
Or burnt in two beneath my red heart's flame
Such are the perils he is cast among.

'But if he can he has a pretty choice
From an anatomy with little to lose
Whether he cut my tongue and take my voice
Or whether it be my round red heart he choose.'

It was the neatest knave that ever was seen
Stepping in perfume from his lady's bower
Who at this word put in his merry mien
And fell on Captain Carpenter like a tower.

I would not knock old fellows in the dust
But there lay Captain Carpenter on his back
His weapons were the old heart in his bust
And a blade shook between rotten teeth alack.

The rogue in scarlet and grey soon knew his mind
He wished to get his trophy and depart
With gentle apology and touch refined
He pierced him and produced the Captain's heart.

God's mercy rest on Captain Carpenter now
I thought him Sirs an honest gentleman
Citizen husband soldier and scholar enow
Let jangling kites eat of him if they can.

But God's deep curses follow after those
That shore him of his goodly nose and ears
His legs and strong arms at the two elbows
And eyes that had not watered seventy years.

The curse of hell upon the sleek upstart
That got the Captain finally on his back
And took the red red vitals of his heart
And made the kites to whet their beaks clack
    clack.

CHRISTOPHER MARLOWE

[1588]   *from* The Tragical History of
            Doctor Faustus (Act V)

from SCENE I
OLD MAN: O gentle Faustus, leave this damned art,
          This magic, that will charm thy soul to hell,
          And quite bereave thee of salvation.
          Though thou hast now offended like a man,
          Do not persever in it like a devil;
          Yet, yet, thou hast an amiable soul,
          If sin by custom grow not into nature:

Then, Faustus, will repentance come too late,
Then thou art banish'd from the sight of heaven;
No mortal can express the pains of hell.
It may be this my exhortation
Seems harsh and all unpleasant; let it not,
For, gentle son, I speak it not in wrath,
Or envy of thee, but in tender love,
And pity of thy future misery.
And so have hope, that this my kind rebuke,
Checking thy body, may amend thy soul.

FAUSTUS: Break heart, drop blood, and mingle it with tears,
Tears falling from repentant heaviness
Of thy most vile and loathsome filthiness,
The stench whereof corrupts the inward soul
With such flagitious crimes of heinous sins
As no commiseration may expel,
But mercy, Faustus, of thy Saviour sweet,
Whose blood alone must wash away thy guilt –
Where art thou, Faustus? wretch, what hast thou
    done?
Damn'd art thou, Faustus, damn'd; despair and
    die!
(*Mephistophilis gives him a dagger.*)
Hell claims his right, and with a roaring voice
Says, 'Faustus, come; thine hour is almost come';
And Faustus now will come to do thee right.

OLD MAN: Oh, stay, good Faustus, stay thy desperate steps!
I see an angel hover o'er thy head,
And, with a vial full of precious grace,
Offers to pour the same into thy soul:
Then call for mercy, and avoid despair.

FAUSTUS: O friend, I feel
Thy words to comfort my distressed soul!
Leave me a while to ponder on my sins.

OLD MAN: Faustus, I leave thee; but with grief of heart,
Fearing the enemy of thy hapless soul.
(*Exit.*)

FAUSTUS: Accursed Faustus, where is mercy now?
I do repent; and yet I do despair:
Hell strives with grace for conquest in my breast:
What shall I do to shun the snares of death?

MEPHISTOPH.: Thou traitor, Faustus, I arrest thy soul
For disobedience to my sovereign lord:
Revolt, or I'll in piecemeal tear thy flesh.

FAUSTUS: I do repent I e'er offended him.
Sweet Mephistophilis, entreat thy lord
To pardon my unjust presumption,
And with my blood again I will confirm
The former vow I made to Lucifer.

MEPHISTOPH.: Do it, then, Faustus, with unfeigned heart,
Lest greater dangers do attend thy drift.
(*Faustus stabs his arm, and writes on a paper with his blood.*)

FAUSTUS: Torment, sweet friend, that base and aged man.
That durst dissuade me from thy Lucifer,
With greatest torments that our hell affords.

MEPHISTOPH.: His faith is great; I cannot touch his soul;
But what I may afflict his body with
I will attempt, which is but little worth.

FAUSTUS: One thing, good servant, let me crave of thee,
To glut the longing of my heart's desire, –
That I may have unto my paramour
That heavenly Helen which I saw of late,
Whose sweet embraces may extinguish clean
Those thoughts that do dissuade me from my vow,
And keep my oath I made to Lucifer.

MEPHISTOPH.: This, or what else, my Faustus shall desire,
Shall be perform'd in twinkling of an eye.
(*Enter Helen again, passing over the stage between two Cupids.*)

FAUSTUS: Was this the face that launch'd a thousand ships,
And burnt the topless towers of Ilium? –

Sweet Helen, make me immortal with a kiss. –
(*She kisses him.*)
Her lips suck forth my soul: see where it flies! –
Come, Helen, come, give me my soul again.
Here will I dwell, for heaven is in these lips,
And all is dross that is not Helena.
(*Enter Old Man.*)
I will be Paris, and for love of thee,
Instead of Troy, shall Wittenberg be sack'd;
And I will combat with weak Menelaus,
And wear thy colours on my plumed crest:
Yea, I will wound Achilles in the heel,
And then return to Helen for a kiss.
O, thou art fairer than the evening's air
Clad in the beauty of a thousand stars;
Brighter art thou than flaming Jupiter
When he appear'd to hapless Semele;
More lovely than the monarch of the sky
In wanton Arethusa's azured arms;
And none but thou shalt be my paramour!
(*Exeunt Faustus, Helen and Cupids.*)
OLD MAN: Accursed Faustus, miserable man,
That from thy soul exclud'st the grace of Heaven,
And fliest the throne of his tribunal-seat!
(*Enter the Devils.*)
Satan begins to sift me with his pride:
As in this furnace God shall try my faith,
My faith, vile hell, shall triumph over thee.
Ambitious fiends, see how the heavens smiles
At your repulse, and laughs your state to scorn!
Hence, hell! for hence I fly unto my God.
(*Exeunt.*)

from SCENE II
Enter the Good Angel and the Bad Angel at several doors.

GOOD ANGEL: Oh, Faustus, if thou hadst given ear to me,
                   Innumerable joys had followed thee.
                   But thou didst love the world.

BAD ANGEL: Gave ear to me,
                   And now must taste hell's pains perpetually.

GOOD ANGEL: O what will all thy riches, pleasures, pomps,
                   Avail thee now?

BAD ANGEL: Nothing but vex thee more,
                   To want in hell, that had on earth such store.
                   (*Music while the throne descends.*)

GOOD ANGEL: O thou hast lost celestial happiness,
                   Pleasures unspeakable, bliss without end.
                   Hadst thou affected sweet divinity,
                   Hell, or the devil, had had no power on thee.
                   Hadst thou kept on that way, Faustus, behold,
                   In what resplendent glory thou hadst sit
                   In yonder throne, like those bright shining
                          saints,
                   And triumph'd over hell: that hast thou lost:
                   And now, poor soul, must thy good angel leave
                          thee,
                   (*The throne ascends.*)
                   The jaws of hell are open to receive thee.
                   (*Exit. Hell is discovered.*)

BAD ANGEL: Now, Faustus, let thine eyes with horror stare
                   Into that vast perpetual torture-house.
                   There are the Furies tossing damned souls
                   On burning forks; their bodies boil in lead:
                   There are live quarters broiling on the coals,
                   That ne'er can die: this ever-burning chair
                   Is for o'er-tortured souls to rest them in;
                   These that are fed with sops of flaming fire,
                   Were gluttons and lov'd only delicates,

And laugh'd to see the poor starve at their gates:
But yet all these are nothing; thou shalt see
Ten thousand tortures that more horrid be.

FAUSTUS: O, I have seen enough to torture me.

BAD ANGEL: Nay, thou must feel them, taste the smart of all:
He that loves pleasure, must for pleasure fall:
And so I leave thee, Faustus, till anon;
Then wilt thou tumble in confusion.
(*Exit. Hell disappears. The clock strikes eleven.*)

FAUSTUS: Ah, Faustus,
Now hast thou but one bare hour to live,
And then thou must be damn'd perpetually!
Stand still, you ever moving spheres of heaven,
That time may cease, and midnight never come;
Fair Nature's eye, rise, rise again, and make
Perpetual day; or let this hour be but
A year, a month, a week, a natural day,
That Faustus may repent and save his soul!

'O run slowly, slowly, *O lente, lente currite, noctis equi!*
horses of the night!' The stars move still, time runs, the clock will
      strike,
The devil will come, and Faustus must be damn'd.
O, I'll leap up to my God! – Who pulls me down? –
See, see, where Christ's blood streams in the
      firmament!
One drop would save my soul, half a drop: ah, my
      Christ! –
Ah, rend not my heart for naming of my Christ!
Yet will I call on him: O, spare me, Lucifer! –
Where is it now? 'tis gone: and see, where God
Stretcheth out his arm, and bends his ireful
      brows!
Mountains and hills, come, come, and fall on me,
And hide me from the heavy wrath of God!
No, no!
Then will I headlong run into the earth:

193

Earth, gape! O, no, it will not harbour me!
You stars that reign'd at my nativity,
Whose influence hath allotted death and hell,
Now draw up Faustus, like a foggy mist,
Into the entrails of yon lab'ring cloud
That, when you vomit forth into the air,
My limbs may issue from your smoky mouths,
So that my soul may but ascend to heaven!
(*The clock strikes.*)
Ah, half the hour is past! 'twill all be passed anon.
O God,
If thou wilt not have mercy on my soul,
Yet for Christ's sake, whose blood hath ransom'd
            me,
Impose some end to my incessant pain;
Let Faustus live in hell a thousand years,
A hundred thousand, and at last be sav'd!
O, no end is limited to damned souls!
Why wert thou not a creature wanting soul?
Or why is this immortal that thou hast?
Ah, Pythagoras' *metempsychosis*, were that true,
This soul should fly from me, and I be changed
Unto some brutish beast! all beasts are happy,
For, when they die,
Their souls are soon dissolved in elements;
But mine must live still to be plagu'd in hell.
Curs'd be the parents that engender'd me!
No, Faustus, curse thyself, curse Lucifer
That hath depriv'd thee of the joys of heaven.
(*The clock striketh twelve.*)
O, it strikes, it strikes! Now, body, turn to air,
Or Lucifer will bear thee quick to hell!
O soul, be changed into little water-drops,
And fall into the ocean, ne'er be found!
(*Thunder and enter the Devils.*)
My God, my God, look not so fierce on me!

Adders and serpents, let me breathe a while!
Ugly hell, gape not! come not, Lucifer!
I'll burn my books! – Ah, Mephistophilis!
(*Exeunt with him.*)

EPILOGUE

Enter Chorus.

CHORUS: Cut is the branch that might have grown full
     straight,
  And burned is Apollo's laurel-bough,
  That sometime grew within this learned man.
  Faustus is gone: regard his hellish fall,
  Whose fiendful fortune may exhort the wise,
  Only to wonder at unlawful things,
  Whose deepness doth entice such forward wits
  To practise more than heavenly power permits.

ANONYMOUS

[traditional]

The Strange Visitor

A wife was sitting at her reel ae night,
wound her yarn   And aye she sat, and aye she reeled, and aye
   she wished for company.

In came a pair o' braid braid soles, and sat down
   at the fireside,
  And aye she sat, and aye she reeled, and aye
   she wished for company.

In came a pair o' sma' sma' legs, and sat down on
   the braid braid soles,
  And aye she sat, and aye she reeled, and aye
   she wished for company.

big

In came a pair o' muckle muckle knees, and sat
　　down on the sma' sma' legs,
　　And aye she sat, and aye she reeled, and aye
　　she wished for company.

thighs

In came a pair o' sma' sma' thees, and sat down
　　on the muckle muckle knees,
　　And aye she sat, and aye she reeled, and aye
　　she wished for company.

In came a pair o' muckle muckle hips, and sat
　　down on the sma' sma' thees,
　　And aye she sat, and aye she reeled, and aye
　　she wished for company.

In came a sma' sma' waist, and sat down on the
　　muckle muckle hips,
　　And aye she sat, and aye she reeled, and aye
　　she wished for company.

In came a pair o' braid braid shouthers, and sat
　　down on the sma' sma' waist,
　　And aye she sat, and aye she reeled, and aye
　　she wished for company.

In came a pair o' sma' sma' arms, and sat down
　　on the braid braid shouthers,
　　And aye she sat, and aye she reeled, and aye
　　she wished for company.

In came a pair o' muckle muckle hands and sat
　　down on the sma' sma' arms,
　　And aye she sat, and aye she reeled, and aye
　　she wished for company.

In came a sma' sma' neck, and sat down on the
　　braid braid shouthers,
　　And aye she sat, and aye she reeled, and aye
　　she wished for company.

In came a great big head, and sat down on the
        sma' sma' neck.

What way hae ye sic braid braid feet? quo' the
        wife.
trampling   Muckle ganging, muckle ganging.
What way hae ye sic sma' sma' legs?
up late and little food Aih-h-h! – late – and wee-e-e moul.
What way hae ye sic muckle muckle knees?
Muckle praying, muckle praying.
What way hae ye sic sma' sma' thees?
Aih-h-h! – late – and wee-e-e – moul.
What way hae ye sic big big hips?
Muckle sitting, muckle sitting.
What way hae ye sic a sma' sma' waist?
Aih-h-h! – late – and wee-e-e – moul.
What way hae ye sic braid braid shouthers?
Wi' carrying broom, wi' carrying broom.
What way hae ye sic sma' sma' arms?
Aih-h-h! – late – and wee-e-e – moul.
What way hae ye sic muckle muckle hands?
Threshing wi' an iron flail, threshing wi' an iron
        flail.
What way hae ye sic a sma' sma' neck?
Aih-h-h! – late – and wee-e-e – moul.
What way hae ye sic a muckle muckle head?
Muckle wit, muckle wit.
What do you come for?
For YOU!

JUDITH WRIGHT

[1949]   ## Eli, Eli

To see them go by drowning in the river –
soldiers and elders drowning in the river,
the pitiful women drowning in the river,

the children's faces staring from the river –
that was his cross, and not the cross they gave
    him.

To hold the invisible wand, and not to save them –
to know them turned to death, and yet not save
    them;
only to cry to them and not to save them,
knowing that no one but themselves could save
    them –
this was the wound, more than the wound they
    dealt him.

To hold out love and know they would not take it,
to hold out faith and know they dared not take it –
the invisible wand, and none would see or take it;
all he could give, and there was none to take it –
thus they betrayed him, not with the tongue's
    betrayal.

He watched, and they were drowning in the
    river;
faces like sodden flowers in the river,
faces of children moving in the river;
and all the while, he knew there was no river.

ANONYMOUS

[15th century]   'Adam lay ibounden'

Adam lay ibounden,
Bounden in a bond:
Foure thousand winter
Thought he not too long.
And all was for an apple,
And apple that he tok,
As clerkes finden
Wreten in here book.

Ne hadde the apple taken ben,
The apple taken ben,
Ne hadde never our Lady
A ben Hevene Quen.
Blissed be the time
That apple taken was!
Therfore we moun singen,
'Thanks be to God'   'Deo gracias!'

ANONYMOUS (OLD ENGLISH)

[8th century or earlier] The Dream of the Rood

Listen! I'll tell the sweetest dream,
That dropped to me from midnight, in the quiet
Time of silence and restful sleep.
    I seemed to see a tree of miracles
Rising in the sky, a shining cross
Wrapped in light. And all that beacon
Was sheathed in gold; jewels were set
Where it touched the earth, and five studded
The shoulder-span. Angels looked on,
The loveliest things in creation. No thief had
    crowned that gibbet;
Holy spirits watched it, and humble
Men, and all glory under the universe.
    It was a tree of victory and splendor, and I
    tainted,
Ulcered with sin. And yet I saw it –
Shining with joy, clothed, adorned,
Covered with gold, the tree of the Lord
Gloriously wrapped in gleaming stones.
And through the gold I saw the stains
Of its ancient agony when blood spilled out
On its right-hand side. I was troubled and afraid
Of the shining sight. Then its garments changed,

And its color; for a moment it was moist with
    blood,
Dripping and stained; then it shone like silver.
  So I lay there in the darkness a long while,
    watching
In stricken grief the Saviour's tree,
Until I suddenly heard it speak.
And these were the words of the holy wood:

  'It was long ago (but I won't forget)
When they came to the forest and cut me down,
Pulled me out of the earth. Ruthless enemies took
    me
And made me a mocking show, forced me to hold
    their thieves.
They swung me up on their shoulders, planted
    me into a hill,
Set me deep and straight. I saw the Lord of the
    world
Boldly rushing to climb upon me
And I could neither bend, nor break
The word of God. I saw the ground
Trembling. I could have crushed them all,
And yet I kept myself erect.
  The young hero, God Himself, threw off His
    garments,
Determined and brave. Proud in the sight of men
    He mounted
The meanest gallows, to make men's souls
    eternally free.
I trembled as His arms went round me. And still I
    could not bend,
Crash to the earth, but had to bear the body of
    God.
I was reared as a cross. I raised the mighty
King of Heaven and could not bend.

They pierced me with vicious nails. I bear the
    scars
Of malicious gashes. But I dared not injure any of
    them.
We were both reviled, we two together. I was
    drenched with the blood that gushed
From the hero's side as His holy spirit swept to
    Heaven.
    Cruel things came to me there
On that hill. I saw the God of Hosts
Stretched on the rack. Clouds rolled
From the darkness to cover over the corpse,
The shining splendor; a livid shadow
Dropped from Heaven. The creation wept,
Bewailed His death. Christ was on the cross.
    From distant lands the eager ones came
To the hero. And I watched it all,
Wrapped as I was in sorrow I bent to their
    reaching hands,
Humble with courage. They carried away
    almighty God,
Raised Him out of His torment. I was abandoned
    of men,
Standing bespattered with blood, driven through
    with spikes.
They laid down the weary-limbed God, stood and
    watched at His head,
Beholding Heaven's King as He lay in quiet sleep,
Exhausted with hardship and pain. And they
    started to carve a sepulchre,
With His slayer watching. They chiselled the
    tomb of the brightest stone
And laid the Lord of victories there. And then
    they sang
A dirge, miserable in the dusk, and wearily began
    the journey

Home, leaving their mighty prince. He was left
   alone.
   Yet after His followers' voices drifted
Away, we crosses went on weeping,
Standing in place. The beautiful corpse
Grew cold. Then they came to cut us
Down. We shuddered with fear, and fell.
They buried us deep in a pit, but the faithful
Heard of my fate, and came, and dug me
Out, and adorned me with silver and gold.
   Only now can you hear, oh Heaven-blessed
      man,
How evil men have brought me pain
And sorrow. For now a season has come
When the men of all the world, and all creation,
Shall honor and worship me far and wide,
Pray to this symbol. The Son of God
Suffered on me, and made me glorious,
Towering on earth, so that every man
Who holds me in awe can be healed at my touch.
I was made to be a bitter punishment,
Loathed by men until I led them
To the road of life, and opened its gates.
Listen! The Father of glory has honored me
Past any forest tree, the Lord
Himself – as He honored His mother, Mary,
Made her, loveliest and best of women,
For every man to bow to and worship.
   And now I tell you, oh trusted of men,
That you shall reveal this sight, disclose
To the world that this is that glorious wood
On which almighty God has suffered
Agony for mankind's millions of sins
And for Adam's ancient fall. On me
He tasted death, and then He rose
As God to save all men with His greatness.

He rose to Heaven. He will hurry here
Again, to seek the souls of this earth,
On the day of doom. As God Himself,
The Ruler of Heaven, gathering His angels,
He will judge you all, He alone who can judge,
Opening to every man eternity
Or Hell, as each has earned in this fleeting
Life. No one will stand unafraid
Of the word the Lord of the world will pronounce.
And He will ask, there among many, for the man
Who would go to death in the name of God
As Christ knew death on this bitter cross.
They will tremble in terror, and few will try
To give an answer to God. But none
Need fear who carries faith in his heart,
The sign of this glorious beacon, for they are given
A power, all through this cross of pain,
That shall carry every soul on earth
To live with the Lord for whom they yearn.'

   Then I offered cheerful prayers to that cross,
Bravely, where I found myself
Again alone. My spirit was eager
To start on a journey for which it has suffered
Endless longing. My hope in life
Is now that I shall see and reverence
That cross of triumph more than other
Men. All my heart's desire
Reaches for that holy tree, and seeks
Its hallowed protection. No mighty patrons
Shelter me here; they've melted in shadows,
Gone from the joys of this world, sought the
    glorious King
And live in Heaven, now, with Him,
Live in His glory. My longing, through every
Day, is for that cross of faith

Which I beheld here on earth
To come and fetch me out of exile
And bring me where exultation is,
Joy in Heaven, where the blessèd of God
Sit at His table, where bliss is eternal,
There to place me in the midst of glory,
To grant me eternal gladness with the host
Of the saints. May God befriend me, He
Who once suffered agony here on earth,
Ascended the gibbet to ransom our sins.
He broke our bonds and gave us life
And a home in Heaven. And hope was renewed
In bliss for those who'd burned in Hell.
The Son triumphed on that journey to darkness,
Smashing Hell's doors. Many men's souls
Rose with Him then, the Ruler of all,
Rising to Heaven and the angels' bliss
And the joy of the saints already enthroned
And dwelling in glory, welcoming almighty
God returned to His shining home.

translated by Burton Raffel

R. S. THOMAS

[1961] Here

I am a man now.
Pass your hand over my brow,
You can feel the place where the brains grow.

I am like a tree,
From my top boughs I can see
The footprints that led up to me.

There is blood in my veins
That has run clear of the stain
Contracted in so many loins.

Why, then, are my hands red
With the blood of so many dead?
Is this where I was misled?

Why are my hands this way
That they will not do as I say?
Does no God hear when I pray?

I have nowhere to go.
The swift satellites show
The clock of my whole being is slow.

It is too late to depart
For destinations not of the heart.
I must stay here with my hurt.

ROBERT SOUTHWELL

[1602] ## The Burning Babe

As I in hoary winter's night stood shivering in the
    snow,
Surprised I was with sudden heat which made my
    heart to glow;
And lifting up a fearful eye to view what fire was
    near,
A pretty Babe all burning bright did in the air
    appear,
Who scorchèd with excessive heat such floods of
    tears did shed,
As though his floods should quench his flames
    which with his tears were bred;
'Alas!' quoth he, 'but newly born, in fiery heats I
    fry,
Yet none approach to warm their hearts or feel
    my fire but I.
My faultless breast the furnace is, the fuel
    wounding thorns;

Love is the fire and sighs the smoke, the ashes
    shames and scorns;
The fuel Justice layeth on, and Mercy blows the
    coals,
The metal in this furnace wrought are men's
    defilèd souls,
For which, as now on fire I am, to work them to
    their good,
So will I melt into a bath, to wash them in my
    blood.'
With this he vanished out of sight, and swiftly
    shrunk away,
And straight I callèd unto mind that it was
    Christmas day.

ANONYMOUS

[16th century] ## The Corpus Christi Carol

Lully, lulley, lully, lulley,
falcon
mate   The fawcon hath born my mak away.

He bare him up, he bare him down,
He bare him into an orchard brown.

In that orchard ther was an hall,
rich purple cloth   That was hanged with purpill and pall.

And in that hall ther was a bed:
It was hanged with gold so red.

And in that bed ther lythe a knight,
His woundes bleding day and night.

maiden   By that bedes side ther kneleth a may,
And she wepeth both night and day.

And by that bedes side ther stondeth a ston,
'The Body of Christ'   'Corpus Christi' wreton theron.

JAMES K. BAXTER

[1969] ## The Maori Jesus

I saw the Maori Jesus
Walking on Wellington Harbour.
He wore blue dungarees.
His beard and hair were long.
His breath smelt of mussels and paraoa.
When he smiled it looked like the dawn.
When he broke wind the little fishes trembled.
When he frowned the ground shook.
When he laughed everybody got drunk.

The Maori Jesus came on shore
And picked out his twelve disciples.
One cleaned toilets in the Railway Station;
His hands were scrubbed red to get the shit out of
    the pores.
One was a call-girl who turned it up for nothing.
One was a housewife who'd forgotten the Pill
And stuck her TV set in the rubbish can.
One was a little office clerk
Who'd tried to set fire to the Government
    Buildings.
Yes, and there were several others;
One was an old sad quean;
One was an alcoholic priest
Going slowly mad in a respectable parish.

The Maori Jesus said, 'Man,
From now on the sun will shine.'

He did no miracles;
He played the guitar sitting on the ground.

The first day he was arrested
For having no lawful means of support.
The second day he was beaten up by the cops

For telling a dee his house was not in order.
The third day he was charged with being a Maori
And given a month in Mount Crawford.
The fourth day he was sent to Porirua
For telling a screw the sun would stop rising.
The fifth day lasted seven years
While he worked in the asylum laundry
Never out of the steam.
The sixth day he told the head doctor,
'I am the Light in the Void;
I am who I am.'
The seventh day he was lobotomized;
The brain of God was cut in half.

On the eighth day the sun did not rise.
It didn't rise the day after.
God was neither alive nor dead.
The darkness of the Void,
Mountainous, mile-deep, civilized darkness
Sat on the earth from then till now.

PATRICK KAVANAGH

[1942]   *from* The Great Hunger

I

Clay is the word and clay is the flesh
Where the potato-gatherers like mechanised
    scarecrows move
Along the side-fall of the hill – Maguire and his
    men.
If we watch them an hour is there anything we
    can prove
Of life as it is broken-backed over the Book
Of Death? Here crows gabble over worms and
    frogs

And the gulls like old newspapers are blown clear
    of the hedges, luckily.
Is there some light of imagination in these wet
    clods?
Or why do we stand here shivering?
              Which of these men
Loved the light and the queen
Too long virgin? Yesterday was summer. Who
    was it promised marriage to himself
Before apples were hung from the ceilings for
    Hallowe'en?
We will wait and watch the tragedy to the last
    curtain,
Till the last soul passively like a bag of wet clay
Rolls down the side of the hill, diverted by the
    angles
Where the plough missed or a spade stands,
    straitening the way.

A dog lying on a torn jacket under a heeled-up
    cart,
A horse nosing along the posied headland,
    trailing
A rusty plough. Three heads hanging between
    wide-apart
Legs. October playing a symphony on a slack wire
    paling.
Maguire watches the drills flattened out
And the flints that lit a candle for him on a June
    altar
Flameless. The drills slipped by and the days
    slipped by
And he trembled his head away and ran free from
    the world's halter,
And thought himself wiser than any man in the
    townland

When he laughed over pints of porter
Of how he came free from every net spread
In the gaps of experience. He shook a knowing
    head
And pretended to his soul
That children are tedious in hurrying fields of
    April
Where men are spanging across wide furrows.
Lost in the passion that never needs a wife –
The pricks that pricked were the pointed pins of
    harrows.
Children scream so loud that the crows could
    bring
The seed of an acre away with crow-rude jeers.
Patrick Maguire, he called his dog and he flung a
    stone in the air
And hallooed the birds away that were the birds
    of the years.

Turn over the weedy clods and tease out the
    tangled skeins.
What is he looking for there?
He thinks it is a potato, but we know better
Than his mud-gloved fingers probe in this
    insensitive hair.

'Move forward the basket and balance it steady
In this hollow. Pull down the shafts of that cart,
    Joe,
And straddle the horse,' Maguire calls.
'The wind's over Brannagan's, now that means
    rain.
Graip up some withered stalks and see that no
    potato falls
Over the tail-board going down the ruckety
    pass –
And *that's* a job we'll have to do in December,

Gravel it and build a kerb on the bog-side. Is that
    Cassidy's ass
Out in my clover? Curse o' God –
Where is that dog?
Never where he's wanted.' Maguire grunts and
    spits
Through a clay-wattled moustache and stares
    about him from the height.
His dream changes again like the cloud-swung
    wind
And he is not so sure now if his mother was right
When she praised the man who made a field his
    bride.

Watch him, watch him, that man on a hill whose
    spirit
Is a wet sack flapping about the knees of time.
He lives that his little fields may stay fertile when
    his own body
Is spread in the bottom of a ditch under two
    coulters crossed in Christ's Name.

He was suspicious in his youth as a rat near
    strange bread,
When girls laughed; when they screamed he
    knew that meant
The cry of fillies in season. He could not walk
The easy road to destiny. He dreamt
The innocence of young brambles to hooked
    treachery.
O the grip, O the grip of irregular fields! No man
    escapes.
It could not be that back of the hills love was free
And ditches straight.
No monster hand lifted up children and put down
    apes
As here.

'O God if I had been wiser!'
That was his sigh like the brown breeze in the
thistles.
He looks towards his house and haggard. 'O God
if I had been wiser!'
But now a crumpled leaf from the whitethorn
bushes
Darts like a frightened robin, and the fence
Shows the green of after-grass through a little
window,
And he knows that his own heart is calling his
mother a liar
God's truth is life – even the grotesque shapes of
its foulest fire.

The horse lifts its head and cranes
Through the whins and stones
To lip late passion in the crawling clover.
In the gap there's a bush weighted with boulders
like morality,
The fools of life bleed if they climb over.

The wind leans from Brady's, and the coltsfoot
leaves are holed with rust,
Rain fills the cart-tracks and the sole-plate
grooves;
A yellow sun reflects in Donaghmoyne
The poignant light in puddles shaped by hooves.

Come with me, imagination, into this iron house
And we will watch from the doorway the years
run back,
And we will know what a peasant's left hand
wrote on the page.
Be easy, October. No cackle hen, horse neigh, tree
sough, duck quack.

VIII

Sitting on a wooden gate,
Sitting on a wooden gate,
Sitting on a wooden gate
He didn't care a damn.
Said whatever came into his head,
Said whatever came into his head,
Said whatever came into his head
And inconsequently sang.
While his world withered away,
He had a cigarette to smoke and a pound to spend
On drink the next Saturday.
His cattle were fat
And his horses all that
Midsummer grass could make them.

The young women ran wild
And dreamed of a child
Joy dreams though the fathers might forsake
        them
But no one would take them,
No one would take them;
No man could ever see
That their skirts had loosed buttons,
O the men were as blind as could be.
And Patrick Maguire
From his purgatory fire
Called the gods of the Christian to prove
That this twisted skein
Was the necessary pain
And not the rope that was strangling true love.

But sitting on a wooden gate
Sometime in July
When he was thirty-four or five
He gloried in the lie:

He made it read the way it should,
He made life read the evil good
While he cursed the ascetic brotherhood
Without knowing why.
Sitting on a wooden gate
All, all alone
He sang and laughed
Like a man quite daft,
Or like a man on a channel raft
He fantasied forth his groan.
Sitting on a wooden gate,
Sitting on a wooden gate,
Sitting on a wooden gate
He rode in day-dream cars.
He locked his body with his knees
When the gate swung too much in the breeze.
But while he caught high ecstasies
Life slipped between the bars.

XII

The fields were bleached white,
The wooden tubs full of water
Were white in the winds
That blew through Brannagan's Gap on their
    way from Siberia;
The cows on the grassless heights
Followed the hay that had wings –
The February fodder that hung itself on the black
    branches
Of the hill-top hedge.
A man stood beside a potato-pit
And clapped his arms
And pranced on the crisp roots
And shouted to warm himself.
Then he buck-leaped about the potatoes

And scooped them into a basket.
He looked like a bucking suck-calf
Whose spine was being tickled.
Sometimes he stared across the bogs
And sometimes he straightened his back and
    vaguely whistled
A tune that weakened his spirit
And saddened his terrier dog's.

[. . .]

O what was I doing when the procession passed?
Where was I looking?
Young women and men
And I might have joined them.
Who bent the coin of my destiny
That it stuck in the slot?
I remember a night we walked.
Through the moon of Donaghmoyne,
Four of us seeking adventure,
It was midsummer forty years ago.
Now I know
The moment that gave the turn to my life.
O Christ! I am locked in a stable with pigs and
    cows for ever.

XIV

We may come out into the October reality,
    Imagination,
The sleety wind no longer slants to the black hill
    where Maguire
And his men are now collecting the scattered
    harness and baskets.
The dog sitting on a wisp of dry stalks
Watches them through the shadows.

'Back in, back in.' One talks to the horse as to a
    brother.
Maguire himself is patting a potato-pit against
    the weather –
An old man fondling a new-piled grave:
'Joe, I hope you didn't forget to hide the spade,
For there's rogues in the townland. Hide it flat in
    a furrow.
I think we ought to be finished by to-morrow.'
Their voices through the darkness sound like
    voices from a cave,
A dull thudding far away, futile, feeble, far away,
First cousins to the ghosts of the townland.

A light stands in a window. Mary Anne
Has the table set and the tea-pot waiting in the
    ashes.
She goes to the door and listens and then she calls
From the top of the haggard-wall:
'What's keeping you
And the cows to be milked and all the other work
    there's to do?'
'All right, all right,
We'll not stay here all night.'

Applause, applause,
The curtain falls.
Applause, applause
From the homing carts and the trees
And the bawling cows at the gates.
From the screeching water-hens
And the mill-race heavy with the Lammas floods
    curving over the weir.
A train at the station blowing off steam
And the hysterical laughter of the defeated
    everywhere.
Night, and the futile cards are shuffled again.

Maguire spreads his legs over the impotent
   cinders that wake no manhood now
And he hardly looks to see which card is trump.
His sister tightens her legs and her lips and
   frizzles up
Like the wick of an oil-less lamp.
The curtain falls –
Applause, applause.

Maguire is not afraid of death, the Church will
   light him a candle
To see his way through the vaults and he'll
   understand the
Quality of the clay that dribbles over his coffin.
He'll know the names of the roots that climb
   down to tickle his feet.
And he will feel no different than when he walked
   through Donaghmoyne.

If he stretches out a hand – a wet clod,
If he opens his nostrils – a dungy smell;
If he opens his eyes once in a million years –
Through a crack in the crust of the earth he may
   see a face nodding in
Or a woman's legs. Shut them again for that sight
   is sin.

He will hardly remember that life happened to
   him –
Something was brighter a moment. Somebody
   sang in the distance.
A procession passed down a mesmerised street.
He remembers names like Easter and Christmas
By the colour his fields were.
Maybe he will be born again, a bird of an angel's
   conceit
To sing the gospel of life

To a music as flightily tangent
As a tune on an oboe.
And the serious look of the fields will have
    changed to the leer of a hobo
Swaggering celestially home to his three wishes
    granted.
Will that be? will that be?
Or is the earth right that laughs haw-haw
And does not believe
In an unearthly law.
The earth that says:
Patrick Maguire, the old peasant, can neither be
    damned nor glorified:
The graveyard in which he will lie will be just a
    deep-drilled potato-field
Where the seed gets no chance to come through
To the fun of the sun.
The tongue in his mouth is the root of a yew.
Silence, silence. The story is done.

He stands in the doorway of his house
A ragged sculpture of the wind,
October creaks the rotted mattress,
The bedposts fall. No hope. No lust.
The hungry fiend
Screams the apocalypse of clay
In every corner of this land.

[1925]

The Hollow Men

A penny for the Old Guy

I

We are the hollow men
We are the stuffed men
Leaning together
Headpiece filled with straw. Alas!
Our dried voices, when
We whisper together
Are quiet and meaningless
As wind in dry grass
Or rats' feet over broken glass
In our dry cellar

Shape without form, shade without colour,
Paralysed force, gesture without motion;

Those who have crossed
With direct eyes, to death's other Kingdom
Remember us – if at all – not as lost
Violent souls, but only
As the hollow men
The stuffed men.

II

Eyes I dare not meet in dreams
In death's dream kingdom
These do not appear:
There, the eyes are
Sunlight on a broken column
There, is a tree swinging
And voices are
In the wind's singing

More distant and more solemn
Than a fading star.

Let me be no nearer
In death's dream kingdom
Let me also wear
Such deliberate disguises
Rat's coat, crowskin, crossed staves
In a field
Behaving as the wind behaves
No nearer –

Not that final meeting
In the twilight kingdom

III

This is the dead land
This is cactus land
Here the stone images
Are raised, here they receive
The supplication of a dead man's hand
Under the twinkle of a fading star.

Is it like this
In death's other kingdom
Waking alone
At the hour when we are
Trembling with tenderness
Lips that would kiss
Form prayers to broken stone.

IV

The eyes are not here
There are no eyes here
In this valley of dying stars

In this hollow valley
This broken jaw of our lost kingdoms

In this last of meeting places
We grope together
And avoid speech
Gathered on this beach of the tumid river

Sightless, unless
The eyes reappear
As the perpetual star
Multifoliate rose
Of death's twilight kingdom
The hope only
Of empty men.

v

Here we go round the prickly pear
Prickly pear prickly pear
Here we go round the prickly pear
At five o'clock in the morning.

Between the idea
And the reality
Between the motion
And the act
Falls the Shadow

For Thine is the Kingdom

Between the conception
And the creation
Between the emotion
And the response
Falls the Shadow

Life is very long

Between the desire
And the spasm
Between the potency
And the existence
Between the essence
And the descent
Falls the Shadow

For Thine is the Kingdom

For Thine is
Life is
For Thine is the

This is the way the world ends
This is the way the world ends
This is the way the world ends
Not with a bang but a whimper.

ISAAC ROSENBERG

[1916] ## Break of Day in the Trenches

The darkness crumbles away.
It is the same old druid Time as ever,
Only a live thing leaps my hand,
A queer sardonic rat,
As I pull the parapet's poppy
To stick behind my ear.
Droll rat, they would shoot you if they knew
Your cosmopolitan sympathies.
Now you have touched this English hand
You will do the same to a German
Soon, no doubt, if it be your pleasure
To cross the sleeping green between.
It seems you inwardly grin as you pass
Strong eyes, fine limbs, haughty athletes,
Less chanced than you for life,

Bonds to the whims of murder,
Sprawled in the bowels of the earth,
The torn fields of France.
What do you see in our eyes
At the shrieking iron and flame
Hurled through still heavens?
What quaver – what heart aghast?
Poppies whose roots are in man's veins
Drop, and are ever dropping;
But mine in my ear is safe –
Just a little white with the dust.

JOHN HEWITT

[1974]

The King's Horses

After fifty years, nearly, I remember,
living then in a quiet leafy suburb,
waking in the darkness, made aware
of a continuous irregular noise,
and groping to the side window to discover
the shadow-shapes which made that muffled
    patter
passing across the end of our avenue,
the black trees and the streetlights shuttering
a straggle of flowing shadows, endless, of horses.

Gypsies they could have been, or tinkers maybe,
mustering to some hosting of their clans,
or horse-dealers heading their charges to the
    docks,
timed to miss the day's traffic and alarms:
a migration the newspapers had not foretold;
some battle's ragged finish, dream repeated:
the last of an age retreating, withdrawing,
leaving us beggared, bereft
of the proud nodding muzzles, the nervous bodies:

gone from us the dark men with their ancient
    skills
of saddle and stirrup, or bridle and breeding.

It was an end, I was sure, but an end of what
I never could tell. It was never reported:
but the echoing hooves persisted. Years after,
in a London hotel in the grey dawn
a serious man concerned with certain duties,
I heard again the metal clatter of hooves staccato
and hurriedly rose to catch a glimpse of my
    horses,
but the pace and beat were utterly different:
I saw by the men astride these were the King's
    horses
going about the King's business, never mine.

ANONYMOUS (IRISH)

[8th century]   ## Pangur Bán

Written by a student of the monastery of Carinthia
on a copy of St Paul's Epistles

I and Pangur Bán, my cat,
'Tis a like task we are at;
Hunting mice is his delight,
Hunting words I sit all night.

Better far than praise of men
'Tis to sit with book and pen;
Pangur bears me no ill-will,
He too plies his simple skill.

'Tis a merry thing to see
At our tasks how glad are we,
When at home we sit and find
Entertainment to our mind.

Oftentimes a mouse will stray
In the hero Pangur's way;
Oftentimes my keen thought set
Takes a meaning in its net.

'Gainst the wall he sets his eye
Full and fierce and sharp and sly;
'Gainst the wall of knowledge I
All my little wisdom try.

When a mouse darts from its den,
O how glad is Pangur then!
O what gladness do I prove
When I solve the doubts I love!

So in peace our tasks we ply,
Pangur Bán, my cat, and I;
In our arts we find our bliss,
I have mine and he has his.

Practice every day has made
Pangur perfect in his trade;
I get wisdom day and night
Turning darkness into light.

translated by Robin Flower

CHRISTOPHER SMART

[*c.* 1760]   *from* Jubilate Deo

For I will consider my Cat Jeoffry.
For he is the servant of the Living God duly and
    daily serving him.
For at the first glance of the glory of God in the
    East he worships in his way.
For is this done by wreathing his body seven
    times round with elegant quickness.
For then he leaps up to catch the musk, which is
    the blessing of God upon his prayer.

For he rolls upon prank to work it in.

For having done duty and received blessing he
begins to consider himself.

For this he performs in ten degrees.

For first he looks upon his fore-paws to see if they
are clean.

For secondly he kicks up behind to clear away
there.

For thirdly he works it upon stretch with the fore-
paws extended.

For fourthly he sharpens his paws by wood.

For fifthly he washes himself.

For Sixthly he rolls upon wash.

For Seventhly he fleas himself, that he may not be
interrupted upon the beat.

For Eighthly he rubs himself against a post.

For Ninthly he looks up for his instructions.

For Tenthly he goes in quest of food.

For having consider'd God and himself he will
consider his neighbour.

For if he meets another cat he will kiss her in
kindness.

For when he takes his prey he plays with it to give
it chance.

For one mouse in seven escapes by his dallying.

For when his day's work is done his business
more properly begins.

For he keeps the Lord's watch in the night against
the adversary.

For he counteracts the powers of darkness by his
electrical skin and glaring eyes.

For he counteracts the Devil, who is death, by
brisking about the life.

For in his morning orisons he loves the sun and
the sun loves him.

For he is of the tribe of Tiger.

For the Cherub Cat is a term of the Angel Tiger.
For he has the subtlety and hissing of a serpent,
   which in goodness he suppresses.
For he will not do destruction, if he is well-fed,
   neither will he spit without provocation.
For he purrs in thankfulness, when God tells him
   he's a good Cat.
For he is an instrument for the children to learn
   benevolence upon.
For every house is incompleat without him and a
   blessing is lacking in the spirit.
For the Lord commanded Moses concerning the
   cats at the departure of the Children of Israel
   from Egypt.
For every family had one cat at least in the bag.
For the English Cats are the best in Europe.
For he is the cleanest in the use of his fore-paws of
   any quadrupede.
For the dexterity of his defence is an instance of
   the love of God to him exceedingly.
For he is the quickest to his mark of any creature.
For he is tenacious of his point.
For he is a mixture of gravity and waggery.
For he knows that God is his Saviour.
For there is nothing sweeter than his peace when
   at rest.
For there is nothing brisker than his life when in
   motion.
For he is of the Lord's poor and so indeed is he
   called by benevolence perpetually – Poor
   Jeoffry! poor Jeoffry! the rat has bit thy throat.
For I bless the name of the Lord Jesus that Jeoffrey
   is better.
For the divine spirit comes about his body to
   sustain it in compleat cat.

For his tongue is exceeding pure so that it has in
    purity what it wants in musick.
For he is docile and can learn certain things.
For he can set up with gravity which is patience
    upon approbation.
For he can fetch and carry, which is patience in
    employment.
For he can jump over a stick which is patience
    upon proof positive.
For he can spraggle upon waggle at the word of
    command.
For he can jump from an eminence into his
    master's bosom.
For he can catch the cork and toss it again.
For he is hated by the hypocrite and miser.
For the former is affraid of detection.
For the latter refuses the charge.
For he camels his back to bear the first notion of
    business.
For he is good to think on, if a man would express
    himself neatly.
For he made a great figure in Egypt for his signal
    services.
For he killed the Ichneumon-rat very pernicious
    by land.
For his ears are so acute that they sting again.
For from this proceeds the passing quickness of
    his attention.
For by stroaking of him I have found out
    electricity.
For I perceived God's light about him both wax
    and fire.
For the Electrical fire is the spiritual substance,
    which God sends from heaven to sustain the
    bodies both of man and beast.

For God has blessed him in the variety of his
    movements.
For, though he cannot fly, he is an excellent
    clamberer.
For his motions upon the face of the earth are
    more than any other quadrupede.
For he can tread to all the measures upon the
    musick.
For he can swim for life.
For he can creep.

ANDREW YOUNG

[1939]   ## A Dead Mole

Strong-shouldered mole,
That so much lived below the ground,
Dug, fought and loved, hunted and fed,
For you to raise a mound
Was as for us to make a hole;
What wonder now that being dead
Your body lies here stout and square
Buried within the blue vault of the air?

MARJORY FLEMING

[c. 1810]   ## A Sonnet on a Monkey

O lovely O most charming pug
Thy graceful air and heavenly mug
The beauties of his mind do shine
And every bit is shaped so fine
Your very tail is most divine
Your teeth is whiter than the snow
beau   You are a great buck and a bow
Your eyes are of so fine a shape
More like a christians than an ape.
His cheeks is like the roses blume

Your hair is like the ravens plume
His noses cast is of the roman
He is a very pretty weoman
I could not get a rhyme for roman
And was obliged to call it weoman.

WILLIAM COWPER

[1784] Epitaph on a Hare

Here lies, whom hound did n'er pursue,
   Nor swifter greyhound follow,
Whose foot ne'er tainted morning dew,
   Nor ear heard huntsman's 'hallo',

Old Tiney, surliest of his kind,
   Who, nursed with tender care,
And to domestic bounds confined,
   Was still a wild jack-hare.

Though duly from my hand he took
   His pittance ev'ry night,
He did it with a jealous look,
   And, when he could, would bite.

His diet was of wheaten bread,
   And milk, and oats, and straw,
Thistles, or lettuces instead,
   With sand to scour his maw.

On twigs of hawthorn he regaled,
   On pippins' russet peel;
And, when his juicy salads failed,
   Sliced carrot pleased him well.

A Turkey carpet was his lawn,
   Whereon he loved to bound,
To skip and gambol like a fawn,
   And swing his rump around.

His frisking was at evening hours,
    For then he lost his fear;
But most before approaching show'rs,
    Or when a storm drew near.

Eight years and five round-rolling moons
    He thus saw steal away,
Dozing out all his idle noons,
    And ev'ry night at play.

I kept him for his humour's sake,
    For he would oft beguile
My heart of thoughts that made it ache,
    And force me to a smile.

But now, beneath this walnut-shade
    He finds his long, last home,
And waits in snug concealment laid,
    Till gentler Puss shall come.

He, still more agèd, feels the shocks
    From which no care can save,
And, partner once of Tiney's box,
    Must soon partake his grave.

NORMAN NICHOLSON

[1948]   Cowper's Tame Hare

She came to him in dreams – her ears
Diddering like antennae, and her eyes
Wide as dark flowers where the dew
Holds and dissolves a purple hoard of shadow.
The thunder clouds crouched back, and the
    world opened
Tiny and bright as a celandine after rain.
A gentle light was on her, so that he
Who saw the talons in the vetch
Remembering now how buttercup and daisy

Would bounce like springs when a child's foot
    stepped off them.
Oh, but never dared he touch –
Her fur was still electric to the fingers.

Yet of all the beasts blazoned in gilt and blood
In the black-bound scriptures of his mind,
Pentecostal dove and paschal lamb,
Eagle, lion, serpent, she alone
Lived also in the noon of ducks and sparrows;
And the cleft-mouthed kiss which plugged the
    night with fever
Was sweetened by a lunch of docks and lettuce.

EDWARD TAYLOR

[late 17th century] ## Upon a Spider Catching a Fly

Thou sorrow, venom Elfe:
    Is this thy play,
To spin a web out of thyselfe
    To Catch a Fly?
        For why?

I saw a pettish wasp
    Fall foule therein:
Whom yet thy whorle pins did not hasp
    Lest he should fling
        His sting.

But as afraid, remote
    Didst stand hereat,
And with thy little fingers stroke
    And gently tap
        His back.

Thus gently him didst treate
    Lest he should pet,
And in a froppish, aspish heate

Should greatly fret
  Thy net.

Whereas the silly Fly,
  Caught by its leg,
Thou by the throate took'st hastily,
  And 'hinde the head
    Bite Dead.

This goes to pot, that not
  Nature doth call.
Strive not above what strength hath got,
  Lest in the brawle
    Thou fall.

This Fray seems thus to us:
  Hells Spider gets
His intrails spun to whip Cords thus,
  And wove to nets,
    And sets.

To tangle Adams race
  In's stratagems
To their Destructions, Spoil'd, made base
  By venom things,
    Damn'd Sins.

But mighty, Gracious Lord,
  Communicate
Thy Grace to breake the Cord; afford
  Us Glorys Gate
    And State.

We'll Nightingaile sing like,
  When pearcht on high
In Glories Cage, thy glory, bright:
  Yea, thankfully,
    For joy.

[1962]

Roman Poem III: A Sparrow's Feather

There was this empty birdcage in the garden.
    And in it, to amuse myself, I had hung
pseudo-Oriental birds constructed of
        glass and tin bits and paper, that squeaked
            sadly
as the wind sometimes disturbed them.
        Suspended
    in melancholy disillusion they sang
of things that had never happened, and never
    could in that cage of artificial existence.
The twittering of these instruments lamenting
    their absent lives resembled threnodies
torn from a falling harp, till the cage filled with
    engineered regret like moonshining cobwebs
as these constructions grieved over not existing.
    The children fed them with flowers. A sudden
        gust
and without sound lifelessly one would die
    scattered in scraps like debris. The wire doors
always hung open, against their improbable
    transfiguration into, say, chaffinches
or even more colourful birds. Myself I found
    the whole game charming, let alone the
        children.
And then, one morning – I do not record a
    matter of cosmic proportions, I assure you,
not an event to flutter the Volscian dovecotes –
    there, askew among those constructed mages
like a lost soul electing to die in Rome,
    its feverish eye transfixed, both wings
        fractured,
lay – I assure you, Catullus – a young sparrow.
    Not long for this world, so heavily breathing

one might have supposed this cage his
    destination
after labouring past seas and holy skies
whence, death not being known there, he had
    flown.
    Of course, there was nothing to do. The
    children
brought breadcrumbs, brought water, brought
    tears in their
    eyes perhaps to restore him, that shivering
    panic
of useless feathers, that tongue-tied little gossip,
    that lying flyer. So there, among its gods
that moaned and whistled in a little wind,
    flapping their paper anatomies like windmills,
wheeling and bowing dutifully to the
    divine intervention of a child's forefinger,
there, at rest and at peace among its monstrous
    idols, the little bird died. And, for my part,
I hope the whole unimportant affair is
    quickly forgotten. The analogies are too trite.

JOHN SKELTON

[c. 1505] *from* Philip Sparrow

Of fortune this the chaunce
Standeth on variaunce:
Oft time after pleasaunce
Trouble and grevaunce;
No man can be sure
Allway to have pleasure:
As well perceive ye maye
How my disport and play
From me was taken away
By Gib, our cat savage,
That in a furious rage

Caught Phillip by the head,
And slew him there starke dead.
'Lord, have mercy'   Kyrie, eleison,
      Christe, eleison,
      Kyrie, eleison!
For Philip Sparowes soule,
prayer-roll   Set in our bederolle,
Let us now whisper
'Our Father'   A Pater noster.
'Praise the Lord, O my soul'   Lauda, anima mea, Dominum!
To wepe with me loke that ye come,
All maner of birdes in your kind;
Se none be left behinde.
mourning   To morninge loke that ye fall
With dolorous songes funerall,
Some to singe, and some to say,
Some to wepe, and some to pray,
tune   Every birde in his laye.
The goldfinche, the wagtaile;
The janglinge jay to raile,
magpie   The fleckid pye to chatter
Of this dolorous mater;
And robin redbrest,
He shall be the preest
The requiem masse to singe,
Softly warbelinge,
reed sparrow   With helpe of the red sparrow,
And the chattringe swallow,
This herse for to halow;
toe   The larke with his longe to;
finch   The spinke, and the martinet also;
shoveller duck   The shovelar with his brode bek;
dolt   The doterell, that folishe pek,
And also the mad coote,
peer at   With a balde face to toote;
snipe   The feldefare, and the snite;

The crowe, and the kite;
The ravin, called Rolfe,
sing   His plaine songe to solfe;
The partriche, the quaile;
The plover with us to waile;
woodpecker   The woodhacke, that singeth 'chur'
catarrh   Horsly, as he had the mur;
The lusty chaunting nightingale;
parrot   The popingay to tell her tale,
peers   That toteth oft in a glasse,
Shal rede the Gospell at masse;
missel-thrush   The mavis with her whistell
epistle   Shal rede there the pistell.
long and short note   But with a large and a longe
To kepe just plaine songe,
cuckoo   Our chaunters shalbe the cuckoue,
stockdove   The culver, the stokedowue,
With 'putwit' the lapwing,
The versicles shall sing.
bittern   The bitter with his 'bumpe,'
trumpet   The crane with his trumpe,
The swan of Menander,
The gose and the gander,
The ducke and the drake,
Shall watche at this wake;
The pecocke so proude,
Because his voice is loude,
And hath a glorious taile,
Gradual   He shall sing the graile;
The owle, that is so foule,
Must helpe us to howle;
The heron so gaunte,
And the cormoraunte,
With the fesaunte,
gabbling gannet   And the gaglinge gaunte,
And the churlisshe chough;

The route and the rough; *a type of goose / sandpiper*
The barnacle, the bussarde,
With the wilde mallarde;
The divendop to slepe; *dabchick*
The water hen to wepe;
The puffin and the tele
Money they shall dele *distribute*
To poore folke at large,
That shall be their charge;
The semewe and the titmose; *seamew*
The wodcocke with the longe nose;
The threstil with her warbling; *throstle*
The starling with her brabling;
The roke, with the ospraye *rook*
That putteth fisshes to a fraye; *fright*
And the denty curlewe, *dainty*
With the turtill most trew.

At this *Placebo* *i.e., stage of liturgy*
We may not well forgo
The countringe of the coe; *accompaniment-singing / jackdaw*
The storke also,
That maketh his nest
In chimneys to rest;
Within those walles
No broken galles *blisters*
May there abide
Of cokoldry side, *i.e., pertaining to cuckoldry*
Or els philosophy
Maketh a great lie.

The estrige, that will eate *ostrich*
An horshowe so great, *horseshoe*
In the stede of meate,
Such fervent heat
His stomacke doth freat; *gnaw*
He can not well fly,
Nor singe tunably,

Yet for a whim
Yet at a braide
He hath well assaide
to sing above high C To solfe above ela,
loafer Fa, lorell, fa, fa;
'Lest whenever by singing badly' *Ne quando*
Male cantando,
The best that we can,
To make him our belman,
And let him ring the bellis;
He can do nothing ellis.
      Chaunteclere, our coke,
Must tell what is of the clocke
By the astrology
That he hath naturally
Conceived and cought,
And was never tought
By Albumazer
The astronomer,
Nor by Ptholomy
Prince of astronomy,
Nor yet by Haly;
And yet he croweth daily
times And nightly the tides
That no man abides,
With Partlot his hen,
Whom now and then
Hee plucketh by the hede
What he doth her trede.
      The birde of Araby,
That potencially
May never die,
And yet there is none
But one alone;
A phenex it is
bless This herse that must blis
With armaticke gummes

239

That cost great summes,
The way of thurification
To make a fumigation,

odor Swete of reflare,

smell And redolent of eire,

the corpse to cense This corse for to sence
With greate reverence,
As patriarke or pope
In a blacke cope;

censes Whiles he senseth the herse,
He shall singe the verse,

'Deliver me' *Libera me*,
In de, la, soll, re,

i.e., sing the flat part Softly bemole
For my sparowes soule.
Plinny sheweth all
In his story naturall
What he doth finde
Of the phenix kinde;
Of whose incineracion
There riseth a new creacion

fashion Of the same facion
Without alteracion,
Saving that olde age

heartiness Is turned into corage
Of fresshe youth againe;
This matter trew and plaine,
Plaine matter indede,
Who so list to rede.
    But for the egle doth flye
Hyest in the skye,

subdean He shall be the sedeane,

to manage the choir The quere to demeane,
As provost principall,

service book To teach them their ordinall;

falcon Also the noble faucon,

240

With the gerfaucon,
tercel   The tarsell gentill,
mourn   They shall morne soft and still
fur-lined hood   In their amisse of gray;
a type of falcon   The sacre with them shall say
i.e., stage of liturgy   *Dirige* for Phillippes soule;
The goshauke shall have a role
choristers   The queresters to controll;
types of falcon   The lanners and the marlions
mourning   Shall stand in their morning gownes;
a type of falcon /   The hobby and the muskette
sparrowhawk
censers / fetch   The sensers and the crosse shall fet;
work   The kestrell in all this warke
clerk   Shall be holy water clarke.
And now the darke cloudy night
Chaseth away Phebus bright,
Taking his course toward the west,
sparrow's   God sende my sparoes sole good rest!
'Give them eternal peace,   *Requiem aeternam dona eis, Domine!*
O Lord'
Fa, fa, fa, mi, re, re,
'by the lower gate'   *A por-ta, in-fe-ri,*
Fa, fa, fa, mi, mi.
'I believe I am seeing the   *Credo videre bona Domini,*
blessing of the Lord'
I pray God Phillip to heven may fly!

IRVING LAYTON

[1958]   ## Cat Dying in Autumn

I put the cat outside to die,
Laying her down
Into a rut of leaves
Cold and bloodsoaked;
Her moan
Coming now more quiet
And brief in October's economy

Till the jaws
Opened and shut on no sound.

Behind the wide pane
I watched the dying cat
Whose fur like a veil of air
The autumn wind stirred
Indifferently with the leaves;
Her form (or was it the wind?)
Still breathing –
A surprise of white.

And I was thinking
Of melting snow in spring
Or a strip of gauze
When a sparrow
Dropped down beside it
Leaning his clean beak
Into the hollow;
Then whirred away, his wings,
You may suppose, shuddering.

Letting me see
From my house
The twisted petal
That fell
Between the ruined paws
To hold or play with,
And the tight smile
Cats have for meeting death.

[*c.* 1608]

'Call for the robin-redbreast and the wren'
from The White Devil

Call for the robin-redbreast and the wren,
Since o'er shady groves they hover
And with leaves and flowers do cover
The friendless bodies of unburied men.
Call unto his funeral dole
The ant, the field-mouse, and the mole,
To rear him hillocks that shall keep him warm
And, when gay tombs are robbed, sustain no
    harm;
But keep the wolf far thence, that's foe to men,
For with his nails he'll dig them up again.

ANONYMOUS

[traditional]

A Lyke-Wake Dirge

This ae nighte, this ae nighte,
    Every night and alle,
Fire, and sleete, and candle lighte,
    And Christe receive thye saule.

When thou from hence away are paste,
    Every night and alle,
To Winny-muir thou comest at laste,
    And Christe receive thye saule.

stockings / shoes If ever thou gavest hosen and shoon,
    Every night and alle,
Sit thee down and put them on,
    And Christe recveive thye saule.

If hosen and shoon thou ne'er gavest name,
    Every night and alle,

The whinnes shall pricke thee to the bare bane,
  And Christe receive thye saule.

From Whinny-muir when thou mayst passe,
  Every night and alle,
To Brigg o' Dread thou comest at laste,
  And Christe receive thye saule.

From Brigg o' Dread when thou mayst passe,
  Every night and alle,
To purgatory fire thou comest at laste,
  And Christe receive thye saule.

If ever thou gavest meat or drink
  Every night and alle,
The fire shall never make thee shrinke,
  And Christe receive thye saule.

If meate or drinke thou never gavest nane,
  Every night and alle,
The fire will burn thee to the bare bane,
  And Christe receive thye saule.

This ae nighte, this ae nighte,
  Every night and alle,
Fire, and sleete, and candle lighte,
  And Christe receive thye saule.

JAMES CLARENCE MANGAN

[1846]   ## Siberia

In Siberia's wastes
  The Ice-wind's breath
Woundeth like the toothèd steel;
Lost Siberia doth reveal
  Only blight and death.

Blight and death alone.
  No Summer shines.

Night is interblent with Day.
In Siberia's wastes alway
    The blood blackens, the heart pines.

In Siberia's wastes
    No tears are shed,
For they freeze within the brain.
Nought is felt but dullest pain,
    Pain acute, yet dead;

Pain as in a dream,
    When years go by
Funeral-paced, yet fugitive,
When man lives, and doth not live,
    Doth not live – nor die.

In Siberia's wastes
    Are sands and rocks.
Nothing blooms of green or soft,
But the snow-peaks rise aloft
    And the gaunt ice-blocks.

And the exile there
    Is one with those;
They are part, and he is part,
For the sands are in his heart,
    And the killing snows.

Therefore, in those wastes
    None curse the Czar.
Each man's tongue is cloven by
The North Blast, that heweth nigh
    With sharp scymitar.

And such doom each drees,
    Till, hunger-gnawn,
And cold-slain, he at length sinks there,
Yet scarce more a corpse than ere
    His last breath was drawn.

[1895]

City of Dreadful Thirst

The stranger came from Narromine and made his
    little joke;
'They say we folks in Narromine are narrow-
    minded, folk;
But all the smartest men down here are puzzled to
    define
A kind of new phenomenon that came to
    Narromine.

'Last summer up in Narromine 'twas gettin'
    rather warm –
Two hundred in the water-bag, and lookin' like a
    storm –
We all were in the private bar, the coolest place in
    town,
When out across the stretch of plain a cloud came
    rollin' down.

'We don't respect the clouds up there, they fill us
    with disgust,
They mostly bring a Bogan shower – three
    raindrops and some dust;
But each man, simultaneous-like, to each man
    said, "I think
That cloud suggests it's up to us to have another
    drink!"

'There's clouds of rain and clouds of dust – we'd
    heard of them before,
And sometimes in the daily press we read of
    "clouds of war".
But – if this ain't the Gospel truth I hope that I
    may burst –

That cloud that came to Narromine was just a
    cloud of thirst.

'It wasn't like a common cloud, 'twas more a sort
    of haze;
It settled down about the street, and stopped for
    days and days;
And not a drop of dew could fall, and not a
    sunbeam shine
To pierce that dismal sort of mist that hung on
    Narromine.

'Oh, Lord! we had a dreadful time beneath that
    cloud of thirst!
We all chucked-up our daily work and went upon
    the burst.
The very blacks about the town, that used to
    cadge for grub,
They made an organized attack and tried to loot
    the pub.

'We couldn't leave the private bar no matter how
    we tried;
Shearers and squatters, union-men and
    blacklegs side by side
Were drinkin' there and dursn't move, for each
    was sure, he said,
Before he'd get a half-a-mile the thirst would
    strike him dead!

'We drank until the drink gave out; we searched
    from room to room,
And round the pub, like drunken ghosts, went
    howling through the gloom.
The shearers found some kerosene and settled
    down again,
But all the squatter chaps and I, we staggered to
    the train.

'And once outside the cloud of thirst we felt as
    right as pie,
But while we stopped about the town we had to
    drink or die.
I hear today it's safe enough; I'm going back to
    work
Because they say the cloud of thirst has shifted on
    to Bourke.

'But when you see those clouds about – like this
    one over here –
All white and frothy at the top, just like a pint of
    beer,
It's time to go and have a drink, for if that cloud
    should burst
You'd find the drink would all be gone, for that's
    a cloud of thirst!'

We stood the man from Narromine a pint of half-
    and-half;
He drank it off without a gasp in one tremendous
    quaff;
'I joined some friends last night,' he said, 'in what
    they called a spree;
But after Narromine 'twas just a holiday to me.'

And now beyond the Western Range, where
    sunset skies are red,
And clouds of dust, and clouds of thirst, go
    drifting overhead,
The railway-train is taking back, along the
    Western Line,
That narrow-minded person on his road to
    Narromine.

WILLIAM MCGONAGALL

[1880?] ## The Tay Bridge Disaster

Beautiful Railway Bridge of the Silv'ry Tay!
Alas! I am very sorry to say
That ninety lives have been taken away
On the last Sabbath day of 1879,
Which will be remember'd for a very long time.

'Twas about seven o'clock at night,
And the wind it blew with all its might,
And the rain came pouring down,
And the dark clouds seem'd to frown,
And the Demon of the air seem'd to say –
'I'll blow down the Bridge of Tay.'

When the train left Edinburgh
The passengers' hearts were light and felt no
    sorrow,
But Boreas blew a terrific gale,
Which made their hearts for to quail,
And many of the passengers with fear did say –
'I hope God will send us safe across the Bridge of
    Tay.'

But when the train came near to Wormit Bay,
Boreas he did loud and angry bray,
And shook the central girders of the Bridge of Tay
On the last Sabbath day of 1879,
Which will be remember'd for a very long time.

So the train sped on with all its might,
And Bonnie Dundee soon hove in sight,
And the passengers' hearts felt light,
Thinking they would enjoy themselves on the
    New Year,
With their friends at home they lov'd most dear,
And wish them all a happy New Year.

So the train mov'd slowly along the Bridge of Tay,
Until it was about midway,
Then the central girders with a crash gave way,
And down went the train and passengers into the
    Tay!
The Storm Fiend did loudly bray,
Because ninety lives had been taken away,
On the last Sabbath day of 1879,
Which will be remember'd for a very long time.

As soon as the catastrophe came to be known
The alarm from mouth to mouth was blown,
And the cry rang out all o'er the town,
Good Heavens! the Tay Bridge is blown down,
And a passenger train from Edinburgh,
Which fill'd all the people's hearts with sorrow,
And made them for to turn pale,
Because none of the passengers were sav'd to tell
    the tale
How the disaster happen'd on the last Sabbath
    day of 1879,
Which will be remember'd for a very long time.

It must have been an awful sight,
To witness in the dusky moonlight,
While the Storm Fiend did laugh, and angry did
    bray,
Along the Railway Bridge of the Silv'ry Tay.
Oh! ill-fated Bridge of the Silv'ry Tay.
I must now conclude my lay
By telling the world fearlessly without the least
    dismay,
That your central girders would not have given
    way,
At least many sensible men do say,
Had they been supported on each side with
    buttresses,

At least many sensible men confesses,
For the stronger we our houses do build,
The less chance we have of being killed.

ANONYMOUS (WELSH)

[10th century]   ## The Wind

Make out who this is:
Formed before the Flood,
Powerful creature,
Fleshless and boneless,
Nerveless and bloodless,
Headless and footless,
No older, no younger,
Than when he began;
He is not put off
By terror or death;
He's never unneeded
By any creature
(Great God, so holy,
What was his origin?
Great are His wonders,
The Man who made him);
He's in field, he's in wood,
Handless and footless,
Ageless, sorrowless,
Forever hurtless;
And he's the same age
As the five epochs;
And he is older
Than many times fifty;
And he is as broad
As the earth's surface;
And he was not born,
And he is not seen,
On sea and on land

He sees not, unseen;
He's unreliable,
Will not come when wanted;
On land and on sea
He's indispensable;
He is unyielding,
He's beyond compare;
From the four corners
He'll not be fought with;
He springs from a nook
Above the sea-cliff;
He's roaring, he's hushed,
He has no manners,
He's savage, he's bold;
When he goes cross-country
He's hushed, he's roaring,
He is boisterous,
The loudest of shouts
On the face of the earth;
He's good, he's wicked;
He is in hiding,
He is on display,
For no eye sees him;
He is here, he is there;
He hurls things about,
He pays no damages,
He makes no amends,
And he is blameless;
He is wet, he is dry,
He comes quite often.
One Man fashioned them,
All created things,
His the beginning
And His is the end.

translated by Joseph P. Clancy

PATRICIA BEER

[1967]

The Postilion has been Struck by Lightning

He was the best postilion
I ever had. That summer in Europe
Came and went
In striding thunder-rain.
His tasselled shoulders bore up
More bad days than he could count
Till he entered his last storm in the mountains.

You to whom a postilion
Means only a cocked hat in a museum
Or a light
Anecdote, pity this one
Burnt at milord's expense far from home
Having seen every sight
But never anyone struck by lightning.

A. E. HOUSMAN

[pub. 1936]

'Oh who is that young sinner'

Oh who is that young sinner with the handcuffs
      on his wrists?
And what has he been after that they groan and
      shake their fists?
And wherefore is he wearing such a conscience-
      stricken air?
Oh they're taking him to prison for the colour of
      his hair.

'Tis a shame to human nature, such a head of
      hair as his;
In the good old time 'twas hanging for the colour
      that it is;

Though hanging isn't bad enough and flaying
    would be fair
For the nameless and abominable colour of his
    hair.

Oh a deal of pains he's taken and a pretty price
    he's paid

crown of the head   To hide his poll or dye it of a mentionable shade;
But they've pulled the beggar's hat off for the
    world to see and stare,
And they're haling him to justice for the colour of
    his hair.

Now 'tis oakum for his fingers and the treadmill
    for his feet
And the quarry-gang on Portland in the cold and
    in the heat,
And between his spells of labour in the time he
    has to spare
He can curse the God that made him for the
    colour of his hair.

OSCAR WILDE

[1898] *from* The Ballad of Reading Gaol

IN MEMORIAM
C. T. W.
Sometime Trooper of the Royal Horse Guards
obit H. M. Prison, Reading, Berkshire
July 7, 1896

I

He did not wear his scarlet coat,
    For blood and wine are red,
And blood and wine were on his hands
    When they found him with the dead,

The poor dead woman whom he loved,
    And murdered in her bed.

He walked amongst the Trial Men
    In a suit of shabby grey;
A cricket cap was on his head,
    And his step seemed light and gay;
But I never saw a man who looked
    So wistfully at the day.

I never saw a man who looked
    With such a wistful eye
Upon that little tent of blue
    Which prisoners call the sky,
And at every drifting cloud that went
    With sails of silver by.

I walked, with other souls in pain,
    Within another ring,
And was wondering if the man had done
    A great or little thing,
When a voice behind me whispered low,
    That fellow's got to swing.

Dear Christ! the very prison walls
    Suddenly seemed to reel,
And the sky above my head became
    Like a casque of scorching steel;
And, though I was a soul in pain,
    My pain I could not feel.

I only knew what hunted thought
    Quickened his step, and why
He looked upon the garish day
    With such a wistful eye;
The man had killed the thing he loved,
    And so he had to die.

        *

Yet each man kills the thing he loves,
  By each let this be heard,
Some do it with a bitter look,
  Some with a flattering word.
The coward does it with a kiss,
  The brave man with a sword!

Some kill their love when they are young,
  And some when they are old;
Some strangle with the hands of Lust,
  Some with the hands of Gold:
The kindest use a knife, because
  The dead so soon grow cold.

Some love too little, some too long,
  Some sell, and others buy;
Some do the deed with many tears,
  And some without a sigh:
For each man kills the thing he loves,
  Yet each man does not die.

He does not die a death of shame
  On a day of dark disgrace,
Nor have a noose about his neck,
  Nor a cloth upon his face,
Nor drop feet foremost through the floor
  Into an empty space.

He does not sit with silent men
  Who watch him night and day;
Who watch him when he tries to weep,
  And when he tries to pray;
Who watch him lest himself should rob
  The prison of its prey.

He does not wake at dawn to see
  Dread figures throng his room,
The shivering Chaplain robed in white,

The Sheriff stern with gloom,
And the Governor all in shiny black,
    With the yellow face of Doom.

He does not rise in piteous haste
    To put on convict-clothes,
While some coarse-mouthed Doctor gloats, and
        notes
    Each new and nerve-twitched pose,
Fingering a watch whose little ticks
    Are like horrible hammer-blows.

He does not feel that sickening thirst
    That sands one's throat, before
The hangman with his gardener's gloves
    Comes through the padded door,
And binds one with three leathern thongs,
    That the throat may thirst no more.

He does not bend his head to hear
    The Burial Office read,
Nor, while the anguish of his soul
    Tells him he is not dead,
Cross his own coffin, as he moves
    Into the hideous shed.

He does not stare upon the air
    Through a little roof of glass:
He does not pray with lips of clay
    For his agony to pass;
Nor feel upon his shuddering cheek
    The kiss of Caiaphas.

II

Six weeks the guardsman walked the yard,
    In the suit of shabby grey:
His cricket cap was on his head,

And his step seemed light and gay,
But I never saw a man who looked
    So wistfully at the day.

I never saw a man who looked
    With such a wistful eye
Upon that little tent of blue
    Which prisoners call the sky,
And at every wandering cloud that trailed
    Its ravelled fleeces by.

He did not wring his hands, as do
    Those witless men who dare
To try to rear the changeling Hope
    In the cave of black Despair:
He only looked upon the sun,
    And drank the morning air.

[. . .]

So with curious eyes and sick surmise
    We watched him day by day,
And wondered if each one of us
    Would end the self-same way,
For none can tell to what red Hell
    His sightless soul may stray.

At last the dead man walked no more
    Amongst the Trial Men,
And I knew that he was standing up
    In the black dock's dreadful pen,
And that never would I see his face
    For weal or woe again.

Like two doomed ships that pass in storm
    We had crossed each other's way:
But we made no sign, we said no word,
    We had no word to say;

For we did not meet in the holy night,
    But in the shameful day.

A prison wall was round us both,
    Two outcast men we were:
The world had thrust us from its heart
    And God from out His care:
trap And the iron gin that waits for Sin
    Had caught us in its snare.

III

In Debtors' Yard the stones are hard,
    And the dripping wall is high,
So it was there he took the air
    Beneath the leaden sky,
And by each side a Warder walked,
    For fear the man might die.

Or else he sat with those who watched
    His anguish night and day;
Who watched him when he rose to weep,
    And when he crouched to pray;
Who watched him lest himself should rob
    Their scaffold of its prey.

The Governor was strong upon
    The Regulations Act:
The Doctor said that Death was but
    A scientific fact:
And twice a day the Chaplain called,
    And left a little tract.

And twice a day he smoked his pipe,
    And drank his quart of beer:
His soul was resolute, and held
    No hiding-place for fear;

259

He often said that he was glad
    The hangman's day was near.

But why he said so strange a thing
    No warder dared to ask:
For he to whom a watcher's doom
    Is given as his task,
Must set a lock upon his lips
    And make his face a mask.

Or else he might be moved, and try
    To comfort or console:
And what should Human Pity do
    Pent up in Murderer's Hole?
What word of grace in such a place
    Could help a brother's soul?

With slouch and swing around the ring
    We trod the Fool's Parade!
We did not care: we knew we were
    The Devil's Own Brigade:
And shaven head and feet of lead
    Make a merry masquerade.

We tore the tarry rope to shreds
    With blunt and bleeding nails;
We rubbed the doors, and scrubbed the floors,
    And cleaned the shining rails:
And, rank by rank, we soaped the plank,
    And clattered with the pails.

We sewed the sacks, we broke the stones,
    We turned the dusty drill:
We banged the tins, and bawled the hymns,
    And sweated on the mill:
But in the heart of every man
    Terror was lying still.

So still it lay that every day
    Crawled like a weed-clogged wave:
And we forgot the bitter lot
    That waits for fool and knave,
Till once, as we tramped in from work,
    We passed an open grave.

With yawning mouth the yellow hole
    Gaped for a living thing;
The very mud cried out for blood
    To the thirsty asphalte ring;
And we knew that ere one dawn grew fair
    Some prisoner had to swing.

Right in we went, with soul intent
    On Death and Dread and Doom:
The hangman, with his little bag,
    Went shuffling through the gloom:
And I trembled as I groped my way
    Into my numbered tomb.

                *

That night the empty corridors
    Were full of forms of Fear,
And up and down the iron town
    Stole feet we could not hear,
And through the bars that hide the stars
    White faces seemed to peer.

He lay as one who lies and dreams
    In a pleasant meadow-land
The watchers watched him as he slept,
    And could not understand
How one could sleep so sweet a sleep
    With a hangman close at hand.

    [...]

IV

There is no chapel on the day
   On which they hang a man:
The Chaplain's heart is far too sick,
   Or his face is far to wan,
Or there is that written in his eyes
   Which none should look upon.

So they kept us close till nigh on noon,
   And then they rang the bell,
And the warders with their jingling keys
   Opened each listening cell,
And down the iron stair we tramped,
   Each from his separate Hell.

Out into God's sweet air we went,
   But not in wonted way,
For this man's face was white with fear,
   And that man's face was grey,
And I never saw sad men who looked
   So wistfully at the day.

I never saw sad men who looked
   With such a wistful eye
Upon that little tent of blue
   We prisoners called the sky,
And at every happy cloud that passed
   In such strange freedom by.

   […]

The warders strutted up and down,
   And watched their herd of brutes,
Their uniforms were spick and span,
   And they wore their Sunday suits,
But we knew the work they had been at,
   By the quicklime on their boots.

For where a grave had opened wide,
    There was no grave at all:
Only a stretch of mud and sand
    By the hideous prison-wall,
And a little heap of burning lime,
    That the man should have his pall.

For he has a pall, this wretched man,
    Such as few men can claim:
Deep down below a prison-yard,
    Naked for greater shame,
He lies, with fetters on each foot,
    Wrapt in a sheet of flame!

And all the while the burning lime
    Eats flesh and bone away,
It eats the brittle bone by night,
    And the soft flesh by day,
It eats the flesh and bone by turns,
    But it eats the heart alway.

                *

For three long years they will not sow
    Or root or seedling there:
For three long years the unblessed spot
    Will sterile be and bare,
And look upon the wondering sky
    With unreproachful stare.

    [. . .]

                V

I know not whether Laws be right,
    Or whether Laws be wrong;
All that we know who lie in gaol
    Is that the wall is strong;

And that each day is like a year,
    A year whose days are long.

But this I know, that every Law
    That men have made for Man,
Since first Man took his brother's life,
    And the sad world began,
But straws the wheat and saves the chaff
    With a most evil fan.

This too I know – and wise it were
    If each could know the same –
That every prison that men build
    Is built with bricks of shame,
And bound with bars lest Christ should see
    How men their brothers maim.

With bars they blur the gracious moon,
    And blind the goodly sun:
And they do well to hide their Hell,
    For in it things are done
That Son of God nor son of Man
    Ever should look upon!

                *

The vilest deeds like poison weeds,
    Bloom well in prison-air;
It is only what is good in Man
    That wastes and withers there:
Pale Anguish keeps the heavy gate,
    And the Warder is Despair.

For they starve the little frightened child
    Till it weeps both night and day:
And they scourge the weak, and flog the fool,
    And gibe the old and grey,
And some grow mad, and all grow bad,
    And none a word may say.

Each narrow cell in which we dwell
    Is a foul and dark latrine,
And the fetid breath of living Death
    Chokes up each grated screen,
And all, but Lust, is turned to dust
    In Humanity's machine.

The brackish water that we drink
    Creeps with a loathsome slime,
And the bitter bread they weigh in scales
    Is full of chalk and lime,
And Sleep will not lie down, but walks
    Wild-eyed, and cries to Time.

    [. . .]

VI

In Reading gaol by Reading town
    There is a pit of shame,
And in it lies a wretched man
    Eaten by teeth of flame,
In a burning winding-sheet he lies,
    And his grave has got no name.

And there, till Christ call forth the dead,
    In silence let him lie:
No need to waste the foolish tear,
    Or heave the windy sigh:
The man had killed the thing he loved,
    And so he had to die.

And all men kill the thing they love,
    By all let this be heard,
Some do it with a bitter look,
    Some with a flattering word,
The coward does it with a kiss,
    The brave man with a sword!

CHIDIOCK TICHBORNE

[1586] ## Elegy for Himself

Written in the Tower before his execution

My prime of youth is but a frost of cares;
   My feast of joy is but a dish of pain;
My crop of corn is but a field of tares;
   And all my good is but vain hope of gain:
The day is past, and yet I saw no sun;
And now I live, and now my life is done.

My tale was heard, and yet it was not told;
   My fruit is fall'n, and yet my leaves are green;
My youth is spent, and yet I am not old;
   I saw the world, and yet I was not seen:
My thread is cut, and yet it is not spun;
And now I live, and now my life is done.

I sought my death, and found it in my womb;
   I looked for life, and saw it was a shade;
I trod the earth, and knew it was my tomb;
   And now I die, and now I was but made;
My glass is full, and now my glass is run;
And now I live, and now my life is done.

DAVID O'BRUADAIR (IRISH)

[17th century] ## A Glass of Beer

The lanky hank of a she in the inn over there
Nearly killed me for asking the loan of a glass of
   beer;
May the devil grip the whey-faced slut by the
   hair,
And beat bad manners out of her skin for a year.

That parboiled ape, with the toughest jaw you
    will see
On virtue's path, and a voice that would rasp the
    dead,
Came roaring and raging the minute she looked
    at me,
And threw me out of the house on the back of my
    head!

If I asked her master he'd give me a cask a day;
But she, with the beer at hand, not a gill would
    arrange!
May she marry a ghost and bear him a kitten, and
    may
The High King of Glory permit her to get the
    mange.

translated by James Stephens

JOHN DAVIDSON

[1894]   ## Thirty Bob a Week

I couldn't touch a stop and turn a screw,
    And set the blooming world a-work for me,
Like such as cut their teeth – I hope, like you –
    On the handle of a skeleton gold key;
I cut mine on a leek, which I eat it every week:
    I'm a clerk at thirty bob as you can see.

But I don't allow it's luck and all a toss;
    There's no such thing as being starred and
        crossed;
It's just the power of some to be a boss,
    And the bally power of others to be bossed:
I face the music, sir; you bet I ain't a cur;
    Strike me lucky if I don't believe I'm lost!

For like a mole I journey in the dark,
    A-travelling along the underground
From my Pillar'd Halls and broad Suburbean
        Park,
    To come the daily dull official round;
And home again at night with my pipe all alight,
    A-scheming how to count ten bob a pound.

And it's often very cold and very wet,
    And my missis stitches towels for a hunks;
And the Pillar'd Halls is half of it to let –
    Three rooms about the size of travelling trunks.
And we cough, my wife and I, to dislocate a sigh,
    When the noisy little kids are in their bunks.

But you never hear her do a growl or whine,
    For she's made of flint and roses, very odd;
And I've got to cut my meaning rather fine,
    Or I'd blubber, for I'm made of greens and sod:
So p'r'aps we are in Hell for all that I can tell,
    And lost and damn'd and served up hot to God.

I ain't blaspheming, Mr Silver-tongue;
    I'm saying things a bit beyond your art:
Of all the rummy starts you ever sprung,
    Thirty bob a week's the rummiest start!
With your science and your books and your
        the'ries about spooks,
    Did you ever hear of looking in your heart?

I didn't mean your pocket, Mr, no:
    I mean that having children and a wife,
With thirty bob on which to come and go,
    Isn't dancing to the tabor and the fife:
When it doesn't make you drink, by Heaven! it
        makes you think,
    And notice curious items about life.

I step into my heart and there I meet
    A god-almighty devil singing small,
Who would like to shout and whistle in the street,
    And squelch the passers flat against the wall;
If the whole world was a cake he had the power to
        take,
    He would take it, ask for more, and eat them all.

And I meet a sort of simpleton beside,
    The kind that life is always giving beans;
With thirty bob a week to keep a bride
    He fell in love and married in his teens:
At thirty bob he stuck; but he knows it isn't luck:
    He knows the seas are deeper than tureens.

And the god-almighty devil and the fool
    That meet me in the High Street on the strike,
When I walk about my heart a-gathering wool,
    Are my good and evil angels if you like.
And both of them together in every kind of
        weather
    Ride me like a double-seated bike.

That's rough a bit and needs its meaning curled.
    But I have a high old hot un in my mind –
A most engrugious notion of the world,
    That leaves your lightning 'rithmetic behind:
I give it at a glance when I say 'There ain't no
        chance,
    Nor nothing of the lucky-lottery kind.'

And it's this way that I make it out to be:
    No fathers, mothers, countries, climates –
        none;
No Adam was responsible for me,
    Nor society, nor systems, nary one:
A little sleeping seed, I woke – I did, indeed –
    A million years before the blooming sun.

I woke because I thought the time had come;
    Beyond my will there was no other cause;
And everywhere I found myself at home,
    Because I chose to be the thing I was;
And in whatever shape of mollusc or of ape
    I always went according to the laws.

I was the love that chose my mother out;
    I joined two lives and from the union burst;
My weakness and my strength without a doubt
    Are mine alone for ever from the first:
It's just the very same with a difference in the
        name
        As 'Thy will be done.' You say it if you durst!

They say it daily up and down the land
    As easy as you take a d rink, it's true;
But the difficultest go to understand,
    And the difficultest job a man can do,
Is to come it brave and meek with thirty bob a
        week,
        And feel that that's the proper thing for you.

It's a naked child against a hungry wolf;
    It's playing bowls upon a splitting wreck;
It's walking on a string across a gulf
    With millstones fore-and-aft about your neck;
But the thing is daily done by many and many a
        one;
        And we fall, face forward, fighting, on the deck.

RUDYARD KIPLING

[1892]   Tommy

I went into a public-'ouse to get a pint o' beer,
The publican 'e up an' sez, 'We serve no red-coats
        here.'

The girls be'ind the bar they laughed an' giggled
    fit to die,
I outs into the street again an' to myself sez I:
    O it's Tommy this, an' Tommy that, an'
        'Tommy, go away';
    But it's 'Thank you, Mister Atkins,' when the
        band begins to play –
    The band begins to play, my boys, the band
        begins to play,
    O it's 'Thank you, Mister Atkins,' when the
        band begins to play.

I went into a theatre as sober as could be,
They gave a drunk civilian room, but 'adn't none
    for me;
They sent me to the gallery or round the music-
    'alls,
But when it comes to fightin', Lord! they'll shove
    me in the stalls!
    For it's Tommy this, an' Tommy that, an'
        'Tommy, wait outside';
    But it's 'Special train for Atkins' when the
        trooper's on the tide –
    The troopship's on the tide, my boys, the
        troopship's on the tide,
    O it's 'Special train for Atkins' when the
        trooper's on the tide.

Yes, makin' mock o' uniforms that guard you
    while you sleep
Is cheaper than them uniforms, an' they're
    starvation cheap;
An' hustlin' drunken soldiers when they're goin'
    large a bit
Is five times better business than paradin' in full
    kit.

Then it's Tommy this, an' Tommy that, an'
'Tommy, 'ow's yer soul?'
But it's 'Thin red line of 'eroes' when the drums
begin to roll –
The drums begin to roll, my boys, the drums
begin to roll.
O it's 'Thin red line of 'eroes' when the drums
begin to roll.

We aren't no thin red 'eroes, nor we aren't no
blackguards too,
But single men in barricks, most remarkable like
you;
An' if sometimes our conduck isn't all your fancy
paints,
Why, single men in barricks don't grow into
plaster saints;
While it's Tommy this, an' Tommy that, an'
'Tommy, fall be'ind,'
But it's 'Please to walk in front, sir,' when
there's trouble in the wind –
There's trouble in the wind, my boys, there's
trouble in the wind,
O it's 'Please to walk in front, sir,' when there's
trouble in the wind.

You talk o' better food for us, an' schools, an'
fires, an' all:
We'll wait for extry rations if you treat us
rational.
Don't mess about the cook-room slops, but prove
it to our face
The Widow's Uniform is not the soldier-man's
disgrace.
For it's Tommy this, an' Tommy that, an'
'Chuck him out, the brute!'

But it's 'Saviour of 'is country' when the guns
  begin to shoot;
An' it's Tommy this, an' Tommy that, an'
  anything you please;
An' Tommy ain't a bloomin' fool – you bet that
  Tommy sees!

ARTHUR HUGH CLOUGH

[1858]   *from* Amours de Voyage

Dulce it is, and *decorum*, no doubt, for the country
  to fall, – to
Offer one's blood an oblation to Freedom, and die
  for the Cause; yet
Still, individual culture is also something, and no
  man
Finds quite distinct the assurance that he of all
  others is called on,
Or would be justified even, in taking away from
  the world that
Precious creature, himself. Nature sent him here
  to abide here;
Else why send him at all? Nature wants him still,
  it is likely;
On the whole, we are meant to look after
  ourselves; it is certain
Each has to eat for himself, digest for himself, and
  in general
Care for his own dear life, and see to his own
  preservation;
Nature's intentions, in most things uncertain, in
  this are decisive;
Which, on the whole, I conjecture the Romans
  will follow, and I shall.
  So we cling to our rocks like limpets; Ocean
  may bluster,

Over and under and round us; we open our shells
    to imbibe our
Nourishment, close them again, and are safe,
    fulfilling the purpose
Nature intended, – a wise one, of course, and a
    noble, we doubt not.
Sweet it may be and decorous, perhaps, for the
    country to die; but,
On the whole, we conclude the Romans won't do
    it, and I sha'n't.

EDWIN MUIR

[1946]   The Castle

All through that summer at ease we lay,
And daily from the turret wall
We watched the mowers in the hay
And the enemy half a mile away.
They seemed no threat to us at all.

For what, we thought, had we to fear
With our arms and provender, load on load,
Our towering battlements, tier on tier,
And friendly allies drawing near
On every leafy summer road.

Our gates were strong, our walls were thick,
So smooth and high, no man could win
A foothold there, no clever trick
Could take us, have us dead or quick.
Only a bird could have got in.

What could they offer us for bait?
Our captain was brave and we were true . . .
There was a little private gate,
A little wicked wicket gate.
The wizened warder let them through.

Oh then our maze of tunnelled stone
Grew thin and treacherous as air.
The cause was lost without a groan,
The famous citadel overthrown,
And all its secret galleries bare.

How can this shameful tale be told?
I will maintain until my death
We could do nothing, being sold;
Our only enemy was gold,
And we had no arms to fight it with.

OLIVER GOLDSMITH

[1770] *from* The Deserted Village

Sweet was the sound, when oft at evening's close
Up yonder hill the village murmur rose;
There, as I passed with careless steps and slow,
The mingling notes came softened from below;
The swain responsive as the milkmaid sung,
The sober herd that lowed to meet their young;
The noisy geese that gabbled o'er the pool,
The playful children just let loose from school;
The watchdog's voice that bayed the whispering
        wind,
And the loud laugh that spoke the vacant mind;
These all in sweet confusion sought the shade,
And filled each pause the nightingale had made.
But now the sounds of population fail,
No cheerful murmurs fluctuate in the gale,
No busy steps the grassgrown foot-way tread,
For all the bloomy flush of life is fled.
All but yon widowed, solitary thing
That feebly bends beside the plashy spring;
She, wretched matron, forced, in age, for bread,
To strip the brook with mantling cresses spread,

To pick her wintry faggot from the thorn,
To seek her nightly shed and weep till morn;
She only left of all the harmless train,
The sad historian of the pensive plain.

   Near yonder copse, where once the garden
      smiled,
And still where many a garden flower grows wild;
There, where a few torn shrubs the place disclose,
The village preacher's modest mansion rose.
A man he was to all the country dear,
And passing rich with forty pounds a year;
Remote from towns he ran his godly race,
Nor e'er had changed, nor wished to change, his
      place;
Unpractised he to fawn, or seek for power,
By doctrines fashioned to the varying hour;
Far other aims his heart had learned to prize,
More skilled to raise the wretched than to rise.
His house was known to all the vagrant train,
He chid their wanderings, but relieved their pain;
The long-remembered beggar was his guest,
Whose beard descending swept his aged breast;
The ruined spendthrift, now no longer proud,
Claimed kindred there and had his claims
      allowed;
The broken soldier, kindly bade to stay,
Sat by his fire and talked the night away;
Wept o'er his wounds or tales of sorrow done,
Shouldered his crutch and showed how fields
      were won.
Pleased with his guests, the good man learned to
      glow,
And quite forgot their vices in their woe;
Careless their merits or their faults to scan,
His pity gave ere charity began.

   Thus to relieve the wretched was his pride,

And even his failings leaned to virtue's side;
But in his duty prompt at every call,
He watched and wept, he prayed and felt, for all.
And, as a bird each fond endearment tries
To tempt its new-fledged offspring to the skies,
He tried each art, reproved each dull delay,
Allured to brighter worlds, and led the way.

Beside the bed where parting life was laid,
And sorrow, guilt, and pain by turns dismayed,
The reverend champion stood. At his control,
Despair and anguish fled the struggling soul;
Comfort came down the trembling wretch to
    raise,
And his last faltering accents whispered praise.

At church, with meek and unaffected grace,
His looks adorned the venerable place;
Truth from his lips prevailed with double sway,
And fools, who came to scoff, remained to pray.
The service past, around the pious man,
With steady zeal each honest rustic ran;
Even children followed with endearing wile,
And plucked his gown, to share the good man's
    smile.
His ready smile a parent's warmth expressed,
Their welfare pleased him and their cares
    distressed;
To them his heart, his love, his griefs were given,
But all his serious thoughts had rest in heaven.
As some tall cliff, that lifts its awful form,
Swells from the vale and midway leaves the
    storm,
Though round its breast the rolling clouds are
    spread,
Eternal sunshine settles on its head.

Beside yon straggling fence that skirts the way,
With blossomed furze unprofitably gay,

There, in his noisy mansion, skilled to rule,
The village master taught his little school;
A man severe he was and stern to view;
I knew him well, and every truant knew;
Well had the boding tremblers learned to trace
The day's disasters in his morning face;
Full well they laughed, with counterfeited glee,
At all his jokes, for many a joke had he;
Full well the busy whisper, circling round,
Conveyed the dismal tidings when he frowned;
Yet he was kind, or, if severe in aught,
The love he bore to learning was in fault;
The village all declared how much he knew;

practise arithmetic   'Twas certain he could write and cipher too;
Lands he could measure, terms and tides presage,

calculate capacity of   And even the story ran that he could gauge.
vessels
In arguing too, the parson owned his skill,
For even though vanquished, he could argue
       still;
While words of learned length and thundering
       sound
Amazed the gazing rustics ranged around,
And still they gazed, and still the wonder grew,
That one small head could carry all he knew.
   But past is all his fame. The very spot,
Where many a time he triumphed, is forgot.
Near yonder thorn, that lifts its head on high,
Where once the signpost caught the passing eye,
Low lies that house where nutbrown draughts
       inspired,
Where greybeard mirth and smiling toil retired,
Where village statesmen talked with looks
       profound,
And news much older than their ale went round.
Imagination fondly stoops to trace
The parlour splendours of that festive place;

The white-washed wall, the nicely sanded floor,
The varnished clock that clicked behind the door;
The chest contrived a double debt to pay,
A bed by night, a chest of drawers by day;
The pictures placed for ornament and use,
The twelve good rules, the royal game of goose;
The hearth, except when winter chilled the day,
With aspen boughs and flowers and fennel gay;
While broken teacups, wisely kept for show,
Ranged o'er the chimney, glistened in a row.

    Vain, transitory splendours! Could not all
Reprieve the tottering mansion from its fall!
Obscure it sinks, nor shall it more impart
An hour's importance to the poor man's heart;
Thither no more the peasant shall repair
To sweet oblivion of his daily care;
No more the farmer's news, the barber's tale,
No more the woodman's ballad shall prevail;
No more the smith his dusky brow shall clear,
Relax his ponderous strength and lean to hear;
The host himself no longer shall be found
Careful to see the mantling bliss go round;
Nor the coy maid, half willing to be pressed,
Shall kiss the cup to pass it to the rest.

    Yes! let the rich deride, the proud disdain,
These simple blessings of the lowly train;
To me more dear, congenial to my heart,
One native charm than all the gloss of art.

GEORGE CHAPMAN

[1614–15]   *from* The Odyssey of Homer (Book XVII)

Such speech they changed; when in the yard
   there lay
A dog, call'd Argus, which, before his way
Assumed for Ilion, Ulysses bred,

Yet stood his pleasure then in little stead,
As being too young, but, growing to his grace,
Young men made choice of him for every chace,
Or of their wild goats, of their hares, or harts.
But, his king gone, and he, now past his parts,
Lay all abjectly on the stable's store,
Before the ox-stall, and mules' stable door,
To keep the clothes cast from the peasants'
    hands,
While they laid compass on Ulysses' lands,
The dog, with ticks (unlook'd to) overgrown.
But by this dog no sooner seen but known
Was wise Ulysses, who new enter'd there,
Up went his dog's laid ears, and, coming near,
Up he himself rose, fawn'd, and wagg'd his stern,
Couch'd close his ears, and lay so; nor discern
Could evermore his dear-loved lord again.
Ulysses saw it, nor had power t' abstain
From shedding tears; which (far-off seeing his
    swain)
He dried from his sight clean; to whom he thus
His grief dissembled: ''Tis miraculous,
That such a dog as this should have his lair
On such a dunghill, for his form is fair.
And yet, I know not, if there were in him
Good pace, or parts, for all his goodly limb;
Or he lived empty of those inward things,
As are those trencher-beagles tending kings,
Whom for their pleasure's, or their glory's, sake,
Or fashion, they into their favours take.'
    'This dog,' said he, 'was servant to one dead
A huge time since. But if he bore his head,
For form and quality, of such a height,
As when Ulysses, bound for th'Ilion fight,
Or quickly after, left him, your rapt eyes
Would then admire to see him use his thighs

In strength and swiftness. He would nothing fly,
Nor anything let 'scape. If once his eye
Seized any wild beast, he knew straight his scent;
Go where he would, away with him he went.
Nor was there ever any savage stood
Amongst the thickets of the deepest wood
Long time before him, but he pull'd him down;
As well by that true hunting to be shown
In such vast coverts, as for speed of pace
In any open lawn. For in deep chace
He was a passing wise and well-nosed hound.
And yet is all this good in him uncrown'd
With any grace here now, nor he more fed
Than any errant cur. His king is dead,
Far from his country; and his servants are
So negligent they lend his hound no care.
Where masters rule not, but let men alone,
You never there see honest service done.
That man's half virtue Jove takes quite away,
That once is sun-burnt with the servile day.'

DUNCAN BAN MACINTYRE (SCOTS GAELIC)

[18th century]   ## Song to the Foxes

> *Ho hù o hó the cunning dogs,*
> > *Not often that we find them!*
> *Ho hù o hó the cunning dogs.*

My blessing on the foxes,
    for their hunting of the sheep.
        Ho hù o hó the cunning dogs, etc.

How could these sheep of brindled head
    set on the world's contention;

to make our land a wilderness
    and yet its rent increasing?

No farmer has a place here,
    the profit's ever shrinking;

No other course but exile
    from the homeland of his people.

settlements   The townships and the shielings
    where once dwelt warmth and kindness –

no houses but the tumbled stones,
    no ploughing of the meadows.

The customs that were followed,
    they have perished now in Gaeldom,

have come to be unnatural
    in hospitable places.

No filly's found or brood mare
    with foal at heel beside her.

There are no two-year heifers
    who will suckle their own calves now.

There is no need for milkmaids,
    when all milking-folds are scattered.

No lad can earn his keep there
    but the minder of the sheep-flocks.

The treasured goats are gone now;
    though a king gave them their freedom.

The small doe of the greenwood
    will not be waked with calling.

No deer comes to the spring there
    now the gentry have lost liking.

They have turned off every stalker,
    without reward of labour.

I'm angered by the fellow
    who speaks ill of the foxes.

Who sets a hound to hunt them
    or scatters them with lead-shot.

May all the foxcubs prosper
    that live within an earth there.

Could they get my earnest wishes,
    they'd thrive there never fearing.

Young foxes would breed youngsters,
    and they'd live till old age killed them.

translated by William Neil

DYLAN THOMAS

[1946]   # Fern Hill

Now as I was young and easy under the apple
    boughs
About the lilting house and happy as the grass
    was green,
    The night above the dingle starry,
      Time let me hail and climb
    Golden in the heydays of his eyes,
And honoured among wagons I was prince of the
    apple towns
And once below a time I lordly had the trees and
    leaves
    Trail with daisies and barley
Down the rivers of the windfall light.

And as I was green and carefree, famous among
    the barns
About the happy yard and singing as the farm
    was home,
    In the sun that is young once only,

Time let me play and be
Golden in the mercy of his means,
And green and golden I was huntsman and
herdsman, the calves
Sang to my horn, the foxes on the hills barked
clear and cold,
And the sabbath rang slowly
In the pebbles of the holy streams.

All the sun long it was running, it was lovely, the
hay
Fields high as the house, the tunes from the
chimneys, it was air
And playing, lovely and watery
And fire green as grass.
And nightly under the simple stars
As I rode to sleep the owls were bearing the farm
away,
All the moon long I heard, blessed among stables,
the nightjars
Flying with the ricks, and the horses
Flashing into the dark.

And then to awake, and the farm, like a wanderer
white
With the dew, come back, the cock on his
shoulder: it was all
Shining, it was Adam and maiden,
The sky gathered again
And the sun grew round that very day.
So it must have been after the birth of the simple
light
In the first, spinning place, the spellbound horses
walking warm
Out of the whinnying green stable
On to the fields of praise.

And honoured among foxes and pheasants by the
    gay house
Under the new made clouds and happy as the
    heart was long,
  In the sun born over and over,
    I ran my heedless ways,
  My wishes raced through the house high hay
And nothing I cared, at my sky blue trades, that
    time allows
In all his tuneful turning so few and such
    morning songs
  Before the children green and golden
    Follow him out of grace,

Nothing I cared, in the lamb white days, that time
    would take me
Up to the swallow thronged loft by the shadow of
    my hand,
  In the moon that is always rising,
    Nor that riding to sleep
  I should hear him fly with the high fields
And wake to the farm forever fled from the
    childless land.
Oh as I was young and easy in the mercy of his
    means,
    Time held me green and dying
    Though I sang in my chains like the sea.

SORLEY MACLEAN (SCOTS GAELIC)

[1954]   Hallaig
           'Time, the deer, is in the wood of Hallaig'

The window is nailed and boarded
through which I saw the West
and my love is at the Burn of Hallaig,
a birch tree, and she has always been

285

between Inver and Milk Hollow,
here and there about Baile-chuirn:
she is a birch, a hazel,
a straight, slender young rowan.

In Screapadal of my people
where Norman and Big Hector were,
their daughters and their sons are a wood
going up beside the stream.

Proud tonight the pine cocks
crowing on the top of Cnoc an Ra,
straight their backs in the moonlight –
they are not the wood I love.

I will wait for the birch wood
until it comes up by the cairn,
until the whole ridge from Beinn na Lice
will be under its shade.

If it does not, I will go down to Hallaig,
to the Sabbath of the dead,
where the people are frequenting,
every single generation gone.

They are still in Hallaig,
MacLeans and MacLeods,
all who were there in the time of Mac Gille
    Chaluim
the dead have been seen alive.

The men lying on the green
at the end of every house that was,
the girls a wood of birches,
straight their backs, bent their heads.

Between the Leac and Fearns
the road is under mild moss

and the girls in silent bands
go to Clachan as in the beginning,

and return from Clachan
from Suisnish and the land of the living;
each one young and lift-stepping,
without the heartbreak of the tale.

From the Burn of Fearns to the raised beach
that is clear in the mystery of the hills,
there is only the congregation of the girls
keeping up the endless walk,

coming back to Hallaig in the evening,
in the dumb living twilight,
filling the steep slopes,
their laughter a mist in my ears,

channels

and their beauty a film on my heart
before the dimness comes on the kyles,
and when the sun goes down behind Dun Cana
a vehement bullet will come from the gun of Love;

and will strike the deer that goes dizzily,
sniffing at the grass-grown ruined homes;
his eye will freeze in the wood,
his blood will not be traced while I live.

translated by the author

ROBERT PENN WARREN

[1969]   Tell Me a Story

[A]

Long ago, in Kentucky, I, a boy, stood
By a dirt road, in first dark, and heard
The great geese hoot northward.

I could not see them, there being no moon
And the stars sparse. I heard them.

I did not know what was happening in my heart.

It was the season before the elderberry blooms,
Therefore they were going north.

The sound was passing northward.

[B]

Tell me a story.

In this century, and moment, of mania,
Tell me a story.

Make it a story of great distances, and starlight.

The name of the story will be Time,
But you must not pronounce its name.

Tell me a story of deep delight.

THOMAS BASTARD

[1598] ## 'Methinks 'tis pretty sport to hear a child'

Methinks 'tis pretty sport to hear a child
Rocking a word in mouth yet undefiled;
The tender racquet rudely plays the sound
Which, weakly bandied, cannot back rebound;
And the soft air the softer roof doth kiss
With a sweet dying and a pretty miss,
Which hears no answer yet from the white rank
Of teeth not risen from their coral bank.
The alphabet is searched for letters soft
To try a word before it can be wrought;
And when it slideth forth, it goes as nice
As when a man doth walk upon the ice.

ROBERT SOUTHEY

[1798]

After Blenheim

It was a summer evening,
   Old Kaspar's work was done,
And he before his cottage door
   Was sitting in the sun;
And by him sported on the green
His little grandchild Wilhelmine.

She saw her brother Peterkin
   Roll something large and round
Which he beside the rivulet
   In playing there had found;
He came to ask what he had found
That was so large and smooth and round.

Old Kaspar took it from the boy
   Who stood expectant by;
And then the old man shook his head,
   And with a natural sigh
''Tis some poor fellow's skull,' said he,
'Who fell in the great victory.

'I find them in the garden,
   For there's many here about,
And often when I go to plough
   The ploughshare turns them out,
For many thousand men,' said he
'Were slain in that great victory.'

'Now tell us what 'twas all about,'
   Young Peterkin he cries;
And little Wilhelmine looks up
   With wonder-waiting eyes;
'Now tell us all about the war,
And what they fought each other for.'

'It was the English,' Kaspar cried,
    'Who put the French to rout;
But what they fought each other for
    I could not well make out.
But everybody said,' quoth he,
'That 'twas a famous victory.

'My father lived at Blenheim then,
    Yon little stream hard by;
They burnt his dwelling to the ground,
    And he was forced to fly:
So with his wife and child he fled,
Nor had he where to rest his head.

'With fire and sword the country round
    Was wasted far and wide,
And many a childing mother then
    And newborn baby died:
But things like that, you know, must be
At every famous victory.

'They say it was a shocking sight
    After the field was won;
For many thousand bodies here
    Lay rotting in the sun:
But things like that, you know, must be
After a famous victory.

'Great praise the Duke of Marlbro' won,
    And our good Prince Eugene.'
'Why 'twas a very wicked thing!'
    Said little Wilhelmine.
'Nay . . . nay . . . my little girl,' quoth he,
'It was a famous victory.

'And everybody praised the Duke
    Who this great fight did win.'
'But what good came of it at last?'

Quoth little Peterkin.
'Why that I cannot tell,' said he
'But 'twas a famous victory.'

WILLIAM CARLOS WILLIAMS

[1963] *from* Pictures from Breughel

I

This is a schoolyard
crowded
with children

of all ages near a village
on a small stream
meandering by

where some boys
are swimming
bare-ass

or climbing a tree in leaf
everything
is motion

elder women are looking
after the small
fry

a play wedding a
christening
nearby one leans

hollering
into
an empty hogshead

II

Little girls
whirling their skirts about
until they stand out flat

tops pinwheels
to run in the wind with
or a toy in 3 tiers to spin

with a piece
of twine to make it go
blindman's-buff follow the

leader stilts
high and low tipcat jacks
bowls hanging by the knees

standing on your head
run the gauntlet
a dozen on their backs

feet together kicking
through which a boy must pass
roll the hoop or a

construction
made of bricks
some mason has abandoned

III

The desperate toys
of children
their

imagination equilibrium
and rocks
which are to be

found
everywhere
and games to drag

the other down
blindfold
to make use of

a swinging
weight
with which

at random
to bash in the
heads about

them
Brueghel saw it all
and with his grim

humor faithfully
recorded
it

ALLEN TATE

[1953] ## The Swimmers
SCENE: *Montgomery County, Kentucky, July 1911*

Kentucky water, clear springs: a boy fleeing
    To water under the dry Kentucky sun,
    His four little friends in tandem with him,
        seeing

Long shadows of grapevine wriggle and run
    Over the green swirl; mullein under the ear
    Soft as Nausicaä's palm; sullen fun

Savage as childhood's thin harmonious tear:
  O fountain, bosom source undying-dead
  Replenish me the spring of love and fear

And give me back the eye that looked and fled
  When a thrush idling in the tulip tree
  Unwound the cold dream of the copperhead.

poisonous snake

– Along the creek the road was winding; we
  Felt the quicksilver sky. I see again
  The shrill companions of that odyssey:

Bill Eaton, Charlie Watson, 'Nigger' Layne
  The doctor's son, Harry Duèsler who played
  The flute, and Tate, with water on the brain.

Dog-days: the dusty leaves where rain delayed
  Hung low on poison-oak and scuppernong
  And we were following the active shade

type of grape

Of water, that bells and bickers all night long.
  'No more'n a mile,' Layne said. All five
    stood still.
  Listening, I heard what seemed at first a
    song;

Peering, I heard the hooves come down the hill.
  The posse passed, twelve horse; the leader's
    face
  Was worn as limestone on an ancient sill.

Then, as sleepwalkers shift from a hard place
  In bed, and rising to keep a formal pledge
  Descend a ladder into empty space,

We scuttled down the bank below a ledge
  And marched stiff-legged in our common
    fright
  Along a hog-track by the riffle's edge:

Into a world where sound shaded the sight
    Dropped the dull hooves again; the
        horsemen came
    Again, all but the leader: it was night

Momently and I feared: eleven same
    Jesus-Christers unmembered and unmade,
    Whose Corpse had died again in dirty
        shame.

The bank then levelling in a speckled glade,
    We stopped to breathe above the
        swimming-hole;
    I gazed at its reticulated shade

Recoiling in blue fear, and felt it roll
    Over my ears and eyes and lift my hair
    Like seaweed tossing on a sunk atoll.

I rose again. Borne on the copper air
    A distant voice green as a funeral wreath
    Against a grave: 'That dead nigger there.'

The melancholy sheriff slouched beneath
    A giant sycamore; shaking his head
    He plucked a sassafras twig and picked his
        teeth:

'We come to late.' He spoke to the tired dead
    Whose ragged shirt soaked up the viscous
        flow
    Of blood in which It lay discomfited.

A butting horse-fly gave one ear a blow
    And glanced off, as the sheriff kicked the
        rope
    Loose from the neck and hooked it with his
        toe

Away from the blood. – I looked back down the
    slope:
    The friends were gone that I had hoped to
      greet. –
    A single horseman came at a slow lope

And pulled up at the hanged man's horny feet;
    The sheriff noosed the feet, the other end
    The stranger tied to his pommel in a neat

Slip-knot. I saw the Negro's body bend
    And straighten, as a fish-line cast transverse
    Yields to the current that it must subtend.

The sheriff's Goddamn was a murmured curse
    Not for the dead but for the blinding dust
    That boxed the cortège in a cloudy hearse

And dragged it towards our town. I knew I must
    Not stay till twilight in that silent road;
    Sliding my bare feet into the warm crust,

I hopped the stonecrop like a panting toad
    Mouth open, following the heaving cloud
    That floated to the court-house square its
      load

Of limber corpse that took the sun for shroud.
    There were three figures in the dying sun
    Whose light were company where three
      was crowd.

My breath crackled the dead air like a shotgun
    As, sheriff and the stranger disappearing,
    The faceless head lay still. I could not run

Or walk, but stood. Alone in the public clearing
    This private thing was owned by all the
      town,

Though never claimed by us within my
hearing.

PADRAIC FALLON

[pub. 1974]   ## A Flask of Brandy

You, said the Lionwoman,
Pliz, this errand, a snipe of brandy
From the first shop. Here's money;
And for you this penny.

And on my way I saw:
Item, a clown who waltzed on stilts;
A bear saluting with a paw;
Two pairs of dancing dogs in kilts;
Eight midget ponies in a single file,
A very piccolo of ponies;
Then the princess far off in her smile;
And the seven beautiful distant ladies:
And then –

Facing after the big bandwagon, he
The boy in spangles, lonely and profound:
Behind him the Ringmaster, a redfaced man,
Followed by silence heavy as a wound,
And empty.

Quickly as two feet can did I come back
To the Lionwoman with her cognac.

You, said the Lionwoman;
Pliz to the window, said foreign gutterals in
The cave of the caravan.
I waited, errand done.

And waiting on one foot saw:
Item: a twitching coloured chintz
Moved by a lemontaloned claw:

And after a woman with her face in paints,
A throat thickened in its round of tan
On shoulders sick and white with nature;
Behind was a pair of bloomers on a line,
Blue; a table with a tin platter:
More else:

A black electric cat, a stove, a pot
Purring, and a wild Red Indian blanket
Crouching sidewise on a bunk;
And some exciting smell that stunk
Till the Lionwoman rising blotted out
All but a breast as heavy as a sigh
That stared at me from one bruised eye.

CHARLES CAUSLEY

[1988] ## Eden Rock

They are waiting for me somewhere beyond Eden
    Rock:
My father, twenty-five, in the same suit
Of Genuine Irish Tweed, his terrier Jack
Still two years old and trembling at his feet.

My mother, twenty-three, in a sprigged dress
Drawn at the waist, ribbon in her straw hat,
Has spread the stiff white cloth over the grass.
Her hair, the colour of wheat, takes on the light.

She pours tea from a Thermos, the milk straight
From an old H.P. sauce-bottle, a screw
Of paper for a cork; slowly sets out
The same three plates, the tin cups painted blue.

The sky whitens as if lit by three suns.
My mother shades her eyes and looks my way
Over the drifted stream. My father spins
A stone along the water. Leisurely,

They beckon to me from the other bank.
I hear them call, 'See where the stream-path is!
Crossing is not as hard as you might think.'

I had not thought that it would be like this.

ANNE BRADSTREET

[1656]

In Reference to Her Children,
23 June, 1656

I had eight birds hatcht in one nest,
Four Cocks there were, and Hens the rest,
I nurst them up with pain and care,
Nor cost, nor labour did I spare,
Till at the last they felt their wing,
Mounted the Trees, and learn'd to sing;
Chief of the Brood then took his flight,
To Regions far, and left me quite:
My mournful chirps I after send,
Till he return, or I do end,
Leave not thy nest, thy Dam and Sire,
Fly back and sing amidst this Quire.
My second bird did take her flight,
And with her mate flew out of sight:
Southward they both their course did bend,
And Seasons twain they there did spend:
Till after blown by *Southern* gales,
They *Norward* steer'd with filled sayles.
A prettier bird was no where seen,
trees   Along the Beach among the treen.
I have a third of colour white,
On whom I plac'd no small delight;
Coupled with mate loving and true,
Hath also bid her Dam adieu:
Dawn   And where *Aurora* first appears,
She now hath percht, to spend her years;

One to the Academy flew
To chat among that learned crew:
Ambition moves still in his breast
That he might chant above the rest,
Striving for more than to do well,
That nightingales he might excell.
My fifth, whose down is yet scarce gone
Is 'mongst the shrubs and bushes flown,
And as his wings increase in strength,
On higher boughs he'l perch at length.
My other three, still with me nest,
Untill they're grown, then as the rest,
Or here or there, they'l take their flight,
As is ordain'd, so shall they light.
If birds could weep, then would my tears
Let others know what are my fears
Lest this my brood some harm should catch,
And be surpriz'd for want of watch,
Whilst pecking corn, and void of care
They fall un'wares in Fowlers snare:
Or whilst on trees they sit and sing,
Some untoward boy at them do fling:
Or whilst allur'd with bell and glass,
The net be spread, and caught, alas.
Or least by Lime-twigs they be foyl'd,
Or by some greedy hawks be spoyl'd.
O would my young, ye saw my breast,
And knew what thoughts there sadly rest,
Great was my pain when I you bred,
Great was my care, when I you fed,
Long did I keep you soft and warm,
And with my wings kept off all harm,
My cares are more, and fears than ever,
My throbs such now, as 'fore were never:
Alas my birds, you wisdome want,
Of perils you are ignorant,

Oft times in grass, on trees, in flight,
Sore accidents on you may light.
O to your safety have an eye,
So happy may you live and die:
Mean while my dayes in tunes I'le spend,
Till my weak layes with me shall end.
In shady woods I'le sit and sing,
And things that past, to mind I'le bring.
Once young and pleasant, as are you,
But former toyes (no joyes) adieu.
My age I will not once lament,
But sing, my time so near is spent.
And from the top bough take my flight,
Into a country beyond sight,
Where old ones instantly grow young,
And there with Seraphims set song:
No seasons cold, nor storms they see;
But spring lasts to eternity,
When each of you shall in your nest
Among your young ones take your rest,
In chirping language, oft them tell,
You had a Dam that lov'd you well,
That did what could be done for young,
And nurst you up till you were strong,
And 'fore she once would let you fly,
She shew'd you joy and misery;
Taught what was good, and what was ill,
What would save life, and what would kill.
Thus gone, amongst you I may live,
And dead, yet speak, and counsel give:
Farwel my birds, farewel adieu,
I happy am, if well with you.

BEN JONSON

[1616] ## On My First Son

Farewell, thou child of my right hand, and joy!
My sin was too much hope of thee, loved boy;
Seven years thou wert lent to me, and I thee pay,
Exacted by thy fate, on the just day.
Oh, could I lose all father now! For why
Will man lament the state he should envy –
To have so soon 'scaped world's and flesh's rage,
And, if no other misery, yet age?
Rest in soft peace, and, asked, say here doth lie
Ben Jonson his best piece of poetry:
For whose sake, henceforth, all his vows be such
As what he loves may never like too much.

ROBERT HAYDEN

[1962] ## Those Winter Sundays

Sundays too my father got up early
and put his clothes on in the blueblack cold,
then with cracked hands that ached
from labor in the weekday weather made
banked fires blaze. No one ever thanked him.

I'd wake and hear the cold splintering, breaking.
When the rooms were warm, he'd call,
and slowly I would rise and dress,
fearing the chronic angers of that house,

Speaking indifferently to him,
who had driven out the cold
and polished my good shoes as well.
What did I know, what did I know
of love's austere and lonely offices?

ANONYMOUS (OLD ENGLISH)

[10th century] ## 'O wen, wen, O little wennikins'

O wen, wen, O little wennikins,
Here shall you build not, here have no abode,
But you must northwards to the nearby hill,
For there, O wretched one, you have a brother,
And he shall lay a leaf upon your head.
Under wolf's foot and under eagle's wing,
'Neath claw of eagle ever may you fade.
May you decrease like coal upon the hearth,
Shrivel away like dirt upon the wall,
Evaporate like water in a pail,
Become as little as a linseed-grain,
Much smaller than a hand-worm's hip-bone is,
And so diminish that you come to nothing.

translated by Richard Hamer

THOMAS CAMPION

[c. 1617] ## 'Thrice toss these oaken ashes in the air'

Thrice toss these oaken ashes in the air,
Thrice sit thou mute in this enchanted chair;
Then thrice-three times tie up this true love's
    knot.
And murmur soft 'She will or she will not.'

Go burn these poisonous weeds in yon blue fire,
These screech-owl's feathers and this prickling
    brier,
This cypress gathered at a dead man's grave,
That all thy fears and cares an end may have.

Then come, you Fairies! dance with me a round!
Melt her hard heart with your melodious
    sound! –

In vain are all the charms I can devise:
She hath an art to break them with her eyes.

ANONYMOUS

[traditional] ## Song of the Cauld Lad of Hylton

Wae's me, wae's me,
The acorn is not yet
Fallen from the tree
That's to grow the wood
That's to make the cradle
That's to rock the bairn
That's to grow to a man
That's to lay me.

ANONYMOUS

[traditional] ## 'There was a man of double deed'

There was a man of double deed
Who sowed his garden full of seed.
When the seed began to grow,
'Twas like a garden full of snow.
When the snow began to melt,
'Twas like a ship without a bell.
When the ship began to sail,
'Twas like a bird without a tail.
When the bird began to fly,
'Twas like an eagle in the sky.
When the sky began to roar,
'Twas like a lion at the door.
When the door began to crack,
'Twas like a stick across my back.
When my back began to smart,
'Twas like a penknife in my heart.
When my heart began to bleed,
'Twas death, and death, and death indeed.

WILLIAM BLAKE

[c. 1803] ## Auguries of Innocence

To see a World in a Grain of Sand
And a Heaven in a Wild Flower,
Hold Infinity in the palm of your hand
And Eternity in an hour.
A Robin Red breast in a Cage
Puts all Heaven in a Rage.
A dove house fill'd with doves & Pigeons
Shudders Hell thro' all its regions.
A dog starv'd at his Master's Gate
Predicts the ruin of the State.
A Horse misus'd upon the Road
Calls to Heaven for Human blood.
Each outcry of the hunted Hare
A fibre from the Brain does tear.
A Skylark wounded in the wing,
A Cherubim does cease to sing.
The Game Cock clip'd & arm'd for fight
Does the Rising Sun affright.
Every Wolf's & Lion's howl
Raises from Hell a Human Soul.
The wild deer, wand'ring here & there,
Keeps the Human Soul from Care.
The Lamb misus'd breeds Public strife
And yet forgives the Butcher's Knife.
The Bat that flits at close of Eve
Has left the Brain that won't Believe.
The Owl that calls upon the Night
Speaks the Unbeliever's fright.
He who shall hurt the little Wren
Shall never be belov'd by Men.
He who the Ox to wrath has mov'd
Shall never be by Woman lov'd.
The wanton Boy that kills the Fly

Shall feel the Spider's enmity.
He who torments the Chafer's sprite
Weaves a Bower in endless Night.
The Catterpiller on the Leaf
Repeats to thee thy Mother's grief.
Kill not the Moth nor Butterfly,
For the Last Judgment draweth nigh.
He who shall train the Horse to War
Shall never pass the Polar Bar.
The Begger's Dog & Widow's Cat,
Feed them & thou wilt grow fat.
The Gnat that sings his Summer's song
Poison gets from Slander's tongue.
The poison of the Snake & Newt
Is the sweat of Envy's Foot.
The Poison of the Honey Bee
Is the Artist's Jelousy.
The Prince's Robes & Beggar's Rags
Are Toadstools on the Miser's Bags.
A truth that's told with bad intent
Beats all the Lies you can invent.
It is right it should be so;
Man was made for Joy & Woe;
And when this we rightly know
Thro' the World we safely go.
Joy & Woe are woven fine,
A Clothing for the Soul divine
Under every grief & pine
Runs a joy with silken twine.
The Babe is more than swadling Bands;
Throughout all these Human Lands
Tools were made, & Born were hands,
Every Farmer Understands.
Every Tear from Every Eye
Becomes a Babe in Eternity;
This is caught by Females bright

And return'd to its own delight.
The Bleat, the Bark, Bellow & Roar
Are Waves that Beat on Heaven's Shore.
The Babe that weeps the Rod beneath
Writes Revenge in realms of death.
The Beggar's Rags, fluttering in Air,
Does to Rags the Heavens tear.
The Soldier, arm'd with Sword & Gun,
Palsied strikes the Summer's Sun.
The poor Man's Farthing is worth more
Than all the Gold on Afric's Shore.
One Mite wrung from the Labrer's hands
Shall buy & sell the Miser's Lands:
Or, if protected from on high,
Does that whole Nation sell & buy.
He who mocks the Infant's Faith
Shall be mock'd in Age & Death.
He who shall teach the Child to Doubt
The rotting Grave shall ne'er get out.
He who respects the Infant's faith
Triumphs over Hell & Death.
The Child's Toys & the Old Man's Reasons
Are the Fruits of the Two seasons.
The Questioner, who sits so sly,
Shall never know how to reply.
He who replies to words of Doubt
Doth put the Light of Knowledge out.
The Strongest Poison ever known
Came from Caesar's Laurel Crown.
Nought can deform the Human Race
Like to the Armour's iron brace.
When Gold & Gems adorn the Plow
To peaceful Arts shall Envy Bow.
A Riddle or the Cricket's Cry
Is to Doubt a fit Reply.
The Emmet's Inch & Eagle's Mile

Make Lame Philosophy to smile.
He who Doubts from what he sees
Will ne're Believe, do what you Please.
If the Sun & Moon should doubt,
They'd immediately Go out.
To be in a Passion you Good may do,
But no Good if a Passion is in you.
The Whore & Gambler, by the State
Licenc'd, build that Nation's Fate.
The Harlot's cry from Street to Street
Shall weave Old England's winding Sheet.
The Winner's Shout, the Loser's Curse,
Dance before dead England's Hearse.
Every Night & every Morn
Some to Misery are Born.
Every Morn & every Night
Some are Born to sweet delight.
Some are Born to sweet delight,
Some are Born to Endless Night.
We are led to Believe a Lie
When we see not Thro' the Eye
Which was Born in a Night to perish in a Night
When the Soul Slept in Beams of Light.
God Appears & God is Light
To those poor Souls who dwell in Night,
But does a Human Form Display
To those who Dwell in Realms of day.

W. H. AUDEN

[1939]   Law Like Love

Law, say the gardeners, is the sun,
Law is the one
All gardeners obey
To-morrow, yesterday, to-day.

Law is the wisdom of the old,
The impotent grandfathers feebly scold;
The grandchildren put out a treble tongue,
Law is the senses of the young.

Law, says the priest with a priestly look,
Expounding to an unpriestly people,
Law is the words in my priestly book,
Law is my pulpit and my steeple.

Law, says the judge as he looks down his nose,
Speaking clearly and most severely,
Law is as I've told you before,
Law is as you know I suppose,
Law is but let me explain it once more,
Law is The Law.

Yet law-abiding scholars write:
Law is neither wrong nor right,
Law is only crimes
Punished by places and by times,
Law is the clothes men wear
Anytime, anywhere,
Law is Good morning and Good night.

Others say, Law is our Fate;
Others say, Law is our State;
Others say, others say
Law is no more,
Law has gone away.

And always the loud angry crowd,
Very angry and very loud,
Law is We,
And always the soft idiot softly Me.

If we, dear, know we know no more
Than they about the Law,
If I no more than you

Know what we should and should not do
Except that all agree
Gladly or miserably
That the Law is
And that all know this,
If therefore thinking it absurd
To identify Law with some other word,
Unlike so many men
I cannot say Law is again,
No more than they can we suppress
The universal wish to guess
Or slip out of our own position
Into an unconcerned condition.
Although I can at least confine
Your vanity and mine
To stating timidly
A timid similarity,
We shall boast anyway:
Like love I say.

Like love we don't know where or why,
Like love we can't compel or fly,
Like love we often weep,
Like love we seldom keep.

DUDLEY RANDALL

[1969] ## Booker T. and W. E. B.
(*Booker T. Washington and W. E. B. Du Bois*)

'It seems to me,' said Booker T.,
'It shows a mighty lot of cheek
To study chemistry and Greek
When Mister Charlie needs a hand
To hoe the cotton on his land.
And when Miss Ann looks for a cook,
Why stick your nose inside a book?'

'I don't agree,' said W. E. B.
'If I should have the drive to seek
Knowledge of chemistry or Greek,
I'll do it. Charles and Miss can look
Another place for hand or cook.
Some men rejoice in skill of hand,
And some in cultivating land,
But there are others who maintain
The right to cultivate the brain.'

'It seems to me,' said Booker T.,
'That all you folks have missed the boat
Who shout about the right to vote,
And spend vain days and sleepless nights
In uproar over civil rights.
Just keep your mouths shut, do not grouse,
But work, and save, and buy a house.'

'I don't agree,' said W. E. B.,
'For what can property avail
If dignity and justice fail?
Unless you help to make the laws,
They'll steal your house with trumped-up clause.
A rope's as tight, a fire as hot,
No matter how much cash you've got.
Speak soft, and try your little plan,
But as for me, I'll be a man.'

'It seems to me,' said Booker T. –

'I don't agree,'
Said W. E. B.

ANONYMOUS

[15th century] ## 'I have a yong suster'

I have a yong suster,
Fer beyonden the se:

love-tokens   Many be the drowryes
That she sente me.

She sente me the cherye
Withouten ony ston;
And so she dede the dove
Withouten ony bon;

briar   She sente me the brer
bark   Withouten ony rinde;
sweetheart   She bad me love my lemman
Withoute longing.

How shuld ony cherye
Be withoute ston?
And how shuld ony dove
Ben withoute bon?

How shuld ony brer
Ben withoute rinde?
How shuld love mine lemman
Without longing?

Whan the cherye was a flowr
Than hadde it non ston;
egg   Whan the dove was an ey
Than hadde it non bon;

in the seed   Whan the brer was onbred
Than hadde it non rinde;
Whan the maiden hath that she loveth
She is without longing.

DAVID GASCOYNE

[1936] ## The Cubical Domes

Indeed indeed it is growing very sultry
The Indian feather pots are scrambling out of the
    room
The slow voice of the tobacconist is like a circle
Drawn on the floor in chalk and containing ants
And indeed there is a shoe upon the table
And indeed it is as regular as clockwork
Demonstrating the variability of the weather
Or denying the existence of manu altogether
For after all why should love resemble a cushion
Why should the stumbling-block float up
    towards the ceiling
And in our attic it is always said
That this is a sombre country the wettest place on
    earth
And then there is the problem of living to be
    considered
With its vast pink parachutes full of underdone
    mutton
Its tableaux of the archbishops dressed in their
    underwear
Have you ever paused to consider why grass is
    green
Yes greener at least it is said than the man in the
    moon
Which is why
The linen of flat countries basks in the tropical
    sun
And the light of the stars is attracted by
    transparent flowers
And at last is forgotten by both man and beast
By helmet and capstan and mermerised nun

For the bounds of my kingdom are truly
    unknown
And its factories work all night long
Producing the strongest canonical wastepaper-
    baskets
And ant-eaters' skiing-shoes
Which follow the glistening murders as far as the
    pond
And then light a magnificent bonfire of old rusty
    nails
And indeed they are paid by the state for their
    crimes
There is room for them all in the conjuror's
    musical-box
There is still enough room for even the hardest of
    faces
For faces are needed to stick on the emperor's
    walls
To roll down the stairs like a party of seafaring
    christians
Whose hearts are on fire in the snow.

ANONYMOUS (WELSH)

[12th century]   Gnomic Stanzas

Mountain snow, everywhere white;
A raven's custom is to sing;
No good comes of too much sleep.

Mountain snow, white the ravine;
By rushing wind trees are bent;
Many a couple love one another
Though they never come together.

Mountain snow, tossed by the wind;
Broad full moon, dockleaves green;
Rarely a knave's without litigation.

Mountain snow, swift the stag;
Usual in Britain are brave chiefs;
There's need of prudence in an exile.

Mountain snow, hunted stag;
Wind whistles above the eaves of a tower;
Heavy, O man, is sin.

Mountain snow, leaping stag:
Wind whistles above a high white wall;
Usually the calm are comely.

Mountain snow, stag in the vale;
Wind whistles above the rooftop;
There's no hiding evil, no matter where.

Mountain snow, stag on the shore;
Old man must feel his loss of youth;
Bad eyesight puts a man in prison.

Mountain snow, stag in the ditch;
Bees are asleep and snug;
Thieves and a long night suit each other.

Mountain snow, deer are nimble;
Waves wetten the brink of the shore;
Let the skilful hide his purpose.

Mountain snow, speckled breast of a goose;
Strong are my arm and shoulder;
I hope I shall not live to a hundred.

Mountain snow, bare tops of reeds;
Bent tips of branches, fish in the deep;
Where there's no learning, cannot be talent.

Mountain snow; red feet of hens;
Where it chatters, water's but shallow;
Big words add to any disgrace.

Mountain snow, swift the stag;
Rarely a thing in the world concerns me;
To warn the unlucky does not save them.

Mountain snow, fleece of white;
It's rare that a relative's face is friendly
If you visit him too often.

Mountain snow, white house-roofs;
If tongue were to tell what the heart may know
Nobody would be neighbours.

Mountain snow, day has come;
Every sad man sick, half-naked the poor;
Every time, a fool gets hurt.

translated by Anthony Conran

LOUISE BOGAN

[1941]   Question in a Field

Pasture, stone wall, and steeple,
What most perturbs the mind:
The heart-rending homely people,
Or the horrible beautiful kind?

E. E. CUMMINGS

[1940]   anyone lived in a pretty how town

anyone lived in a pretty how town
(with up so floating many bells down)
spring summer autumn winter
he sang his didn't he danced his did.

Women and men (both little and small)
cared for anyone not at all
they sowed their isn't they reaped their same
sun moon stars rain

children guessed (but only a few
and down they forgot as up they grew
autumn winter spring summer)
that noone loved him more by more

when by now and tree by leaf
she laughed his joy she cried his grief
bird by snow and stir by still
anyone's any was all to her

someones married their everyones
laughed their cryings and did their dance
(sleep wake hope and then) they
said their nevers they slept their dream

stars rain sun moon
(and only the snow can begin to explain
how children are apt to forget to remember
with up so floating many bells down)

one day anyone died i guess
(and noone stooped to kiss his face)
busy folk buried them side by side
little by little and was by was

all by all and deep by deep
and more by more they dream their sleep
noone and anyone earth by april
wish by spirit and if by yes.

Women and men (both dong and ding)
summer autumn winter spring
reaped their sowing and went their came
sun moon stars rain

[1954] ## The Umbrella

To Conrad Aiken

Because, in the hot countries,
They worshipped trees; because,
Under the sacred figs, Gautama
Became a god; because of the rain,
Because the sun beats down.
Because we followed orders, building a tent
'Of ten curtains of fine twined linen,
And blue and purple and scarlet.' And because
The ark required protection, with four pillars
Holding the curtains up, and 'the veil
Shall divide unto you between the holy place
And the most holy.' – I planted the seed
Of an elm and watered it. Rest
In the shelter of this shade. Black spines
Of metal and a tent of cloth
Are blooming where a tree stood up.

Discs float above the heads
Of the images
Of Indian gods. Sometimes
There are three of them, and each
Smaller than the one
That goes beneath. And sometimes
These tiers of aureoles
Are gone: umbrellas
Crown them in their place.

Two thousand years before the birth of Christ,
If there is any believing Chinese legend,
The wife of a carpenter named Lou Pan
Said to her husband one morning: 'You and your
    father

Before you have built well My Lord. But your
    houses
Are rigid, immovable. Now that the grass
Goes brown with autumn, I will build roofs
One can carry about. I will build a pagoda
On a stick, to give shelter wherever one goes.'
And this she proceeded to do.
                            When the Son
Of Heaven strode to the hunt, twenty-four
    umbrellas
Went before him. The Mikado proceeded in
    similar fashion
Under a red silk sunshade: emblem of 'absolute
    power.'
Protectors of kings and princes, floating
Over triumphal processions and battlefields,
Moving like a sea of tossing waves.
And in India, in 1877, the Prince of Wales
(Later Edward VII) moved in stately procession
Mounted on an elephant,
A gold umbrella before him. The Greeks
Hinted at secret rites of the umbrella cult.
At the Scirophoria, a priestess and a priest
'Went from the Acropolis to a place called Scira
Walking under a great white baldachino.'
And during the Thesmophoria, slaves
Carried parasols over the heads of the women
Who brought gifts to Persephone at the temple,
Desiring fertility. – And when we left the corpses
Out of doors, we put umbrellas over them,
Not to shield them from the sun, but rather
To protect the sunlight against pollution
By the dead. The Pope's was carried by a man in
    armor
On a white horse. The English and the French
Trimmed them with ruches, valances, pompons,

Tassels, fringes, frills of lace, glass beads,
Sequins, artificial flowers, ostrich feathers,
God knows what else.

Over the empty harbor, gray and motionless,
The clouds have been gathering all afternoon,
    and now
The sea is pitted with rain. Wind shakes the
    house.
Here from this window lashed with spray, I
    watch
A black umbrella, ripped apart and wrong side
    out,
Go lurching wildly down the beach; a sudden
    gust
Carries it upward, upside down,
Over the water, flapping and free,
Into the heart of the storm.

[10th century]   Cuckoo

Abandoned unborn by my begetters
I was still dead a few spring days ago:
no beat in the breast, no breath in me.

A kinswoman covered me in the clothes she
    wore,
no kind but kind indeed. I was coddled &
    swaddled
as close as I had been a baby of her own,
until, as had been shaped, so shielded, though no
    kin,
the unguessed guest grew great with life.

She fended for me, fostered me, she fed me up,
till I was of a size to set my bounds

further afield. She had fewer dear
sons and daughters because she did so.

translated by Michael Alexander

RALPH WALDO EMERSON

[1847]   **Blight**

Give me truths;
For I am weary of the surfaces,
And die of inanition. If I knew
Only the herbs and simples of the wood,
Rue, cinquefoil, gill, vervain and agrimony,
Blue-vetch and trillium, hawkweed, sassafras,
Milkweeds and murky brakes, quaint pipes and
      sundew,
And rare and virtuous roots, which in these
      woods
Draw untold juices from the common earth,
Untold, unknown, and I could surely spell
Their fragrance, and their chemistry apply
By sweet affinities to human flesh,
Driving the foe and stablishing the friend, –
O, that were much, and I could be a part
Of the round day, related to the sun
And planted world, and full executor
Of their imperfect functions.
But these young scholars, who invade our hills,
Bold as the engineer who fells the wood,
And travelling often in the cut he makes,
Love not the flower they pluck, and know it not,
And all their botany is Latin names.
The old men studied magic in the flowers,
And human fortunes in astronomy,
And an omnipotence in chemistry,
Preferring things to names, for these were men,
Were unitarians of the united world,

And, wheresoever their clear eye-beams fell,
They caught the footsteps of the SAME. Our eyes
Are armed, but we are strangers to the stars,
And strangers to the mystic beast and bird,
And strangers to the plant and to the mine.
The injured elements say, 'Not in us';
And night and day, ocean and continent,
Fire, plant and mineral say, 'Not in us';
And haughtily return us stare for stare.
For we invade them impiously for gain;
We devastate them unreligiously,
And coldly ask their pottage, not their love.
Therefore they shove us from them, yield to us
Only what to our griping toil is due;
But the sweet affluence of love and song,
The rich results of the divine consents
Of man and earth, of world beloved and lover,
The nectar and ambrosia, are withheld;
And in the midst of spoils and slaves, we thieves
And pirates of the universe, shut out
Daily to a more thin and outward rind,
Turn pale and starve. Therefore, to our sick eyes,
The stunted trees look sick, the summer short,
Clouds shade the sun, which will not tan our hay,
And nothing thrives to reach its natural term;
And life, shorn of its venerable length,
Even at its greatest space is a defeat,
And dies in anger that it was a dupe;
And, in its highest noon and wantonness,
Is early frugal, like a beggar's child;
Even in the hot pursuit of the best aims
And prizes of ambition, checks its hand,
Like Alpine cataracts frozen as they leaped,
Chilled with a miserly comparison
Of the toy's purchase with the length of life.

ALLEN CURNOW

[1988] ## Continuum

The moon rolls over the roof and falls behind
my house, and the moon does neither of these
        things,
I am talking about myself.

It's not possible to get off to sleep or
the subject or the planet, nor to think thoughts.
Better barefoot it out the front

door and lean from the porch across the privets
and the palms into the washed-out creation,
a dark place with two particular

bright clouds dusted (query) by the moon, one's
        mine
the other's an adversary, which may depend
on the wind, or something.

A long moment stretches, the next one is not
on time. Not unaccountably the chill of
the planking underfoot rises

in the throat, for its part the night sky empties
the whole of its contents down. Turn on a bare
heel, close the door behind

on the author, cringing demiurge, who picks up
his litter and his tools and paces me back
to bed, stealthily in step.

THEODORE ROETHKE

[1951] ## The Waking

I wake to sleep, and take my waking slow.
I feel my fate in what I cannot fear.
I learn by going where I have to go.

We think by feeling. What is there to know?
I hear my being dance from ear to ear.
I wake to sleep, and take my waking slow.

Of those so close beside me, which are you?
God bless the Ground! I shall walk softly there,
And learn by going where I have to go.

Light takes the Tree; but who can tell us how?
The lowly worm climbs up a winding stair;
I wake to sleep, and take my waking slow.

Great Nature has another thing to do
To you and me; so take the lively air,
And, lovely, learn by going where to go.

This shaking keeps me steady. I should know.
What falls away is always. And is near.
I wake to sleep, and take my waking slow.
I learn by going where I have to go.

ROBERT LOWELL

[1967]   # Waking Early Sunday Morning

O to break loose, like the chinook
salmon jumping and falling back,
nosing up to the impossible
stone and bone-crushing waterfall –
raw-jawed, weak-fleshed there, stopped by ten
steps of the roaring ladder, and then
to clear the top on the last try,
alive enough to spawn and die.

Stop, back off. The salmon breaks
water, and now my body wakes
to feel the unpolluted joy
and criminal leisure of a boy –
no rainbow smashing a dry fly

in the white run is free as I,
here squatting like a dragon on
time's hoard before the day's begun!

Vermin run for their unstopped holes;
in some dark nook a fieldmouse rolls
a marble, hours on end, then stops;
the termite in the woodwork sleeps –
listen, the creatures of the night
obsessive, casual, sure of foot,
go on grinding, while the sun's
daily remorseful blackout dawns.

Fierce, fireless mind, running downhill.
Look up and see the harbor fill:
business as usual in eclipse
goes down to the sea in ships –
wake of refuse, dacron rope,
bound for Bermuda or Good Hope,
all bright before the morning watch
the wine-dark hulls of yawl and ketch.

I watch a glass of water wet
with a fine fuzz of icy sweat,
silvery colors touched with sky,
serene in their neutrality –
yet if I shift, or change my mood,
I see some object made of wood,
background behind it of brown grain,
to darken it, but not to stain.

O that the spirit could remain
tinged but untarnished by its strain!
Better dressed and stacking birch,
or lost with the Faithful at Church –
anywhere, but somewhere else!
And now the new electric bells,

clearly chiming, 'Faith of our fathers,'
and now the congregation gathers.

O Bible chopped and crucified
in hymns we hear but do not read,
none of the milder subtleties
of grace or art will sweeten these
stiff quatrains shoveled out four-squre –
they sing of peace, and preach despair;
yet they gave darkness some control,
and left a loophole for the soul.

No, put old clothes on, and explore
the corners of the woodshed for
its dregs and dreck: tools with no handle,
ten candle-ends not worth a candle,
old lumber banished from the Temple,
damned by Paul's precept and example,
cast from the kingdom, banned in Israel,
the wordless sign, the tinkling cymbal.

When will we see Him face to face?
Each day, He shines through darker glass.
In this small town where everything
is known, I see His vanishing
emblems, His white spire and flag-
pole sticking out above the fog,
like old white china doorknobs, sad,
slight, useless things to calm the mad.

Hammering military splendor,
top-heavy Goliath in full armor –
little redemption in the mass
liquidations of their brass,
elephant and phalanx moving
with the times and still improving,
when that kingdom hit the crash:
a million foreskins stacked like trash . . .

Sing softer! But what if a new
diminuendo brings no true
tenderness, only restlessness,
excess, the hunger for success,
sanity of self-deception
fixed and kicked by reckless caution,
while we listen to the bells –
anywhere, but somewhere else!

O to break loose. All life's grandeur
is something with a girl in summer . . .
elated as the President
girdled by his establishment
this Sunday morning, free to chaff
his own thoughts with his bear-cuffed staff,
swimming nude, unbuttoned, sick
of his ghost-written rhetoric!

No weekends for the gods now. Wars
flicker, earth licks its open sores,
fresh breakage, fresh promotions, chance
assassinations, no advance.
Only man thinning out his kind
sounds through the Sabbath noon, the blind
swipe of the pruner and his knife
busy about the tree of life . . .

Pity the planet, all joy gone
from this sweet volcanic cone;
peace to our children when they fall
in small war on the heels of small
war – until the end of time
to police the earth, a ghost
orbiting forever lost
in our monotonous sublime.

WILLIAM EMPSON

[1962]

Let It Go

It is this deep blankness is the real thing strange.
The more things happen to you the more you
can't
Tell or remember even what they were.

The contradictions cover such a range.
The talk would talk and go so far aslant.
You don't want madhouse and the whole
thing there.

WILLIAM DUNBAR

[late 16th/early 17th
century]

On His Heid-ake

ache

My heid did yak yester nicht,

write poetry

this day to mak that I na micht,

headache / disable

so sair the magryme dois me menyie,

arrow

perseing my brow as ony ganyie,
that scant I luik may on the licht.

sire / mass

And now, schir, laitlie, eftir mes,
to dyt thocht I begowthe to dres,

difficult

the sentence lay full evill till find,

not having slept

unsleipit in my heid behind,
dullit in dulnes and distres.

Full oft at morrow I upryse,

when / spirit

quhen that my curage sleipeing lyis,
for mirth, for menstrallie and play,

revelry

for din nor danceing nor deray,
it will nocht walkin me no wise.

328

STEPHEN CRANE

[1896] ## 'In the desert'

In the desert
I saw a creature, naked, bestial,
Who, squatting upon the ground,
Held his heart in his hands,
And ate of it.
I said: 'Is it good, friend?'
'It is bitter – bitter,' he answered;
'But I like it
Because it is bitter,
And because it is my heart.'

ALEXANDER POPE

[1735] ## Epistle to Dr Arbuthnot

Shut, shut the door, good John! fatigued, I said;
Tie up the knocker, say I'm sick, I'm dead.
The dog-star rages! nay 'tis past a doubt,
All Bedlam, or Parnassus, is let out:
Fire in each eye, and papers in each hand,
They rave, recite, and madden round the land.
   What walls can guard me, or what shades can
     hide?

grotto They pierce my thickets, through my grot they
     glide,
By land, by water, they renew the charge,
They stop the chariot, and they board the barge.
No place is sacred, not the church is free,
Ev'n Sunday shines no Sabbath-day to me:

sanctuary for insolvent Then from the Mint walks forth the man of
debtors   rhyme,
Happy! to catch me, just at dinner-time.
   Is there a parson, much bemused in beer,
A maudlin poetess, a rhyming peer,

A clerk, foredoomed his father's soul to cross,
Who pens a stanza, when he should engross?
Is there, who, locked from ink and paper, scrawls
With desp'rate charcoal round his darkened walls?
Twickenham
All fly to Twit'nam, and in humble strain
Apply to me, to keep them mad or vain.
Arthur, whose giddy son neglects the laws,
Imputes to me and my damned works the cause:
Poor Cornus sees his frantic wife elope,
And curses wit, and poetry, and Pope.
   Friend to my life (which did not you prolong,
The world had wanted many an idle song),
What drop or nostrum can this plague remove?
Or which must end me, a fool's wrath or love?
A dire dilemma! either way I'm sped,
If foes, they write, if friends, they read me dead.
Seized and tied down to judge, how wretched I!
Who can't be silent, and who will not lie;
To laugh, were want of goodness and of grace,
And to be grave, exceeds all pow'r of face.
I sit with sad civility, I read
With honest anguish, and an aching head;
And drop at last, but in unwilling ears,
This saving counsel, 'Keep your piece nine years.'
   'Nine years!' cries he, who, high in Drury Lane,
Lulled by soft zephyrs through the broken pane,
Rhymes ere he wakes, and prints before Term
         ends,
Obliged by hunger, and request of friends:
'The piece, you think, is incorrect? why take it,
I'm all submission; what you'd have it, make it.'
   Three things another's modest wishes bound,
My friendship, and a prologue, and ten pound.
   Pitholeon sends to me: 'You know his Grace,
I want a patron; ask him for a place.'
Pitholeon libelled me – 'But here's a letter

330

Informs you, Sir, 'twas when he knew no better.
Dare you refuse him? Curll invites to dine,

become a clergyman

He'll write a journal, or he'll turn divine.'
   Bless me! a packet. ''Tis a stranger sues,
A virgin tragedy, an orphan Muse.'
If I dislike it, 'Furies, death and rage!'
If I approve, 'Commend it to the stage.'
There (thank my stars) my whole commission
     ends,
The play'rs and I are, luckily, no friends.
Fired that the house reject him, ''Sdeath, I'll print
     it,
And shame the fools – Your interest, Sir, with
     Lintot.'
Lintot, dull rogue! will think your price too much:
'Not, Sir, if you revise it, and retouch.'
All my demurs but double his attacks:

divide the profits

And last he whispers, 'Do, and we go snacks.'
Glad of a quarrel, straight I clap the door:
Sir, let me see your works and you no more.
   'Tis sung, when Midas' ears began to spring
(Midas, a sacred person and a king),
His very minister who spied them first
(Some say his queen) was forced to speak or
     burst:
And is not mine, my friend, a sorer case,
When every coxcomb perks them in my face?
'Good friend, forbear! you deal in dang'rous
     things,
I'd never name queens, ministers, or kings;

be discreet

Keep close to ears, and those let asses prick,
'Tis nothing' – Nothing! if they bite and kick?
Out with it, *Dunciad*! let the secret pass,
That secret to each fool, that he's an ass:
The truth once told (and wherefore should we
     lie?)

The queen of Midas slept, and so may I.
  You think this cruel? Take it for a rule,
No creature smarts so little as a fool.
Let peals of laughter, Codrus! round thee break,
Thou unconcerned canst hear the mighty crack.
Pit, box, and gallery in convulsions hurled,
Thou stand'st unshook amidst a bursting world.
Who shames a scribbler? break one cobweb
        through,
He spins the slight, self-pleasing thread anew;
Destroy his fib or sophistry; in vain,
The creature's at his dirty work again,
Throned in the centre of his thin designs,
Proud of a vast extent of flimsy lines.
Whom have I hurt? has poet yet, or peer,
Lost the arched eyebrow, or Parnassian sneer?
And has not Colley still his lord, and whore?
His butchers Henley, his freemasons Moore?
Does not one table Bavius still admit?
Still to one bishop Philips seem a wit?
Still Sappho – 'Hold! for God's sake – you'll offend:
No names – be calm – learn prudence of a friend:
I too could write, and I am twice as tall,
But foes like these!' – One flatt'rer's worse than
        all;
Of all mad creatures, if the learned are right,
It is the slaver kills, and not the bite.
A fool quite angry is quite innocent;
Alas! 'tis ten times worse when they repent.
  One dedicates in high heroic prose,
And ridicules beyond a hundred foes;
One from all Grub Street will my fame defend,
And, more abusive, calls himself my friend.
This prints my letters, that expects a bribe,
And others roar aloud, 'Subscribe, subscribe.'
  There are, who to my person pay their court,

i.e., hack writers

I cough like Horace, and, though lean, am short;
Ammon's great son one shoulder had too high,
Such Ovid's nose, – and 'Sir! you have an eye – '.
Go on, obliging creatures, make me see
All that disgraced my betters met in me:
Say, for my comfort, languishing in bed,
'Just so immortal Maro held his head';
And, when I die, be sure you let me know
Great Homer died three thousand years ago.

   Why did I write? what sin to me unknown
Dipped me in ink, my parents', or my own?
As yet a child, nor yet a fool to fame,
I lisped in numbers, for the numbers came.
I left no calling for this idle trade,
No duty broke, no father disobeyed.
The Muse but served to ease some friend, not
      wife,
To help me through this long disease, my life;
To second, Arbuthnot! thy art and care,
And teach the being you preserved to bear.

   But why then publish? Granville the polite,
And knowing Walsh, would tell me I could write;
Well-natured Garth inflamed with early praise,
And Congreve loved, and Swift endured my lays;
The courtly Talbot, Somers, Sheffield read,
Ev'n mitred Rochester would nod the head,
And St John's self (great Dryden's friends before)
With open arms received one poet more.
Happy my studies, when by these approved!
Happier their author, when by these beloved!
From these the world will judge of men and
      books,
Not from the Burnets, Oldmixons, and Cookes.

   Soft were my numbers; who could take offence
While pure description held the place of sense?
Like gentle Fanny's was my flow'ry theme,

A painted mistress, or a purling stream.
Yet then did Gildon draw his venal quill;
I wished the man a dinner, and sat still:
Yet then did Dennis rave in furious fret;
I never answered, I was not in debt:
If want provoked, or madness made them print,
I waged no war with Bedlam or the Mint.

Did some more sober critic come abroad?
If wrong, I smiled; if right, I kissed the rod.
Pains, reading, study are their just pretence,
And all they want is spirit, taste, and sense.
Commas and points they set exactly right,
And 'twere a sin to rob them of their mite.
Yet ne'er one sprig of laurel graced these ribalds,
From slashing Bentley down to piddling Tibbalds.
Each wight who reads not, and but scans and
    spells,
Each word-catcher that lives on syllables,
Ev'n such small critics, some regard may claim,
Preserved in Milton's or in Shakespeare's name.
Pretty! in amber to observe the forms
Of hairs, or straws, or dirt, or grubs, or worms;
The things, we know, are neither rich nor rare,
But wonder how the devil they got there.

Were others angry? I excused them too;
Well might they rage; I gave them but their due.
A man's true merit 'tis not hard to find,
But each man's secret standard in his mind,
That casting-weight pride adds to emptiness,
This, who can gratify, for who can guess?
The bard whom pilfered pastorals renown,
Who turns a Persian tale for half-a-crown,
Just writes to make his barrenness appear,
And strains from hard-bound brains eight lines a
    year;
He, who still wanting, though he lives on theft,

person

334

Steals much, spends little, yet has nothing left;
And he, who now to sense, now nonsense
    leaning,
Means not, but blunders round about a meaning;
And he, whose fustian's so sublimely bad,
It is not poetry, but prose run mad:
All these, my modest satire bade translate,
And owned that nine such poets made a Tate.
How did they fume, and stamp, and roar, and
    chafe!
And swear, not Addison himself was safe.
    Peace to all such! but were there one whose
    fires
True genius kindles, and fair fame inspires,
Blest with each talent and each art to please,
And born to write, converse, and live with ease:

eager Should such a man, too fond to rule alone,
Bear, like the Turk, no brother near the throne,
View him with scornful, yet with jealous eyes,
And hate for arts that caused himself to rise;
Damn with faint praise, assent with civil leer,
And, without sneering, teach the rest to sneer;
Willing to wound, and yet afraid to strike,
Just hint a fault, and hesitate dislike;
Alike reserved to blame, or to commend,
A tim'rous foe, and a suspicious friend,
Dreading ev'n fools, by flatterers besieged,
And so obliging that he ne'er obliged;
Like Cato, give his little senate laws,
And sit attentive to his own applause;
While wits and Templars every sentence raise,
And wonder with a foolish face of praise.
Who but must laugh, if such a man there be?
Who would not weep, if Atticus were he?

advertised (using red- What though my name stood rubric on the
letter title pages)   walls,

335

posters
Or plastered posts, with claps in capitals?
Or smoking forth, a hundred hawkers load,
On wings of winds came flying all abroad?
I sought no homage from the race that write;
I kept, like Asian monarchs, from their sight:
Poems I heeded (now be-rhymed so long)
No more than thou, great George! a birthday
    song.
I ne'er with wits or witlings passed my days,
To spread about the itch of verse and praise;

trailed
Nor like a puppy daggled through the town,
To fetch and carry sing-song up and down;
Nor at rehearsals sweat, and mouthed, and cried,
With handkerchief and orange at my side:
But sick of fops, and poetry, and prate,

i.e., domain of poetry
To Bufo left the whole Castalian state.
    Proud as Apollo on his forkèd hill,
Sat full-blown Bufo, puffed by every quill;
Fed with soft dedication all day long,
Horace and he went hand in hand in song.
His library (where busts of poets dead
And a true Pindar stood without a head)
Received of wits an undistinguished race,
Who first his judgement asked, and then a place:

residence
Much they extolled his pictures, much his seat,
And flattered every day, and some days eat:
Till grown more frugal in his riper days,
He paid some bards with port, and some with
    praise,
To some a dry rehearsal was assigned,
And others (harder still) he paid in kind.
Dryden alone (what wonder?) came not nigh,
Dryden alone escaped this judging eye:
But still the great have kindness in reserve,
He helped to bury whom he helped to starve.

336

May some choice patron bless each grey goose
    quill!
May every Bavius have his Bufo still!
So when a statesman wants a day's defence,
Or envy holds a whole week's war with sense,
Or simple pride for flatt'ry makes demands,
May dunce by dunce be whistled off my hands!
Blessed be the great! for those they take away,
And those they left me – for they left me Gay;
Left me to see neglected genius bloom,
Neglected die, and tell it on his tomb;
Of all thy blameless life the sole return
My verse, and Queensb'ry weeping o'er thy urn!
    Oh let me live my own, and die so too!
('To live and die is all I have to do:')
Maintain a poet's dignity and ease,
And see what friends, and read what books I
    please.
Above a patron, though I condescend
Sometimes to call a minister my friend:
I was not born for courts or great affairs,
I pay my debts, believe, and say my pray'rs,
Can sleep without a poem in my head,
Nor know if Dennis be alive or dead.
    Why am I asked what next shall see the light?
Heav'ns! was I born for nothing but to write?
Has life no joys for me? or (to be grave)
Have I no friend to serve, no soul to save?
'I found him close with Swift' – 'Indeed? no doubt'
(Cries prating Balbus) 'something will come out.'
'Tis all in vain, deny it as I will:
'No, such a genius never can lie still';
And then for mine obligingly mistakes
The first lampoon Sir Will or Bubo makes.
Poor guiltless I! and can I choose but smile,
When ev'ry coxcomb knows me by my style?

Cursed be the verse, how well soe'er it flow,
That tends to make one worthy man my foe,
Give virtue scandal, innocence a fear,
Or from the soft-eyed virgin steal a tear!
But he who hurts a harmless neighbour's peace,
Insults fall'n worth, or beauty in distress,
Who loves a lie, lame slander helps about,
Who writes a libel, or who copies out;
That fop, whose pride affects a patron's name,
Yet absent, wounds an author's honest fame;
Who can your merit selfishly approve,
And show the sense of it without the love;
Who has the vanity to call you friend,
Yet wants the honour, injured, to defend;
Who tells whate'er you think, whate'er you say,
And, if he lie not, must at least betray;

i.e., chapel bell Who to the dean and silver bell can swear,
And sees at Cannons what was never there;
Who reads, but with a lust to misapply,
Makes satire a lampoon, and fiction lie:
A lash like mine no honest man shall dread,
But all such babbling blockheads in his stead.

Let Sporus tremble – 'What? that thing of silk,
Sporus, that mere white curd of ass's milk?
Satire or sense, alas! can Sporus feel?
Who breaks a butterfly upon a wheel?'
Yet let me flap this bug with gilded wings,
This painted child of dirt, that stinks and stings;
Whose buzz the witty and the fair annoys,
Yet wit ne'er tastes and beauty ne'er enjoys:
So well-bred spaniels civilly delight
In mumbling of the game they dare not bite.
Eternal smiles his emptiness betray,
As shallow streams run dimpling all the way.
Whether in florid impotence he speaks,

And, as the prompter breathes, the puppet
    squeaks;
Or at the ear of Eve, familiar toad,
Half froth, half venom, spits himself abroad,
In puns, or politics, or tales, or lies,
Or spite, or smut, or rhymes, or blasphemies.
His wit all see-saw, between that and this,
Now high, now low, now master up, now miss,
And he himself one vile antithesis.
Amphibious thing! that acting either part,
The trifling head, or the corrupted heart!
Fop at the toilet, flatt'rer at the board,
Now trips a lady, and now struts a lord.
Eve's tempter thus the rabbins have expressed,
A cherub's face, a reptile all the rest;
Beauty that shocks you, parts that none will trust,
Wit that can creep, and pride that licks the dust.

    Not Fortune's worshipper, nor Fashion's fool,
Not Lucre's madman, nor Ambition's tool,
Not proud, nor servile; be one poet's praise,
That, if he pleased, he pleased by manly ways;
That flatt'ry, ev'n to kings, he held a shame,
And thought a lie in verse or prose the same;
That not in Fancy's maze he wandered long,
But stooped to Truth, and moralised his song:
That not for fame, but Virtue's better end,
He stood the furious foe, the timid friend,
The damning critic, half-approving wit,
The coxcomb hit, or fearing to be hit;
Laughed at the loss of friends he never had,
The dull, the proud, the wicked, and the mad;
The distant threats of vengeance on his head,
The blow unfelt, the tear he never shed;
The tale revived, the lie so oft o'erthrown;
Th' imputed trash, and dullness not his own;
The morals blackened when the writings 'scape;

rabbis / described

swooped down on

The libelled person, and the pictured shape;
Abuse, on all he loved, or loved him, spread,
A friend in exile, or a father dead;
The whisper, that to greatness still too near,
Perhaps yet vibrates on his Sovereign's ear –
Welcome for thee, fair Virtue! welcome ev'n the
    last!
   'But why insult the poor, affront the great?'
A knave's a knave, to me, in ev'ry state;
Alike my scorn, if he succeed or fail,
Sporus at court, or Japhet in a jail,
A hireling scribbler, or a hireling peer,
Knight of the Post corrupt, or of the Shire;
If on a pillory, or near a throne,
He gain his prince's ear, or lose his own.
   Yet soft by nature, more a dupe than wit,
Sappho can tell you how this man was bit:
This dreaded sat'rist Dennis will confess
Foe to his pride, but friend to his distress:
So humble, he has knocked at Tibbald's door,
Has drunk with Cibber, nay has rhymed for
    Moore.
Full ten years slandered, did he once reply?
Three thousand suns went down on Welsted's lie;
To please a mistress one aspersed his life;
He lashed him not, but let her be his wife;
Let Budgell charge low Grub Street on his quill,
And write what'er he pleased, except his will;
Let the two Curlls of town and court abuse
His father, mother, body, soul, and Muse.
Yet why? that father held it for a rule,
It was a sin to call our neighbour fool;
That harmless mother thought no wife a whore, –
Hear this, and spare his family, James Moore!
Unspotted names, and memorable long!
If there be force in virtue, or in song.

Of gentle blood (part shed in honour's cause,
While yet in Britain honour had applause)
Each parent sprung – 'What fortune, pray?' –
　　Their own,
And better got than Bestia's from the throne.
Born to no pride, inheriting no strife,
Nor marrying discord in a noble wife,
Stranger to civil and religious rage,
The good man walked innoxious through his age.
No courts he saw, no suits would ever try,
Nor dared an oath, nor hazarded a lie:
Unlearned, he knew no schoolman's subtle art,
No language, but the language of the heart.
By nature honest, by experience wise,
Healthy by temp'rance and by exercise,
His life, though long, to sickness passed
　　unknown,
His death was instant, and without a groan.
O grant me thus to live, and thus to die!
Who sprung from kings shall know less joy than I.
　　O friend! may each domestic bliss be thine!
Be no unpleasing melancholy mine:
Me, let the tender office long engage
To rock the cradle of reposing age,
With lenient arts extend a mother's breath,
Make languor smile, and smooth the bed of death,
Explore the thought, explain the asking eye,
And keep awhile one parent from the sky!
On cares like these if length of days attend,
May heav'n, to bless those days, preserve my
　　friend,
Preserve him social, cheerful, and serene,
And just as rich as when he served a queen.
Whether that blessing be denied or giv'n,
Thus far was right, the rest belongs to heav'n.

[1964] *from* Dream Songs

4

Filling her compact & delicious body
with chicken páprika, she glanced at me
twice.
Fainting with interest, I hungered back
and only the fact of her husband & four other
    people
kept me from springing on her

or falling at her little feet and crying
'You are the hottest one for years of night
Henry's dazed eyes
have enjoyed, Brilliance.' I advanced upon
(despairing) my spumoni. – Sir Bones: is stuffed,
de world, wif feeding girls.

– Black hair, complexion Latin, jewelled eyes
downcast . . . The slob beside her   feasts . . .
    What wonders is
she sitting on, over there?
The restaurant buzzes. She might as well be on
    Mars.
Where did it all go wrong? There ought to be a
    law against Henry.
– Mr. Bones: there is.

14

Life, friends, is boring. We must not say so.
After all, the sky flashes, the great sea yearns,
we ourselves flash and yearn,
and moreover my mother told me as a boy

(repeatedly) 'Ever to confess you're bored
means you have no

Inner Resources.' I conclude now I have no
inner resources, because I am heavy bored.
Peoples bore me,
literature bores me, especially great literature,
Henry bores me, with his plights & gripes
as bad as achilles,

who loves people and valiant art, which bores
    me.
And the tranquil hills, & gin, look like a drag
and somehow a dog
has taken itself & its tail considerably away
into mountains or sea or sky, leaving
behind: me, wag.

63

Bats have no bankers and they do not drink
and cannot be arrested and pay no tax
and, in general, bats have it made.
Henry for joining the human race is *bats*,
known to be so, by few them who think,
out of the cave.

Instead of the cave! ah lovely-chilly, dark,
ur-moist his cousins hang in hundreds or swerve
with personal radar,
crisisless, kid. Instead of the cave? I serve,
inside, my blind term. Filthy four-foot lights
reflect on the whites of our eyes.

He then salutes for sixty years of it
just now a one of valor and insights,
a theatrical man,
O scholar & Legionnaire who as quickly might

have killed as cast you. *Olè*. Stormed with years
he tranquil commands and appears.

67

I don't operate often. When I do,
persons take note.
Nurses look amazed. They pale.
The patient is brought back to life, or so.
The reason I don't do this more (I quote)
is: I have a living to fail —

because of my wife & son – to keep from earning.
– Mr Bones, I sees that.
They for these operations thanks you, what?
not pays you. – Right.
You have seldom been so understanding.
now there is further a difficulty with the light:

I am obliged to perform in complete darkness
operations of great delicacy
on my self.
– Mr Bones, you terrifies me.
No wonder they don't pay you. Will you die?
– My
        friend, I succeeded. Later.

75

Turning it over, considering, like a madman
Henry put forth a book.
No harm resulted from this.
Neither the menstruating   stars (nor man) was
    moved
at once.
Bare dogs drew closer for a second look

and performed their friendly operations there.
Refreshed, the bark rejoiced.
Seasons went and came.
Leaves fell, but only a few.
Something remarkable about this
unshedding bulky bole-proud blue-green moist

thing made by savage & thoughtful
surviving Henry
began to strike the passers from despair
so that sore on their shoulders old men hoisted
six-foot sons and polished women called
small girls to dream awhile toward the flashing &
     bursting tree!

EDWIN ARLINGTON ROBINSON

[1924] ## Miniver Cheevy

Miniver Cheevy, child of scorn,
    Grew lean while he assailed the seasons;
He wept that he was ever born,
    And he had reasons.

Miniver loved the days of old
    When swords were bright and steeds were
        prancing;
The vision of a warrior bold
    Would set him dancing.

Miniver sighed for what was not,
    And dreamed, and rested from his labors;
He dreamed of Thebes and Camelot,
    And Priam's neighbors.

Miniver mourned the ripe renown
    That made so many a name so fragrant;
He mourned Romance, now on the town,
    And Art, a vagrant.

Miniver loved the Medici,
   Albeit he had never seen one;
He would have sinned incessantly
   Could he have been one.

Miniver cursed the commonplace
   And eyed a khaki suit with loathing;
He missed the mediaeval grace
   Of iron clothing.

Miniver scorned the gold he sought,
   But sore annoyed was he without it;
Miniver thought, and thought, and thought,
   And thought about it.

Miniver Cheevy, born too late,
   Scratched his head and kept on thinking;
Miniver coughed and called it fate,
   And kept on drinking.

JOHN WILMOT, EARL OF ROCHESTER

[1691]   ## The Maim'd Debauchee

As some brave *Admiral*, in former War
   Depriv'd of Force, but prest with Courage still,
Two Rival Fleets appearing from afar,
   Crawls to the top of an adjacent Hill;

From whence (with Thoughts full of Concern) he
     views
   The wise and daring Conduct of the Fight:
And each bold Action to his Mind renews,
   His present Glory, and his past Delight.

From his fierce Eyes Flashes of Rage he throws,
   As from black Clouds when Lightning breaks
     away,

Transported thinks himself amidst his Foes,
    And absent, yet enjoys the bloody Day.

So when my Days of Impotence approach,
    And I'm by Love and Wine's unlucky chance
Driv'n from the pleasing Billows of Debauch,
    On the dull Shoar of lazy Temperance;

My Pains at last some Respite shall afford,
    While I behold the Battels you maintain:
When Fleets of Glases sail around the Board,
    From whose Broad-sides Volleys of Wit shall
        rain.

Nor shall the sight of honourable Scars,
    Which my too forward Valour did procure,
Frighten new-listed Soldiers from the Wars;
    Past Joys have more than paid what I endure.

Shou'd some brave Youth (worth being drunk)

reluctant   prove nice,
    And from his fair Inviter meanly shrink,
'Twould please the Ghost of my departed Vice,
    If, at my Counsel, he repent and drink.

Or shou'd some cold-complexion'd Sot forbid,
    With his dull Morals, our Night's brisk
        Alarms;
I'll fire his Blood, by telling what I did,
    When I was strong, and able to bear Arms.

I'll tell of Whores attack'd their Lords at home,
    Bawds Quarters beaten up, and Fortress won;
Windows demolish'd, Watches overcome,
    And handsom Ills by my Contrivance done.

With Tales like these I will such Heat inspire,
    As to important Mischief shall incline;

I'll make him long some ancient Church to fire,
    And fear no Lewdness they're call'd to by Wine.

Thus Statesman-like I'll saucily impose,
    And, safe from Danger, valiantly advise;
Shelter'd in Impotence urge you to Blows,
    And, being good for nothing else, be Wise.

J. T. 'FUNNY PAPER' SMITH

[1930]   Seven Sisters

They tell me Seven Sisters in New Orleans, that
    can really fix a man up right,
And I'm headed for New Orleans, Louisiana, I'm
    traveling both day and night.
I hear them say the oldest sister look like she's
    just twenty-one
And said she can look right in your eyes and tell
    you exactly what you want done.
They tell me they been hung, been bled and been
    crucified
But I just want enough help to stand on the water
    and rule the tide.
It's bound to be Seven Sisters 'cause I've heard it
    by everybody else.
'Course I'd love to take their word, but I'd rather
    go and see for myself.
When I leave the Seven Sisters I'm piling stones
    all around
And go to my baby and tell her there's another
    Seven-Sister man in town.
Good mornin' Seven Sisters, just thought I'd
    come down and see
Will you build me up where I'm torn down and
    make me strong where I'm weak?

348

I went to New Orleans, Louisiana, just on
  account of something I heard.
The Seven Sisters told me everything I wanted to
  know and they wouldn't let me speak a word.
Now it's Sara, Minnie, Bertha, Holly, Dolly, Betty
  and Jane –
You can't know them sisters apart because they
  all looks just the same
The Seven Sisters sent me away happy, 'round
  the corner I met another little girl;
She looked at me and smiled and said: Go devil
  and destroy the world.
[Spoken: I'm gonna destroy it, too . . . I'm all right
  now]
Seven times you hear the Seven Sisters, will visit
  me in my sleep,
And they said I won't have no more trouble, and
  said I'll live twelve days in a week.
Boy go down in Louisiana, and get the lead right
  outta your being.
If Seven Sisters can't do anything in Louisiana,
  bet you'll have to go to New Orleans.

CATHAL BUÍ MAC GIOLLA GHUNNA (IRISH)

[early 18th century]   The Yellow Bittern

Yellow bittern, I'm sad it's over.
  Your bones are frozen and all caved in.
It wasn't hunger but thirst and craving
  That left you foundering on the shore.
What odds is it now about Troy's destruction
  With you on the flagstones upside down,
Who never injured or hurt a creature
  And preferred bog-water to any wine?

349

Bittern, bittern, your end was awful,
    Your perished skull there on the road,
You that would call me every morning
    With your gargler's song as you guzzled mud.
And that's what's ahead of your brother Cahal
    (You know what they say about me and the
        stuff),
But they've got it wrong, and the truth is simple:
    A drop would have saved that croaker's life.

I am saddened, bittern, and broken-hearted
    To find you in scrags in the rushy tufts
And the big rats scampering down the ratpaths
    To wake your carcass and have their fun.
If you could have got word to me in time, bird,
    That you were in trouble and craved a sup
I'd have struck the fetters off those lough waters
    And have wet your thrapple with the blow I
        struck.

Your common birds do not concern me,
    The blackbird, say, or the thrush or crane,
But the yellow bittern, my heartsome namesake
    With my looks and locks, he's the one I
        mourn.
Constantly he was drinking, drinking,
    And by all accounts I am just the same,
But every drop I get I'll down it
    For fear I might get my end from drouth.

The woman I love says to give it up now
    Or else I'll go to an early grave,
But I say no and keep resisting
    For taking drink's what prolongs your days.
You saw for yourselves a while ago
    What happened the bird when its throat went
        dry;

So, my friends and neighbours, let it flow:
You'll be stood no rounds in eternity.

translated by Seamus Heaney

ROBERT BURNS

[1790]   # Tam o' Shanter

Of Brownyis and of Bogillis full is this buke.
GAWIN DOUGLAS

street traders   When chapman billies leave the street,
thirsty   And drouthy neebors, neebors meet,
As market-days are wearing late,
An' folk begin to tak the gate;
ale   While we sit bousing at the nappy,
drunk / extremely   And getting fou and unco happy,
We think na on the lang Scots miles,
bogs / passes   The mosses,waters, slaps, and styles,
That lie between us and our hame,
Where sits our sulky sullen dame,
Gathering her brows like gathering storm,
Nursing her wrath to keep it warm.

This truth fand honest *Tam o' Shanter*,
As he frae Ayr ae night did canter,
(Auld Ayr, wham ne'er a town surpasses,
For honest men and bonny lasses.)

O *Tam*! hadst thou but been sae wise,
As ta'en thy ain wife *Kate*'s advice!
rascal   She tauld thee weel thou was a skellum,
babbler   A blethering, blustering, drunken blellum;
That frae November till October,
Ae market-day thou was nae sober;
every meal-grinding   That ilka melder, wi' the miller,
Thou sat as lang as thou had siller;
horse / shod   That every naig was ca'd a shoe on,

The smith and thee gat roaring fou on;
That at the L–d's house, even on Sunday,
Thou drank wi' Kirkton Jean till Monday.
She prophesied that late or soon,
Thou would be found deep drown'd in Doon;
evil spirits / dark   Or catch'd wi' warlocks in the mirk,
By *Alloway*'s auld haunted kirk.

makes me weep   Ah, gentle dames! it gars me greet,
To think how mony counsels sweet,
How mony lengthen'd sage advices,
The husband frae the wife despises!

But to our tale: Ae market-night,
Tam had got planted unco right;
Fast by an ingle, bleezing finely,
frothing ale   Wi' reaming swats, that drank divinely;
shoe-maker   And at his elbow, Souter *Johnny*,
His ancient, trusty, drouthy crony;
Tam lo'ed him like a vera brither;
They had been fou for weeks thegither.
The night drave on wi' sangs and clatter;
And ay the ale was growing better:
The landlady and *Tam* grew gracious,
Wi' favours, secret, sweet, and precious:
The Souter tauld his queerest stories;
The landlord's laugh was ready chorus:
The storm without might rair and rustle,
Tam did na mind the storm a whistle.

Care, mad to see a man sae happy,
E'en drown'd himsel amang the nappy:
As bees flee hame wi' lades o' treasure,
The minutes wing'd their way wi' pleasure:
Kings may be blest, but *Tam* was glorious,
O'er a' the ills o' life victorious!

But pleasures are like poppies spread,
You seize the flower, its bloom is shed;
Or like the snow falls in the river,
A moment white – then melts for ever;
Or like the borealis race,
That flit ere you can point their place;
Or like the rainbow's lovely form
Evanishing amid the storm. –
Nae man can tether time or tide;

must The hour approaches *Tam* maun ride;
That hour, o' night's black arch the key-stane,
That dreary hour he mounts his beast in;
And sic a night he taks the road in,
As ne'er poor sinner was abroad in.

The wind blew as 'twad blawn its last;
The rattling showers rose on the blast;
The speedy gleams the darkness swallow'd;
Loud, deep, and lang, the thunder bellow'd:
That night, a child might understand,
The Deil had business on his hand.

Weel mounted on his gray mare, *Meg*,
A better never lifted leg,

hurried / puddle *Tam* skelpit on thro' dub and mire,
Despising wind, and rain, and fire;

at times Whiles holding fast his gude blue bonnet;
Whiles crooning o'er some auld Scots sonnet;
Whiles glowring round wi' prudent cares,

phantoms Lest bogles catch him unawares:
Kirk-Alloway was drawing nigh,

owlets Whare ghaists and houlets nightly cry.–

By this time he was cross the ford,
was smothered Whare, in the snaw, the chapman smoor'd;
birches / big And past the birks and meikle stane,
Whare drunken *Charlie* brak 's neck-bane;

353

And thro' the whins, and by the cairn,
Whare hunters fand the murder'd bairn;
And near the thorn, aboon the well,
Whare *Mungo*'s mither hang'd hersel.–
Before him *Doon* pours all his floods;
The doubling storm roars thro' the woods;
The lightnings flash from pole to pole;
Near and more near the thunders roll:
When, glimmering thro' the groaning trees,
Kirk-Alloway seem'd in a bleeze;

aperture Thro' ilka bore the beams were glancing;
And loud resounded mirth and dancing. –

Inspiring bold *John Barleycorn*!
What dangers thou canst make us scorn!
two-penny ale Wi' tippeny, we fear nae evil;
whisky Wi' usquabae, we'll face the devil!–
The swats sae ream'd in *Tammie*'s noddle,
not a farthing for devils Fair play, he car'd na deils a boddle.
But *Maggie* stood right sair astonish'd,
Till, by the heel and hand admonish'd,
She ventured forward on the light;
And, vow! *Tam* saw an unco sight!
Warlocks and witches in a dance;
brand Nae cotillion brent new frae *France*,
But hornpipes, jigs, strathspeys, and reels,
Put life and mettle in their heels.
window-seat A winnock-bunker in the east,
There sat auld Nick, in shape o' beast;
shaggy A towzie tyke, black, grim, and large,
To gie them music was his charge:
He screw'd the pipes and gart them skirl,
vibrate Till roof and rafters a' did dirl. –
Coffins stood round, like open presses,
That shaw'd the dead in their last dresses;
magic And by some devilish cantraip slight

354

Each in its cauld hand held a light. –
By which heroic *Tam* was able
To note upon the haly table,

A murderer's banes in gibbet airns;
Twa span-lang, wee, unchristen'd bairns;
A thief, new-cutted frae a rape,
Wi' his last gasp his gab did gape;
Five tomahawks, wi' blude red-rusted;
Five scymitars, wi' murder crusted;
A garter, which a babe had strangled;
A knife, a father's throat had mangled,
Whom his ain son o' life bereft,
The grey hairs yet stack to the heft;
Wi' mair o' horrible and awefu',
Which even to name wad be unlawfu'.

As *Tammie* glow'rd, amaz'd, and curious,
The mirth and fun grew fast and furious:
The piper loud and louder blew;
The dancers quick and quicker flew;

joined arms   They reel'd, they set, they cross'd, they cleekit,
woman   Till ilka carlin swat and reckit,
cast off her clothes   And coost her duddies to the wark,
went quickly / shift   And linket at it in her sark!

Now, *Tam*, O *Tam*! had thae been queans,
A' plump and strapping in their teens,

greasy flannel   Their sarks, instead o' creeshie flannen,
Been snaw-white seventeen hunder linnen!

these   Thir breeks o' mine, my only pair,
That ance were plush, o' gude blue hair,

buttocks   I wad hae gi'en them off my hurdies,
girls   For ae blink o' the bonie burdies!

But wither'd beldams, auld and droll,

wretched / wean   Rigwoodie hags wad spean a foal,

crooked staff	Lowping and flinging on a crummock,
	I wonder didna turn thy stomach.
well	But *Tam* kend what was what fu' brawlie,
comely	There was ae winsome wench and wawlie,
corps	That night enlisted in the core,
known	(Lang after kend on *Carrick* shore;
	For mony a beast to dead she shot,
	And perish'd mony a bony boat,
barley	And shook baith meikle corn and bear,
	And kept the country-side in fear:)
short / coarse cloth	Her cutty sark, o' Paisley harn,
	That while a lassie she had worn,
	In longitude tho' sorely scanty,
haughty	It was her best, and she was vauntie. –
	Ah! little kend thy reverend grannie,
bought	That sark she coft for her wee Nannie,
	Wi' twa pund Scots, ('twas a' her riches),
	Wad ever grac'd a dance of witches!
lower	But here my Muse her wing maun cour;
	Sic flights are far beyond her pow'r;
	To sing how Nannie lap and flang,
	(A souple jade she was, and strang),
	And how *Tam* stood, like ane bewitch'd,
	And thought his very een enrich'd;
fidgeted	Even Satan glowr'd, and fidg'd fu' fain,
jerked	And hotch'd and blew wi' might and main:
	Till first ae caper, syne anither,
lost	*Tam* tint his reason a' thegither,
	And roars out, 'Weel done, Cutty-sark!'
	And in an instant all was dark:
	And scarcely had he Maggie rallied,
	When out the hellish legion sallied.
fuss	As bees bizz out wi' angry fyke,
hive	When plundering herds assail their byke;

As open pussie's mortal foes,
When, pop! she starts before their nose;
As eager runs the market-crowd,
When 'Catch the thief!' resounds aloud;
So Maggie runs, the witches follow,
Wi' mony an eldritch skreech and hollow.

Ah, *Tam*! Ah, *Tam*! thou'll get thy fairin!
In hell they'll roast thee like a herrin!
In vain thy *Kate* awaits thy comin!
Kate soon will be a woefu' woman!
Now, do thy speedy utmost, Meg,
And win the key-stane of the brig;
There at them thou thy tail may toss,
A running stream they dare na cross.
But ere the key-stane she could make,
The fient a tail she had to shake!
For Nannie, far before the rest,
Hard upon noble Maggie prest,
And flew at *Tam* wi' furious ettle;
But little wist she Maggie's mettle–
Ae spring brought off her master hale,
But left behind her ain gray tail:
The carlin claught her by the rump,
And left poor Maggie scarce a stump.

Now, wha this tale o' truth shall read,
Ilk man and mother's son, take heed:
Whene'er to drink you are inclin'd,
Or cutty-sarks run in your mind,
Think, ye may buy the joys o'er dear,
Remember Tam o' Shanter's mare.

hare's

hideous

gift from a fair, i.e. just deserts

devil

purpose

whole

[1780] *from* The Midnight Court

I used to wade through heavy dews
On the riverbank, in the grassy meadows,
Beside the woods, in a glen apart
As the morning light lit sky and heart
And sky and heart kept growing lighter
At the sight of Graney's clear lough water.
The lift of the mountains there! Their brows
Shining and stern in serried rows!
My withered heart would start to quicken,
Everything small in me, hardbitten,
Everything hurt and needy and shrewd
Lifted its eyes to the top of the wood
Past flocks of ducks on a glassy bay
And a swan there too in all her glory;
Jumping fish in the heady light
And the perch's belly flashing white.
The sheen of the lough, the grumble and roar
Of the blue-black waves as they rolled ashore.
There'd be chirruping birds from tree to tree
And leaping deer in the woods nearby,
Sounding of horns, the dashing crowd
As the hounds gave tongue and Reynard fled.

Yesterday morning the sky was clear,
The sun flamed up in the house of Cancer
With the night behind it, fit to take on
The work of the day that had to be done.
Leafy branches were all around me,
Shooting grasses and growths abounded;
There were green plants climbing and worts and
    weeds
That would gladden your mind and clear your
    head.

I was tired out, dead sleepy and slack,
So I lay at my length on the flat of my back
With my head well propped, my limbs at ease
In a nest in a ditch beside the trees.
The minute I closed my eyes, I drowsed.
My lids were locked, I couldn't be roused.
I was hidden from flies, felt safe and sound
When a nightmare swarmed and gathered
    around,
Battered me, flattened me, dragged me down
Through weltering sleep and left me stunned.
But my rest was short for next there comes
A sound from the ground like the roll of drums,
A wind from the north, a furious rout
And the lough in a sulphurous thunderlight.
And then comes looming into view
And steering towards me along the bay
This hefty menacing dangerwoman,
Bony and huge, a terrible hallion.
Her height, I'd say, to the nearest measure,
Was six or seven yards or more,
muck / spatters   With a swatch of her shawl all clabber and japs
muddy gaps   Streeling behind in the muck and slaps.
It was awe-inspiring just to see her,
So hatchet-faced and scarred and sour –
yawning   With her ganting gums and her mouth in a twist
She'd have put the wind up man or beast.
And Lord of Fates! Her hand was a vise
Clamped on a towering staff or mace
With a spike on top and a flange of brass
That indicated her bailiff's powers.

Her words were grim when she got started.
'Get up,' she said, 'and on your feet!
What do you think gives you the right
To shun the crowds and the sitting court?

A court of justice, truly founded,
And not the usual rigged charade,
But a fair and clement court of women
Of the gentlest stock and regimen.
The Irish race should be grateful always
For such a bench, agreed and wise,
That's been sitting now two days and a night
In the spacious fort on Graney Height.

Their king, moreover, has taken to heart
The state of the country; he feels its hurt
As if it were his own, and all
His entourage are aghast as well.
It's goodbye to freedom and ancient right,
To honest dealing and leadership:
The ground ripped off and nothing put back,
Weeds in the field once crop is stacked.
With the best of the people leaving the land,
Graft has the under- and upper hand.
Just line your pockets, a wink and a nod,
And to hell with the poor! Their backs are broad.
Alas for the plight of the underclass
And the system's victims who seek redress:
Their one recourse is the licensed robber
With his legalese and his fancy slabber,
Lawyers corrupt, their standards gone,
Favouritism the way it's done,
The bar disgraced, truth compromised,
Nothing but kick-backs, bribes and lies.

To add to which, the whole assembly
Decreed on the Bible this very day:
The youth has failed, declined, gone fallow –
A censure, sir, that pertains to you.
In living memory, with birth rates fallen
And marriage in Ireland on the wane,
The country's life has been dissipated,

Pillage and death have left it wasted.
Blame arrogant kings, blame emigration,
But it's you and your spunkless generation.
You're a source blocked off that won't refill.
You have failed your women, one and all.

Think of the way they're made and moulded,
The flush and zest in their flesh and blood –
Those easy ladies half on offer
And the big strait-laced ones, all ignored.
Why aren't they all consoled and gravid,
In full proud sail with their breasts in bud?
Say but the word and the clustered fruit
Will be piled like windfalls round your feet.

So the meeting pondered the country's crisis
And the best opinions agreed on this:
That one of their own should be deputed
To come back here to adjudicate.
Then Aevill rises, as Munster's guardian
And Craglee's peerless fairy queen
And offers to leave the fairy palace
And go to Thomond to hear the case.
And, honest princess, she makes a promise
To come down hard on the law's abuse.
Might without right to be defeated
And right as right reinstated straight.
So take it from me, you can grease the palm
Of pimp or madam or sycophant
But it won't avail for it's not an inch
Now that Her Grace is boss of the bench.
Already at Feakle the court's in session
That you must answer. So move. Shove on!
Move it. Faster! Don't whinge or blurt.
Move, or I'll drag your ass in the dirt.'

With that she stuck her crook in my cape
And hooked me behind and heaved me up
And we went like hell over glen and hill
To Moinmoy Church, by the gable wall.

And there (I am sure) lit torches showed
A handsome, grand, well-built abode,
A stately, steadfast, glittering space,
Accessible and commodious.
And I saw a lovely vision woman
Ensconced on the bench of law and freedom,
And saw her fierce, fleet guard of honour
Rank upon rank in throngs around her.
I saw then too rooms filling full,
Crowding with women from wall to wall,
And saw this other heavenly beauty
With her lazy eye, on her dignity,
Seductive, pouting, with curling locks,
Biding her time in the witness box.
Her hair spilled down, loosed tress on tress,
And a hurt expression marked her face;
She was full of fight, with a glinting eye,
Hot on the boil, ill-set and angry –
Yet for all her spasms, she couldn't speak
For her hefts and huffing had made her weak.
She looked like death or a living death wish
She was so cried out; but straight as a rush,
She stood to the fore as a witness stands
Flailing and wailing and wringing hands.
And she kept it up; she raved and screeched
Till sighing restored her powers of speech.
Then her downlook went, her colour rose,
She dried her eyes and commenced as follows:

'A thousand welcomes! And bless Your Highness!
Aevill of Crag, our prophetess!
Our daylight's light, our moon forever,

Our hope of life when the weeping's over!
O head of all the hosted sisters,
endure Thomond can thole no more! Assist us!
My cause, my case, the reason why
My plea's prolonged so endlessly
Until I'm raving and round the twist
Like a maenad whirled in a swirl of mist –
The reason why is the unattached
And unprovided for, unmatched
Women I know, like flowers in a bed
Nobody's dibbled or mulched or weeded
Or trimmed or watered or ever tended;
So here they are, unhusbanded,
Unasked, untouched, beyond conception –
And, needless to say, I'm no exception.
I'm scorched and tossed, a sorry case
Of nerves and drives and neediness,
Depressed, obsessed, awake at night,
Unused, unsoothed, disconsolate,
A throbbing ache, a dumb discord,
My mind and bed like a kneading board.
O Warden of the Crag, incline!
Observe the plight of Ireland's women,
For if things go on like this, then look it!
The men will have to be abducted!'

[. . .]

Bathed in an aura of morning light,
Her Grace on the bench got up to her feet;
Beautiful, youthful, full of poise,
She cleared her throat and raised her voice,
Then clenched her fists with definite menace
And ordered the bailiff to call for silence.
The court complied; they sat entranced
As her lovely fluent lips pronounced:

'To my mind, girl, you've stated your case
With point and force. You deserve redress.
So I here enact a law for women:
Men not mated by twenty-one
To be sought, pursued, and hunted down,
Tied to this tree beside the headstone,
Their vests stripped off, their jackets ripped,
Their backs and asses scourged and whipped.
But the long-in-the-tooth and the dry-in-
    marrow,
The ones whose harrow-pins won't harrow,
Who pen the pent and lock away
The ram that's rampant in their body,
Keeping in hand what should go the rounds
And fencing off the pleasure grounds –
Their nemesis I leave to you
Whose hearths they'd neither fan nor blow.
Dear natural sexual women, think!
Consult your gender, mind and instinct.
Take cognizance. Co-operate.
For I here invest you with the right
(To be exercised to the breaking point)
And powers of violent punishment.'

[...]

She stopped, but still her starry gaze
Transfixed me in a kind of daze
I couldn't shake off. My head went light,
I suffered cramps and a fainting fit.
The whole earth seemed to tilt and swing,
My two ears sang from the tongue-lashing
And then the awful targe who'd brought me,
The plank-armed bailiff, reached and caught me
Up by the ears and scruff of the neck
And dragged me struggling into the dock.
Where next comes skipping, clapping hands,

The lass who had aired her love-demands
And says to my face, 'You hardened chaw,
I've waited long, now I'll curry you raw!

[. . .]

And you, dear women, you must assist.
So rope him, Una, and all the rest –
Anna, Maura – take hold and bind him.
Double twist his arms behind him.
Remember all the sentence called for
And execute it to the letter.
Maeve and Sive and Sheila! Maureen!
Knot the rope till it tears the skin.
Let Mr Brian take what we give,
Let him have it. Flay him alive
And don't draw back when you're drawing
    blood.
Test all of your whips against his manhood.
Cut deep. No mercy. Make him squeal.
Leave him in strips from head to heel
Until every single mother's son
In the land of Ireland learns the lesson.

And it only seems both right and fitting
To note the date of this special sitting
So calm your nerves and start computing:
A thousand minus a hundred and ten –
Take what that gives you, double it, then
Your product's the year.' She'd lifted her pen
And her hand was poised to ratify
The fate that was looking me straight in the eye.
She was writing it down, the household guard
Sat at attention, staring hard
As I stared back. Then my dreaming ceased
And I started up, awake, released.

translated by Seamus Heaney

365

[1940–42]

Behaviour of Money

Money was once well known, like a townhall or
    the sky
or a river East and West, and you lived one side or
    the other;
Love and Death dealt shocks,
but for all the money that passed, the wise man
    knew his brother.

But money changed. Money came jerking
    roughly alive;
went battering round the town with a boozy,
    zigzag tread.
A clear case for arrest;
and the crowds milled and killed for the pound
    notes that he shed.

And the town changed, and the mean and the
    little lovers of gain
inflated like a dropsy, and gone were the
    courtesies
that eased the market day;
saying, 'buyer' and 'seller' was saying, 'enemies'.

The poor were shunted nearer to beasts. The cops
    recruited.
The rich became a foreign community. Up there
    leaped
quiet folk gone nasty,
quite strangely distorted, like a photograph that
    has slipped.

Hearing the drunken roars of Money from down
    the street,
'What's to become of us?' the people in bed would
    cry:

'And oh, the thought strikes chill;
what's to become of the world if Money should
    suddenly die?

Should suddenly take a toss and go down crack
    on his head?
If the dance suddenly finished, if they stopped the
    runaway bus,
if the trees stopped racing away?
If our hopes come true and he dies, what's to
    become of us?

Shall we recognize each other, crowding around
    the body?
And as we go stealing off in search of the town we
    have known
– what a job for the Sanitary Officials;
the sprawled body of Money, dead, stinking,
    alone!'

Will X contrive to lose the weasel look in his eyes?
Will the metal go out of the voice of Y? Shall we all
    turn back
to men, like Circe's beasts?
Or die? Or dance in the street the day that the
    world goes crack?

ABRAHAM COWLEY

[1656]   Drinking

The thirsty Earth soaks up the Rain,
And drinks, and gapes for drink again.
The Plants soak up the Earth, and are
With constant drinking fresh and fair.
The Sea itself, which one would think
Should have but little need of Drink,
Drinks ten thousand Rivers up,

So filled that they o'erflow the Cup.
The busy Sun (and one would guess
By his drunken fiery face no less)
Drinks up the Sea, and when he has done,
The Moon and Stars drink up the Sun.
They drink and dance by their own light,
They drink and revel all the night.
Nothing in Nature's sober found,
But an eternal Health goes round.
Fill up the Bowl, then fill it high,
Fill all the Glasses there, for why
Should every creature drink but I,
Why, Man of Morals, tell me why?

ANONYMOUS (IRISH)

[12th century] ## The Vision of Mac Conglinne

A vision that appeared to me,
An apparition wonderful
    I tell to all:
There was a coracle all of lard
Within a Port of New-Milk Lake
    Upon the world's smooth sea.

We went into that man-of-war,
'Twas warrior-like to take the road
    O'er ocean's heaving waves.
Our oar-strokes then we pulled
Across the level of the main,
Throwing the sea's harvest up
    Like honey, the sea-soil.

The fort we reached was beautiful,
With works of custards thick,
    Beyond the lake.
Fresh butter was the bridge in front,

The rubble dyke was fair white wheat,
  Bacon the palisade.

Stately, pleasantly it sat,
A compact house and strong.
  Then I went in:
The door of it was hung beef,
The threshold was dry bread,
  Cheese-curds the walls . . .

Behind it was a well of wine,

drink of ale and honey   Beer and bragget in streams,
  Each full pool to the taste.
Malt in smooth wavy sea
Over a lard-spring's brink
  Flowed through the floor . . .

A row of fragrant apple-trees,
An orchard in its pink-tipped bloom,
  Between it and the hill.
A forest tall of real leeks,
Of onions and of carrots, stood
  Behind the house.

Within, a household generous,
A welcome of red, firm-fed men,
  Around the fire:
Seven bead-strings and necklets seven
Of cheeses and of bits of tripe
  Round each man's neck.

The Chief in cloak of beefy fat
Beside his noble wife and fair
  I then beheld.
Below the lofty cauldron's spit
Then the Dispenser I beheld,
  His fleshfork on his back.

      translated by Kuno Meyer

JOHN DAVIES OF HEREFORD

[early 17th century]   'If there were, oh! an Hellespont
of cream'

If there were, oh! an Hellespont of cream
Between us, milk-white mistress, I would swim
To you, to show to both my love's extreme,
Leander-like, – yea! dive from brim to brim.
But met I with a buttered pippin-pie
Floating upon 't, that would I make my boat
To waft me to you without jeopardy,
Though sea-sick I might be while it did float.
Yet if a storm should rise, by night or day,
Of sugar-snows and hail of caraways,
Then, if I found a pancake in my way,
It like a plank should bring me to your kays;
    Which having found, if they tobacco kept,
    The smoke should dry me well before I slept.

JONATHAN SWIFT

[1739]   *from* Verses on the Death of Dr Swift

The time is not remote, when I
Must by the course of nature die;
When I foresee my special friends
Will try to find their private ends,
Though it is hardly understood
Which way my death can do them good;
Yet thus, methinks, I hear 'em speak:
'See, how the Dean begins to break:
Poor gentleman, he droops apace,
You plainly find it in his face;
That old vertigo in his head
Will never leave him, till he's dead.
Besides, his memory decays,
He recollects not what he says;

He cannot call his friends to mind,
Forgets the place where last he dined;
Plies you with stories o'er and o'er:
He told them fifty times before.
How does he fancy we can sit
To hear his out-of-fashioned wit?
But he takes up with younger folks,
Who for his wine will bear his jokes:
Faith, he must make his stories shorter,
Or change his comrades once a quarter;
In half the time, he talks them round;
There must another set be found.

   'For poetry, he's past his prime,
He takes an hour to find a rhyme:
His fire is out, his wit decayed,
His fancy sunk, his Muse a jade.
I'd have him throw away his pen;
But there's no talking to some men.'

   And then their tenderness appears,
By adding largely to my years:
'He's older than he would be reckoned,
And well remembers Charles the Second.

   'He hardly drinks a pint of wine;
And that, I doubt, is no good sign.
His stomach too begins to fail:
Last year we thought him strong and hale;
But now he's quite another thing;
I wish he may hold out till spring.'

   Then hug themselves, and reason thus:
'It is not yet so bad with us.'

[...]

   Behold the fatal day arrive!
'How is the Dean?' 'He's just alive.'
Now the departing prayer is read.
'He hardly breathes.' 'The Dean is dead.'

Before the passing-bell begun,
The news through half the town has run.
'O, may we all for death prepare!
What has he left? And who's his heir?'
'I know no more than what the news is,
'Tis all bequeathed to public uses.'
'To public use! A perfect whim!
What had the public done for him?
Mere envy, avarice, and pride!
He gave it all. – But first he died.
And had the Dean, in all the nation,
No worthy friend, no poor relation?
So ready to do strangers good,
Forgetting his own flesh and blood?'

[. . .]

 'He gave the little wealth he had
To build a house for fools and mad,
And showed by one satiric touch,
No nation wanted it so much. [. . .]'

ANONYMOUS (IRISH)

from The Lament of the Old Woman of Beare

Youth's summer in which we were
I have spent with its autumn:
Winter-age which overwhelms all men,
To me has come its beginning.

Amen! Woe is me!
Every acorn has to drop.
After feasting by shining candles
To be in the gloom of a prayer-house!

I had my day with kings
Drinking mead and wine:

Today I drink whey-water
Among shrivelled old hags.

I see upon my cloak the hair of old age,
My reason has beguiled me:
Grey is the hair that grows through my skin –
'Tis thus I am an old hag.

The flood-wave
And the second ebb-tide –
They have all reached me,
So that I know them well.

The flood-wave
Will not reach the silence of my kitchen:
Though many are my company in darkness,
A hand has been laid upon them all.

O happy the isle of the great sea
Which the flood reaches after the ebb!
As for me, I do not expect
Flood after ebb to come to me.

There is scarce a little place today
That I can recognise:
What was on flood
Is all on ebb.

translated by Kuno Meyer

ANTHONY RAFTERY

[early 19th century] ### 'I am Raftery the poet'

I am Raftery the poet,
Full of hope and love,
My eyes without sight,
My mind without torment.

Going west on my journey
By the light of my heart,

Tired and weary
To the end of the road.

Behold me now
With my back to the wall,
Playing music
To empty pockets.

translated by James Stephens

ANONYMOUS

[1600]   ## Fine Knacks for Ladies

Fine knacks for ladies, cheap, choice, brave and
    new!
   Good pennyworths, – but money cannot move:
I keep a fair but for the Fair to view, –
   A beggar may be liberal of love.
Though all my wares be trash, the heart is true,
           The heart is true.

Great gifts are guiles and look for gifts again;
   My trifles come as treasures from my mind:
It is a precious jewel to be plain;
   Sometimes in shell the orient'st pearls we find.
Of others take a sheaf, of me a grain!
           Of me a grain!

Within this pack pins, points, laces, and gloves,
   And divers toys fitting a country fair;
But in my heart, where duty serves and loves,
   Turtles and twins, court's brood, a heavenly
    pair –
Happy the heart that thinks of no removes!
           Of no removes!

[13th century] ## 'I am Taliesin. I sing perfect metre'

I am Taliesin. I sing perfect metre,
Which will last to the end of the world.
My patron is Elphin ...

I know why there is an echo in a hollow;
Why silver gleams; why breath is black; why liver
  is bloody;
Why a cow has horns; why a woman is
  affectionate;
Why milk is white; why holly is green;
Why a kid is bearded; why the cow-parsnip is
  hollow;
Why brine is salt; why ale is bitter;
Why the linnet is green and berries red;
Why a cuckoo complains; why it sings;
I know where the cuckoos of summer are in
  winter.
I know what beasts there are at the bottom of the
  sea;
How many spears in battle; how many drops in a
  shower;
Why a river drowned Pharaoh's people;
Why fishes have scales,
Why a white swan has black feet ...

I have been a blue salmon,
I have been a dog, a stag, a roebuck on the
  mountain,
A stock, a spade, an axe in the hand,
A stallion, a bull, a buck,
A grain which grew on a hill,
I was reaped, and placed in an oven,
I fell to the ground when I was being roasted
And a hen swallowed me.

For nine nights was I in her crop.
I have been dead, I have been alive,
I am Taliesin.

translated by Ifor Williams

WALT WHITMAN

[1855]   *from* Song of Myself

I

I celebrate myself, and sing myself,
And what I assume you shall assume,
For every atom belonging to me as good belongs
     to you.

I loafe and invite my soul,
I lean and loafe at my ease observing a spear of
     summer grass.
My tongue, every atom of my blood, form'd from
     this soil, this air,
Born here of parents born here from parents the
     same, and their parents the same,
I, now thirty-seven years old in perfect health
     begin,
Hoping to cease not till death.

Creeds and schools in abeyance,
Retiring back a while sufficed at what they are,
     but never forgotten,
I harbor for good or bad, I permit to speak at every
     hazard,
Nature without check with original energy.

II

Houses and rooms are full of perfumes, the
     shelves are crowded with perfumes,

I breathe the fragrance myself and know it and
    like it,
The distillation would intoxicate me also, but I
    shall not let it.

The atmosphere is not a perfume, it has no taste
    of the distillation, it is odorless,
It is for my mouth forever, I am in love with it,
I will go to the bank by the wood and become
    undisguised and naked,
I am mad for it to be in contact with me.
The smoke of my own breath,
Echoes, ripples, buzz'd whispers, love-root, silk-
    thread, crotch and vine,
My respiration and inspiration, the beating of my
    heart, the passing of blood and air through my
    lungs,
The sniff of green leaves and dry leaves, and of the
    shore and dark-color'd sea-rocks, and of hay in
    the barn,
The sound of the belch'd words of my voice loos'd
    to the eddies of the wind,
A few light kisses, a few embraces, a reaching
    around of arms,
The play of shine and shade on the trees as the
    supple boughs wag,
The delight alone or in the rush of the streets, or
    along the fields and hill-sides,
The feeling of health, the full-noon trill, the song
    of me rising from bed and meeting the sun.

Have you reckon'd a thousand acres much? have
    you reckon'd the earth much?
Have you practis'd so long to learn to read?
Have you felt so proud to get at the meaning of
    poems?

Stop this day and night with me and you shall
    possess the origin of all poems,
You shall possess the good of the earth and sun,
    (there are millions of suns left,)
You shall no longer take things at second or third
    hand, nor look through the eyes of the dead,
    nor feed on the spectres in books,
You shall not look through my eyes either, nor
    take things from me,
You shall listen to all sides and filter them from
    your self.

III

I have heard what the talkers were talking, the
    talk of the beginning and the end,
But I do not talk of the beginning or the end.

There was never any more inception than there is
    now,
Nor any more youth or age than there is now,
And will never be any more perfection than there
    is now,
Nor any more heaven or hell than there is now.

Urge and urge and urge,
Always the procreant urge of the world.

Out of the dimness opposite equals advance,
    always substance and increase, always sex,
Always a knit of identity, always distinction,
    always a breed of life.

To elaborate is no avail, learn'd and unlearn'd
    feel that it is so.

Sure as the most certain sure, plumb in the
    uprights, well entretied, braced in the beams,
Stout as a horse, affectionate, haughty, electrical,
I and this mystery here we stand.

Clear and sweet is my soul, and clear and sweet is
all that is not my soul.

Lack one lacks both, and the unseen is proved by
the seen,
Till that becomes unseen and receives proof in its
turn.

Showing the best and dividing it from the worst
age vexes age,
Knowing the perfect fitness and equanimity of
things, while they discuss I am silent, and go
bathe and admire myself.

Welcome is every organ and attribute of me, and
of any man hearty and clean,
Not an inch nor a particle of an inch is vile, and
none shall be less familiar than the rest.

I am satisfied – I see, dance, laugh, sing;
As the hugging and loving bed-fellow sleeps at
my side through the night, and withdraws at
the peep of the day with stealthy tread,
Leaving me baskets cover'd with white towels
swelling the house with their plenty.
Shall I postpone my acceptation and realization
and scream at my eyes,
That they turn from gazing after and down the
road,
And forthwith cipher and show me to a cent,
Exactly the value of one and exactly the value of
two, and which is ahead?

IV

Trippers and askers surround me,
People I meet, the effect upon me of my early life
or the ward and city I live in, or the nation,

The latest dates, discoveries, inventions,
  societies, authors old and new,
My dinner, dress, associates, looks, compliments,
  dues,
The real or fancied indifference of some man or
  woman I love,
The sickness of one of my folks or of myself, or ill-
  doing or loss or lack of money, or depressions
  or exaltations,
Battles, the horrors of fratricidal war, the fever of
  doubtful news, the fitful events:
These come to me days and nights and go from
  me again,
But they are not the Me myself.

Apart from the pulling and hauling stands what I
  am,
Stands amused, complacent, compassionating,
  idle, unitary,
Looks down, is erect, or bends an arm on an
  impalpable certain rest,
Looking with side-curved head curious what will
  come next,
Both in and out of the game and watching and
  wondering at it.

Backward I see in my own days where I sweated
  through fog with linguists and contenders,
I have no mockings or arguments, I witness and
  wait.

v

I believe in you my soul, the other I am must not
  abase itself to you,
And you must not be abased to the other.

Loafe with me on the grass, loose the stop from
    your throat,
Not words, not music or rhyme I want, not
    custom or lecture, not even the best,
Only the lull I like, the hum of your valvèd voice.

I mind how once we lay such a transparent
    summer morning,
How you settled your head athwart my hips and
    gently turn'd over upon me,
And parted the shirt from my bosom-bone, and
    plunged your tongue to my bare-stript heart,
And reach'd till you felt my beard, and reach'd till
    you held my feet.

Swiftly arose and spread around me the peace
    and knowledge that pass all the argument of
    the earth,
And I know that the hand of God is the promise of
    my own,
And I know that the spirit of God is the brother of
    my own,
And that all the men ever born are also my
    brothers, and the women my sisters and lovers,
And that a kelson of the creation is love,
And limitless are leaves stiff or drooping in the
    fields,
And brown ants in the little wells beneath them,
And mossy scabs of the worm fence, heap'd
    stones, elder, mullein and poke-weed.

VI

A child said *What is the grass?* fetching it to me
    with full hands;
How could I answer the child? I do not know
    what it is any more than he.

I guess it must be the flag of my disposition, out of
    hopeful green stuff woven.

Or I guess it is the handkerchief of the Lord,
A scented gift and remembrancer designedly
    dropt,
Bearing the owner's name someway in the
    corners, that we may see and remark, and say
    Whose?

Or I guess the grass is itself a child, the produced
    babe of the vegetation.

Or I guess it is a uniform hieroglyphic,
And it means, Sprouting alike in broad zones and
    narrow zones,
Growing among black folks as among white,
Kanuck, Tuckahoe, Congressman, Cuff, I give
    them the same, I receive them the same.

And now it seems to me the beautiful uncut hair
    of graves.

Tenderly will I use you curling grass,
It may be you transpire from the breasts of young
    men,
It may be if I had known them I would have loved
    them,
It may be you are from old people, or from
    offspring taken soon out of their mothers' laps,
And here you are the mothers' laps.

This grass is very dark to be from the white heads
    of old mothers,
Darker than the colorless beards of old men,
Dark to come from under the faint red roofs of
    mouths.

O I perceive after all so many uttering tongues,
And I perceive they do not come from the roofs of
   mouths for nothing.

I wish I could translate the hints about the dead
   young men and women,
And the hints about old men and mothers, and
   the offspring taken soon out of their laps.

What do you think has become of the young and
   old men?
And what do you think has become of the women
   and children?

They are alive and well somewhere,
The smallest sprout shows there is really no
   death,
And if ever there was it led forward life, and does
   not wait at the end to arrest it,
And ceas'd the moment life appear'd.

All goes onward and outward, nothing collapses,
And to die is different from what any one
   supposed, and luckier.

VII

Has any one supposed it lucky to be born?
I hasten to inform him or her it is just as lucky to
   die, and I know it.

I pass death with the dying and birth with the
   new-wash'd babe, and am not contain'd
   between my hat and boots,
And peruse manifold objects, no two alike and
   every one good,
The earth good and the stars good, and their
   adjuncts all good.

I am not an earth nor an adjunct of an earth,
I am the mate and companion of people, all just as
    immortal and fathomless as myself,
(They do not know how immortal, but I know.)

Every kind for itself and its own, for me mine male
    and female,
For me those that have been boys and that love
    women,
For me the man that is proud and feels how it
    stings to be slighted,
For me the sweet-heart and the old maid, for me
    mothers and the mothers of mothers,
For me lips that have smiles, eyes that have shed
    tears,
For me children and the begetters of children.

Undrape! you are not guilty to me, nor stale nor
    discarded,
I see through the broadcloth and gingham
    whether or no,
And am around, tenacious, acquisitive, tireless,
    and cannot be shaken away.

VIII

The little one sleeps in its cradle,
I lift the gauze and look a long time, and silently
    brush away flies with my hand.
The youngster and the red-faced girl turn aside
    up the busy hill,
I peeringly view them from the top.

The suicide sprawls on the bloody floor of the
    bedroom,
I witness the corpse with its dabbled hair, I note
    where the pistol has fallen.

The blab of the pave, tires of carts, sluff of boot-
soles, talk of the promenaders.
The heavy omnibus, the driver with his
interrogating thumb, the clank of the shod
horses on the granite floor,
The snow-sleighs, clinking, shouted jokes, pelts
of snow-balls,
The hurrahs for popular favorites, the fury of
rous'd mobs,
The flap of the curtain'd litter, a sick man inside
borne to the hospital,
The meeting of enemies, the sudden oath, the
blows and fall,
The excited crowd, the policeman with his star
quickly working his passage to the centre of
the crowd,
The impassive stones that receive and return so
many echoes,
What groans of over-fed or half-starv'd who fall
sunstruck or in fits,
What exclamations of women taken suddenly
who hurry home and give birth to babes,
What living and buried speech is always
vibrating here, what howls restrain'd by
decorum,
Arrests of criminals, slights, adulterous offers
made, acceptances, rejections with convex
lips,
I mind them or the show or resonance of them – I
come and I depart.

IX

The big doors of the country barn stand open and
ready,

The dried grass of the harvest-time loads the
    slow-drawn wagon,
The clear light plays on the brown gray and green
    intertinged,
The armfuls are pack'd to the sagging mow.

I am there, I help, I came stretch'd atop of the
    load,
I felt its soft jolts, one leg reclined on the other,
I jump from the cross-beams and seize the clover
    and timothy,
And roll head over heels and tangle my hair full of
    wisps.

X

Alone far in the wilds and mountains I hunt,
Wandering amazed at my own lightness and
    glee,
In the late afternoon choosing a safe spot to pass
    the night,
Kindling a fire and broiling the fresh-kill'd game,
Falling asleep on the gather'd leaves with my dog
    and gun by my side.

The Yankee clipper is under her sky-sails, she
    cuts the sparkle and scud,
My eyes settle the land, I bend at her prow or
    shout joyously from the deck.

The boatmen and clam-diggers arose early and
    stopt for me,
I tuck'd my trowser-ends in my boots and went
    and had a good time;
You should have been with us that day round the
    chowder-kettle.

I saw the marriage of the trapper in the open air
in the far west, the bride was a red girl,
Her father and his friends sat near cross-legged
and dumbly smoking, they had moccasins to
their feet and large thick blankets hanging
from their shoulders,
On a bank lounged the trapper, he was drest
mostly in skins, his luxuriant beard and curls
protected his neck, he held his bride by the
hand,
She had long eyelashes, her head was bare, her
coarse straight locks descended upon her
voluptuous limbs and reach'd to her feet.

The runaway slave came to my house and stopt
outside,
I heard his motions crackling the twigs of the
woodpile,
Through the swung half-door of the kitchen I
saw him limpsy and weak,
And went where he sat on a log and led him in
and assured him,
And brought water and fill'd a tub for his sweated
body and bruis'd feet,
And gave him a room that enter'd from my own,
and gave him some coarse clean clothes,
And remember perfectly well his revolving eyes
and his awkwardness,
And remember putting plasters on the galls of his
neck and ankles;
He staid with me a week before he was
recuperated and pass'd north,
I had him sit next me at table, my fire-lock lean'd
in the corner.

Twenty-eight young men bathe by the shore,
Twenty-eight young men and all so friendly;
Twenty-eight years of womanly life and all so
   lonesome.

She owns the fine house by the rise of the bank,
She hides handsome and richly drest aft the
   blinds of the window.

Which of the young men does she like the best?
Ah the homeliest of them is beautiful to her.

Where are you off to, lady? for I see you,
You splash in the water there, yet stay stock still
   in your room.

Dancing and laughing along the beach came the
   twenty-ninth bather,
The rest did not see her, but she saw them and
   loved them.

The beards of the young men glisten'd with wet,
   it ran from their long hair,
Little streams pass'd all over their bodies.

An unseen hand also pass'd over their bodies,
It descended tremblingly from their temples and
   ribs.

The young men float on their backs, their white
   bellies bulge to the sun, they do not ask who
   seizes fast to them,
They do not know who puffs and declines with
   pendant and bending arch,
They do not think whom they souse with spray.

The butcher-boy puts off his killing-clothes, or
    sharpens his knife at the stall in the market,
I loiter enjoying his repartee and his shuffle and
    break-down.

Blacksmiths with grimed and hairy chests
    environ the anvil,
Each has his main-sledge, they are all out, there
    is a great heat in the fire,

From the cinder-strew'd threshold I follow their
    movements,
The lithe sheer of their waists plays even with
    their massive arms,
Overhand the hammers swing, overhand so slow,
    overhand so sure,
They do not hasten, each man hits in his place.

XIII

The negro holds firmly the reins of his four
    horses, the block swags underneath on its tied-
    over chain,
The negro that drives the long dray of the stone-
    yard, steady and tall he stands pois'd on one leg
    on the string-piece,
His blue shirt exposes his ample neck and breast
    and loosens over his hip-band,
His glance is calm and commanding, he tosses
    the slouch of his hat away from his forehead,
The sun falls on his crispy hair and mustache,
    falls on the black of his polish'd and perfect
    limbs.

I behold the picturesque giant and love him, and I
do not stop there,
I go with the team also.

In me the caresser of life whenever moving,
backward as well as forward sluing,
To niches aside and junior bending, not a person
or object missing,
Absorbing all to myself and for this song.

Oxen that rattle the yoke and chain or halt in the
leafy shade, what is that you express in your
eyes?
It seems to me more than all the print I have read
in my life.

My tread scares the wood-drake and wood-duck
on my distant and day-long ramble,
They rise together, they slowly circle around.

I believe in those wing'd purposes,
And acknowledge red, yellow, white, playing
within me,
And consider green and violet and the tufted
crown intentional,
And do not call the tortoise unworthy because
she is not something else,
And the jay in the woods never studied the
gamut, yet trills pretty well to me,
And the look of the bay mare shames silliness out
of me.

XIV

The wild gander leads his flock through the cool
night,
Ya-honk he says, and sounds it down to me like an
invitation,

The pert may suppose it meaningless, but I
    listening close,
Find its purpose and place up there toward the
    wintry sky.

The sharp-hoof'd moose of the north, the cat on
    the house-sill, the chickadee, the prairie-dog,
The litter of the grunting sow as they tug at her
    teats,
The brood of the turkey-hen and she with her
    half-spread wings,
I see in them and myself the same old law.
The press of my foot to the earth springs a
    hundred affections,
They scorn the best I can do to relate them.

I am enamour'd of growing out-doors,
Of men that live among cattle or taste of the
    ocean or woods,
Of the builders and steerers of ships and the
    wielders of axes and mauls, and the drivers of
    horses,
I can eat and sleep with them week in and week
    out.

What is commonest, cheapest, nearest, easiest, is
    Me,
Me going in for my chances, spending for vast
    returns,
Adorning myself to bestow myself on the first that
    will take me,
Not asking the sky to come down to my good will,
Scattering it freely forever.

XV

The pure contralto sings in the organ loft,
The carpenter dresses his plank, the tongue of his
    foreplane whistles its wild ascending lisp,
The married and unmarried children ride home
    to their Thanksgiving dinner,
The pilot seizes the king-pin, he heaves down
    with a strong arm,
The mate stands braced in the whale-boat, lance
    and harpoon are ready,
The duck-shooter walks by silent and cautious
    stretches,
The deacons are ordain'd with cross'd hands at
    the altar,
The spinning-girl retreats and advances to the
    hum of the big wheel,
The farmer stops by the bars as he walks on a
    First-day loafe and looks at the oats and rye,
The lunatic is carried at last to the asylum a
    confirm'd case,
(He will never sleep any more as he did in the cot
    in his mother's bed-room;)
The jour printer with gray head and gaunt jaws
    works at his case,
He turns his quid of tobacco while his eyes blurr
    with the manuscript;
The malform'd limbs are tied to the surgeon's
    table,
What is removed drops, horribly in a pail;
The quadroon girl is sold at the auction-stand,
    the drunkard nods by the bar-room stove,
The machinist rolls up his sleeves, the policeman
    travels his beat, the gate-keeper marks who
    pass,

The young fellow drives the express-wagon, (I
love him, though I do not know him;)
The half-breed straps on his light boots to
compete in the race,
The western turkey-shooting draws old and
young, some lean on their rifles, some sit on
logs,
Out from the crowd steps the marksman, takes
his position, levels his piece;
The groups of newly-come immigrants cover the
wharf or levee,
As the woolly-pates hoe in the sugar-field, the
overseer views them from his saddle,
The bugle calls in the ball-room, the gentlemen
run for their partners, the dancers bow to each
other,
The youth lies awake in the cedar-roof'd garret
and harks to the musical rain,
The Wolverine sets traps on the creek that helps
fill the Huron,
The squaw wrapt in her yellow-hemm'd cloth is
offering moccasins and bead-bags for sale,
The connoisseur peers along the exhibition-
gallery with half-shut eyes bent sideways,
As the deck-hands make fast the steamboat the
plank is thrown for the shore-going
passengers,
The young sister holds out the skein while the
elder sister winds it off in a ball, and stops now
and then for the knots,
The one-year wife is recovering and happy
having a week ago borne her first child,
The clean-hair'd Yankee girl works with her
sewing-machine or in the factory or mill,
The paving-man leans on his two-handed
rammer, the reporter's lead flies swiftly over

the note-book, the sign-painter is lettering
     with blue and gold,
The canal boy trots on the tow-path, the book-
     keeper counts at his desk, the shoemaker
     waxes his thread,
The conductor beats time for the band and all the
     performers follow him,
The child is baptized, the convert is making his
     first professions,
The regatta is spread on the bay, the race is
     begun, (how the white sails sparkle!)
The drover watching his drove sings out to them
     that would stray,
The pedler sweats with his pack on his back, (the
     purchaser higgling about the odd cent;)
The bride unrumples her white dress, the minute-
     hand of the clock moves slowly,
The opium-eater reclines with rigid head and
     just-open'd lips,
The prostitute draggles her shawl, her bonnet
     bobs on her tipsy and pimpled neck,
The crowd laugh at her blackguard oaths, the
     men jeer and wink to each other,
(Miserable! I do not laugh at your oaths nor jeer
     you;)
The President holding a cabinet council is
     surrounded by the great Secretaries,
On the piazza walk three matrons stately and
     friendly with twined arms,
The crew of the fish-smack pack repeated layers
     of halibut in the hold,
The Missourian crosses the plains toting his
     wares and his cattle,
As the fare-collector goes through the train he
     gives notice by the jingling of loose change,

The floor-men are laying the floor, the tinners are tinning the roof, the masons are calling for mortar,
In single file each shouldering his hod pass onward the laborers;
Seasons pursuing each other the indescribable crowd is gather'd, it is the fourth of Seventh-month, (what salutes of cannon and small arms!)
Seasons pursuing each other the plougher ploughs, the mower mows, and the winter-grain falls in the ground;
Off on the lakes the pike-fisher watches and waits by the hole in the frozen surface,
The stumps stand thick round the clearing, the squatter strikes deep with his axe,
Flatboatmen make fast towards dusk near the cotton-wood or pecan-trees,
Coon-seekers go through the regions of the Red river or through those drain'd by the Tennessee, or through those of the Arkansas,
Torches shine in the dark that hangs on the Chattahooche or Altamahaw,
Patriarchs sit at supper with sons and grandsons and great-grandsons around them,
In walls of adobie, in canvas tents, rest hunters and trappers after their day's sport,
The city sleeps and the country sleeps,
The living sleep for their time, the dead sleep for their time,
The old husband sleeps by his wife and the young husband sleeps by his wife;
And these tend inward to me, and I tend outward to them,

And such as it is to be of these more or less I am,
And of these one and all I weave the song of
myself.

ALLEN GINSBERG

[1956] A Supermarket in California

What thoughts I have of you tonight, Walt
Whitman, for I walked down the sidestreets
under the trees with a headache self-conscious
looking at the full moon.

In my hungry fatigue, and shopping for
images, I went into the neon fruit supermarket,
dreaming of your enumerations!

What peaches and what penumbras! Whole fa-
milies shopping at night! Aisles full of husbands!
Wives in the avocados, babies in the tomatoes! –
and you, Garcia Lorca, what were you doing
down by the watermelons?

I saw you, Walt Whitman, childless, lonely old
grubber, poking among the meats in the refrig-
erator and eyeing the grocery boys.

I heard you asking questions of each: Who
killed the pork chops? What price bananas? Are
you my Angel?

I wandered in and out of the brilliant stacks of
cans following you, and followed in my ima-
gination by the store detective.

We strode down the open corridors together in
our solitary fancy tasting artichokes, possessing
every frozen delicacy, and never passing the
cashier.

Where are we going, Walt Whitman? The
doors close in an hour. Which way does your
beard point tonight?

(I touch your book and dream of our odyssey in the supermarket and feel absurd.)

Will we walk all night through solitary streets? The trees add shade to shade, lights out in the houses, we'll both be lonely.

Will we stroll dreaming of the lost America of love past blue automobiles in driveways, home to our silent cottage?

Ah, dear father, graybeard, lonely old courage-teacher, what America did you have when Charon quit poling his ferry and you got out on a smoking bank and stood watching the boat disappear on the black waters of Lethe?

WILLIAM LANGLAND (MIDDLE ENGLISH)

[14th century]   *from* Piers Plowman

In a summer season when the sun was mild
I clad myself in clothes as I'd become a sheep;
In the habit of a hermit unholy of works
Walked wide in this world, watching for wonders.
And on a May morning, on Malvern Hills,
There befell me as by magic a marvelous thing:
I was weary of wandering and went to rest
At the bottom of a broad bank by a brook's side,
And as I lay lazily looking in the water
I slipped into a slumber, it sounded so pleasant.
There came to me reclining there a most curious
        dream
That I was in a wilderness, nowhere that I knew;
But as I looked into the east, up high toward the
        sun,
I saw a tower on a hill-top, trimly built,
A deep dale beneath, a dungeon tower in it,
With ditches deep and dark and dreadful to look
        at.

A fair field full of folk I found between them,
Of human beings of all sorts, the high and the low,
Working and wandering as the world requires.
  Some applied themselves to plowing, played
      very rarely,
Sowing seeds and setting plants worked very
      hard;
Won what wasters gluttonously consume.
And some pursued pride, put on proud clothing,
Came all got up in garments garish to see.
To prayers and penance many put themselves,
All for love of our Lord lived hard lives,
Hoping thereafter to have Heaven's bliss –
Such as hermits and anchorites that hold to their
      cells,
Don't care to go cavorting about the countryside,
With some lush livelihood delighting their bodies.
And some made themselves merchants – they
      managed better,
As it seems to our sight that such men prosper.
And some make mirth as minstrels can
And get gold for their music, guiltless, I think.
But jokers and word jugglers, Judas' children,
Invent fantasies to tell about and make fools of
      themselves,
And have whatever wits they need to work if they
      wanted.
What Paul preaches of them I don't dare repeat
      here:

'Who speaks filthy
language'

Qui loquitur turpiloquium is Lucifer's henchman.
Beadsmen and beggars bustled about
Till both their bellies and their bags were
      crammed to the brim;
Staged flytings for their food, fought over beer.
In gluttony, God knows, they go to bed.
And rise up with ribaldry, those Robert's boys.

Sleep and sloth pursue them always.
   Pilgrims and palmers made pacts with each
      other
To seek out Saint James and saints at Rome.
They went on their way with many wise stories,
And had leave to lie all their lives after.
I saw some that said they'd sought after saints:
In every tale they told their tongues were tuned
      to lie
More than to tell the truth – such talk was theirs.
A heap of hermits with hooked staffs
Went off to Walsingham, with their wenches
      behind them.
Great long lubbers that don't like to work
Dressed up in cleric's dress to look different from
      other men
And behaved as they were hermits, to have an
      easy life.
I found friars there – all four of the orders –
Preaching to the people for their own paunches'
      welfare,
Making glosses of the Gospel that would look
      good for themselves;
Coveting copes, they construed it as they pleased.
Many of these Masters may clothe themselves
      richly,
For their money and their merchandise march
      hand in hand.
Since Charity has proved a peddler and
      principally shrives lords,
Many marvels have been manifest within a few
      years.
Unless Holy Church and friars' orders hold
      together better,
The worst misfortune in the world will be welling
      up soon.

A pardoner preached there as if he had priest's
    rights,
Brought out a bull with bishop's seals,
And said he himself could absolve them all
Of failure to fast, of vows they'd broken.
Unlearned men believed him and liked his words,
Came crowding up on knees to kiss his bulls.
He banged them with his brevet and bleared their
    eyes,
And raked in with his parchment-roll rings and
    brooches.
Thus you give your gold for gluttons' well-being,
And squander it on scoundrels schooled in
    lechery.
If the bishop were blessed and worth both his ears,
His seal should not be sent out to deceive the
    people.
– It's nothing to the bishop that the blackguard
    preaches,
And the parish priest and the pardoner split the
    money
That the poor people of the parish would have but
    for them.
  Parsons and parish priests complained to the
    bishop
That their parishes were poor since the
    pestilence-time,
Asked for license and leave to live in London,
And sing Masses there for simony, for silver is
    sweet.
Bishop and Bachelors, both Masters and Doctors,
Who have cures under Christ and their crowns
    shaven
As a sign that they should shrive their
    parishioners,

Preach and pray for them, and provide for the
     poor,
Take lodging in London in Lent and other
     seasons.
Some serve the king and oversee his treasury,
In the Exchequer and in Chancery press charges
     for debts
Involving wards' estates and city-wards, waifs
     and strays.

[. . .]

Yet scores of men stood there in silken coifs
Who seemed to be law-sergeants that served at
     the bar,
Pleaded cases for pennies and impounded the
     law,
And not for love of our Lord once unloosed their
     lips:
You might better measure mist on Malvern Hills
Than get a 'mum' from their mouths till money's
     on the table.
Barons and burgesses and bondmen also
I saw in this assemblage, as you shall hear later;
Bakers and brewers and butchers aplenty,
Weavers of wool and weavers of linen,
Tailors, tinkers, tax-collectors in markets,
Masons, miners, many other craftsmen.
Of all living laborers there leapt forth some,
Such as diggers of ditches that do their jobs badly,
And dawdle away the long day with '*Dieu save
     dame Emme.*'
Cooks and their kitchen-boys kept crying, 'Hot
     pies, hot!
Good geese and pork! Let's go and dine!'
Tavern-keepers told them a tale of the same sort:
'White wine of Alsace and wine of Gascony,

Of the Rhine and of La Rochelle, to wash the roast
    down with.'
All this I saw sleeping, and seven times more.

translated by E. Talbot Donaldson

FRANK O'HARA

[1964]

A Step Away from Them

It's my lunch hour, so I go
for a walk among the hum-colored
cabs. First, down the sidewalk
where laborers feed their dirty
glistening torsos sandwiches
and Coca-Cola, with yellow helmets
on. They protect them from falling
bricks, I guess. Then onto the
avenue where skirts are flipping
above heels and blow up over
grates. The sun is hot, but the
cabs stir up the air. I look
at bargains in wristwatches. There
are cats playing in sawdust.
                    On
to Times Square, where the sign
blows smoke over my head, and higher
the waterfall pours lightly. A
Negro stands in a doorway with a
toothpick, languorously agitating.
A blonde chorus girl clicks: he
smiles and rubs his chin. Everything
suddenly honks: it is 12:40 of
a Thursday.
            Neon in daylight is a
great pleasure, as Edwin Denby would
write, as are light bulbs in daylight.
I stop for a cheeseburger at JULIET'S

Giulietta Masina, wife of
'she's a fine actress' Federico Fellini, *è bell' attrice.*
And chocolate malted. A lady in
foxes on such a day puts her poodle
in a cab.
            There are several Puerto
Ricans on the avenue today, which
makes it beautiful and warm. First
Bunny died, then John Latouche,
then Jackson Pollock. But is the
earth as full as life was full, of them?
And one has eaten and one walks,
past the magazines with nudes
and the posters for BULLFIGHT and
the Manhattan Storage Warehouse,
which they'll soon tear down. I
used to think they had the Armory
Show there.
            A glass of papaya juice
and back to work. My heart is in my
pocket, it is Poems by Pierre Reverdy.

THOMAS GRAY

[1751] ## Elegy Written in a Country Churchyard

The curfew tolls the knell of parting day,
The lowing herd wind slowly o'er the lea,
The ploughman homeward plods his weary way,
And leaves the world to darkness and to me.

Now fades the glimmering landscape on the
    sight,
And all the air a solemn stillness holds,
Save where the beetle wheels his droning flight,
And drowsy tinklings lull the distant folds;

Save that from yonder ivy-mantled tow'r
The moping owl does to the moon complain
Of such as, wand'ring near her secret bow'r,
Molest her ancient solitary reign.

Beneath those rugged elms, that yew-tree's
     shade,
Where heaves the turf in many a mould'ring
     heap,
Each in his narrow cell for ever laid,
The rude forefathers of the hamlet sleep.

The breezy call of incense-breathing morn,
The swallow twitt'ring from the straw-built shed,
The cock's shrill clarion or the echoing horn,
No more shall rouse them from their lowly bed.

For them no more the blazing hearth shall burn,
Or busy housewife ply her evening care:
No children run to lisp their sire's return,
Or climb his knees the envied kiss to share.

Oft did the harvest to their sickle yield,
Their furrow oft the stubborn glebe has broke;
How jocund did they drive their team afield!
How bowed the woods beneath their sturdy
     stroke!

Let not Ambition mock their useful toil,
Their homely joys and destiny obscure;
Nor Grandeur hear, with a disdainful smile,
The short and simple annals of the poor.

The boast of heraldry, the pomp of pow'r,
And all that beauty, all that wealth e'er gave,
Awaits alike the inevitable hour.
The paths of glory lead but to the grave.

Nor you, ye Proud, impute to these the fault,
If Mem'ry o'er their tomb no trophies raise,
Where through the long-drawn aisle and fretted
    vault
The pealing anthem swells the note of praise.

Can storied urn or animated bust
Back to its mansion call the fleeting breath?
Can Honour's voice provoke the silent dust,
Or Flatt'ry soothe the dull cold ear of Death?

Perhaps in this neglected spot is laid
Some heart once pregnant with celestial fire;
Hands that the rod of empire might have swayed,
Or waked to ecstasy the living lyre.

But Knowledge to their eyes her ample page
Rich with the spoils of time did ne'er unroll;
Chill Penury repressed their noble rage,
And froze the genial current of the soul.

Full many a gem of purest ray serene
The dark unfathomed caves of ocean bear:
Full many a flower is born to blush unseen
And waste its sweetness on the desert air.

Some village-Hampden that with dauntless
    breast
The little tyrant of his fields withstood;
Some mute inglorious Milton here may rest,
Some Cromwell guiltless of his country's blood.

Th' applause of list'ning senates to command,
The threats of pain and ruin to despise,
To scatter plenty o'er a smiling land,
And read their hist'ry in a nation's eyes,

Their lot forbade: nor circumscribed alone
Their growing virtues, but their crimes confined;

Forbade to wade through slaughter to a throne,
And shut the gates of mercy on mankind,

The struggling pangs of conscious truth to hide,
To quench the blushes of ingenuous shame,
Or heap the shrine of Luxury and Pride
With incense kindled at the Muse's flame.

Far from the madding crowd's ignoble strife
Their sober wishes never learned to stray;
Along the cool sequestered vale of life
They kept the noiseless tenor of their way.

Yet ev'n these bones from insult to protect
Some frail memorial still erected nigh,
With uncouth rhymes and shapeless sculpture
    decked,
Implores the passing tribute of a sigh.

Their name, their years, spelt by th' unlettered
    muse,
The place of fame and elegy supply:
And many a holy text around she strews,
That teach the rustic moralist to die.

For who to dumb Forgetfulness a prey,
This pleasing anxious being e'er resigned,
Left the warm precincts of the cheerful day,
Nor cast one longing ling'ring look behind?

On some fond breast the parting soul relies,
Some pious drops the closing eye requires;
Ev'n from the tomb the voice of Nature cries,
Ev'n in our ashes live their wonted fires.

For thee who, mindful of th' unhonoured dead,
Dost in these lines their artless tale relate;
If chance, by lonely Contemplation led,
Some kindred spirit shall inquire thy fate,

Haply some hoary-headed swain may say,
'Oft have we seen him at the peep of dawn
Brushing with hasty steps the dews away
To meet the sun upon the upland lawn.

'There at the foot of yonder nodding beech
That wreathes its old fantastic roots so high,
His listless length at noontide would he stretch,
And pore upon the brook that babbles by.

'Hard by yon wood, now smiling as in scorn,
Muttering his wayward fancies he would rove,
Now drooping, woeful wan, like one forlorn,
Or crazed with care, or crossed in hopeless love.

'One morn I missed him on the customed hill,
Along the heath and near his fav'rite tree;
Another came; nor yet beside the rill,
Nor up the lawn, nor at the wood was he;

'The next with dirges due in sad array
Slow through the church-way path we saw him
   borne.
Approach and read (for thou canst read) the lay,
Graved on the stone beneath yon aged thorn.'

THE EPITAPH

Here rests his head upon the lap of earth
A youth to fortune and to fame unknown.
Fair Science frowned not on his humble birth,
And Melancholy marked him for her own.

Large was his bounty and his soul sincere,
Heaven did a recompense as largely send:
He gave to Mis'ry all he had, a tear,
He gained from heav'n ('twas all he wished) a
   friend.

No farther seek his merits to disclose,
Or draw his frailties from their dread abode
(There they alike in trembling hope repose),
The bosom of his Father and his God.

CHARLES OLSON

[1953] At Yorktown

1

At Yorktown the church

at Yorktown the dead

at Yorktown the grass

are live

      at York-town the earth

piles itself in shallows,

declares itself, like water,

by pools and mounds

2

At Yorktown the dead

are soil

at Yorktown the church

is marl

at Yorktown the swallows

dive where it is greenest,

      the hollows

are eyes are flowers, the heather,

equally accurate, is hands

    at Yorktown only the flies

dawdle, like history,

in the sun

  3

at Yorktown the earthworks

braw

at Yorktown the mortars

of brass, weathered green, of mermaids

for handles, of Latin

for texts, scream

without noise

like a gull

  4

At Yorktown the long dead

loosen the earth, heels

sink in, over an abatis

a bird wheels

and time is a shine caught blue

from a martin's

back

ROBERT SEMPILL OF BELTREES

[early 17th century] ## The Life and Death of Habbie Simson, the Piper of Kilbarchan

Kilbarchan now may say alas!
For she hath lost her game and grace,
Both *Trixie* and *The Maiden Trace*;
help   But what remead?
For no man can supply his place:
     Hab Simson's dead.

Now who shall play *The Day it Dawis*,
Or *Hunt's Up*, when the cock he craws?
Or who can for our kirk-town cause
     Stand us in stead?
On bagpipes now nobody blaws
since   Sen Habbie's dead.

Or wha will cause our shearers shear?
play the war-tunes   Wha will bend up the brags of weir,
play more   Bring in the bells, or good play meir
     In time of need?
ask   Hab Simson cou'd, what needs you speir?
     But now he's dead.

nearest   So kindly to his neighbours neast
At Beltan and St Barchan's feast
He blew, and then held up his breast,
feverish   As he were weid:
stop   But now we need not him arrest,
     For Habbie's dead.

At fairs he play'd before the spear-men
kitted-out   All gaily graithed in their gear men:
Steel bonnets, jacks, and swords so clear then
ring of folk   Like any bead:
warriors   Now wha shall play before such weir-men
     Sen Habbie's dead?

At clark-plays when he wont to come
plays composed or acted by clerics or school-men

His Pipe play'd trimly to the drum;
Like bikes of bees he gart it bum,
    And tun'd his reed:
Now all our pipers may sing dumb,
    Sen Habbie's dead.

And at horse races many a day,
Before the black, the brown, the gray,
He gart his pipe, when he did play,
    Baith skirl and skreed:
Now all such pastime's quite away
    Sen Habbie's dead.

He counted was a weil'd wight-man,
And fiercely at football he ran:
At every game the gree he wan
    For pith and speed.
The like of Habbie was na than,
    But now he's dead.

And than, besides his valiant acts,
At bridals he won many placks;
He bobbed ay behind fo'k's backs
    And shook his head.
Now we want many merry cracks
    Sen Habbie's dead.

He was convoyer of the bride,
With Kittock hinging at his side;
About the kirk he thought a pride
    The ring to lead:
But now we may gae but a guide,
    For Habbie's dead.

So well's he keeped his decorum
And all the stots of _Whip-meg-morum_;
He slew a man, and wae's me for him,

put up with the feud	And bure the fead!
got	But yet the man wan hame before him,
	And was not dead.
	And whan he play'd the lasses leugh
tough	To see him teethless, auld, and teugh,
earned	He wan his pipes beside Barcleugh,
	Withouten dread!
plenty wealth	Which after wan him gear eneugh;
	But now he's dead.
urchins gathered	Ay when he play'd the gaitlings gedder'd,
old man boasted	And when he spake, the carl bledder'd,
	On Sabbath days his cap was fedder'd,
proper outfit	A seemly weid;
	In the kirk-yeard his mare stood tedder'd
	Where he lies dead.
	Alas! for him my heart is saur,
dance-tune / share	For of his spring I gat a skair,
	At every play, race, feast, and fair,
without	But guile or greed;
	We need not look for pyping mair,
	Sen Habbie's dead.

SAMUEL JOHNSON

[1740]   An Epitaph upon the Celebrated Claudy
Philips, Musician, Who Died Very Poor

Philips, whose touch harmonious could remove
The pangs of guilty pow'r, and hapless love,
Rest here, distress'd by poverty no more,
Here find that calm, thou gav'st so oft before.
Sleep, undisturb'd, within this peaceful shrine,
Till angels wake thee, with a note like thine.

ANONYMOUS

[traditional]

Johnny, I Hardly Knew Ye

While going the road to sweet Athy,
   Hurroo! Hurroo!
While going the road to sweet Athy,
   Hurroo! Hurroo!
While going the road to sweet Athy,
A stick in my hand and a drop in my eye,
A doleful damsel I heard cry: –
   'Och, Johnny, I hardly knew ye!
With drums and guns, and guns and drums,
   The enemy nearly slew ye,
   My darling dear, you look so queer,
   Och, Johnny, I hardly knew ye!

'Where are your eyes that looked so mild?
   Hurroo! Hurroo!
Where are your eyes that looked so mild?
   Hurroo! Hurroo!
Where are your eyes that looked so mild
When my poor heart you first beguiled?
Why did you run from me and the child?
   Och, Johnny, I hardly knew ye!

'Where are the legs with which you run?
   Hurroo! Hurroo!
Where are the legs with which you run?
   Hurroo! Hurroo!
Where are the legs with which you run
When you went to carry a gun? –
Indeed your dancing days are done!
   Och, Johnny, I hardly knew ye!

'It grieved my heart to see you sail,
   Hurroo! Hurroo!
It grieved my heart to see you sail,

Hurroo! Hurroo!
It grieved my heart to see you sail
Though from my heart you took leg bail, –
Like a cod you're doubled up head and tail.
　　Och, Johnny, I hardly knew ye!

'You haven't an arm and you haven't a leg,
　　Hurroo! Hurroo!
You haven't an arm and you haven't a leg,
　　Hurroo! Hurroo!
You haven't an arm and you haven't a leg,
You're an eyeless, noseless, chickenless egg:
You'll have to be put in a bowl to beg;
　　Och, Johnny, I hardly knew ye!

'I'm happy for to see you home,
　　Hurroo! Hurroo!
I'm happy for to see you home,
　　Hurroo! Hurroo!
I'm happy for to see you home,
All from the island of Sulloon,
So low in flesh, so high in bone,
　　Och, Johnny, I hardly knew ye!

'But sad as it is to see you so,
　　Hurroo! Hurroo!
But sad as it is to see you so,
　　Hurroo! Hurroo!
But sad as it is to see you so,
And to think of you now as an object of woe,
Your Peggy'll still keep ye on as her beau;
　　Och, Johnny, I hardly knew ye!
With drums and guns, and guns and drums,
　　The enemy nearly slew ye,
　　My darling dear, you look so queer,
　　Och, Johnny, I hardly knew ye!'

ROBERT HENRYSON

[1532]

from The Testament of Cresseid

'Lovers be war and tak gude heid about
whom quhome that ye lufe, for quohome ye suffer paine.
existing I lat yow wit, thair is richt few thairout
quhome ye may traist to have trew lufe agane.
test Preif quhen ye will, your labour is in vaine.
advise Thairfoir, I reid, ye tak thame as ye find,
steady for thay ar sad as Widdercock in Wind,

'Because I knaw the greit unstabilnes
brittle brukkill as glas, into my self I say,
traisting in uther als greit unfaithfulnes,
faith Als unconstant, and als untrew of fay,
thocht sum be trew, I wait richt few ar thay:
praise quha findis treuth lat him his Lady ruse:
nane but my self as now I will accuse.'

Quhen this was said, with Paper scho sat doun,
and on this maneir maid hir Testament.
bequeath 'Heir I beteiche my Corps and Carioun
toads with Wormis and with Taidis to be rent.
My Cop and Clapper and myne Ornament,
and all my gold the Lipper folk sall have,
quhen I am deid, to burie me in grave.

'This Royal Ring, set with this Rubie reid,
which quhilk Troylus in drowrie to me send,
to him agane I leif it quhen I am deid,
sorrowful / known to mak my cairfull deid unto him kend:
thus I conclude schortlie and make ane end,
my Spreit I leif to Diane quhair scho dwellis,
marshes to walk with hir in waist Woddis and Wellis.

'O Diomeid, thou hes baith Broche and Belt,
as tokens quhilk Troylus gave me in takning
died of his trew lufe,' and with that word scho swelt,

and sone ane Lipper man tuik of the Ring,
then
syne buryit hir withouttin tarying:
to Troylus furthwith the Ring he bair,
and of Cresseid the deith he can declair.

Quhen he had hard hir greit infirmitie,
his Legacie and Lamentatioun,
and how scho endit in sic povertie,
he swelt for wo, and fell doun in ane swoun,
ready
for greit sorrow his hart to brist was boun:
sighing
siching full sadlie, said: 'I can no moir,
scho was untrew, and wo is me thairfoir.'

Sum said he maid ane Tomb of Merbell gray,
and wrait hir name and superscriptioun,
and laid it on hir grave quhair that scho lay,
in goldin Letteris, conteining this ressoun:
'Lo, fair Ladyis, Cresseid, of Troyis toun,
sumtyme countit the flour of Womanheid,
under this stane lait Lipper lyis deid.'

Now, worthie Wemen, in this Ballet schort,
made for your worschip and Instructioun,
admonish
of Cheritie, I monische and exhort,
mingle
ming not your lufe with fals deceptioun.
Beir in your mynd this schort conclusioun
of fair Cresseid, as I have said befoir.
Sen scho is deid, I speik of hir no moir.

ANONYMOUS (IRISH)

[traditional] # Donal Óg

It is late last night the dog was speaking of you;
the snipe was speaking of you in her deep marsh.
It is you are the lonely bird through the woods;
and that you may be without a mate until you
    find me.

You promised me, and you said a lie to me,
that you would be before me where the sheep are
    flocked;
I gave a whistle and three hundred cries to you,
and I found nothing there but a bleating lamb.

You promised me a thing that was hard for you,
a ship of gold under a silver mast;
twelve towns with a market in all of them,
and a fine white court by the side of the sea.

You promised me a thing that is not possible,
that you would give me gloves of the skin of a fish;
that you would give me shoes of the skin of a bird;
and a suit of the dearest silk in Ireland.

When I go by myself to the Well of Loneliness,
I sit down and I go through my trouble;
when I see the world and do not see my boy,
he that has an amber shade in his hair.

It was on that Sunday I gave my love to you;
the Sunday that is last before Easter Sunday.
And myself on my knees reading the Passion;
and my two eyes giving love to you for ever.

My mother said to me not to be talking with you
    today,
or tomorrow, or on the Sunday;
it was a bad time she took for telling me that;
it was shutting the door after the house was
    robbed.

My heart is as black as the blackness of the sloe,
or as the black coal that is on the smith's forge;
or as the sole of a shoe left in white halls;
it was you put that darkness over my life.

You have taken the east from me; you have taken
the west from me;
you have taken what is before me and what is
behind me;
you have taken the moon, you have taken the
sun from me;
and my fear is great that you have taken God
from me!

translated by Lady Augusta Gregory

ANONYMOUS

[traditional]   ## The Daemon Lover

'O where have you been, my long, long love,
This long seven years and more?'
'O I'm come to seek my former vows
Ye granted me before.'

'O hold your tongue of your former vows,
For they will breed sad strife;
O hold your tongue of your former vows,
For I am become a wife.'

He turned him right and round about,
And the tear blinded his ee:
'I wad never hae trodden on Irish ground,
If it had not been for thee.

'I might hae had a king's daughter,
Far, far beyond the sea;
I might have had a king's daughter,
Had it not been for love o thee.'

'If ye might have had a king's daughter,
Yersel ye had to blame;

Ye might have taken the king's daughter,
    For ye kend that I was nane.

            *

'If I was to leave my husband dear,
    And my two babes also,
O what have you to take me to,
    If with you I should go?'

'I hae seven ships upon the sea –
    The eighth brought me to land –
With four-and-twenty bold mariners,
    And music on every hand.'

She has taken up her two little babes,
    Kissd them baith cheek and chin:
'O fair ye weel, my ain two babes,
    For I'll never see you again.'

She set her foot upon the ship,
    No mariners could she behold;
But the sails were o' the taffetie,
    And the masts o' the beaten gold.

She had not sailed a league, a league,
    A league but barely three,
When dismal grew his countenance,
cloudy, troubled   And drumlie grew his ee.

            *

They had not sailed a league, a league,
    A league but barely three,
Until she espied his cloven foot,
    And she wept right bitterlie.

'O hold your tongue of your weeping,' says he,
    'Of your weeping now let me be;

I will shew you how the lilies grow
   On the banks of Italy.'

'O what hills are yon, yon pleasant hills,
   That the sun shines sweetly on?'
'O yon are the hills of heaven,' he said,
   Where you will never win.'

'O whaten a mountain is yon,' she said,
   'All so dreary wi frost and snow?'
'O yon is the mountain of hell,' he cried,
   'Where you and I will go.'

     *

He strack the tap-mast wi his hand,
   The fore'mast wi his knee,
And he brake that gallant ship in twain,
   And sank her in the sea.

WILLIAM ALLINGHAM

[1850]   The Fairies

Up the airy mountain,
   Down the rushy glen,
We daren't go a-hunting
   For fear of little men;
Wee folk, good folk,
   Trooping all together;
Green jacket, red cap,
   And white owl's feather!

Down along the rocky shore
   Some make their home,
They live on crispy pancakes
   Of yellow tide-foam;
Some in the reeds
   Of the black mountain lake,

With frogs for their watch-dogs,
　All night awake.

High on the hill-top
　The old King sits;
He is now so old and gray
　He's nigh lost his wits.
With a bridge of white mist
　Columbkill he crosses,
On his stately journeys
　From Slieveleague to Rosses;
Or going up with music
　On cold starry nights,
To sup with the Queen
　Of the gay Northern Lights.

They stole little Bridget
　For seven years long;
When she came down again
　Her friends were all gone.
They took her lightly back,
　Between the night and morrow,
They thought that she was fast asleep,
　But she was dead with sorrow.
They have kept her ever since
　Deep within the lake,
On a bed of flag-leaves,
　Watching till she wake.

By the craggy hill-side,
　Through the mosses bare,
They have planted thorn-trees
　For pleasure here and there.
Is any man so daring
　As dig them up in spite,
He shall find their sharpest thorns
　In his bed at night.

Up the airy mountain,
  Down the rushy glen,
We daren't go a-hunting
  For fear of little men;
Wee folk, good folk,
  Trooping all together;
Green jacket, red cap,
  And white owl's feather!

ANONYMOUS

[traditional]

The Fause Knicht upon the Road

going   'O whare are ye gaun?'
false   Quo' the fause knicht upon the road;
            'I'm gaun to the scule,'
                Quo' the wee boy, and still he stude.

            'What is that upon your back?'
                Quo' the fause knicht upon the road;
know well 'Atweel it is my bukes,'
                Quo' the wee boy, and still he stude.

            'What's that ye've got in your arm?'
                Quo' the fause knicht upon the road;
            'Atweel it is my peit,'
                Quo' the wee boy, and still he stude.

who owns   'Wha's aucht they sheep?'
                Quo' the fause knicht upon the road;
            'They're mine and my mither's,'
                Quo' the wee boy, and still he stude.

            'How monie o' them are mine?'
                Quo' the fause knicht upon the road;
            'A' they that hae blue tails,'
                Quo' the wee boy, and still he stude.

'I wiss ye were on yon tree:'
  Quo' the fause knicht upon the road;
'And a gude ladder under me,'
  Quo' the wee boy, and still he stude.

'And the ladder for to break'
  Quo' the fause knicht upon the road;
'And you for to fa' down,'
  Quo' the wee boy, and still he stude.

sea 'I wish ye were in yon sie,'
  Quo' the fause knicht upon the road;
boat 'And a gude bottom under me,'
  Quo' the wee boy, and still he stude.

'And the bottom for to break,'
  Quo' the fause knicht upon the road;
'And ye to be drowned,'
  Quo' the wee boy, and still he stude.

JOHN CLARE

[1835–7]   ## The Badger

The badger grunting on his woodland track
striped With shaggy hide and sharp nose scrowed with
    black
Roots in the bushes and the woods and makes
A great hugh burrow in the ferns and brakes
With nose on ground he runs a awkard pace
And anything will beat him in the race
The shepherds dog will run him to his den
Followed and hooted by the dogs and men
The woodman when the hunting comes about
Go round at night to stop the foxes out
And hurrying through the bushes ferns and
    brakes
Nor sees the many holes the badger makes

And often through the bushes to the chin
Breaks the old holes and tumbles headlong in.

When midnight comes a host of dogs and men
Go out and track the badger to his den
And put a sack within the hole and lye
Till the old grunting badger passes bye
He comes and hears they let the strongest loose
The old fox hears the noise and drops the goose
The poacher shoots and hurrys from the cry
And the old hare half wounded buzzes bye
They get a forked stick to bear him down
And clapt the dogs and bore him to the town
And bait him all the day with many dogs
And laugh and shout and fright the scampering
    hogs
He runs along and bites at all he meets
They shout and hollo down the noisey streets.

He turns about to face the loud uproar
And drives the rebels to their very doors
The frequent stone is hurled where ere they go
When badgers fight and every ones a foe
The dogs are clapt and urged to join the fray
The badger turns and drives them all away
Though scarcely half as big dimute and small
He fights with dogs for hours and beats them all
The heavy mastiff savage in the fray
Lies down and licks his feet and turns away
The bull dog knows his match and waxes cold
The badger grins and never leaves his hold
He drives the crowd and follows at their heels
And bites them though the drunkard swears and
    reels.

The frighted women takes the boys away
The blackguard laughs and hurrys on the fray

He tries to reach the woods a awkard race
But sticks and cudgels quickly stop the chace
He turns agen and drives the noisey crowd
And beats the many dogs in noises loud
He drives away and beats them every one
And then they loose them all and set them on
He falls as dead and kicked by boys and men
Then starts and grins and drives the crowd agen
Till kicked and torn and beaten out he lies
And leaves his hold and cackles groans and dies.

Some keep a baited badger tame as hog
And tame him till he follows like the dog
They urge him on like dogs and show fair play
He beats and scarcely wounded goes away
Lapt up as if asleep he scorns to fly
And siezes any dog that ventures nigh
Clapt like a dog he never bites the men
But worrys dogs and hurrys to his den
They let him out and turn a harrow down
And there he fights the host of all the town
He licks the patting hand and trys to play
And never trys to bite or run away
And runs away from noise in hollow trees
Burnt by the boys to get a swarm of bees.

HUW LLWYD (WELSH)

[late 16th century] The Fox

Good morning, fox of the cave,
Every tame fowl's arch-foeman,
Your ripple I recognize,
Welcome to fertile country.
Describe, in the fair meadow,
Your life, bold soft-bellied beast.

Fair and clean, you are noted,
And shapely in every part:
You were dyed with dark colour,
Red and gold that will not fade;
Your narrow nose is savage,
Your teeth, they are marvellous,
Strange pincers, swiftly gripping,
And able to crunch through bones;
And your eye's glowering look
You turn like an old traitor.
On your head, fine beast, always,
Is the semblance of stiff stumps;
Your neck beneath was well-dressed,
Shaped like a ridge, you're splendid;
Bulging belly in coarse cloth,
A belly full of malice!
Short leg, bold through thick-branched grove,
Keen trotter towards weak lambkins.
Your tail, the length of mid-day,
Thick coarse cloth, is your pillow;
That tail is a yard-long brush,
A roll extremely swollen.
Kindling on the cairn's summit,
Kindled lad in a stout den,
Well-designed is your dwelling,
A hide-out from terriers.

Sorry scheme, you live yonder,
Paunchy lad, by plundering,
Pilfering, when it's quiet,
And strolling through leaves all day:
Kid's meat, when it's to be had,
Ewes, if they're for the taking;
A fine life, when there are lambs,
Blameless for you to tithe them.
Take hereafter, yours freely,

A goose and hen, unrebuked:
Clever you are, bird-snatching,
Hillside or bog, wild and tame.

All accomplishments your gift,
When closed in, you're a lion.
And if you come with twilight
Is there one so full of sense,
Or any with tricks slicker
Than yours, savage-snarling fox?
Nowhere, I know, in the grove,
Will I find shrewder judgment.
I am a man unwelcomed,
Disheartened, speechless, unloved,
No malice, no violence,
Strengthless in every struggle:
Yours, today, well-earned honours,
Teach me, a gift, how to live;
If you will give good counsel,
Forever I'll sing your praise.

'Be still, sound man, no clamour,
No search for help, no complaint.
See that there are, and take heed,
Two paths for your protection:
One true path, straight is its course;
Another one through falsehood.

'Seeking success, preferment?
I'd wish you to live like me.
One who's simple and peaceful,
Without malice, he'll not mount,
And integrity today,
In the world's view, is foolish.
Pillage or hazard the world,
Try cunning for the moment;
Learn to keep watch, look for faults,

Spare not one nor the other.
Remember, basic lesson,
Remember gain, the world's rule.
Devise, beware of a frown,
Traps for all, know all evil.
Do a kindness to no one
All your life, lest life be lost.
Make yourself known where you go,
From fear, cause much gift-giving.

'Hard to live, no denying,
Today by what's gained from love.
If you wish to live for long,
Go with praise, learn to flatter,
And by lauding each small thing
Learn the art of deception.
Speak sweetly on each errand,
Let no profit slip your hand.
Speak nothing but pious words,
Your malice in your belly.
Let not a man who's been born
Know any place your purpose:
That's the way a fool is known,
He reveals what he's thinking.
To prey on the weak's the way;
Treat the strong with smooth talking.
Do wrong, make no amendment:
To you, man, a good day comes.
Do all this, you'll not founder,
With deception as your guide.

'I have nothing more to tell:
The other path, consider.
I see the hounds in pursuit,
Hard for me to speak further

Or stay here on the hillside.
Farewell, I must flee above.'

translated by Joseph P. Clancy

BASIL BUNTING

[1966] *from* Briggflatts

Heart slow, nerves numb and memory, he lay
on glistening moss by a spring;
as a woodman dazed by an adder's sting
barely within recall
tests the rebate tossed to him, so he
ascertained moss and bracken,
a cold squirm snaking his flank
and breath leaked to his ear:
I am neither snake nor lizard,
I am the slowworm.

Ripe wheat is my lodging. I polish
my side on pillars of its transept,
gleam in its occasional light.
Its swaying
copies my gait.

Vaults stored with slugs to relish,
my quilt a litter of husks, I prosper
lying low, little concerned.
My eyes sharpen
when I blink.

Good luck to reaper and miller!
Grubs adhere even to stubble.
Come plowtime
the ditch is near.

Sycamore seed twirling,
O, writhe to its measure!
Dust swirling trims pleasure.

Thorns prance in a gale.
In air snow flickers,
twigs tap,
elms drip.

Swaggering, shimmering fall,
drench and towel us all!

So he rose and led home silently through clean
   woodland
where every bough repeated the slowworm's
   song.

SEÁN Ó RIORDÁIN (IRISH)

[1952] ## Switch

'Come here,' said Turnbull, 'till you see the
      sadness
   In the horse's eyes,
If you had such big hooves under you there'd be
      sadness
   In your eyes too.'

It was clear that he understood so well the
      sadness
   In the horse's eyes,
And had pondered it so long that in the end he'd
      plunged
   Into the horse's mind.

I looked at the horse to see the sadness
   Obvious in its eyes,
And saw Turnbull's eyes looking in my direction
   From the horse's head.

I looked at Turnbull one last time
   And saw on his face

Outsize eyes that were dumb with sadness –
    The horse's eyes.

                                    translated by Patrick Crotty

SIÔN PHYLIP (WELSH)

[late 16th/early 17th century]

The Seagull

Fair gull on the water's bank,
Bright-plumed breast, well-provided,
Hawk does not seize or pursue,
Water drown, nor man own you.
Nun feasting on the ocean,
Green sea's corners' coarse-voiced girl,
Thrusting wide through the lake's neck;
And then shaking a herring,
Salt water's clear white sunlight,
You're the banner of the shore,
The blessed godchild are you,
Below the bank, of Neptune:
A sorrow for you, the change
Of your life, cold your christening,
Brave white bird in rough waters,
Once a girl in a man's arms.

Halcyon, fair slim-browed maiden,
You were called in your kind land,
And after your man, good cause,
To the waves then you ventured,
And to the wild strait's seagull
You were changed, weak-footed bird.
You live, quick fish-feeding girl,
Below the slope and billows,
And the same cry for your mate
You screech loudly till doomsday.

Was there ever on the sea
A more submissive swimmer?

Hear my cry, wise and white-cloaked,
The hurt of the bare sea's bard:
My breast is pained with passion,
Pining for love of a girl.
I have begged from my boyhood
That she'd make one tryst with me,
And the tryst was for today:
Great was grief, it was wasted.
Swim, forget not my complaint,
To the dear maiden's region;
Fly to the shore, brave brightness,
And say where I was held fast
By the mouth, no gentle wave,
Of rough Bermo, cold foaming,
In all moods a sorry spot,
A cold black sea for sailing.

I rose, I travelled as day was
Breaking towards that dear bright face.
Dawn came on a thorny seastrand,
A cold day from the south-east.
A foul wind winnowed gravel,
Stripping stones, the whirlwind's nest.
The signs grew darker with dawn,
Twrch Trwydd drenching the beaches.
Inky was the wind's gullet
Where the western wind draws breath.

Harsh is the shore in conflict
If the western inlet's rough:
The sea spews, turning rocks green,
From the east spews fresh water.
Deep heaves from the ocean-bed,
In pain the pale moon's swooning.
The green pond is heaved abroad,
A snake's heave, sick from surfeit.
Sad heave where I saw tide ebb,

Rain's drivel that came pouring,
Cold black bed between two slopes,
Salt-filled briny sea-water.
Furnace dregs, draff of hell-spit,
Mouth sucking drops from the stars,
A winter night's greedy mouth,
Greed on the face of night-time,
Crock-shaped wet-edged enclosure,
A ban between bard and girl,
Foul hollow gap, raging pit,
Foggy land's filthy cranny,
Cromlech of every sickness,
Narrow pit of the world's plagues.
The pit was the sea-pool's haunt,
High it leaped, pool of prickles.
As high as the shelf it climbs,
Spew of the storm-path's anguish.
It never ebbs, will not turn:
I could not cross the current.

Three waters could flow eastwards,
Three oceans, these are the ones:
The Euxin, where rain wets us,
The Adriatic, black look,
The flood that runs to Rhuddallt,
Ancient Noah's flood turned salt.
The water-gate at Bermo,
Tide and shelf, may it turn land!

translated by Joseph P. Clancy

WILLIAM FOWLER

[late 16th/early 17th century]

'Ship-broken men whom stormy seas sore toss'

Ship-broken men whom stormy seas sore toss
Protests with oaths not to adventure more;

Bot all their perils, promises, and loss
They quite forget when they come to the shore:
Even so, fair dame, whiles sadly I deplore
The shipwreck of my wits procured by you,
Your looks rekindleth love as of before,
And dois revive which I did disavow;
So all my former vows I disallow,
And buries in oblivion's grave, but groans;
Yea, I forgive, hereafter, even as now
My fears, my tears, my cares, my sobs, and
        moans,
once In hope if anes I be to shipwreck driven,
allow Ye will me thole to anchor in your heaven.

CLAUDE MCKAY

[1953]   # The Harlem Dancer

Applauding youths laughed with young
        prostitutes
And watched her perfect, half-clothed body
        sway;
Her voice was like the sound of blended flutes
Blown by black players upon a picnic day.
She sang and danced on gracefully and calm,
The light gauze hanging loose about her form;
To me she seemed a proudly-swaying palm
Grown lovelier for passing through a storm.
Upon her swarthy neck black shiny curls
Luxuriant fell; and tossing coins in praise,
The wine-flushed, bold-eyed boys, and even the
        girls,
Devoured her shape with eager, passionate gaze;
But looking at her falsely smiling face,
I knew her self was not in that strange place.

from THE SONG OF SOLOMON

[1611]   CHAPTER 2

I am the rose of Sharon, and the lily of the valleys.

As the lily among thorns, so is my love among the daughters.

As the apple tree among the trees of the wood, so *is* my beloved among the sons. I sat down under his shadow with great delight, and his fruit *was* sweet to my taste.

He brought me to the banqueting house, and his banner over me was love.

Stay me with flagons, comfort me with apples: for I am sick of love.

His left hand is under my head, and his right hand doth embrace me.

I charge you, O ye daughters of Jerusalem, by the roes, and by the hinds of the field, that ye stir not up, nor awake my love, till he please.

The voice of my beloved! behold, he cometh leaping upon the mountains, skipping upon the hills.

My beloved is like a roe or a young hart: behold, he standeth behind our wall, he looketh forth at the windows, shewing himself through the lattice.

My beloved spake, and said unto me, Rise up, my love, my fair one, and come away.

For, lo, the winter is past, the rain is over and gone;

The flowers appear on the earth; the time of the singing of birds is come, and the voice of the turtle is heard in our land;

The fig tree putteth forth her green figs, and the vines with the tender grape give a good smell. Arise, my love, my fair one, and come away.

O my dove, that art in the clefts of the rock, in the secret places of the stairs, let me see thy countenance, let me hear thy voice; for sweet is thy voice, and thy countenance is comely.

Take us the foxes, the little foxes, that spoil the vines: for our vines have tender grapes.

My beloved is mine, and I am his: he feedeth among the lilies.

Until the day break, and the shadows flee away, turn, my beloved, and be thou like a roe or a young hart upon the mountains of Bether.

CHAPTER 3

By night on my bed I sought him whom my soul loveth: I sought him, but I found him not.

I will rise now, and go about the city in the streets, and in the broad ways I will seek him whom my soul loveth; I sought him, but I found him not.

The watchmen that go about the city found me: to whom I said, Saw ye him whom my soul loveth?

It was but a little that I passed from them, but I found him whom my soul loveth: I held him, and would not let him go, until I had brought him into my mother's house, and into the chamber of her that conceived me.

I charge you, O ye daughters of Jerusalem, by the roes, and by the hinds of the field, that ye stir not up, nor awake my love, till he please.

Who *is* this that cometh out of the wilderness like pillars of smoke, perfumed with myrrh and frankincense, with all powders of the merchant?

Behold his bed, which is Solomon's; threescore valiant men are about it, of the valiant of Israel.

They all hold swords, being expert in war: every man hath his sword upon his thigh because of fear in the night.

King Solomon made himself a chariot of the wood of Lebanon.

He made the pillars thereof of silver, the bottom thereof of gold, the covering of it of purple, the midst thereof being paved with love, for the daughters of Jerusalem.

Go forth, O ye daughters of Zion, and behold King Solomon with the crown wherewith his mother crowned him in the day of his espousals, and in the day of the gladness of his heart.

CHAPTER 5

I am come into my garden, my sister, my spouse: I have gathered my myrrh with my spice; I have eaten my honeycomb with my honey; I have drunk my wine with my milk: eat, O friends; drink, yea, drink abundantly, O beloved.

I sleep, but my heart waketh: it is the voice of my beloved that knocketh, saying, Open to me, my sister, my love, my dove, my undefiled: for my head is filled with dew, and my locks with the drops of the night.

I have put off my coat; how shall I put it on? I have washed my feet; how shall I defile them?

My beloved put in his hand by the hole of the door, and my bowels were moved for him.

I rose up to open to my beloved; and my hands dropped with myrrh, and my fingers with sweet smelling myrrh, upon the handles of the lock.

I opened to my beloved; but my beloved had withdrawn himself, and was gone: my soul failed when he spake: I sought him, but I could not find him; I called him, but he gave me no answer.

The watchmen that went about the city found me, they smote me, they wounded me; the keepers of the walls took away my veil from me.

I charge you, O daughters of Jerusalem, if ye find my beloved, that ye tell him, that I am sick of love.

What *is* thy beloved more than another beloved, O thou fairest among women? what *is* thy beloved more than *another* beloved, that thou dost so charge us?

My beloved is white and ruddy, the chiefest among ten thousand.

His head is as the most fine gold, his locks are bushy, and black as a raven.

His eyes are as the eyes of doves by the rivers of waters, washed with milk, and fitly set.

His cheeks are as a bed of spices, as sweet flowers: his lips like lilies, dropping sweet smelling myrrh.

His hands are as gold rings set with the beryl: his belly is as bright ivory overlaid with sapphires.

His legs are as pillars of marble, set upon sockets of fine gold: his countenance is as Lebanon, excellent as the cedars.

His mouth is most sweet: yea, he is altogether lovely. This is my beloved, and this is my friend, O daughters of Jerusalem.

ROBERT HERRICK

[1648]   ## Delight in Disorder

A sweet disorder in the dresse
Kindles in cloathes a wantonnesse:

A Lawne about the shoulders thrown
Into a fine distraction:
An erring Lace, which here and there
Enthralls the Crimson Stomacher:
A Cuffe neglectfull, and thereby
Ribbands to flow confusedly:
A winning wave (deserving Note)
In the tempestuous petticote:
A carelesse shooe-string, in whose tye
I see a wilde civility:
Doe more bewitch me, then when Art
Is too precise in every part.

RICHARD WILBUR

[1957]   Piazza di Spagna, Early Morning

    I can't forget
  How she stood at the top of that long marble
    stair
  Amazed, and then with a sleepy pirouette
Went dancing slowly down to the fountain-
    quieted square;

    Nothing upon her face
But some impersonal loneliness, – not then a girl,
  But as it were a reverie of the place,
    A called-for falling glide and whirl;

  As when a leaf, petal, or thin chip
Is drawn to the falls of a pool and, circling a
    moment above it,
    Rides on over the lip –
Perfectly beautiful, perfectly ignorant of it.

PADRAIC COLUM

[1917] ## She Moved through the Fair

My young love said to me, 'My brothers won't
    mind,
And my parents won't slight you for your lack of
    kind.'
Then she stepped away from me, and this she did
    say,
'It will not be long, love, till our wedding day.'

She stepped away from me and she moved
    through the fair,
And fondly I watched her go here and go there,
Then she went her way homeward with one star
    awake,
As the swan in the evening moves over the lake.

The people were saying no two were e'er wed
But one had a sorrow that never was said,
And I smiled as she passed with her goods and her
    gear,
And that was the last that I saw of my dear.

I dreamt it last night that my young love came in,
So softly she entered, her feet made no din;
She came close beside me, and this she did say,
'It will not be long, love, till our wedding day.'

HOWARD NEMEROV

[1955] ## I Only am Escaped Alone to Tell Thee

I tell you that I see her still
At the dark entrance of the hall.
One gas lamp burning near her shoulder
Shone also from her other side
Where hung the long inaccurate glass

Whose pictures were as troubled water.
An immense shadow had its hand
Between us on the floor, and seemed
To hump the knuckles nervously,
A giant crab readying to walk,
Or a blanket moving in its sleep.

You will remember, with a smile
Instructed by movies to reminisce,
How strict her corsets must have been,
How the huge arrangements of her hair
Would certainly betray the least
Impassionate displacement there.
It was no rig for dallying,
And maybe only marriage could
Derange that queenly scaffolding –
As when a great ship, coming home,
Coasts in the harbor, dropping sail
And loosing all the tackle that had laced
Her in the long lanes . . .
                                    I know
We need not draw this figure out
But all that whalebone came from whales
And all the whales lived in the sea,
In calm beneath the troubled glass,
Until the needle drew their blood.

I see her standing in the hall,
Where the mirror's lashed to blood and foam,
And the black flukes of agony
Beat at the air till the light blows out.

AEMELIA LANYER

[1610]   *from* Salve Deus Rex Judaeorum

Till now your indiscretion sets us free,
And makes our former fault much lesse appeare;

441

Our Mother *Eve*, who tasted of the Tree,
Giving to *Adam* what shee held most deare,
Was simply good, and had no powre to see,
The after-comming harme did not appeare:
    The subtile Serpent that our Sex betraide,
    Before our fall so sure a plot had laide.

That undiscerning Ignorance perceav'd
No guile, or craft that was by him intended;
For had she knowne, of what we were bereav'd,
To his request she had not condiscended.
But she (poore soule) by cunning was deceav'd,
No hurt therein her harmelesse Heart intended:
    For she alleadg'd Gods word, which he denies,
    That they should die, but even as Gods, be wise.

But surely *Adam* can not be excusde,
Her fault though great, yet hee was most too
      blame;
What Weaknesse offerd, Strength might have
      refusde,
Being Lord of all, the greater was his shame:
Although the Serpents craft had her abusde,
Gods holy word ought all his actions frame,
    For he was Lord and King of all the earth,
    Before poore *Eve* had either life or breath.

Who being fram'd by Gods eternall hand,
The perfect'st man that ever breath'd on earth;
And from Gods mouth receiv'd that strait
      command,
The breach whereof he knew was present death:
Yea having powre to rule both Sea and Land,
Yet with one Apple wonne to loose that breath
    Which God had breathed in his beauteous face,
    Bringing us all in danger and disgrace.

And then to lay the fault on Patience backe,
That we (poore women) must endure it all;
We know right well he did discretion lacke,
Beeing not perswaded thereunto at all;
If *Eve* did erre, it was for knowledge sake,
The fruit beeing faire perswaded him to fall:
    No subtill Serpents falshood did betray him,
    If he would eate it, who had powre to stay him?

Not *Eve*, whose fault was onely too much love,
Which made her give this present to her Deare,
That what shee tasted, he likewise might prove,
Whereby his knowledge might become more
    cleare;
He never sought her weaknesse to reprove,
With those sharpe words, which he of God did
    heare:
    Yet Men will boast of Knowledge, which he
    tooke
    From *Eves* faire hand, as from a learned Booke.

If any Evill did in her remaine,
Beeing made of him, he was the ground of all;
If one of many Worlds could lay a staine
Upon our Sexe, and worke so great a fall

trickery

To wretched Man, by Satans subtill traine;
What will so fowle a fault amongst you all?
    Her weakenesse did the Serpents words obay;
    But you in malice Gods deare Sonne betray.

Whom, if unjustly you condemne to die,
Her sinne was small, to what you doe commit;
All mortall sinnes that doe for vengeance crie,
Are not to be compared unto it:
If many worlds would altogether trie,
By all their sinnes the wrath of God to get;

This sinne of yours, surmounts them all as
    farre
As doth the Sunne, another little starre.

Then let us have our Libertie againe,
And challenge to your selves no Sov'raigntie;
You came not in the world without our paine,
Make that a barre against your crueltie;
Your fault beeing greater, why should you
    disdaine
Our beeing your equals, free from tyranny?
    If one weake woman simply did offend,
    This sinne of yours, hath no excuse, nor end.

SIR HENRY WOTTON

[1619]

On His Mistress, the Queen of Bohemia

You meaner beauties of the night,
    That poorly satisfy our eyes
More by your number than your light;
    You common people of the skies,
    What are you when the sun shall rise?

You curious chanters of the wood,
    That warble forth Dame Nature's lays,
Thinking your voices understood
    By your weak accents; what's your praise
    When Philomel her voice shall raise?

You violets that first appear,
    By your pure purple mantles known,
Like the proud virgins of the year,
    As if the spring were all your own;
    What are you when the rose is blown?

So, when my Mistress shall be seen
    In form and beauty of her mind,
By virtue first, then choice, a Queen,

Tell me, if she were not designed
The eclipse and glory of her kind?

EDNA ST VINCENT MILLAY

[1939]

The Princess Recalls Her One Adventure

Hard is my pillow
Of down from the duck's breast,
Harsh the linen cover;
I cannot rest.

Fall down, my tears,
Upon the fine hem,
Upon the lonely letters
Of my long name;
Drown the sigh of them.

We stood by the lake
And we neither kissed nor spoke;
We heard how the small waves
Lurched and broke,
And chuckled in the rock.

We spoke and turned away.
We never kissed at all.
Fall down, my tears.
I wish that you might fall
On the road by the lake,
Where my cob went lame,
And I stood with the groom
Till the carriage came.

ANONYMOUS

[traditional]

Kiss'd Yestreen

Kiss'd yestreen, and kiss'd yestreen,
Up the Gallowgate, down the Green.

I've woo'd wi' lords, and woo'd wi' lairds,

common men / tinkers   I've mool'd wi' carles and mell'd wi' cairds,

I've kiss'd wi' priests – 'twas done i' the dark,

shift   Twice in my gown and thrice in my sark.

boy   But priest nor lord nor loon can gie

Sic kindly kisses as he gae me.

ANONYMOUS

[14th century] ### 'Maiden in the mor lay'

Maiden in the mor lay,
   In the mor lay,

seven nights   Sevenist fulle, sevenist fulle,

Maiden in the mor lay,
   In the mor lay,

Sevenistes fulle ant a day.

food   Welle was hire mete.
   Wat was hire mete?

primrose   The primerole ant the –

The primerole ant the –

Welle was hire mete.
   Wat was hire mete?

The primerole ant the violet.

drink   Welle was hire dring.
   Wat was hire dring?

cold   The chelde water of the –

The chelde water of the –

Welle was hire dring.
   Wat was hire dring?

The chelde water of the welle-spring.

Welle was hire bowr.
   Wat was hire bowr?

The rede rose an the –

The rede rose an the –

Welle was hire bowr.
   Wat was hire bowr?
The rede rose an the lilye flowr.

ANNE FINCH, COUNTESS OF WINCHILSEA

[c. 1700] A Nocturnal Reverie

In such a night, when every louder wind
Is to its distant cavern safe confined;
And only gentle zephyr fans his wings,
And lonely Philomel, still waking, sings;
Or from some tree, famed for the owl's delight,
She, holloaing clear, directs the wanderers right:
In such a night, when passing clouds give place,
Or thinly veil the heaven's mysterious face;
When in some river, overhung with green,
The waving moon and trembling leaves are seen;
When freshened grass now bears itself upright,
And makes cool banks to pleasing rest invite,
Whence springs the woodbind, and the bramble-
   rose,
And where the sleepy cowslip sheltered grows;
Whilst now a paler hue the foxglove takes,
Yet chequers still with red the dusky brakes:
When scattered glow-worms, but in twilight fine,
Show trivial beauties watch their hour to shine;
Whilst Salisbury stands the test of every light,
In perfect charms and perfect virtue bright.
When odours, which declined repelling day,
Thro' temperate air uninterrupted stray;
When darkened groves their softest shadows
   wear
And falling waters we distinctly hear;
When through the gloom more venerable shows
Some ancient fabric, awful in repose,

While sunburnt hills their swarthy looks
   conceal,
And swelling haycocks thicken up the vale:
When the loosed horse now, as his pasture leads,
Comes slowly grazing through the adjoining
   meads.
Whose stealing pace, and lengthened shade we
   fear,
Till torn-up forage in his teeth we hear:
When nibbling sheep at large pursue their food,
And unmolested kine re-chew the cud;
When curlews cry beneath the village walls,
And to her straggling brood the partridge calls;
Their short-lived jubilee the creatures keep,
Which but endures, while tyrant man does sleep:
When a sedate content the spirit feels,
And no fierce light disturbs, whilst it reveals;
But silent musings urge the mind to seek
Something, too high for syllables to speak;
Till the free soul to a composedness charmed,
Finding the elements of rage disarmed,
O'er all below a solemn quiet grown,
Joys in the inferior world, and thinks it like her
   own:
In such a night let me abroad remain,
Till morning breaks, and all's confused again;
Our cares, our toils, our clamours are renewed,
Our pleasures, seldom reached, again pursued.

EMILY BRONTË

[1845] ## 'Silent is the house'

Silent is the house: all are laid asleep:
One alone looks out o'er the snow-wreaths deep,
Watching every cloud, dreading every breeze

That whirls the wildering drift, and bends the
    groaning trees.

Cheerful is the hearth, soft the matted floor;
Not one shivering gust creeps through pane or
    door;
The little lamp burns straight, its rays shoot
    strong and far:
I trim it well, to be the wanderer's guiding-star.

Frown, my haughty sire; chide, my angry dame:
Set your slaves to spy; threaten me with shame!
But neither sire, nor dame, nor prying serf shall
    know,
What angel nightly tracks that waste of frozen
    snow.

What I love shall come like visitant of air,
Safe in secret power from lurking human snare;
What loves me, no word of mine shall e'er betray,
Though for faith unstained my life must forfeit
    pay.

Burn, then, little lamp; glimmer straight and
    clear –
Hush! a rustling wing stirs, methinks, the air:
He for whom I wait, thus ever comes to me;
Strange Power! I trust thy might; trust thou my
    constancy.

PHILIP LARKIN

[1946]   ## Wedding-Wind

The wind blew all my wedding-day,
And my wedding-night was the night of the high
    wind;
And a stable door was banging, again and again,
That he must go and shut it, leaving me

Stupid in candlelight, hearing rain,
Seeing my face in the twisted candlestick,
Yet seeing nothing. When he came back
He said the horses were restless, and I was sad
That any man or beast that night should lack
The happiness I had.

                     Now in the day
All's ravelled under the sun by the wind's
    blowing.
He has gone to look at the floods, and I
Carry a chipped pail to the chicken-run,
Set it down, and stare. All is the wind
Hunting through clouds and forests, thrashing
My apron and the hanging cloths on the line.
Can it be borne, this bodying-forth by wind
Of joy my actions turn on, like a thread
Carrying beads? Shall I be let to sleep
Now this perpetual morning shares my bed?
Can even death dry up
These new delighted lakes, conclude
Our kneeling as cattle by all-generous waters?

ANONYMOUS

[early 16th century] 'Westron winde, when will thou blow'

Westron winde, when will thou blow,
The smalle raine downe can raine?
Christ if my love were in my armes,
And I in my bed againe.

Wulf and Eadwacer

The men of my tribe would treat him as game:
if he comes to the camp they will kill him
    outright.

      Our fate is forked.

Wulf is on one island, I on another.
Mine is a fastness: the fens girdle it
and it is defended by the fiercest men.
If he comes to the camp they will kill him for sure.

      Our fate is forked.

It was rainy weather, and I wept by the hearth,
thinking of my Wulf's far wanderings;
one of the captains caught me in his arms.
It gladdened me then; but it grieved me too.

Wulf, my Wulf, it was wanting you
that made me sick, your seldom coming,
the hollowness at heart; not the hunger I spoke
    of.

Do you hear, Eadwacer? Our whelp
    Wulf shall take to the wood.
What was never bound is broken easily,
    our song together.

translated by Michael Alexander

SIDNEY KEYES

The Walking Woman

There's a hard wind yet and a sad road
Between the walking woman
And her deadly spouse, the iron lover.
O my hair has fallen and my man

Has fallen and my fruitful time is over:
There is a hard wind and a sad road.

There's a jangled verse, a cry
Beating behind that woman's face.
O my eyes are drowned and my man
Is drowned. Who loves a dead man's grace,
A drowned man's kisses or a blind man's eye?
Cries the unsatisfied, the walking woman.

There's all the angry air, the sea,
Between that woman and her hope:
O once I had a house, a fire
Until my man's proud faring broke
My house and heart. So I'll desire
Lovers of iron or dead men's constancy,
Cries the still passionate, the walking woman.

EGAN O'RAHILLY (IRISH)

[c. 1700]

The Reverie

One morning before Titan thought of stirring his
    feet
  I climbed alone to a hill where the air was kind,
And saw a throng of magical girls go by
  That had lived to the north in Croghan time
    out of mind.

All over the land from Galway to Cork of the ships,
  It seemed that a bright enchanted mist came
    down,
Acorns on oaks and clear cold honey on stones,
  Fruit upon every tree from root to crown.

They lit three candles that shone in the mist like
    stars
  On a high hilltop in Connello and then were
    gone,

But I followed through Thomond the track of the
    hooded queens
    And asked them the cause of the zeal of their
      office at dawn.

The tall queen, Eevul, so bright of countenance,
    said
    'The reason we light three candles on every
      strand
Is to guide the king that will come to us over the
    sea
    And make us happy and reign in a fortunate
      land.'

And then, so suddenly did I start from my sleep,
    They seemed to be true, the words that had
      been so sweet –
It was just that my soul was sick and spent with
    grief
    One morning before Titan thought of stirring
      his feet.

translated by Frank O'Connor

ANONYMOUS

[early 14th century]   **'Icham of Irlaunde'**

I am   Icham of Irlaunde
    Ant of the holy londe
    Of Irlande.

    Gode sire, pray ich the,
    For of saynte charite,
    Come ant daunce wyt me
    In Irlaunde.

THOMAS MOORE

[c. 1807] ### 'Dear Harp of my Country!'

Dear Harp of my Country! in darkness I found
    thee,
    The cold chain of silence had hung o'er thee
      long,
When proudly, my own Island Harp, I unbound
    thee,
    And gave all thy chords to light, freedom, and
      song!

The warm lay of love and the light note of
    gladness
    Have waken'd thy fondest, thy liveliest thrill;
But, so oft hast thou echo'd the deep sigh of
    sadness,
    That ev'n in thy mirth it will steal from thee
    still.

Dear Harp of my Country! farewell to thy
    numbers,
    This sweet wreath of song is the last we shall
    twine!
Go, sleep with the sunshine of Fame on thy
    slumbers,
    Till touch'd by some hand less unworthy than
    mine;

If the pulse of the patriot, soldier, or lover,
    Have throbb'd at our lay, 'tis thy glory alone;
I was *but* as the wind, passing heedlessly over,
    And all the wild sweetness I wak'd was thy
    own.

SIR JOHN BETJEMAN

[1966] Ireland's Own *or,*
The Burial of Thomas Moore

In the churchyard of Bromham the yews
    intertwine
O'er a smooth granite cross of a Celtic design,
Looking quite out of place in surroundings like
    these
In a corner of Wilts 'twixt the chalk and the
    cheese.

I can but account you neglected and poor,
Dear bard of my boyhood, mellifluous Moore,
That far from the land which of all you loved best
In a village of England your bones should have
    rest.

I had rather they lay where the Blackwater glides
When the light of the evening doth burnish its
    tides
And St Carthage Cathedral's meticulous spire
Is tipped like the Castle with sun-setting fire.

I had rather some gate-lodge of plaster and
    thatch
With slim pointed windows and porches to match
Had last seen your coffin drawn out on the road
From a great Irish house to its final abode.

fortified enclosure Or maybe a rath with a round tower near
And the whispering Shannon delighting the ear
And the bog all around and the width of the sky
Is the place where your bones should deservedly
    lie.

The critics may scorn you and Hazlitt may carp
At the 'Musical Snuff-box' you made of the Harp;

455

The Regency drawing-rooms that thrilled with
    your song
Are not the true world to which now you belong.

No! the lough and the mountain, the ruins and
    rain
And purple-blue distances bound your demesne,
For the tunes to the elegant measures you trod
Have chords of deep longing for Ireland and God.

ANONYMOUS

[*c.* 1798] 'General wonder in our land'

General wonder in our land,
    And general consternation;
General gale on Bantry strand,
    For general preservation.

General rich he shook with awe
    At general insurrection;
General poor his sword did draw,
    With general disaffection.

General blood was just at hand,
    As General Hoche appeared;
General woe fled through our land,
    As general want was feared.

General gale our fears dispersed,
    He conquered general dread;
General joy each heart has swelled,
    As General Hoche has fled.

General love no blood has shed,
    He left us general ease,
General horror he has fled,
    Let God get general praise.

To that great General of the skies,
    That sent us general gale,
With general love our voices rise
    In one great general peal.

ANONYMOUS

The Croppy Boy

It was early, early in the spring,
The birds did whistle and sweetly sing,
Changing their notes from tree to tree
And the song they sang was 'Old Ireland Free'.

It was early, early in the night,
The Yeoman cavalry gave me a fright,
The Yeoman cavalry was my downfall
And I was taken by Lord Cornwall.

It was in the coach house that I was laid
And in the parlour that I was tried.
My sentence passed and my courage low
As to Duncannon I was forced to go.

As I was going up Wexford Street
My own first cousin I chanced to meet.
My own first cousin did me betray
And for one bare guinea swore my life away.

As I was passing my father's door
My brother William stood in the door,
My aged father stood there before
And my own dear mother her hair she tore.

As I was going up Wexford Hill
Oh who would blame me to cry my fill?
I looked behind and I looked before
And my own dear mother I shall ne'er see more.

As I was standing on the scaffold high
My own dear father was standing nigh.
My own dear father did me deny
And the name he gave me was 'The Croppy Boy'.

It was in Duncannon this young man died
And in Duncannon his body was laid.
Now all good people that do pass by
O spare a tear for 'The Croppy Boy'.

GAVIN DOUGLAS

[1513]   *from* Virgil's *The Aeneid* (Book I)

The batalis and the man I will discrive
fra Troyis boundis first that fugitive

fate / Italy / Lavinian shore   by fait to Ytail come and cost Lavyne,
sea / compelled / hardship   our land and sey katchit with mekil pine
gods above / place   by fors of goddis abufe, from every steid,
undying anger   of cruell Juno throu ald remembrit fede.
Gret pane in batail sufferit he alsso
before   or he his goddis brocht in Latio
built / whom   and belt the cite fra quham, of nobill fame,
the Latyne pepill takyn heth thar name,
fathers   and eik the faderis, princes of Alba,
battlements   cam, and the wallaris of gret Rome alswa.

O thou my Muse, declare the causis quhy,
quhat majeste offendit schaw quham by,
cruel   or yit quharfor of goddis the drery queyn
indignant / trials   sa feil dangeris, sik travell maid susteyn
a worthy man fulfillit of piete.
rancour   Is thare sik greif in hevynly myndis on hie?
called   Thare was ane ancyant cite hecht Cartage,
quham hynys of Tyre held intill heritage,
ennymy to Itail, standand fair and plane
far away   the mouth of lang Tibir our forgane,
possessions / warlike skills   mighty of moblys, full of sculys seyr,

458

war
and maist expert in crafty fait of weir,
of quhilk a land Juno, as it is said,
as to hir special abuf al otheris maid.

put second
Hir native land for it postponyt sche
Sames / seat of power
callit Same – in Cartage sett hir see.
chariot
Thair war hir armys and here stude eik hir chair.
destiny
This goddess ettillit, gif werdis war nocht
opposed
    contrar,
this realme tobe superior and mastres
to all landis, bot certis netheles
knew
the fatale sisteris revolve and schaw, scho kend,
of Trojane blude a pepill suld discend,
war / far and wide / later
Villiant in were, to ryng wydquhar, and syne
ruin
Cartage suld bring ontill finale rewyne,
and clene distroy the realme of Lybia.
This dredand Juno, and forthirmor alswa
remembring on the ancyant mortell weir
beloved
that for the Grekis, to hir leif and deir,
at Troy lang time scho led befor that day –
origins of conflict
for yit the causys of wreth war nocht away
nor cruell harm foryet ne out of mind,
ful deip engravyn in hir breist onkynd
the jugement of Paris, quhou that he
preferrit Venus, dispisying hir bewte.
Als Trojane blude till hir was odyus,
for Jupiter engenderit Dardanus
(fra quham the Trojanis cam) in adultry,
ravished
and Ganymedes revist abuf the sky,
daughter's
maid him his butler, quhilk was hir douchteris
    office –
troublesome situations
Juno inflambit, musing on thir casis nice
the quhile our sey that salit the Trojanys
quhilkis had the ded eschapit and remanys
fierce
onslane of Grekis or of the fers Achill,
scatters
scho thame fordryvis and causys oft ga will
away from
frawart Latium, quhilk now is Italy,

459

strange fate be fremmyt werd ful mony yeris tharby
catchit and blaw wydquhar all seys about.
Lo, quhou gret cure, quhat travell, pane and
    dowt
was to begin the worthy Romanys blude!

ANEIRIN (WELSH)

[6th century] *from* The Gododdin

I

Men went to Catraeth, keen their war-band.
Pale mead their portion, it was poison.
Three hundred under orders to fight.
And after celebration, silence.
Though they went to churches for shriving,
True is the tale, death confronted them.

2

Men went to Catraeth at dawn:
Their high spirits lessened their life-spans.
They drank mead, gold and sweet, ensnaring;
For a year the minstrels were merry.
Red their swords, let the blades remain
Uncleansed, white shields and four-sided
    spearheads,
Before Mynyddawg Mwynfawr's men.

3

Men went to Catraeth, they were renowned.
Wine and mead from gold cups was their drink,
A year in noble ceremonial,
Three hundred and sixty-three gold-torqued men.
Of all those who charged, after too much drink,

But three won free through courage in strife,
Aeron's two war-hounds and tough Cynon,
And myself, soaked in blood, for my song's sake.

4

Gododdin's war-band on shaggy mounts,
Steeds the hue of swans, in full harness,
Fighting for Eidin's treasure and mead.
On Mynyddawg's orders
Shields were battered to bits,
Sword-blades descended
On pallid cheeks.
They loved combat, broad line of attack:
They bore no disgrace, men who stood firm.

5

Man's mettle, youth's years,
Courage for combat:
Swift thick-maned stallions
Beneath a fine stripling's thighs,
Broad lightweight buckler
On a slim steed's crupper,
Glittering blue blades,
Gold-bordered garments.
Never will there be
Bitterness between us:
Rather I make of you
Song that will praise you.
The blood-soaked field
Before the marriage-feast,
Foodstuff for crows
Before the burial.
A dear comrade, Owain;
Vile, his cover of crows.

Ghastly to me that ground,
Slain, Marro's only son.

6

Diademed, to the fore at all times,
Breathless before a maid, he earned mead.
Rent the front of his shield, when he heard
The war-cry, he spared none he pursued.
He'd not turn from a battle till blood
Flowed, like rushes hewed men who'd not flee.
At court the Gododdin say there came
Before Madawg's tent on his return
But a single man in a hundred.

7

Issac, much-honoured man from the South,
Like the incoming ocean his ways,
　　Genial and generous,
　　Well-mannered over mead.
　　Where he buried his weapons
　　　He called it quits.
Not stained, stainless; not faulty, faultless.
His sword rang in the heads of mothers.
A wall in war, Gwydneu's son was praised.

8

A shame the shield was pierced
Of kind-hearted Cynwal.
A shame he set his thighs
On a long-legged steed.
Dark his brown spear-shaft,
Darker his saddle.
In his den a Saxon
Munches on a goat's

Leg: may he seldom
Have spoils in his purse.

9

Warriors rose together, formed ranks.
With a single mind they assaulted.
Short their lives, long their kinsmen long for
   them.
Seven times their sum of English they slew:
Their fighting turned wives into widows;
Many a mother with tear-filled eyelids.

10

Because of wine-feast and mead-feast they
   charged,
Men famed in fighting, heedless of life.
Bright ranks around cups, they joined to feast.
Wine and mead and bragget, these were theirs.
From Mynyddawg's banquet, grief-stricken my
   mind,
Many I lost of my true comrades.
Of three hundred champions who charged on
   Catraeth,
It is tragic, but one man came back.

11

When thoughts in throngs
Come upon me, mournful of mind,
My breath is faint
As in running, and then I weep.
One dear I mourn,
One dear whom I loved, noble stag,
Grief for the man
Who was ever in Argoed's ranks.

He gave his all
For countrymen, for a lord's sake,
For rough-hewn wood,
For a flood of grief, for the feasts.
Friends about him he bore us to a blazing fire,
And to seats of white skins and to sparkling wine.
Gereint from the South gave the war-cry,
Bright and fair, fair-formed was his face,
Generous spear-lord, praiseworthy lord,
So gracious, well I know his nature,
Well I knew Gereint: kind, noble, he was.

12

Three hundred golden-torqued men attacked:
Contending for the land was cruel.
Although they were being slain, they slew;
Till the world ends, they will be honoured.
Of the comrades who went together,
Tragic, but a single man returned.

translated and arranged by Joseph P. Clancy

JULIA WARD HOWE

[1862] ## Battle-Hymn of the Republic

Mine eyes have seen the glory of the coming of
    the Lord;
He is trampling out the vintage where the grapes
    of wrath are stored;
He hath loosed the fateful lightning of His terrible
    swift sword;
        His truth is marching on.

I have seen Him in the watch-fires of a hundred
    circling camps;
They have builded Him an altar in the evening
    dews and damps;

I can read his righteous sentence by the dim and
    flaring lamps;
        His day is marching on.

I have read a fiery gospel, writ in burnished rows
    of steel:
'As ye deal with my contemners, so with you my
    grace shall deal;
Let the Hero, born of woman, crush the serpent
    with his heel,
        Since God is marching on.'

He has sounded forth the trumpet that shall
    never call retreat;
He is sifting out the hearts of men before His
    judgment-seat;
Oh, be swift, my soul, to answer Him! be jubilant,
    my feet!
        Our God is marching on.

In the beauty of the lilies Christ was born across
    the sea,
With a glory in His bosom that transfigures you
    and me:
As He died to make men holy, let us die to make
    men free,
        While God is marching on.

GEORGE GORDON, LORD BYRON

[1816]   *from* Childe Harold's Pilgrimage
       (Eve of Waterloo)

There was a sound of revelry by night,
    And Belgium's Capital had gathered then
    Her Beauty and her Chivalry, and bright
    The lamps shone o'er fair women and brave
       men;

A thousand hearts beat happily; and when
Music arose with its voluptuous swell,
Soft eyes looked love to eyes which spake
    again,
And all went merry as a marriage bell;
But hush! hark! a deep sound strikes like a rising
    knell!

Did ye not hear it? – No; 'twas but the wind,
    Or the car rattling o'er the stony street;
    On with the dance! let joy be unconfined;
    No sleep till morn, when Youth and Pleasure
        meet
    To chase the glowing Hours with flying feet –
    But hark! – that heavy sound breaks in once
        more,
    As if the clouds its echo would repeat;
    And nearer, clearer, deadlier than before!
Arm! Arm! it is – it is – the cannon's opening roar!

Within a windowed niche of that high hall
    Sate Brunswick's fated chieftain; he did hear
    That sound the first amidst the festival,
    And caught its tone with Death's prophetic
        ear;
    And when they smiled because he deemed it
        near,
    His heart more truly knew that peal too well
    Which stretched his father on a bloody bier,
    And roused the vengeance blood alone could
        quell;
He rushed into the field, and, foremost fighting,
    fell.

Ah! then and there was hurrying to and fro,
    And gathering tears, and tremblings of
        distress,

And cheeks all pale, which but an hour ago
Blushed at the praise of their own loveliness;
And there were sudden partings, such as
    press
The life from out young hearts, and choking
    sighs
Which ne'er might be repeated; who could
    guess
If ever more should meet those mutual eyes,
Since upon night so sweet such awful morn could
    rise!

And there was mounting in hot haste: the steed,
    The mustering squadron, and the clattering
        car,
    Went pouring forward with impetuous speed,
    And swiftly forming in the ranks of war;
    And the deep thunder peal on peal afar;
    And near, the beat of the alarming drum
    Roused up the soldier ere the morning star;
    While thronged the citizens with terror dumb,
Or whispering, with white lips – 'The foe! They
        come! they come!'

And wild and high the 'Cameron's Gathering'
        rose!
    The war-note of Lochiel, which Albyn's hills
    Have heard, and heard, too, have her Saxon
        foes: –
    How in the noon of night that pibroch thrills,
    Savage and shrill! But with the breath which
        fills
    Their mountain-pipe, so fill the mountaineers
    With the fierce native daring which instils
    The stirring memory of a thousand years,
And Evan's, Donald's fame rings in each
        clansman's ears!

And Ardennes waves above them her green
    leaves,
    Dewy with nature's tear-drops, as they pass,
    Grieving, if aught inanimate e'er grieves,
    Over the unreturning brave, – alas!
    Ere evening to be trodden like the grass
    Which now beneath them, but above shall
        grow
    In its next verdure, when this fiery mass
    Of living valour, rolling on the foe
And burning with high hope, shall moulder cold
    and low.

Last noon beheld them full of lusty life,
    Last eve in Beauty's circle proudly gay,
    The midnight brought the signal-sound of
        strife,
    The morn the marshalling in arms, – the day
    Battle's magnificently-stern array!
    The thunder-clouds close o'er it, which when
        rent
    The earth is covered thick with other clay
    Which her own clay shall cover, heaped and
        pent,
Rider and horse, – friend, foe, – in one red burial
    blent!

IVOR GURNEY

[1919/22] ## The Silent One

Who died on the wires, and hung there, one of
    two –
Who for his hours of life had chattered through
Infinite lovely chatter of Bucks accent:
Yet faced unbroken wires; stepped over, and
    went

A noble fool, faithful to his stripes – and ended.
But I weak, hungry, and willing only for the
   chance
Of line – to fight in the line, lay down under
   unbroken
Wires, and saw the flashes and kept unshaken,
Till the politest voice – a finicking accent, said:
'Do you think you might crawl through there:
   there's a hole.'
Darkness, shot at: I smiled, as politely replied –
'I'm afraid not, Sir.' There was no hole no way to
   be seen
Nothing but chance of death, after tearing of
   clothes.
Kept flat, and watched the darkness, hearing
   bullets whizzing –
And thought of music – and swore deep heart's
   deep oaths
(Polite to God) and retreated and came on again,
Again retreated – and a second time faced the
   screen.

DAVID JONES

[1937] *from* In Parenthesis (Part 7)

Mother of Christ under the tree
reduce our dimensional vulnerability to the
   minimum –
cover the spines of us
let us creep back dark-bellied where he can't see
don't let it.
There, there, it can't, won't hurt – nothing
shall harm my beautiful.
   But on its screaming passage
their numbers writ
and stout canvas tatters drop as if they'd salvoed

grape to the mizzen-sheets and the shaped ash
grip rocket-sticks out of the evening sky right
back by Bright Trench
and clots and a twisted clout
on the bowed back of the F.O.O. bent to his
    instrument.
     . . . theirs . . . H.E. . . . fairly, fifty yards to my
front . . . he's bumping the Quadrangle . . . 2025
hours? – thanks – nicely . . . X 29b25 . . . 10.5
cm. gun . . . 35 degrees left . . . he's definitely
livening.
    and then the next packet – and Major Knacks-
bull blames the unresponsive wire.
    And linesmen go out from his presence to seek,
and make whole with adhesive tape, tweezer the
copper with deft hands: there's a bad break on the
Bright Trench line – buzz us when you're
through.

And the storm rises higher
and all who do their business in the valley
do it quickly
and up in the night-shades
where death is closer packed
in the tangled avenues
    fair Balder falleth everywhere
and thunder-besom breakings
bright the wood
and a Golden Bough for
Johnny and Jack
and blasted oaks for Jerry
and shrapnel the swift Jupiter for each expectant
    tree;
after what hypostases uniting:
withered limbs for the chosen
for the fore-chosen.

Take care the black brush-fall
in the night-rides
where they deploy for the final objective.
  Dark baulks sundered, bear down,
beat down, ahurtle through the fractured
    growings green,
pile high an heaped diversity.
Brast, break, bough-break the backs of them,
every bone of the white wounded who wait
    patiently –
looking toward that hope:
for the feet of the carriers long coming
bringing palanquins
to spread worshipful beds for heroes.

You can hear him,
suppliant, under his bowery smother
but who can you get to lift him away
lift him away
a half-platoon can't.
How many mortal men
to bear the Acorn-Sprite –
She's got long Tom
and Major Lillywhite,
        they're jelly-bags with the weight of it:
        and they'll Carry out Deth tomorrow.

    [. . .]

It's difficult with the weight of the rifle.
Leave it – under the oak.
Leave it for a salvage-bloke
let it lie bruised for a monument
dispense the authenticated fragments to the
    faithful.
It's the thunder-besom for us
it's the bright bough borne

it's the tensioned yew for a Genoese jammed arbalest and a scarlet square for a mounted *mareschal*, it's that county-mob back to back. Majuba mountain and Mons Cherubim and spreaded mats for Sydney Street East, and come to Bisley for a Silver Dish. It's R.S.M. O'Grady says, it's the soldier's best friend if you care for the working parts and let us be 'aving those springs released smartly in Company billets on wet forenoons and clickerty-click and one up the spout and you men must really cultivate the habit of treating this weapon with the very greatest care and there should be a healthy rivalry among you – it should be a matter of very proper pride and

Marry it man! Marry it!
Cherish her, she's your very own.

Coax it man coax it – it's delicately and ingeniously made – it's an instrument of precision – it costs us tax-payers, money – I want you men to remember that.

Fondle it like a granny – talk to it – consider it as you would a friend – and when you ground these arms she's not a rooky's gas-pipe for greenhorns to tarnish.

You've known her hot and cold.
You would choose her from among many.
You know her by her bias, and by her exact error at 300, and by the deep scar at the small, by the fair flaw in the grain, above the lower sling-swivel –
but leave it under the oak.

Slung so, it swings its full weight. With you going blindly on all paws, it slews its whole length, to hang at your bowed neck like the Mariner's white oblation.

You drag past the four bright stones at the turn
of Wood Support.

It is not to be broken on the brown stone under
the gracious tree.
  It is not to be hidden under your failing body.
  Slung so, it troubles your painful crawling like
a fugitive's irons.

KENNETH SLESSOR

[1944] ## Beach Burial

Softly and humbly to the Gulf of Arabs
The convoys of dead sailors come;
At night they sway and wander in the waters far
  under,
But morning rolls them in the foam.

Between the sob and clubbing of the gunfire
Someone, it seems, has time for this,
To pluck them from the shallows and bury them
  in burrows
And tread the sand upon their nakedness;

And each cross, the driven stake of tidewood,
Bears the last signature of men,
Written with such perplexity, with such
  bewildered pity,
The words choke as they begin –

'*Unknown seaman*' – the ghostly pencil
Wavers and fades, the purple drips,
The breath of the wet season has washed their
  inscriptions
As blue as drowned men's lips,

Dead seamen, gone in search of the same landfall,
Whether as enemies they fought,

473

Or fought with us, or neither; the sand joins them
    together,
Enlisted on the other front.

El Alamein

ANONYMOUS

[traditional]

The Twa Corbies

As I was walking all alane

ravens / moan   I heard twa corbies making a mane;
The tane unto the t'other say,
'Where sall we gang and dine to-day?'

wall of turf   ' – In behint yon auld fail dyke,
know   I wot there lies a new-slain Knight;
And naebody kens that he lies there,
But his hawk, his hound, and lady fair.

'His hound is to the hunting gane,
His hawk to fetch the wild-fowl hame,
His lady's ta'en another mate,
So we may make our dinner sweet.

neck-bone   'Ye'll sit on his white hause-bane,
And I'll pick out his bonny blue een:
Wi' ae lock o' his gowden hair
thatch   We'll theek our nest when it grows bare.

'Mony a one for him makes mane,
But nane sall ken where he is gane;
O'er his white banes, when they are bare,
The wind sall blaw for evermair.'

[1773] *from* The Lament for Arthur O'Leary

I

My love forever!
The day I first saw you
At the end of the market-house,
My eye observed you,
My heart approved you,
I fled from my father with you,
Far from my home with you.

II

I never repented it:
You whitened a parlour for me,
Painted rooms for me,
Reddened ovens for me,
Baked fine bread for me,
Basted meat for me,
Slaughtered beasts for me;
I slept in ducks' feathers
Till midday milking-time,
Or more if it pleased me.

III

My friend forever!
My mind remembers
That fine spring day
How well your hat suited you,
Bright gold banded,
Sword silver-hilted –
Right hand steady –
Threatening aspect –
Trembling terror

475

On treacherous enemy –
You poised for a canter
On your slender bay horse.
The Saxons bowed to you,
Down to the ground to you,
Not for love of you
But for deadly fear of you,
Though you lost your life to them,
Oh my soul's darling.

VII

My friend you were forever!
I knew nothing of your murder
Till your horse came to the stable
With the reins beneath her trailing,
And your heart's blood on her shoulders
Staining the tooled saddle
Where you used to sit and stand.
My first leap reached the threshold,
My second reached the gateway,
My third leap reached the saddle.

VIII

I struck my hands together
And I made the bay horse gallop
As fast as I was able,
Till I found you dead before me
Beside a little furze-bush.
Without Pope or bishop,
Without priest or cleric
To read the death-psalms for you,
But a spent old woman only
Who spread her cloak to shroud you –
Your heart's blood was still flowing;

I did not stay to wipe it
But filled my hands and drank it.

XVII

My friend and my treasure!
It's bad treatment for a hero
To lie hooded in a coffin,
The warm-hearted rider
That fished in bright rivers,
That drank in great houses
With white-breasted women.
My thousand sorrows
That I've lost my companion.

XVIII

Bad luck and misfortune
Come down on you, Morris!
That snatched my protector,
My unborn child's father:
Two of them walking
And the third still within me,
And not likely I'll bear it.

XIX

My friend and my pleasure!
When you went out through the gateway
You turned and came back quickly,
You kissed your two children,
You kissed me on the forehead,
You said: 'Eileen, rise up quickly,
Put your affairs in order
With speed and with decision.
I am leaving home now
And there's no telling if I'll return.'

I mocked this way of talking,
He had said it to me so often.

XX

My friend and my dear!
Oh bright-sworded rider,
Rise up this moment,
Put on your fine suit
Of clean, noble cloth,
Put on your black beaver,
Pull on your gauntlets.
Up with your whip;
Outside your mare is waiting.
Take the narrow road east,
Where the trees thin before you,
Where streams narrow before you,
Where men and women will bow before you,
If they keep their old manners –
But I fear they have lost them.

XXXV

My love and my dear!
Your stooks are standing,
Your yellow cows milking;
On my heart is such sorrow
That all Munster could not cure it,
Nor the wisdom of the sages.
Till Art O'Leary returns
There will be no end to the grief
That presses down on my heart,
Closed up tight and firm
Like a trunk that is locked
And the key is mislaid.

XXXVI

All you women out there weeping,
Wait a little longer;
We'll drink to Art son of Connor
And the souls of all the dead,
Before he enters the school –
Not learning wisdom or music
But weighed down by earth and stones.

translated by Eilís Dillon

KEITH DOUGLAS

[1941] ## Simplify Me When I'm Dead

Remember me when I am dead
and simplify me when I'm dead.

As the processes of earth
strip off the colour and the skin:
take the brown hair and blue eye

and leave me simpler than at birth,
when hairless I came howling in
as the moon entered the cold sky.

Of my skeleton perhaps,
so stripped, a learned man will say
'He was of such a type and intelligence,' no more.

Thus when in a year collapse
particular memories, you may
deduce, from the long pain I bore

the opinions I held, who was my foe
and what I left, even my appearance
but incidents will be no guide.

Time's wrong-way telescope will show
a minute man ten years hence
and by distance simplified.

Through that lens see if I seem
substance or nothing: of the world
deserving mention or charitable oblivion,

not by momentary spleen
or love into decision hurled,
leisurely arrive at an opinion.

Remember me when I am dead
and simplify me when I'm dead.

THOMAS HOOD

[1824]   Faithless Nelly Gray

Ben Battle was a soldier bold,
    And used to war's alarms:
But a cannon-ball took off his legs,
    So he laid down his arms!

Now, as they bore him off the field,
    Said he, 'Let others shoot,
For here I leave my second leg,
    And the Forty-second Foot!'

The army-surgeons made him limbs:
    Said he, – 'They're only pegs:
But there's as wooden members quite
    As represent my legs!'

Now Ben he loved a pretty maid,
    Her name was Nelly Gray;
So he went to pay her his devours
    When he'd devoured his pay!

But when he called on Nelly Gray,
   She made him quite a scoff;
And when she saw his wooden legs,
   Began to take them off!

'O Nelly Gray! O Nelly Gray!
   Is this your love so warm?
The love that loves a scarlet coat,
   Should be more uniform!'

Said she, 'I loved a soldier once,
   For he was blithe and brave;
But I will never have a man
   With both legs in the grave!

'Before you had those timber toes,
   Your love I did allow,
But then, you know, you stand upon
   Another footing now!'

'O Nelly Gray! O Nelly Gray!
   For all your jeering speeches,
At duty's call I left my legs
   In Badajos's *breaches*!'

'Why, then,' said she, 'you've lost the feet
   Of legs in war's alarms,
And now you cannot wear your shoes
   Upon your feats of arms!'

'O, false and fickle Nelly Gray;
   I know why you refuse: –
Though I've no feet – some other man
   Is standing in my shoes!

'I wish I ne'er had seen your face;
   But, now, a long farewell!
For you will be my death; – alas!
   You will not be my *Nell*!'

Now when he went from Nelly Gray,
    His heart so heavy got –
And life was such a burthen grown,
    It made him take a knot!

So round his melancholy neck
    A rope he did entwine,
And, for his second time in life,
    Enlisted in the Line!

One end he tied around a beam,
    And then removed his pegs,
And, as his legs were off, – of course,
    He soon was off his legs!

And there he hung till he was dead
    As any nail in town, –
For though distress had cut him up,
    It could not cut him down!

A dozen men sat on his corpse,
    To find out why he died –
And they buried Ben in four cross-roads,
    With a *stake* in his inside!

ANONYMOUS (OLD ENGLISH)

[10th century]   *from* Beowulf

    Then, on the headland, the Geats prepared a
        mighty pyre
for Beowulf, hung round with helmets and shields
and shining mail, in accordance with his wishes;
and then the mourning warriors laid
their dear lord, the famous prince, upon it.
    And there on Whaleness, the heroes kindled
the most mighty of pyres; the dark wood-smoke
soared over the fire, the roaring flames

mingled with weeping – the winds' tumult
    subsided –
until the body became ash, consumed even
to its core. The heart's cup overflowed;
they mourned their loss, the death of their lord.
And, likewise, a maiden of the Geats,
with her tresses swept up, intoned
a dirge for Beowulf time after time,
declared she lived in dread of days to come
dark with carnage and keening, terror of the
    enemy,
humiliation and captivity.
                        Heaven swallowed the
                                  smoke.

  Then the Geats built a barrow on the
    headland –
it was high and broad, visible from far
to all seafarers; in ten days they built the beacon
for that courageous man; and they constructed
as noble an enclosure as wise men
could devise, to enshrine the ashes.
They buried rings and brooches in the barrow,
all those adornments that brave men
had brought out from the hoard after Beowulf
    died.
They bequeathed the gleaming gold, treasure of
    men,
to the earth, and there it still remains
as useless to men as it was before.
  Then twelve brave warriors, sons of heroes,
rode round the barrow, sorrowing;
they mourned their king, chanted
an elegy, spoke about that great man:
they exalted his heroic life, lauded
his daring deeds; it is fitting for a man,
when his lord and friend must leave this life,

to mouth words in his praise
and to cherish his memory.
Thus the Geats, his hearth-companions,
grieved over the death of their lord;
they said that of all kings on earth
he was the kindest, the most gentle,
the most just to his people, the most eager for
    fame.

translated by Kevin Crossley-Holland

LEWIS CARROLL

[pub. 1872] ## Jabberwocky

'Twas brillig, and the slithy toves
  Did gyre and gimble in the wabe:
All mimsy were the borogroves,
  And the mome raths outgrabe.

'Beware the Jabberwock, my son!
  The jaws that bite, the claws that catch!
Beware the Jubjub bird, and shun
  The frumious Bandersnatch!'

He took his vorpal sword in hand:
  Long time the manxome foe he sought –
So rested he by the Tumtum tree,
  And stood awhile in thought.

And, as in uffish thought he stood,
  The Jabberwock, with eyes of flame,
Came whiffling through the tulgey wood,
  And burbled as it came!

One, two! One, two! And through and through
  The vorpal blade went snicker-snack!
He left it dead, and with its head
  He went galumphing back.

'And hast thou slain the Jabberwock?
    Come to my arms, my beamish boy!
O frabjous day! Callooh! Callay!'
    He chortled in his joy.

'Twas brillig, and the slithy toves
    Did gyre and gimble in the wabe:
All mimsy were the borogoves,
    And the mome raths outgrabe.

ANONYMOUS (THE 'PEARL POET')

[late 14th century]   *from* Sir Gawain and the Green Knight

[The New Year feast at King Arthur's Court is interrupted by the entry of a
Green Knight, on a green horse, who challenges any of Arthur's knights to
chop off his head and agree to submit to the same blow, from the Green
Knight, at the Green Chapel, one year later. Sir Gawain takes up the
challenge. In the following passage Gawain arrives at the Green Chapel to
keep his word.]

Then he spurred Gringolet, and took up the trail.
Trees overhung him, the steep slope close to his
        shoulder.
He pushed on down through the rough, to the
        gorge-bottom.
Wherever he turned his eyes, it looked wilder.
Nothing anywhere near that could be a shelter.
Only cliffy brinks, beetling above him,
Knuckled and broken outcrops, with horned
        crags.
Clouds dragging low, torn by the scouts.
There he reined in his horse and puzzled awhile.
Turning his doubts over, he searched for the
        Chapel.
Still he could see nothing. He thought it strange.
Only a little mound, a tump, in a clearing,

Between the slope and the edge of the river, a
      knoll,
Over the river's edge, at a crossing place,
The burn bubbling under as if it boiled.
The Knight urged his horse and came closer.
He dismounted there, light as a dancer,
And tethered his costly beast to a rough branch.
Then he turned to the tump. He walked all round
      it,
Debating in himself what it might be.
Shaggy and overgrown with clumps of grass,
It had a hole in the end, and on each side.
Hollow within, nothing but an old cave
Or old gappy rock-heap, it could be either
     Or neither.
    'Ah God!' sighed Gawain,
    'Is the Green Chapel here?
    Here, about midnight,
    Satan could say a prayer.'

'Surely,' he muttered, 'This is desolation.
This oratory is ugly, under its weeds.
The right crypt for that ogre, in his greenery,
To deal with his devotions devil-fashion.
My five wits warn me, this is the evil one,
Who bound me on oath to be here, to destroy me.
The chapel of Mischance – God see it demolished!
It is the worst-cursed Church I ever attended.'
With his helmet on his head, and his lance in his
      hand,
He clambered up on top of the bushy cell
And heard coming off the hill, from a face of rock,
The far side of the stream, a ferocious din.
What! It screeched in the crag, as if it would split
      it!
It sounded like a scythe a-shriek on a grind-stone!

What! It grumbled and scoured, like water in a
      mill!
What! It rushed and it rang, painful to hear!
'By God!' thought Gawain, 'I think that scummer
Is done in your honour, Knight, to welcome you
    As you deserve.
  Let God have his way! Ah well,
  It helps me not one bit.
  What if I lose my life?
  No noise is going to scare me.'

Then the Knight shouted, at the top of his voice:
'Is nobody at home, to collect my debt?
Gawain is here, now, walking about.
If any man is willing, get here quickly.
It is now or never, if he wants payment.'
'Be patient,' came a voice from the crag
      overhead,
'And I shall satisfy you, as I promised.'
Then he was back at his racket, with fresh fury,
Wanting to finish his whetting, before he came
      down.
But suddenly he was there, from under a cliff,
Bounding out of a den with a frightful weapon –
A Dane's axe, new fettled to settle the wager.
It had a massive head hooking back to the helve,
Ground bright with a file, and four foot long.
It measured as much by the rich thong that hung
      from it.
That giant, all got up in green as before,
Both the face and the legs, the hair and the beard,
Came down with plunging strides, in a big hurry,
Planting the axe to the earth and striding beside
      it.
When he got to the water he would not wade it,
He vaulted across on his axe, and loomed up,

Bursting into the clearing, where he stood
    On the snow.
    Sir Gawain knew how to greet him –
    But not too friendly.
    While the other replied: 'I see, Sir Sweetness,
    A man can keep his word.'

'Gawain,' said the Green Man, 'God protect you.
Let me welcome you, Knight, to my small holding.
You have timed your coming, as a true man
        should.
I see you honour the contract sealed between us.
This time twelvemonth back you took a thing
        from me.
So now, at this New Year, I shall reclaim it.
We have this lonely valley to ourselves.
No Knights are here to part us. We fight as we
        please.
Get that helmet off, and take your payment.
And give me no more talk than I gave you
When you whipped off my head with a single
        swipe.'
'Nay,' said Gawain, 'By God that gave me my soul,
I shall not grudge one jot of the damage coming.
Stick to the single stroke and I shall not move
Nor utter a word to warn you from whatever
    You choose.'
    He stretched his neck and bowed
    And bared the white flesh,
    Pretending to fear nothing.
    He would not dare to be fearful.

The Man in Green was eager, and all ready,
Grasping that ugly tool, to hit Gawain.
With all his body's might he hoisted it high,
Aimed it murderously for the utmost hurt.
And if he had brought it down as he had aimed it

The Knight who had never flinched would have
    been headless.
But Gawain skewed a sidelong glance at the
    weapon
As it came down to cut him off from the earth,
And shrank his shoulders a little from the sharp
    iron.
That other checked his stroke. He deflected the
    blade.
Then he reproached the prince with shaming
    words:
'You are not Gawain,' he said, 'whose name is so
    great,
Who never quailed in his life, by hill nor by vale.
Here you are wincing for fear before I touch you.
I never heard such cowardice of that hero.
When you hit me, I never fluttered an eyelid.
I never let out a squeak, in Arthur's hall.
My head rolled over the floor, but I did not flinch.
Before you are touched, your heart jumps out of
    your body.
It seems to me that I am a warrior far
    Far better.'
    Said Gawain: 'I winced once.
    And that once is the last.
    Though my head rolling on earth
    Can never be replaced.

'But hurry up, warrior, for God's sake come to the
    point.
Deal me my destiny, and do it quickly.
I shall stand to your stroke with not one stir
Till your axe-head hits me. I give you my word.'
'Then here it comes,' cried the other, and heaved
    it upwards
With a gargoyle grimace as if he were mad,

And with all his strength hauled down, yet never
    touched him.
He stopped the blade mid-stroke, before it could
    harm.
Gawain patiently waited, not a nerve twitched.
He stood there still as a rock or some stiff stump
That grips the stony ground with a hundred
    roots.
Then the Man in Green spoke pleasantly:
'Now that your heart is whole again, may I ask
    you,
Let your high rank, that Arthur gave you,
    preserve you
And recover your neck from my stroke, if it is able.
Then Gawain ground his teeth and shouted in
    anger:
'Why, hack away, you savage, you threaten too
    long.
I think you have frightened yourself with your
    bragging.'
'What's this?' cried the other, 'Rough words from
    Sir Gawain?
I will no longer withhold from such an appeal
    Justice.'
    And he braced himself for the stroke –
    Clenching both lip and brow.
    No wonder he did not like it
    Who saw no rescue now.

Lightly he lifted the weapon, then let it down
    deftly
With the barb of the bit by the bare neck,
And though he swung full strength he hardly
    hurt him,
But snicked him on that side, so the sheer edge

Sliced through skin and fine white fat to the
      muscle,
Then over his shoulders the bright blood shot to
      the earth.
When Gawain saw his blood blink on the snow
He sprang a spear's length forward, in one great
      stride,
Snatched up his helmet as he went, and crammed
      it on his head.
A shunt of his shoulders brought his shield to the
      front
And his sword flashed out as he spoke fiercely:
Since he was first a man born of his mother
Never in this world was he half as happy.
'That's enough, warrior. I take no more.
I have taken the payment blow, without
      resistance.
If you fetch me another, I shall match it.
I shall repay it promptly, you can trust me,
      And in full.
   I owed a single cut.
   That was our covenant
   Agreed in Arthur's Hall –
   So now, Sir, what about it?'

The Knight in Green stepped back, and leaned on
      his axe.
Setting the shaft in the snow, he rested on the
      head
And gazed awhile at the prince who stood before
      him:
Armed, calm, fearless, undaunted. He had to
      admire him.
Now as he spoke, his voice was big and cheerful:
'What a brave fellow you are. Do not be angry.

Nobody here has misused you, or done you
    dishonour.
We kept to the terms agreed in the King's Court.
I promised a blow. You have it. You are well paid.
And I require from you no other quittance.
If I had wanted it, I could have grieved you.
I could have exacted a cut, perhaps, far worse.
But see how I teased you, my worst was a playful
    feint.
I did not maim you with a gash. I took only justice,
For the contract we agreed on that first night.
You have kept faith with me and the bond
    between us,
And all that you took you returned – as a good
    man should.'

translated by Ted Hughes

JOHN LYLY

[1589]

'Pan's Syrinx was a girl indeed'

Pan's Syrinx was a girl indeed,
Though now she's turned into a reed;
From that dear reed Pan's pipe does come,
A pipe that strikes Apollo dumb;
Nor flute, nor lute, nor gittern can
So chant it as the pipe of Pan:
Cross-gartered swains and dairy girls,

smooth   With faces smug and round as pearls,
When Pan's shrill pipe begins to play,
With dancing wear out night and day:
The bagpipe's drone his hum lays by
When Pan sounds up his minstrelsy;
His minstrelsy! oh, base! this quill –
Which at my mouth with wind I fill –
Puts me in mind, though her I miss,
That still my Syrinx' lips I kiss.

SAINT COLUMCILLE

[11th century] ### 'My hand is weary with writing'

My hand is weary with writing,
My sharp quill is not steady,
My slender-beaked pen jets forth
A black draught of shining dark-blue ink.

A stream of wisdom of blessed God
Springs from my fair-brown shapely hand:
On the page it squirts its draught
Of ink of the green-skinned holly.

My little dripping pen travels
Across the plain of shining books,
Without ceasing for the wealth of the great –
Whence my hand is weary with writing.

translated by Kuno Meyer

SAMUEL BECKETT

[1988] ### What is the Word

folly –
folly for to –
for to –
what is the word –
folly from this –
all this –
folly from all this –
given –
folly given all this –
seeing –
folly seeing all this –
this –
what is the word –
this this –
this this here –

493

all this this here –
folly given all this –
seeing –
folly seeing all this this here –
for to –
what is the word –
see –
glimpse –
seem to glimpse –
need to seem to glimpse –
folly for to need to seem to glimpse –
what –
what is the word –
and where –
folly for to need to seem to glimpse what where –
where –
what is the word –
there –
over there –
away over there –
afar –
afar away over there –
afaint –
afaint afar away over there what –
what –
what is the word –
seeing all this –
all this this –
all this this here –
folly for to see what –
glimpse –
seem to glimpse –
need to seem to glimpse –
afaint afar away over there what –
folly for to need to seem to glimpse afaint afar
    away over there what –

what –
what is the word –

what is the word

[10th century] ## Bookworm

A worm ate words. I thought that wonderfully
Strange – a miracle – when they told me a
   crawling
Insect had swallowed noble songs,
A night-time thief had stolen writing
So famous, so weighty. But the bug was foolish
Still, though its belly was full of thought.

translated by Michael Alexander

TADHG ÓG O'HUIGINN (IRISH)

[15th century] ## *from* Lament for Fergal Rua

Through his death, I realize
How I value poetry:
O hut of our mystery, empty
And isolated always.

Aine's son is dead.
Poetry is daunted.
A stave of the barrel is smashed
And the wall of learning broken.

translated by Seamus Heaney

[1833] *from* In Memoriam

II

Old Yew, which graspest at the stones
    That name the under-lying dead,
    Thy fibres net the dreamless head,
Thy roots are wrapt about the bones.

The seasons bring the flower again,
    And bring the firstling to the flock;
    And in the dusk of thee, the clock
Beats out the little lives of men.

O not for thee the glow, the bloom,
    Who changest not in any gale,
    Nor branding summer suns avail
To touch thy thousand years of gloom:

And gazing on thee, sullen tree,
    Sick for thy stubborn hardihood,
    I seem to fail from out my blood
And grow incorporate into thee.

V

I sometimes hold it half a sin
    To put in words the grief I feel;
    For words, like Nature, half reveal
And half conceal the Soul within.

But, for the unquiet heart and brain,
    A use in measured language lies;
    The sad mechanic exercise,
Like dull narcotics, numbing pain.

In words, like weeds, I'll wrap me o'er,
    Like coarsest clothes against the cold:

But that large grief which these enfold
Is given in outline and no more.

VII

Dark house, by which once more I stand
　　Here in the long unlovely street,
　　Doors, where my heart was used to beat
So quickly, waiting for a hand,

A hand that can be clasp'd no more –
　　Behold me, for I cannot sleep,
　　And like a guilty thing I creep
At earliest morning to the door.

He is not here; but far away
　　The noise of life begins again,
　　And ghastly thro' the drizzling rain
On the bald street breaks the blank day.

IX

Fair ship, that from the Italian shore
　　Sailest the placid ocean-plains
　　With my lost Arthur's loved remains,
Spread thy full wings, and waft him o'er.

So draw him home to those that mourn
　　In vain; a favourable speed
　　Ruffle thy mirror'd mast, and lead
Thro' prosperous floods his holy urn.

All night no ruder air perplex
　　Thy sliding keel, till Phosphor, bright
　　As our pure love, thro' early light
Shall glimmer on the dewy decks.

Sphere all your lights around, above;
　　Sleep, gentle heavens, before the prow;

Sleep, gentle winds, as he sleeps now,
My friend, the brother of my love;

My Arthur, whom I shall not see
    Till all my widow'd race be run;
    Dear as the mother to the son,
More than my brothers are to me.

XI

Calm is the morn without a sound,
    Calm as to suit a calmer grief,
    And only thro' the faded leaf
The chestnut pattering to the ground:

Calm and deep peace on this high wold,
    And on these dews that drench the furze,
    And all the silvery gossamers
That twinkle into green and gold:

Calm and still light on yon great plain
    That sweeps with all its autumn bowers,
    And crowded farms and lessening towers,
To mingle with the bounding main:

Calm and deep peace in this wide air,
    These leaves that redden to the fall;
    And in my heart, if calm at all,
If any calm, a calm despair:

Calm on the seas, and silver sleep,
    And waves that sway themselves in rest,
    And dead calm in that noble breast
Which heaves but with the heaving deep.

XIV

If one should bring me this report,
    That thou hadst touch'd the land to-day,

And I went down unto the quay,
And found thee lying in the port;

And standing, muffled round with woe,
    Should see thy passengers in rank
    Come stepping lightly down the plank,
And beckoning unto those they know;

And if along with these should come
    The man I held as half-divine;
    Should strike a sudden hand in mine,
And ask a thousand things of home;

And I should tell him all my pain,
    And how my life had droop'd of late,
    And he should sorrow o'er my state
And marvel what possess'd my brain;

And I perceived no touch of change,
    No hint of death in all his frame,
    But found him all in all the same,
I should not feel it to be strange.

XV

To-night the winds begin to rise
    And roar from yonder dropping day:
    The last red leaf is whirl'd away,
The rooks are blown about the skies;

The forest crack'd, the waters curl'd,
    The cattle huddled on the lea;
    And wildly dash'd on tower and tree
The sunbeam strikes along the world:

And but for fancies, which aver
    That all thy motions gently pass
    Athwart a plane of molten glass,
I scarce could brook the strain and stir

That makes the barren branches loud;
　　And but for fear it is not so,
　　The wild unrest that lives in woe
Would dote and pore on yonder cloud

That rises upward always higher,
　　And onward drags a labouring breast,
　　And topples round the dreary west,
A looming bastion fringed with fire.

XXVIII

The time draws near the birth of Christ:
　　The moon is hid; the night is still;
　　The Christmas bells from hill to hill
Answer each other in the mist.

Four voices of four hamlets round,
　　From far and near, on mead and moor,
　　Swell out and fail, as if a door
Where shut between me and the sound:

Each voice four changes on the wind,
　　That now dilate, and now decrease,
　　Peace and goodwill, goodwill and peace,
Peace and goodwill, to all mankind.

This year I slept and woke with pain,
　　I almost wish'd no more to wake,
　　And that my hold on life would break
Before I heard those bells again:

But they my troubled spirit rule,
　　For they controll'd me when a boy;
　　They bring me sorrow touch'd with joy,
The merry merry bells of Yule.

XXX

With trembling fingers did we weave
    The holly round the Christmas hearth;
    A rainy cloud possess'd the earth,
And sadly fell our Christmas-eve.

At our old pastimes in the hall
    We gambol'd, making vain pretence
    Of gladness, with an awful sense
Of one mute Shadow watching all.

We paused: the winds were in the beech:
    We heard them sweep the winter land;
    And in a circle hand-in-hand
Sat silent, looking each at each.

Then echo-like our voices rang;
    We sung, tho' every eye was dim,
    A merry song we sang with him
Last year: impetuously we sang:

We ceased: a gentler feeling crept
    Upon us: surely rest is meet:
    'They rest,' we said, 'their sleep is sweet,'
And silence follow'd, and we wept.

Our voices took a higher range;
    Once more we sang: 'They do not die
    Nor lose their mortal sympathy,
Nor change to us, although they change;

'Rapt from the fickle and the frail
    With gather'd power, yet the same,
    Pierces the keen seraphic flame
From orb to orb, from veil to veil.'

Rise, happy morn, rise, holy morn,
    Draw forth the cheerful day from night:
    O Father, touch the east, and light
The light that shone when Hope was born.

L

Be near me when my light is low,
    When the blood creeps, and the nerves prick
    And tingle; and the heart is sick,
And all the wheels of Being slow.

Be near me when the sensuous frame
    Is rack'd with pangs that conquer trust;
    And Time, a maniac scattering dust,
And Life, a Fury slinging flame.

Be near me when my faith is dry,
    And men the flies of latter spring,
    That lay their eggs, and sting and sing
And weave their petty cells and die.

Be near me when I fade away,
    To point the term of human strife,
    And on the low dark verge of life
The twilight of eternal day.

LIV

Oh yet we trust that somehow good
    Will be the final goals of ill,
    To pangs of nature, sins of will,
Defects of doubt, and taints of blood;

That nothing walks with aimless feet;
    That not one life shall be destroy'd,
    Or cast as rubbish to the void,
When God hath made the pile complete;

That not a worm is cloven in vain;
　　That not a moth with vain desire
　　Is shrivell'd in a fruitless fire,
Or but subserves another's gain.

Behold, we know not anything;
　　I can but trust that good shall fall
　　At last – far off – at last, to all,
And every winter change to spring.

So runs my dream: but what am I?
　　An infant crying in the night:
　　An infant crying for the light:
And with no language but a cry.

LXVII

When on my bed the moonlight falls,
　　I know that in thy place of rest
　　By that broad water of the west,
There comes a glory on the walls:

Thy marble bright in dark appears,
　　As slowly steals a silver flame
　　Along the letters of thy name,
And o'er the number of thy years.

The mystic glory swims away;
　　From off my bed the moonlight dies;
　　And closing eaves of wearied eyes
I sleep till dusk is dipt in gray:

And then I know the mist is drawn
　　A lucid veil from coast to coast,
　　And in the dark church like a ghost
Thy tablet glimmers to the dawn.

LXXXVII

I past beside the reverend walls
In which of old I wore the gown;
I roved at random thro' the town,
And saw the tumult of the halls;

chapels

And heard once more in college fanes
The storm their high-built organs make,
And thunder-music, rolling, shake
The prophet blazon'd on the panes;

And caught once more the distant shout,
The measured pulse of racing oars
Among the willows; paced the shores
And many a bridge, and all about

The same gray flats again, and felt
The same, but not the same; and last
Up that long walk of limes I past
To see the rooms in which he dwelt.

Another name was on the door:
I linger'd; all within was noise
Of songs, and clapping hands, and boys
That crash'd the glass and beat the floor;

Where once we held debate, a band
Of youthful friends, on mind and art,
And labour, and the changing mart,
And all the framework of the land;

When one would aim an arrow fair,
But send it slackly from the string;
And one would pierce an outer ring,
And one an inner, here and there;

And last the master-bowman, he,
        Would cleave the mark. A willing ear
        We lent him. Who, but hung to hear
The rapt oration flowing free

From point to point, with power and grace
        And music in the bounds of law,
        To those conclusions when we saw
The God within him light his face,

And seem to lift the form, and glow
        In azure orbits heavenly-wise;
        And over those ethereal eyes
The bar of Michael Angelo.

xcv

By night we linger'd on the lawn,
        For underfoot the herb was dry;
        And genial warmth; and o'er the sky
The silvery haze of summer drawn;

And calm that let the tapers burn
        Unwavering: not a cricket chirr'd:
        The brook alone far-off was heard,
And on the board the fluttering urn:

And bats went round in fragrant skies,
        And wheel'd or lit the filmy shapes
        That haunt the dusk, with ermine capes
And woolly breasts and beaded eyes;

While now we sang old songs that peal'd
        From knoll to knoll, where, couch'd at ease,
        The white kine glimmer'd, and the trees
Laid their dark arms about the field.

But when those others, one by one,
        Withdrew themselves from me and night,

And in the house light after light
Went out, and I was all alone,

A hunger seized my heart; I read
      Of that glad year which once had been,
      In those fall'n leaves which kept their
         green,
The noble letters of the dead:

And strangely on the silence broke
      The silent-speaking words, and strange
      Was love's dumb cry defying change
To test his worth; and strangely spoke

The faith, the vigour, bold to dwell
      On doubts that drive the coward back,
      And keen thro' wordy snares to track
Suggestion to her inmost cell.

So word by word, and line by line,
      The dead man touch'd me from the past,
      And all at once it seem'd at last
The living soul was flash'd on mine,

And mine in this was wound, and whirl'd
      About empyreal heights of thought,
      And came on that which is, and caught
The deep pulsations of the world,

Æonian music measuring out
      The steps of Time – the shocks of Chance –
      The blows of Death. At length my trance
Was cancell'd, stricken thro' with doubt.

Vague words! but ah, how hard to frame
      In matter-moulded forms of speech,
      Or ev'n for intellect to reach
Thro' memory that which I became:

Till now the doubtful dusk reveal'd
      The knolls once more where, couch'd at
         ease,
      The white kine glimmer'd, and the trees
Laid their dark arms about the field:

And suck'd from out the distant gloom
      A breeze began to tremble o'er
      The large leaves of the sycamore,
And fluctuate all the still perfume,

And gathering freshlier overhead,
      Rock'd the full-foliaged elms, and swung
      The heavy-folded rose, and flung
The lilies to and fro, and said

'The dawn, the dawn,' and died away;
      And East and West, without a breath,
      Mixt their dim lights, like life and death,
To broaden into boundless day.

CVI

Ring out, wild bells, to the wild sky,
      The flying cloud, the frosty light:
      The year is dying in the night;
Ring out, wild bells, and let him die.

Ring out the old, ring in the new,
      Ring, happy bells, across the snow:
      The year is going, let him go;
Ring out the false, ring in the true.

Ring out the grief that saps the mind,
      For those that here we see no more;
      Ring out the feud of rich and poor,
Ring in redress to all mankind.

Ring out a slowly dying cause,
      And ancient forms of party strife;
      Ring in the nobler modes of life,
With sweeter manners, purer laws.

Ring out the want, the care, the sin,
      The faithless coldness of the times;
      Ring out, ring out my mournful rhymes,
But ring the fuller minstrel in.

Ring out false pride in place and blood,
      The civic slander and the spite;
      Ring in the love of truth and right,
Ring in the common love of good.

Ring out old shapes of foul disease;
      Ring out the narrowing lust of gold;
      Ring out the thousand wars of old,
Ring in the thousand years of peace.

Ring in the valiant man and free,
      The larger heart, the kindlier hand;
      Ring out the darkness of the land,
Ring in the Christ that is to be.

FRANCIS LEDWIDGE

[1917]   Lament for Thomas MacDonagh

He shall not hear the bittern cry
In the wild sky, where he is lain,
Nor voices of the sweeter birds
Above the wailing of the rain.

Nor shall he know when loud March blows
Thro' slanting snows her fanfare shrill,
Blowing to flame the golden cup
Of many an upset daffodil.

But when the Dark Cow leaves the moor,
And pastures poor with greedy weeds,
Perhaps he'll hear her low at morn
Lifting her horn in pleasant meads.

JOHN MILTON

[1637]

Lycidas

Yet once more, O ye laurels, and once more
Ye myrtles brown, with ivy never sere,
I come to pluck your berries harsh and crude,
And with forced fingers rude,
Shatter your leaves before the mellowing year.
Bitter constraint, and sad occasion dear,
Compels me to disturb your season due:
For Lycidas is dead, dead ere his prime,
Young Lycidas, and hath not left his peer:
Who would not sing for Lycidas? he knew
Himself to sing, and build the lofty rhyme.
He must not float upon his watery bier
Unwept, and welter to the parching wind,
reward   Without the meed of some melodious tear.
   Begin then, sisters of the sacred well,
That from beneath the seat of Jove doth spring,
Begin, and somewhat loudly sweep the string.
Hence with denial vain, and coy excuse,
So may some gentle muse
With lucky words favour my destined urn,
And as he passes turn,
And bid fair peace be to my sable shroud.
For we were nursed upon the self-same hill,
Fed the same flock; by fountain, shade, and rill.
   Together both, ere the high lawns appeared
Under the opening eye-lids of the morn,
We drove a-field, and both together heard
What time the grey-fly winds her sultry horn,

Battening our flocks with the fresh dews of night,
Oft till the star that rose, at evening, bright,
Toward heaven's descent had sloped his
    westering wheel.
Meanwhile the rural ditties were not mute,
Tempered to the oaten flute,
Rough satyrs danced, and fauns with cloven heel,
From the glad sound would not be absent long,
And old Damaetas loved to hear our song.

   But O the heavy change, now thou art gone,
Now thou art gone, and never must return!
Thee shepherd, thee the woods, and desert caves,
With wild thyme and the gadding vine o'ergrown,
And all their echoes mourn.
The willows, and the hazel copses green,
Shall now no more be seen,
Fanning their joyous leaves to thy soft lays.
As killing as the canker to the rose,
Or taint-worm to the weanling herds that graze,
Or frost to flowers, that their gay wardrobe wear,
When first the white-thorn blows;
Such, Lycidas, thy loss to shepherd's ear.

   Where were ye nymphs when the remorseless
    deep
Closed o'er the head of your loved Lycidas?
For neither were ye playing on the steep,
Where your old bards, the famous Druids, lie,
Nor on the shaggy top of Mona high,
Nor yet where Deva spreads her wizard stream:
Ay me, I fondly dream!
Had ye been there . . . for what could that have
    done?
What could the muse herself that Orpheus bore,
The muse herself for her enchanting son
Whom universal nature did lament,
When by the rout that made the hideous roar,

His gory visage down the stream was sent,
Down the swift Hebrus to the Lesbian shore.
   Alas! What boots it with uncessant care
To tend the homely slighted shepherd's trade,
And strictly meditate the thankless muse,
Were it not better done as others use,
To sport with Amaryllis in the shade,
Or with the tangles of Neaera's hair?
Fame is the spur that the clear spirit doth raise
(That last infirmity of noble mind)
To scorn delights, and live laborious days;
But the fair guerdon when we hope to find,
And think to burst out into sudden blaze,
Comes the blind Fury with th' abhorred shears,
And slits the thin-spun life. But not the praise,
Phoebus replied, and touched my trembling ears;
Fame is no plant that grows on mortal soil,
Nor in the glistering foil
Set off to the world, nor in broad rumour lies,
But lives and spreads aloft by those pure eyes,
And perfect witness of all-judging Jove;
As he pronounces lastly on each deed,
Of so much fame in heaven expect thy meed.
   O fountain Arethuse, and thou honoured
      flood,
Smooth-sliding Mincius, crowned with vocal
      reeds,
That strain I heard was of a higher mood:
flute, pipe But now my oat proceeds,
And listens to the herald of the sea
That came in Neptune's plea,
He asked the waves, and asked the felon winds,
What hard mishap hath doomed this gentle
      swain?
And questioned every gust of rugged wings
That blows from off each beaked promontory;

They knew not of his story,
And sage Hippotades their answer brings,
That not a blast was from his dungeon strayed,
The air was calm, and on the level brine,
Sleek Panope with all her sisters played.
It was that fatal and perfidious bark
Built in the eclipse, and rigged with curses dark,
That sunk so low that sacred head of thine.
   Next Camus, reverend sire, went footing
      slow,
His mantle hairy, and his bonnet sedge,
Inwrought with figures dim, and on the edge
Like to that sanguine flower inscribed with woe.
Ah; who hath reft (quoth he) my dearest pledge?
Last came, and last did go,
The pilot of the Galilean lake,
Two massy keys he bore of metals twain,
(The golden opes, the iron shuts amain)
He shook his mitred locks, and stern bespake,
How well could I have spared for thee, young
    swain,
Enow of such as for their bellies' sake,
Creep and intrude, and climb into the fold?
Of other care they little reckoning make,
Than how to scramble at the shearers' feast,
And shove away the worthy bidden guest;
Blind mouths! that scarce themselves know how
   to hold
A sheep-hook, or have learned aught else the
   least
That to the faithful herdman's art belongs!
concerns What recks it them? What need they? They are
   sped;
And when they list, their lean and flashy songs
Grate on their scrannel pipes of wretched straw,
The hungry sheep look up, and are not fed,

But swoll'n with wind, and the rank mist they
    draw,
Rot inwardly, and foul contagion spread:
Besides what the grim wolf with privy paw
Daily devours apace, and nothing said,
But that two-handed engine at the door,
Stands ready to smite once, and smite no more.
    Return Alpheus, the dread voice is past,
That shrunk thy steams; return Sicilian muse,
And call the vales, and bid them hither cast
Their bells, and flowrets of a thousand hues.
Ye valleys low where the mild whispers use,
Of shades and wanton winds, and gushing
    brooks,
On whose fresh lap the swart star sparely looks,
Throw hither all your quaint enamelled eyes,
That on the green turf suck the honied showers,
And purple all the ground with vernal flowers.
early   Bring the rathe primrose that forsaken dies,
The tufted crow-toe, and pale jessamine,
The white pink, and the pansy freaked with jet,
The glowing violet
The musk-rose, and the well-attired woodbine,
With cowslips wan that hang the pensive head,
And every flower that sad embroidery wears:
Bid amaranthus all his beauty shed,
And daffadillies fill their cups with tears,
To strew the laureate hearse where Lycid lies.
For so to interpose a little ease,
Let our frail thoughts dally with false surmise.
Ay me! Whilst thee the shores, and sounding seas
Wash far away, where'er thy bones are hurled,
Whether beyond the stormy Hebrides
Where thou perhaps under the whelming tide
Visit'st the bottom of the monstrous world;
Or whether thou to our moist vows denied,

Sleep'st by the fable of Bellerus old,

i.e., St Michael's Mount Where the great vision of the guarded mount
fortress Looks toward Namancos and Bayona's hold;
Look homeward angel now, and melt with ruth.
And, O ye dolphins, waft the hapless youth.

    Weep no more, woeful shepherds weep no more,
For Lycidas your sorrow is not dead,
Sunk though he be beneath the watery floor,
So sinks the day-star in the ocean bed,
And yet anon repairs his drooping head,
And tricks his beams, and with new spangled ore,
Flames in the forehead of the morning sky:
So Lycidas sunk low, but mounted high,
Through the dear might of him that walked the
      waves;
Where other groves, and other streams along,
With nectar pure his oozy locks he laves,
And hears the unexpressive nuptial song,
In the blest kingdoms meek of joy and love.
There entertain him all the saints above,
In solemn troops, and sweet societies
That sing, and singing in their glory move,
And wipe the tears for ever from his eyes.
Now, Lycidas, the shepherds weep no more;
Henceforth thou art the genius of the shore,
In thy large recompense, and shalt be good
To all that wander in that perilous flood.

unknown   Thus sang the uncouth swain to the oaks and
      rills,
While the still morn went out with sandals grey,
He touched the tender stops of various quills,
With eager thought warbling his Doric lay:
And now the sun had stretched out all the hills,
And now was dropped into the western bay;
At last he rose, and twitched his mantle blue:
Tomorrow to fresh woods, and pastures new.

[1959]

Last Look

His mind, as he was going out of it,
Looked emptier, shabbier than it used to be:
A secret look to which he had no key,
Something misplaced, something that did not fit.

Windows without their curtains seemed to stare
Inward – but surely once they had looked out.
Someone had moved the furniture about
And changed the photographs: the frames were
    there,

But idiot faces never seen before
Leered back at him. He knew there should have
    been
A carpet on the boards, not these obscene
Clusters of toadstools sprouting through the
    floor.

Yet Arabella's portrait on the wall
Followed him just as usual with its eyes.
Was it reproach or pleading, or surprise,
Or love perhaps, or something of them all?

Watching her lips, he saw them part; could just
Catch the thin sibilance of her concern:
'O Richard, Richard, why would you not learn
I was the only soul that you could trust?'

Carefully, carefully, seeming not to know,
He added this remembrance to his store.
Conscience, in uniform beside the door,
Coughed and remarked that it was time to go.

High time indeed! He heard their tramping feet.
To have stayed even so long, he knew, was rash.

The mob was in the house. He heard the crash
Of furniture hurled down into the street.

'This way!' the warder said. 'You must be quick.
You will be safe with us' – He turned to go
And saw too late the gaping void below.
Someone behind him laughed. A brutal kick

Caught him below the shoulders and he fell.
Quite slowly, clutching at the passing air,
He plunged towards the source of his despair
Down the smooth funnel of an endless well.

THOMAS TRAHERNE

[late 17th century]   Shadows in the Water

In unexperienc'd Infancy
Many a sweet Mistake doth lye:
Mistake tho false, intending true;
A *Seeming* somewhat more than *View*;
        That doth instruct the Mind
        In Things that lye behind,
And many Secrets to us show
Which afterwards we com to know.

Thus did I by the Water's brink
Another World beneath me think;
And while the lofty spacious Skies
Reversed there abus'd mine Eyes,
        I fancy'd other Feet
        Came mine to touch or meet;
As by som Puddle I did play
Another World within it lay.

Beneath the Water People drown'd,
Yet with another Hev'n crown'd,
In spacious Regions seem'd to go
As freely moving to and fro:

In bright and open Space
I saw their very face;
Eyes, Hands, and Feet they had like mine;
Another Sun did with them shine.

'Twas strange that People there should walk,
And yet I could not hear them talk:
That thro a little watry Chink,
Which one dry Ox or Horse might drink,
We other Worlds should see,
Yet not admitted be;
And other Confines there behold
Of Light and Darkness, Heat and Cold.

I call'd them oft, but call'd in vain;
No Speeches we could entertain:
Yet did I there expect to find
Some other World, to please my Mind.
I plainly saw by these
A new *Antipodes*,
Whom, tho they were so plainly seen,
A Film kept off that stood between.

By walking Men's reversed Feet
I chanc'd another World to meet;
Tho it did not to View exceed
A Phantasm, 'tis a World indeed,
Where Skies beneath us shine,
And Earth by Art divine
Another face presents below
Where People's feet against Ours go.

Within the Regions of the Air,
Compass'd about with Hev'ns fair,
Great Tracts of Land there may be found
Enricht with Fields and fertil Ground;
Where many num'rous Hosts,
In those far distant Coasts,

For other great and glorious Ends,
Inhabit, my yet unknown Friends.

O ye that stand upon the Brink,
Whom I so near me, thro the Chink,
With Wonder see: What Faces there,
Whose Feet, whose Bodies, do ye wear?
    I my Companions see
    In You, another Me.
They seemed Others, but are We;
Our second Selves those Shadows be.

Look how far off those lower Skies
Extend themselves! scarce with mine Eyes
I can them reach. O ye my Friends,
What *Secret* borders on those Ends?
    Are lofty Hevens hurl'd
    'Bout your inferior World?
Are ye the Representatives
Of other People's distant Lives?

Of all the Play-mates which I knew
That here I do the Image view
In other Selves; what can it mean?
But that below the purling Stream
    Some unknown Joys there be
    Laid up in store for me;
To which I shall, when that thin Skin
Is broken, be admitted in.

JAMES MCAULEY

One Tuesday in Summer

That sultry afternoon the world went strange.
Under a violet and leaden bruise
The air was filled with sinister yellow light;
Trees, houses, grass took on unnatural hues.

Thunder rolled near. The intensity grew and grew
Like doom itself with lightnings on its face.
And Mr Pitt, the grocer's order-man,
Who made his call on Tuesdays at our place,

Said to my mother, looking at the sky,
'You'd think the ending of the world had come.'
A leathern little man, with bicycle-clips
Around his ankles, doing our weekly sum,

He too looked strange in that uncanny light;
As in the Bible ordinary men
Turn out to be angelic messengers,
Pronouncing the Lord's judgments why and
     when.

I watched the scurry of the small black ants
That sensed the storm. What Mr Pitt had said
I didn't quite believe, or disbelieve;
But still the words had got into my head,

For nothing less seemed worthy of the scene.
The darkening imminence hung on and on,
Till suddenly, with lightning-stroke and rain,
Apocalypse exploded, and was gone.

By nightfall things had their familiar look.
But I had seen the world stand in dismay
Under the aspect of another meaning
That rain or time would hardly wash away.

HENRY VAUGHAN

[1650]   'They are all gone into the world of light'

They are all gone into the world of light!
     And I alone sit lingring here;
Their very memory is fair and bright,
     And my sad thoughts doth clear.

It glows and glitters in my cloudy brest
    Like stars upon some gloomy grove,
Or those faint beams in which this hill is drest,
    After the Sun's remove.

I see them walking in an Air of glory,
    Whose light doth trample on my days:
My days, which are at best but dull and hoary,
    Meer glimering and decays.

O holy hope! and high humility,
    High as the Heavens above!
These are your walks, and you have shew'd them me
    To kindle my cold love,

Dear, beauteous death! the Jewel of the Just,
    Shining no where, but in the dark;
What mysteries do lie beyond thy dust;
    Could man outlook that mark!

He that hath found some fledg'd birds nest, may know
    At first sight, if the bird be flown;
But what fair Well, or Grove he sings in now,
    That is to him unknown.

And yet, as Angels in some brighter dreams
    Call to the soul, when man doth sleep:
So some strange thoughts transcend our wonted theams,
    And into glory peep.

If a star were confin'd into a Tomb
    Her captive flames must needs burn there;
But when the hand that lockt her up, gives room,
    She'l shine through all the sphære.

O Father of eternal life, and all
    Created glories under thee!
Resume thy spirit from this world of thrall
    Into true liberty.

Either disperse these mists, which blot and fill
    My perspective (still) as they pass,
Or else remove me hence unto that hill
    Where I shall need no glass.

ANONYMOUS (OLD ENGLISH)

[10th century or
earlier]

Deor

Weland that famous swordsmith
Endured the gull and the wave.
He blew his fists in winter,
He looked for a foreign grave.
He trudged about the headlands,
A cripple and a slave.
           That sorrow withered, so may this

Beadohild wept when death
Cold on her brothers was snowing.
And sorrow grew. No gown
Could hide from public showing
The glebe of her body rich
From Weland's reckless sowing.
           That sorrow withered, so may this

The stranger paused. He marvelled
At a heart-rooted pain.
The thorn ran deep, the bud
Spread a crimson stain.
He would not pluck it, for fear
The rose scattered like rain.
           That sorrow withered, so may this

Earmonric the tyrant
Sat like a wolf by the wall.
Secret mouths round the board
Drank to the beast's fall.
He licked long lazy chops.
The ale grew bitter as gall.
> *That sorrow withered, so may this*

Deor the poet's my name.
I enchanted the leaves of June
Till Heorrend Honeythroat came
And warbled me out of tune,
And sang my fields away,
And shaped a purer rune.
> *All sorrows wither, so may this*
>> *translated by George Mackay Brown*

SIR THOMAS WYATT

[c. 1557]   ### 'They flee from me, that sometime did me seek'

They flee from me, that sometime did me seek
With naked foot stalking in my chamber.
I have seen them gentle, tame, and meek
That now are wild, and do not remember
That sometime they have put themself in danger
To take bread at my hand; and now they range,
Busily seeking with a continual change.

Thanked be fortune it hath been otherwise
Twenty times better, but once in special,
In thin array after a pleasant guise
When her loose gown did from her shoulders fall,
And she me caught in her arms long and small,
Therewithal sweetly did me kiss,
And softly said, 'Dear heart, how like you this?'

It was no dream: I lay broad waking
But all is turned thorough my gentleness
Into a strange fashion of forsaking,
And I have leave to go of her goodness,
And she also to use newfangleness.
But since that I so kindly am served,
I would fain know what she hath deserved.

ROBERT FROST

[1924] ## To Earthward

Love at the lips was touch
As sweet as I could bear;
And once that seemed too much;
I lived on air

That crossed me from sweet things,
The flow of – was it musk
From hidden grapevine springs
Down-hill at dusk?

I had the swirl and ache
From sprays of honeysuckle
That when they're gathered shake
Dew on the knuckle.

I craved strong sweets, but those
Seemed strong when I was young;
The petal of the rose
It was that stung.

Now no joy but lacks salt,
That is not dashed with pain
And weariness and fault;
I crave the stain

Of tears, the aftermark
Of almost too much love,
The sweet of bitter bark
And burning clove.

When stiff and sore and scarred
I take away my hand
From leaning on it hard
In grass and sand,

The hurt is not enough:
I long for weight and strength
To feel the earth as rough
To all my length.

QUEEN ELIZABETH I

[1582] ## On Monsieur's Departure

I grieve and dare not show my discontent,
I love and yet am forced to seem to hate,
I do, yet dare not say I ever meant,
I seem stark mute yet inwardly do prate.
    I am and not, I freeze and yet am burned,
    Since from myself my other self I turned.

My care is like my shadow in the sun,
Follows me flying, flies when I pursue it,
Stands and lies by me, doth what I have done.
His too familiar care doth make me rue it.
    No means I find to rid him from my breast,
    Till by the end of things it be supprest.

Some gentler passions slide into my mind,
For I am soft and made of melting snow;
Or be more cruel, love, and so be kind.
Let me or float or sink, be high or low.
    Or let me live with some more sweet content,
    Or die and so forget what love ere meant.

MICHAEL DRAYTON

[1619]

'Since there's no help, come let us kiss and part'

Since there's no help, come let us kiss and part –
Nay, I have done: you get no more of me;
And I am glad, yea, glad with all my heart,
That thus so cleanly I myself can free.
Shake hands for ever, cancel all our vows,
And when we meet at any time again,
Be it not seen in either of our brows
That we one jot of former love retain.
Now at the last gasp of love's latest breath,
When, his pulse failing, Passion speechless lies,
When Faith is kneeling by his bed of death,
And Innocence is closing up his eyes, –
  Now, if thou wouldst, when all have given
    him over,
  From death to life thou might'st him yet
    recover!

SIR PHILIP SIDNEY

[1598]

'With how sad steps, O Moon, thou climb'st the skies'

With how sad steps, O Moon, thou climb'st the
  skies!
How silently, and with how wan a face!
What! may it be that even in heavenly place
That busy archer his sharp arrows tries?
Sure, if that long-with-love-acquainted eyes
Can judge of love, thou feel'st a lover's case:
I read it in thy looks; thy languished grace
To me, that feel the like, thy state descries.

Then, even of fellowship, O Moon, tell me,
Is constant love deemed there but want of wit?
Are beauties there as proud as here they be?
Do they above love to be loved, and yet
Those lovers scorn whom that love doth possess?
Do they call virtue there ungratefulness?

AITHBHREAC INGHEAN CORCADAIL
(SCOTS GAELIC)

[15th century]

'O rosary that recalled my tear'

O rosary that recalled my tear,
dear was the finger in my sight,
that touched you once, beloved the heart
of him who owned you till tonight.

I grieve the death of him whose hand
you did entwine each hour of prayer;
my grief that it is lifeless now
and I no longer see it there.

My heart is sick, the day has reached
its end for us two, brief the span
that I was given to enjoy
the converse of this goodly man.

Lips whose speech made pleasant sound,
in every land beguiling all,
hawk of Islay of smooth plains,
lion of Mull of the white wall.

His memory for songs was keen,
no poet left him without fee,
nobly generous, courteous, calm,
of princely character was he.

Poets came from Dun an Óir,
and from the Boyne, to him whose hair

was all in curls, drawn by his fame;
to each he gave a generous share.

Slim handsome hawk of Sliabh Gaoil,
who satisfied the clergy's hopes,
salmon of Sanas of quiet stream,
dragon of Lewis of sun-drenched slopes.

Bereft of this man, all alone
I live, and take no part in play,
enjoy no kindly talk, nor mirth,
now that his smiles have gone away.

Niall Og is dead; none of his clan
can hold my interest for long;
the ladies droop, their mirth is stilled,
I cannot hope for joy in song.

Gigha of smooth soil is bereft,
no need of music Dun Suibhne feels,
the grass grows green round the heroes' fort;
they know the sorrow of the MacNeills.

The fort that brought us mirth, each time
we made our way there; now the sight
of it is more than I can bear
as I look on it from each height.

If Thou, Son of the living God,
hast breached the cluster on the tree,
Thou hast taken from us our choicest nut,
and plucked the greatest of the three.

The topmost nut of the bunch is plucked,
Clan Neill has newly lost its head:
often the best of the generous men
descends to the MacNeills' last bed.

His death, the finest of them all,
has sapped my strength, and cost me dear,

taking away my darling spouse,
O rosary that recalled my tear.

My heart is broken in my breast,
and will not heal till death, I fear,
now that the dark-eyed one is dead,
O rosary that recalled my tear.

May Mary Mother, the King's nurse,
guard each path I follow here,
and may Her Son watch over me,
O rosary that recalled my tear.

translated by Derick Thomson

HENRY KING

[pub. 1657]   ## The Exequy

Accept thou Shrine of my dead Saint,
Insteed of Dirges this complaint;
And for sweet flowres to crown thy hearse,
Receive a strew of weeping verse
From thy griev'd friend, whom thou might'st see
Quite melted into tears for thee.

Dear loss! since thy untimely fate
My task hath been to meditate
On thee, on thee: thou art the book,
The library whereon I look
Though almost blind. For thee (lov'd clay)
I languish out not live the day,
Using no other exercise
But what I practise with mine eyes:
By which wet glasses I find out
How lazily time creeps about
To one that mourns: this, onely this
My exercise and bus'ness is:

So I compute the weary houres
With sighs dissolved into showres.

    Nor wonder if my time go thus
Backward and most preposterous;
Thou hast benighted me, thy set
This Eve of blackness did beget,
Who was't my day, (though overcast
Before thou had'st thy Noon-tide past)
And I remember must in tears,
Thou scarce had'st seen so many years
As Day tells houres. By thy cleer Sun
My love and fortune first did run;
But thou wilt never more appear
Folded within my Hemisphear,
Since both thy light and motion
Like a fled Star is fall'n and gon,
And twixt me and my soules dear wish
The earth now interposed is,
With such a strange eclipse doth make
As ne're was read in Almanake.

    I could allow thee for a time
To darken me and my sad Clime,
Were it a month, a year, or ten,
I would thy exile live till then;
And all that space my mirth adjourn,
So thou wouldst promise to return;
And putting off thy ashy shrowd
At length disperse this sorrows cloud.

    But woe is me! the longest date
Too narrow is to calculate
These empty hopes: never shall I
Be so much blest as to descry
A glimpse of thee, till that day come
Which shall the earth to cinders doome,

And a fierce Feaver must calcine
The body of this world like thine,
(My Little World!) that fit of fire
Once off, our bodies shall aspire
To our soules bliss: then we shall rise,
And view our selves with cleerer eyes
In that calm Region, where no night
Can hide us from each others sight.

Mean time, thou hast her earth: much good
May my harm do thee. Since it stood
With Heavens will I might not call
Her longer mine, I give thee all
My short-liv'd right and interest
In her, whom living I lov'd best:
With a most free and bounteous grief,
I give thee what I could not keep.
Be kind to her, and prethee look
Thou write into thy Dooms-day book
Each parcell of this Rarity
Which in thy Casket shrin'd doth ly:
See that thou make thy reck'ning streight,
And yield her back again by weight;
For thou must audit on thy trust
Each graine and atome of this dust,
As thou wilt answer *Him* that lent,
Not gave thee my dear Monument.

So close the ground, and 'bout her shade
Black curtains draw, my *Bride* is laid.

Sleep on my *Love* in thy cold bed
Never to be disquieted!
My last good night! Thou wilt not wake
Till I thy fate shall overtake:
Till age, or grief, or sickness must
Marry my body to that dust

It so much loves; and fill the room
My heart keeps empty in thy Tomb.
Stay for me there; I will not faile
To meet thee in that hallow Vale.
And think not much of my delay;
I am already on the way,
And follow thee with all the speed
Desire can make, or sorrows breed.
Each minute is a short degree,
And ev'ry houre a step towards thee.
At night when I betake to rest,
Next morn I rise neerer my West
Of life, almost by eight houres saile,
Then when sleep breath'd his drowsie gale.

    Thus from the Sun my Bottom stears,
And my dayes Compass downward bears:
Nor labour I to stemme the tide
Through which to *Thee* I swiftly glide.

    'Tis true, with shame and grief I yield,
Thou like the *Vann* first took'st the field,
And gotten hast the victory
In thus adventuring to dy
Before me, whose more years might crave
A just precedence in the grave.
But heark! My pulse like a soft Drum
Beats my approach, tells *Thee* I come;
And slow howere my marches be,
I shall at last sit down by *Thee*.

    The thought of this bids me go on,
And wait my dissolution
With hope and comfort. *Dear* (forgive
The crime) I am content to live
Divided, with but half a heart,
Till we shall meet and never part.

[traditional] ## The Unquiet Grave

'The wind doth blow today, my love,
  And a few small drops of rain;
I never had but one true-love,
  In cold grave she was lain.

'I'll do as much for my true-love
  As any young man may;
I'll sit and mourn all at her grave
  For a twelvemonth and a day.'

The twelvemonth and a day being up,
  The dead began to speak:
'Oh who sits weeping on my grave,
  And will not let me sleep?'

''Tis I, my love, sits on your grave,
  And will not let you sleep;
For I crave one kiss of your clay-cold lips,
  And that is all I seek.'

'You crave one kiss of my clay-cold lips;
  But my breath smells earthy strong;
If you have one kiss of my clay-cold lips,
  Your time will not be long.

''Tis down in yonder garden green,
  Love, where we used to walk,
The finest flower that e'er was seen
  Is withered to a stalk.

'The stalk is withered dry, my love,
  So will our hearts decay;
So make yourself content, my love,
  Till God calls you away.'

LAURA RIDING

[1930s] ## The Wind Suffers

The wind suffers of blowing,
The sea suffers of water,
And fire suffers of burning,
And I of a living name.

As stone suffers of stoniness,
As light of its shiningness,
As birds of their wingedness,
So I of my whoness.

And what the cure of all this?
What the not and not suffering?
What the better and later of this?
What the more me of me?

How for the pain-world to be
More world and no pain?
How for the faithful rain to fall
More wet and more dry?

How for the wilful blood to run
More salt-red and sweet-white?
And how for me in my actualness
To more shriek and more smile?

By no other miracles,
By the same knowing poison,
By an improved anguish,
By my further dying.

LOUIS MACNEICE

[1941] ## Meeting Point

Time was away and somewhere else,
There were two glasses and two chairs

And two people with the one pulse
(Somebody stopped the moving stairs):
Time was away and somewhere else.

And they were neither up nor down;
The stream's music did not stop
Flowing through heather, limpid brown,
Although they sat in a coffee shop
And they were neither up nor down.

The bell was silent in the air
Holding its inverted poise –
Between the clang and clang a flower,
A brazen calyx of no noise:
The bell was silent in the air.

The camels crossed the miles of sand
That stretched around the cups and plates;
The desert was their own, they planned
To portion out the stars and dates:
The camels crossed the miles of sand.

Time was away and somewhere else.
The waiter did not come, the clock
Forgot them and the radio waltz
Came out like water from a rock:
Time was away and somewhere else.

Her fingers flicked away the ash
That bloomed again in tropic trees:
Not caring if the markets crash
When they had forests such as these,
Her fingers flicked away the ash.

God or whatever means the Good
Be praised that time can stop like this,
That what the heart has understood
Can verify in the body's peace
God or whatever means the Good.

Time was away and she was here
And life no longer what it was,
The bell was silent in the air
And all the room one glow because
Time was away and she was here.

ROBERT GRAVES

[1919] Lost Love

His eyes are quickened so with grief,
He can watch a grass or leaf
Every instant grow; he can
Clearly through a flint wall see,
Or watch the startled spirit flee
From the throat of a dead man.
    Across two counties he can hear,
And catch your words before you speak.
The woodlouse, or the maggot's weak
Clamour rings in his sad ear;
And noise so slight it would surpass
Credence: – drinking sound of grass,
Worm talk, clashing jaws of moth
Chumbling holes in cloth:
The groan of ants who undertake
Gigantic loads for honour's sake,
Their sinews creak, their breath comes thin:
Whir of spiders when they spin,
And minute whispering, mumbling, sighs
Of idle grubs and flies.
    This man is quickened so with grief,
He wanders god-like or like thief
Inside and out, below, above,
Without relief seeking lost love.

ANONYMOUS

[late 13th century]   'Foweles in the frith'

wood   Foweles in the frith,
river   The fisses in the flod,
go mad   And I mon waxe wod:
           Mulch sorw I walke with
           For beste of bon and blod.

ANONYMOUS

[1600]   'Thulë, the period of cosmography,'

furthest point on map   Thulë, the period of cosmography,
           Doth vaunt of Hecla, whose sulphureous fire
           Doth melt the frozen clime and thaw the sky;
           Trinacrian Etna's flames ascend not higher:
           These things seem wondrous, yet more wondrous
           I,
           Whose heart with fear doth freeze, with love doth
           fry.

           The Andalusian merchant, that returns
           Laden with cochineal and china dishes,
           Reports in Spain how strangely Fogo burns
           Amidst an ocean full of flying fishes:
           These things seem wondrous, yet more wondrous
           I,
           Whose heart with fear doth freeze, with love doth
           fry.

FULKE GREVILLE, LORD BROOKE

[1590s]   'When all this All doth pass from age
           to age'

           When all this All doth pass from age to age,
           And revolution in a circle turn,

Then heavenly justice doth appear like rage,
The caves do roar, the very seas do burn,
  Glory grows dark, the sun becomes a night,
  And makes this great world feel a greater
    might.

When love doth change his seat from heart to
    heart,
And worth about the Wheel of Fortune goes,
Grace is diseas'd, desert seems overthwart,
Vows are forlorn, and truth doth credit lose,
  Chance then gives law, desire must be wise,
  And look more ways than one, or lose her
    eyes.

My age of joy is past, of woe begun,
Absence my presence is, strangeness my grace,
With them that walk against me, is my sun:
The wheel is turn'd, I hold the lowest place,
  What can be good to me since my love is,
  To do me harm, content to do amiss?

PERCY BYSSHE SHELLEY

[1819] Ode to the West Wind

I

O, wild West Wind, thou breath of Autumn's
    being,
Thou, from whose unseen presence the leaves
    dead
Are driven, like ghosts from an enchanter fleeing,

Yellow, and black, and pale, and hectic red,
Pestilence-stricken multitudes: O, thou,
Who chariotest to their dark wintry bed

The wingèd seeds, where they lie cold and low,
Each like a corpse within its grave, until
Thine azure sister of the Spring shall blow

Her clarion o'er the dreaming earth, and fill
(Driving sweet buds like flocks to feed in air)
With living hues and odours plain and hill:

Wild Spirit, which art moving everywhere;
Destroyer and preserver; hear, O hear!

II

Thou on whose stream, mid the steep sky's
    commotion,
Loose clouds like earth's decaying leaves are
    shed,
Shook from the tangled boughs of Heaven and
    Ocean,

Angels of rain and lightning: there are spread
On the blue surface of thine aëry surge,
Like the bright hair uplifted from the head

Of some fierce Maenad, even from the dim verge
Of the horizon to the zenith's height
The locks of the approaching storm. Thou dirge

Of the dying year, to which this closing night
Will be the dome of a vast sepulchre,
Vaulted with all thy congregated might

Of vapours, from whose solid atmosphere
Black rain, and fire, and hail will burst: O hear!

III

Thou who didst waken from his summer dreams
The blue Mediterranean, where he lay,
Lulled by the coil of his crystàlline streams,

Beside a pumice isle in Baiae's bay,
And saw in sleep old palaces and towers
Quivering within the wave's intenser day,

All overgrown with azure moss and flowers
So sweet, the sense faints picturing them! Thou
For whose path the Atlantic's level powers

Cleave themselves into chasms, while far below
The sea-blooms and the oozy woods which wear
The sapless foliage of the ocean, know

Thy voice, and suddenly grow grey with fear,
And tremble and despoil themselves: O hear!

IV

If I were a dead leaf thou mightest bear;
If I were a swift cloud to fly with thee;
A wave to pant beneath thy power, and share

The impulse of thy strength, only less free
Than thou, O uncontrollable! If even
I were as in my boyhood, and could be

The comrade of thy wanderings over Heaven,
As then, when to outstrip thy skiey speed
Scarce seemed a vision; I would ne'er have
    striven

As thus with thee in prayer in my sore need.
Oh, lift me as a wave, a leaf, a cloud!
I fall upon the thorns of life! I bleed!

A heavy weight of hours has chained and bowed
One too like thee: tameless, and swift, and proud.

V

Make me thy lyre, even as the forest is:
What if my leaves are falling like its own!
The tumult of thy mighty harmonies

Will take from both a deep, autumnal tone,
Sweet though in sadness. Be thou, Spirit fierce,
My spirit! Be thou me, impetuous one!

Drive my dead thoughts over the universe
Like withered leaves to quicken a new birth!
And, by the incantation of this verse,

Scatter, as from an unextinguished hearth
Ashes and sparks, my words among mankind!
Be through my lips to unawakened earth

The trumpet of a prophecy! O, Wind,
If Winter comes, can Spring be far behind?

WILLIAM DRUMMOND OF HAWTHORNDEN

[1656]   'This Life, which seems so fair'

This Life, which seems so fair,
  Is like a bubble blown up in the air
   By sporting children's breath,
   Who chase it everywhere,
And strive who can most motion it bequeath.
And though it sometimes seem of its own might
Like to an eye of gold to be fixed there,
And firm to hover in that empty height,
That only is because it is so light.
 But in that pomp it doth not long appear;
For when 'tis most admirèd – in a thought,
Because it erst was nought, it turns to nought.

GWENDOLYN BROOKS

[1945] # The Rites for Cousin Vit

Carried her unprotesting out the door.
Kicked back the casket-stand. But it can't hold
    her,
That stuff and satin aiming to enfold her,
The lid's contrition nor the bolts before.
Oh oh. Too much. Too much. Even now, surmise,
She rises in the sunshine. There she goes,
Back to the bars she knew and the repose
In love-rooms and the things in people's eyes.
Too vital and too squeaking. Must emerge.
Even now she does the snake-hips with a hiss,
Slops the bad wine across her shantung, talks
Of pregnancy, guitars and bridgework, walks
In parks or alleys, comes haply on the verge
Of happiness, haply hysterics. Is.

ROSEMARY DOBSON

[1984] # Folding the Sheets

You and I will fold the sheets
Advancing towards each other
From Burma, from Lapland,

From India where the sheets have been washed
    in the river
And pounded upon stones:
Together we will match the corners.

From China where women on either side of the
    river
Have washed their pale cloth in the White Stone
    Shallows
'Under the shining moon'.

We meet as though in the formal steps of a dance
To fold the sheets together, put them to air
In wind, in sun over bushes, or by the fire.

We stretch and pull from one side and then the
    other –
Your turn. Now mine.
We fold them and put them away until they are
    needed.

A wish for all people when they lie down in bed –
Smooth linen, cool cotton, the fragrance and stir
    of herbs
And the faint but perceptible scent of sweet clear
    water.

HUGH MACDIARMID

[1925]   ## The Bonnie Broukit Bairn
For Peggy

handsome / crimson   Mars is braw in crammasy,
Venus in a green silk goun,
The auld mune shak's her gowden feathers,
pack of nonsense   Their starry talk's a wheen o' blethers,
Nane for thee a thochtie sparin',
neglected child   Earth, thou bonnie broukit bairn!
weep   *—But greet, an' in your tears ye'll droun*
collection   *The haill clanjamfrie!*

ROBERT TANNAHILL

[1807]   ## The Tap-room

world   This warl's a tap-room owre and owre,
    Whaur ilk ane tak's his caper,
Some taste the sweet, some drink the sour,
    As waiter Fate sees proper;
Let mankind live, ae social core,

An drap a' selfish quar'ling,
An whan the Landlord ca's his score,

money   May ilk ane's clink be sterling.

CYRIL TOURNEUR

[1607] *from* The Revenger's Tragedy

VINDICE: (*holding the poisoned skull*)
Does every proud and self-affecting dame
Camphor her face for this, and grieve her maker
In sinful baths of milk, when many an infant
    starves
For her superfluous outside – all for this?
Who now bids twenty pound a night, prepares
Music, perfumes and sweetmeats? All are
    hushed,
Thou may'st lie chaste now! It were fine methinks
To have thee seen at revels, forgetful feasts
And unclean brothels; sure 'twould fright the
    sinner
And make him a good coward, put a reveller
Out of his antic amble
And cloy an epicure with empty dishes.
Here might a scornful and ambitious woman
Look through and through herself; see, ladies,
    with false forms
You deceive men but cannot deceive worms.
Now to my tragic business. Look you brother,
I have not fashioned this only for show
And useless property, no – it shall bear a part
E'en in its own revenge. This very skull,
Whose mistress the duke poisoned with this drug,
The mortal curse of the earth, shall be revenged
In the like strain and kiss his lips to death.
As much as the dumb thing can, he shall feel;
What fails in poison we'll supply in steel.

543

LLYWELYN GOCH AP MEURIG HEN (WELSH)

[14th century]   ## The Skull

THE BARD   Perfect skull, whom none will praise,
Pock-marked, withered-up headpiece,
Secret shame, foe of the fair
Wanton whose pale skin withered,
No gold does your cheeks homage,
Grave of sorry, mortal flesh.
Who placed you, impolitely,
Setting you to mock at me,
Out of vile, spiteful hatred,
On the wall there, dreary wretch?

THE SKULL   There's no nose, only ruins,
There is neither lip nor tooth,
There's no ear left, foul fracas,
There's no brow nor brilliant glance,
There's not an eye is left me,
And not a breath in my mouth.
Naught remains of eyes but dust
And pits brimful of blackness,
No hair, there is no mantle,
No skin to cover my face.

THE BARD   Much mortified is our land,
Cold sight, to look upon you.
Make, to conceal your forehead,
Your way to your bed of clay.
Allow, chilling all the rest,
Me my clever cywyddau.

THE SKULL   I have, I will not go back,
Lain long in a field's belly,
In fear, hiding my favour,
With the worms crowding me close.
I'll keep, though I may not drink,

My place, warning my parish.
From my niche I preach better
Than Saint Austin, or as well;
There's no man skilled at hoodwinks
May look upon me and laugh;
Grief of man, who will ask me,
Face of pain, to give him birth?
Clean contrary to feasting,
The sight of my naked skull,
Where once could be seen like silk
Auburn hair in small ringlets,
A glowing, soft, smooth forehead,
A falcon's eye and fair brows,
Lips skilled in conversation,
A fair, sweet, neatly shaped nose,
Pretty gums' honeyed language,
Clever courtly tongue and teeth,
Having on the lovely earth
A girl's faith in great passion,
A tryst among young birches,
O Jesus Christ, and a kiss.
For an earthly tare, futile,
By God, how great is man's pride,
To build a sinful burden,
A strange place for vanity.
Busy sprout, no proud passage,
Ponder your time, be not proud.

translated by Joseph P. Clancy

ANONYMOUS (WELSH)

[9th century]   *from* Hateful Old Age

Wooden staff, it is autumn.
Brown the bracken, the stubble yellow;
What once I loved I've said farewell to.

Wooden staff, it is winter.
Men are loud-tongued over their drink;
None puts in at my bed's brink.

Wooden staff, it is spring.
Cuckoos are hidden, clear their plaintive call;
Girls have no use for me at all.

Wooden staff, it is early summer.
Brown the furrow, curly the young corn;
The sight of your crook makes me groan.

translated by Gwyn Jones

THOMAS NASHE

[*c.* 1592] 'Adieu! farewell earth's bliss!'

Adieu! farewell earth's bliss!
This world uncertain is:
Fond are life's lustful joys,
Death proves them all but toys.
None from his darts can fly:
I am sick, I must die –
  Lord, have mercy on us!

Rich men, trust not in wealth,
Gold cannot buy you health;
Physic himself must fade;
All things to end are made;
The plague full swift goes by:
I am sick, I must die –
  Lord, have mercy on us!

Beauty is but a flower
Which wrinkles will devour:
Brightness falls from the air;
Queens have died young and fair

Dust hath closed Helen's eye:
I am sick, I must die –
  Lord, have mercy on us!

Strength stoops unto the grave
Worms feed on Hector brave;
Sword may not fight with fate;
Earth still holds ope her gate;
Come! come! the bells do cry:
I am sick, I must die –
  Lord, have mercy on us!

Wit with his wantonness,
Tasteth death's bitterness;
Hell's executioner
Hath no ears for to hear
What vain art can reply.
I am sick, I must die –
  Lord, have mercy on us!

Haste, therefore, each degree
To welcome destiny!
Heaven is our heritage;
Earth but a player's stage.
Mount we unto the sky!
I am sick, I must die –
  Lord, have mercy on us!

ANONYMOUS (IRISH)

[pre-6th century]   'The *rath* in front of the oak wood'

fortified enclosure   The *rath* in front of the oak wood
belonged to Bruidge, and Cathal,
belonged to Aedh, and Ailill,
belonged to Conaing, and Cuilíne
and to Mael Dúin before them
– all kings in their turn.

547

The *rath* survives; the kings
are covered in clay.

translated by Thomas Kinsella

JEAN ELLIOT

[18th century]   The Flowers of the Forest

ewe   I've heard them lilting at our yowe-milking –
      Lasses a-lilting before dawn of day;

land where cows are milked   But now they are moaning on ilka green
      loaning –

withered   The Flowers of the Forest are a' wede away.

cattle-pens   At buchts, in the morning, nae blythe lads are
      scorning;

sad   Lasses are lonely and dowie and wae; –
dallying   Nae daffin', nae gabbin' – but sighing and sabbing
milk-pail   Ilk ane lifts her leglin and hies her away.

harvest   In hairst, at the shearing, nae youths now are
      jerring –

binders / grizzled   Bandsters are runkled and lyart or grey:
At fair or at preaching, nae wooing, nae
flattering   fleeching –
      The Flowers of the Forest are a' wede away.

smart young fellows   At e'en, in the gloaming, nae swankies are
      roaming,

hide-and-seek   'Bout stacks with the lasses at bogle to play;
But ilk maid sits drearie, lamenting her dearie –
      The Flowers of the Forest are a' wede away.

grief   Dool and wae for the order sent our lads to the
      Border!
      The English, for ance, by guile wan the day; –
The Flowers of the Forest, that foucht aye the
      foremost –
      The prime of our land – are cauld in the clay.

We'll hear nae mair lilting at the yowe-milking;
Women and bairns are heartless and wae,
Sighing and moaning on ilka green loaning –
The Flowers of the Forest are a' wede away.

ANONYMOUS (OLD ENGLISH)

[pre-10th century]   Widsith

Widsith spoke, unlocked his word-hoard,
he, most travelled of men upon earth
among famous folk; in hall often took
splendid treasure. His forbears sprang
from the Myrging tribe. Together with Ealhhild,
gracious peace-weaver, for the first time,
east out of Angeln, Eormanric's
home he sought, that savage king,
fierce and faithless. He spoke at length:
    'I have heard much of the rulers of men!
A lord ought to live by custom and law;
one *eorl* rule a realm after another,
who wishes his princely throne to thrive.
Of these was Hwala the best for a time,
and Alexander mightiest of all,
of the race of men, and he prospered most
of those I have heard about over the earth.
Ætla ruled the Huns, Eormanric the Goths,
Becca the Banings, Gifeca the Burgundians.
Caesar ruled the Greeks and Cælic the Finns,
Hagena the Island-Rugians and Heoden the
    Gloms.
Witta ruled the Swabians, Wade the Hælsings,
Meaca the Myrgings, Mearchalf the Hundings.
Theodric ruled the Franks, Thyle the Rondings,
Breoca the Brondings, Billing the Werns.
Oswine ruled the Eows, and Gefwulf the Jutes;
Fin Folcwalding the tribe of the Frisians.

549

Sigehere ruled the Sea-Danes longest,
Hnæf the Hocings, Helm the Wulfings,
Wald the Woings, Wod the Thuringians,
Sæferth the Secgs, Ongentheow the Swedes,
Sceafthere the Ymbers, Sceafa the Lombards,
Hun the Hætwars, and Holen the Wrosns.
The Raiders' king was called Hringweald.
Offa ruled Angeln, Alewih the Danes:
he was the bravest of all those men,
but, in heroism, not better than Offa;
for Offa was first among men to win
by battle the greatest realm, while young.
No one at his age accomplished greater
heroism. He, with his single sword,
marked out the frontier with the Myrgings
at Fifeldor. It was later held
by Angles and Swabians, as Offa struck it.
Hrothwulf and Hrothgar longest kept
peace together, nephew and uncle,
after they routed the Viking tribe,
humbled Ingeld's vanguard and hewed
down at Heorot the Heathobard host.

    Thus I fared through many foreign lands,
over the wild world. Weal and woe
I suffered there, severed from family,
far from free kinsmen, wandering widely.
So I may sing and utter a measure;
recite before company in the mead hall
how royal dispensers gave to me freely.
I was with the Huns and with the Goths,
with the Swedes and with the Geats and with the
    South-Danes.
I was with the Wendels and with the Wærns and
    with the Vikings.
I was with the Gepids and with the Wends and
    with the Gefflegs.

I was with the Angles and with the Swabians and
with the Ænenes.
I was with the Saxons and with the Secgs and
with the Swordmen.
I was with the Whalemen and with the Danes
and the Heathoreams.
I was with the Thuringians and with the men of
Drontheim
and with the Burgundians where I took a torque;
there Guthhere gave me gleaming treasures
in reward for my song; that was no sluggish king!
I was with the Franks and with the Frisians and
with the Frumtings.
I was with the Rugians and with the Glomms and
with the Romans.
I was also in Italy with Ælfwine,
Eadwine's son; I have heard that he,
of all mankind, had the quickest hand
at gaining renown in giving out rings,
gleaming bracelets, a most generous heart.
I was with the Saracens and with the Seres.
I was with the Greeks and with the Finns and
with Caesar,
who had festive cities in his power,
riches, treasures, and the realm of Wales.
I was with the Scots and with the Picts and with
the Scridefinns.
I was with the Bretons and with the Leons and
with the Lombards,
with the heathens and with the heroes, and with
the Hundings.
I was with the Israelites and with the Assyrians,
with the Hebrews and with the Indians and with
the Egyptians.
I was with the Medes and with the Persians and
with the Myrgings,

and with the Mofdings, and against the
    Myrgings,
and with the Amothings. I was with the East-
    Thuringians
and with the Eols and with the Ests and with the
    Idumings.
    And I was with Eormanric all the time,
where the king of the Goths treated me
    graciously;
he, ruler of the cities, gave me a ring
in which there was reckoned to be six hundred
pieces of pure gold counted in shillings;
I gave that into the keeping of Eadgils,
to my protector, when I came home,
as meed to the loved one, lord of the Myrgings,
for he granted me land, my father's estate.
And Eadwine's daughter, Ealhhild, a queen
noble in majesty, then gave me another.
Her praise was bruited through many lands,
when in song I had to tell
where under heaven I knew best
a gold-adorned queen grant gifts.
When Scilling and I with clear voice raised
the song before our victorious lord –
loud to the lyre our lay resounded –
then many men, proud of mind,
who knew well, declared in words
they never had heard a better song.
    Thence all through the land of the Goths
I fared; the best of comrades always sought,
such were the household of Eormanric.
I sought Hethca and Beadeca, and the Herelings.
I sought Emerca and Fridla, and East-Gota,
the wise and good father of Unwen.
I sought Secca and Becca, Seafola and Theodric,
Heathoric and Sifeca, Hlithe and Incgentheow.

I sought Eadwine and Elsa, Ægelmund and
    Hungar,
and the proud band of the Withmyrgings.
I sought Wulfhere and Wyrmhere: not often was
    there rest from war
when the Goths with strong swords
were forced to defend their ancient domain
against Attila's folk by Vistula-wood.
I sought Rædhere and Rondhere, Rumstan and
    Gislhere,
Withergield and Freotheric and Wudga and
    Hama;
those were not the worst of comrades,
though I should name them last of all.
Full often from that band flew screaming,
the whistling spear against hostile hosts;
there Wudga and Hama, wanderers, had sway
over men and women with twisted gold.
So I have always found it in my wayfaring
that he is dearest to land-dwellers
to whom God grants dominion over men
to hold as long as he lives here.'
    Roving thus, as is their destiny,
men's minstrels wander over many lands;
they tell their need, speak words of thanks;
likewise, south or north, they find some one
skilled in song, generous in gifts,
who wishes to exalt his fame before his retinue,
do heroic deeds, till light and life
in ruin fall together: has renown,
gains enduring glory under heaven.

translated by Louis J. Rodrigues

[1921]

The Negro Speaks of Rivers

I've known rivers:
I've known rivers ancient as the world and older
    than the flow of human blood in human veins.

My soul has grown deep like the rivers.

I bathed in the Euphrates when dawns were
    young.
I built my hut near the Congo and it lulled me to
    sleep.
I looked upon the Nile and raised the pyramids
    above it.
I heard the singing of the Mississippi when Abe
    Lincoln went down to New Orleans, and I've
    seen its muddy bosom turn all golden in the
    sunset.

I've known rivers:
Ancient, dusky rivers.

My soul has grown deep like the rivers.

ANONYMOUS

[traditional]

The Bonnie Earl of Moray

Ye Highlands and ye Lawlands,
    Oh! where hae ye been?
They hae slain the Earl of Moray,
    And hae laid him on the green.

Now wae be to thee, Huntly,
    And wherefore did you sae?
I bade you bring him wi' you,
    But forbade you him to slay.

He was a braw gallant,
    And he rid at the ring;
And the bonnie Earl of Moray,
    Oh! he might hae been a king.

He was a braw gallant,
    And he play'd at the ba';
And the bonnie Earl of Moray
    Was the flower amang them a'.

He was a braw gallant,
    And he play'd at the glove;
And the bonnie Earl of Moray,
    Oh! he was the Queen's luve.

Oh! lang will his lady
    Look owre the castle Doune,
Ere she see the Earl of Moray
    Come sounding thro' the toun.

WALLACE STEVENS

[1954]   The World as Meditation

J'ai passé trop de temps à travailler mon violon, à voyager.
Mais l'exercice essentiel du compositeur – la méditation – rien
ne l'a jamais suspendu en moi . . . Je vis un rêve permanent, qui
ne s'arrête ni nuit ni jour.

GEORGES ENESCO

Is it Ulysses that approaches from the east,
The interminable adventurer? The trees are
    mended.
That winter is washed away. Someone is moving

On the horizon and lifting himself up above it.
A form of fire approaches the cretonnes of
    Penelope,
Whose mere savage presence awakens the world
    in which she dwells.

She has composed, so long, a self with which to
    welcome him,
Companion to his self for her, which she
    imagined,
Two in a deep-founded sheltering, friend and
    dear friend.

The trees had been mended, as an essential
    exercise
In an inhuman meditation, larger than her own.
No winds like dogs watched over her at night.

She wanted nothing he could not bring her by
    coming alone.
She wanted no fetchings. His arms would be her
    necklace
And her belt, the final fortune of their desire.

But was it Ulysses? Or was it only the warmth of
    the sun
On her pillow? The thought kept beating in her
    like her heart.
The two kept beating together. It was only day.

It was Ulysses and it was not. Yet they had met,
Friend and dear friend and a planet's
    encouragement.
The barbarous strength within her would never
    fail.

She would talk a little to herself as she combed
    her hair,
Repeating his name with its patient syllables,
Never forgetting him that kept coming
    constantly so near.

[1933]   ## The Truly Great

I think continually of those who were truly great.
Who, from the womb, remembered the soul's
    history
Through corridors of light, where the hours are
    suns,
Endless and singing. Whose lovely ambition
Was that their lips, still touched with fire,
Should tell of the Spirit, clothed from head to foot
    in song.
And who hoarded from the Spring branches
The desires falling across their bodies like
    blossoms.

What is precious, is never to forget
The essential delight of the blood drawn from
    ageless springs
Breaking through rocks in worlds before our earth.
Never to deny its pleasure in the morning simple
    light
Nor its grave evening demand for love.
Never to allow gradually the traffic to smother
With noise and fog, the flowering of the spirit.

Near the snow, near the sun, in the highest fields,
See how these names are fêted by the waving
    grass
And by the streamers of white cloud
And whispers of wind in the listening sky.
The names of those who in their lives fought for
    life,
Who wore at their hearts the fire's centre.
Born of the sun, they travelled a short while
    toward the sun
And left the vivid air signed with their honour.

JOHN MARSTON

[1598]   ## To Everlasting Oblivion

Thou mighty gulf, insatiate cormorant,
Deride me not, though I seem petulant
To fall into thy chops. Let others pray
Forever their fair poems flourish may.
But as for me, hungry Oblivion,
Devour me quick, accept my orison,
  My earnest prayers, which do importune thee,
  With gloomy shade of thy still empery
  To veil both me and my rude poesy.

Far worthier lines in silence of thy state
Do sleep securely, free from love or hate,
From which this living ne'er can be exempt,
But whilst it breathes will hate and fury tempt.
Then close his eyes with thy all-dimming hand,
Which not right glorious actions can withstand.
Peace, hateful tongues, I now in silence pace;
Unless some hound do wake me from my place,
  I with this sharp, yet well-meant poesy,
  Will sleep secure, right free from injury
  Of cankered hate or rankest villainy.

THOMAS HARDY

[1917]   ## Afterwards

When the Present has latched its postern behind
    my tremulous stay,
  And the May month flaps its glad green leaves
    like wings,
Delicate-filmed as new-spun silk, will the
    neighbours say,
  'He was a man who used to notice such
    things'?

If it be in the dusk when, like an eyelid's
    soundless blink,
  The dewfall-hawk comes crossing the shades
    to alight
Upon the wind-warped upland thorn, a gazer
    may think,
  'To him this must have been a familiar sight.'

If I pass during some nocturnal blackness, mothy
    and warm,
  When the hedgehog travels furtively over the
    lawn,
One may say, 'He strove that such innocent
    creatures should come to no harm,
  But he could do little for them; and now he is
    gone.'

If, when hearing that I have been stilled at last,
    they stand at the door,
  Watching the full-starred heavens that
    winter sees,
Will this thought rise on those who will meet my
    face no more,
  'He was one who had an eye for such
    mysteries'?

And will any say when my bell of quittance is
    heard in the gloom,
  And a crossing breeze cuts a pause in its
    outrollings,
Till they rise again, as they were a new bell's
    boom,
  'He hears it not now, but used to notice such
    things'?

EMILY DICKINSON

[c.1863]   ## 'Because I could not stop for Death'

Because I could not stop for Death –
He kindly stopped for me –
The Carriage held but just Ourselves –
And Immortality.

We slowly drove – He knew no haste
And I had put away
My labor and my leisure too,
For His Civility –

We passed the School, where Children strove
At Recess – in the Ring –
We passed the Fields of Gazing Grain –
We passed the Setting Sun –

Or rather – He passed Us –
The Dews drew quivering and chill –
For only Gossamer, my Gown –
My Tippet – only Tulle –

We paused before a House that seemed
A Swelling of the Ground –
The Roof was scarcely visible –
The Cornice – in the Ground –

Since then – 'tis Centuries – and yet
Feels shorter than the Day
I first surmised the Horses' Heads
Were toward Eternity –

JOHN DRYDEN

[1700] *from* The Secular Masque

| | MOMUS: | All, all of a piece throughout: |

MOMUS: All, all of a piece throughout:
     (*Pointing to Diana.*)

Secular: celebrated once in an age, here referring to the turn of the century

     Thy chase had a beast in view;
     (*To Mars.*)
     Thy wars brought nothing about;
     (*To Venus.*)
     Thy lovers were all untrue.

JANUS: 'Tis well an old age is out.

CHRONOS: And time to begin a new.

CHORUS: All, all of a piece throughout;
     Thy chase had a beast in view:
     Thy wars brought nothing about;
     Thy lovers were all untrue.
     'Tis well an old age is out,
     And time to begin a new.
     (*Dance of huntsmen, nymphs, warriors, and lovers.*)

AFTERWORD: MEMORISING POEMS *by* Ted Hughes

There are many reasons for learning poems. But memorising them should be like a game. It should be a pleasure.

For those of us who need help (nearly all of us), the method most commonly used in schools is *learning by rote*. This is only one of several memorising techniques. And for most people it is the least effective. The tedium of learning by rote was long thought to be a good thing in English classrooms: disciplinary and character-building. But the cost can be heavy, since it creates an aversion to learning and to poetry.

Those who dislike rote-learning yet still wish to gain the many powers that come with knowledge can choose from an array of other less laborious, more productive, more amusing techniques.

These techniques systematically exploit the brain's natural tactics for remembering. Recently I heard one sound technician in a theatre questioning another about the letters GBH, which kept appearing in some music-schedule for a play. It was explained: GBH was one of the actors. But instead of trying to remember the actor's name, the technician had simply dubbed him Ginger Beer Hair. This is the sort of thing we all do almost without thinking about it.

But why should the actor's name be so forgettable, while the idea of his head being a foaming mass of Ginger Beer Hair is instantly and without effort unforgettable – and amusing into the bargain?

One of the brain's spontaneous techniques for fixing anything in the conscious memory, in other words for making it easy to recall, is to connect it with a vivid visual image. And the more absurd, exaggerated, grotesque that image is, the more unforgettable is the thing to which we connect it. One easy technique for memorising poems uses visualised images in this way.

Basically, this particular technique is good for memorising lists. For example:

A peaty burn (stream)
A brown horse
An avalanche
A roaring lion
A hen-coop
A comb
A fleece
Foam
A flute
A lake
Home

might be dealt with as follows:

For 'peaty burn' it might be enough simply to imagine, like a frame in a colour film, a dark torrential mountain stream coming down among boulders. But to make sure it is 'burn' and not 'stream' that you remember, it might be better to imagine the stream actually burning, sending up flames and smoke: a cascade of dark fire, scorching the banks.

The next item, 'brown horse', now has to be connected to the burning stream. The most obvious shortcut is to put the horse in the torrent of fire, trying to scramble out – possibly with its mane in flames.

The next item, 'avalanche', now has to be connected to the brown horse. One easy solution would be to imagine the stream as an avalanche, with the horse galloping among the big rolling rocks, its mane smoking.

The next item, 'a roaring lion', has to be connected to the avalanche. The torrent of boulders could be imagined pouring down onto the head of a huge sleepy lion, who wakes up shaking them from his mane, and roaring.

The next item, 'a hen-coop', has to be connected to that lion. Again the short cut is to jam the lion inside the hen-coop – perhaps chewing the hen.

The next item, 'a comb', has to be connected to the coop. The lion has burst from the coop and gone. So now you construct a rickety, awkward, great comb out of the splintered slats of the hen-coop – try combing your own hair with it.

And so on. If each image is 'photographed' mentally, as on a screen, it will not be forgotten easily. And each image will bring on the next, which has been connected to it. Even when you are remembering a very long list, the procedure is quite small-scale and automatic, because you are never remembering more than one connection at a time, and each connection provides you with the next. The rolling rocks produce – surprise – the lion. The lion produces – out of nowhere, and against all expectations – the hen-coop. The hen-coop produces – can it be right? – the ridiculous wooden comb.

Theoretically, if each connecting image is visualised success-fully, the list can be endless, because each step will always produce the next.

The same technique is used by professional memorisers for mem-orising poems. Some readers might have recognised the list above. The first two lines of Hopkins' poem 'Inversnaid' go:

This darksome burn, horseback brown,
His rollrock highroad roaring down

Using the simple technique described, the lines can be memorised phrase by phrase by converting the poem to a kind of list: the same list as above, now based on the words of the poem.

The first item, 'This darksome burn', is connected to that image of a flaming, smoky mountain torrent of dark fire.

Next item: 'horseback brown' is converted to a brown horse simply, and the brown horse is connected to the 'burn' by seeing him in the torrent, as above, trying to scramble out of the dark flames and up the bank.

Next item: 'His rollrock highroad' is converted to that avalanche of big rocks coming down a steep rough road. This image is con-nected to the brown horse more painfully by visualising the horse high-stepping among the colliding boulders, trying to save its thin legs.

Next item: 'roaring' – a word that could easily be replaced by others in this position – is fixed by converting it to the huge lion roaring. The lion is then connected to that previous image, the avalanche, by letting the whole torrent of rocks pour down on its head, waking it from sleep and making it roar, as it shakes the boulders from its mane.

And so on, through the next two lines:

In coop and in comb the fleece of his foam
Flutes and low to the lake falls home.

In each case the visual image will be enough to do two things: to bring back the verbal phrase in which it is now rooted, and to bring on the next image. Once visually fixed, whenever the sequence is started with the image of the mountain torrent of dark fire the whole film will replay itself, and the words of the poem will come with it as the sound-track.

Hopkins's poem is made up of solid objects. With poems composed in more abstract language the memoriser has to use more ingenuity – but since anything is permitted a way can always be found.

Some may meet a difficulty in releasing the imagination enough to produce the visual images for the cartoon. But practice helps. The release of playful imagination also releases energy, and the brain soon becomes skilful at what it enjoys.

Others may feel reluctant to add such an arbitrary cartoon accompaniment to the sacred words of a solemn poem. But the cartoon is only a first stage. The whole point is to get the poem, by any means, foul or fair, into the head. After a few replays, the words enter the long-term memory, and the cartoon begins to fall away.

In this description I have assumed that the memoriser's mental film of unforgettable images will always supply the perfect wording of each phrase. How does this happen, if each unforgettable image is anchored, as a rule, to no more than one key word in the phrase to which it corresponds? Is that one key word really enough to trigger the memory of all the other words in the phrase? In practice, for most people, where the text being learned is a poem worth learning, the answer is yes. Conscious use of visual imagination brings us to the key-word – but at that point another kind of imagination takes over. Without conscious effort, what then comes to our help is musical or audial memory. In many people, the audial memory is much stronger than the visual. It is wide open to any distinct pattern of sounds. It likes such patterns, and has an extraordinary ability to hang on to them whether we want them or not – as with musical melodies.

The closest thing to a musical melody in a line of verse is the pattern of sounds made by the sequence of syllables. That pattern includes rhythm and overall inflection along with the alternation of vowels and consonants. The stronger the pattern is, the more memorable the line will be. I remember back in 1959 Heinz held a competition for a catch-phrase to advertise their beans. Following the precedent of old oral poetry, using alliteration, assonance and internal rhyme, I came up with 'Whoever minds how he dines demands Heinz'. I realised this was cumbersome, but I still couldn't get it out of my head, so I took it no further, and sent it in. What they ended up with, of course, was the inspired 'Beanz meanz Heinz' – using exactly the same principle as I had, but in that simpler, more concentrated pattern.

Even nonsense becomes unforgettable if the sound pattern is strong enough. The line in Wilfred Owen's poem 'Strange Meeting'

None will break ranks though nations trek from progress

is not exactly meaningless, but is so rhetorically overblown that only two things justify its place in the poem: it sounds magnificent and it is unforgettable. The interplay of 'breakra-', 'trekfro-' and 'progress' is glaringly contrived but, as in the old Welsh poetry from which Owen drew the system, it does what it is meant to do – it roots itself directly in the nerves of the ear.

These examples rely on a dominant pattern in the interwoven texture of the syllables. But a line can be just as unforgettable where the dominant pattern is one of rhythm, as in 'Tom, Tom, the piper's son'. Or where it is one of inflection, as in: 'Och, Johnny, I hardly knew ye!' which Yeats called the most passionate phrase in the language.

Where lines of verse are less strikingly patterned, it may be that the audial imagination grasps them less tenaciously, less automatically. But in most verse worth remembering, the lines always yield some kind of pattern, though often the pattern is hidden, and not so much 'heard' as 'sensed through hearing'. In our own language verbal sounds are organically linked to the vast system of root-meanings and related associations, deep in the subsoil of psychological life, beyond our immediate awareness or conscious manipulation. It is the distinction of poetry to create strong patterns in these hidden meanings as well as in the clearly audible sounds. The hidden patterns are, if anything, much the stronger. The audial memory picks up those patterns in the depths from what it hears at the surface. And they too are difficult to forget. We feel them almost as a physical momentum of inevitability, a current of syntactical force purposefully directed like the flight of an arrow in the dark. What is essential, then, in memorising verse, is to keep the audial faculty wide open, and not so much look at the words as listen for them – listening as widely, deeply and keenly as possible, testing every whisper on the air in the echo-chamber of your whole body, as you bend more narrowly over the job of making that film of brightly-coloured images.

Memory techniques of the kind I have described, using strongly visualised imagery, were invented in the ancient world and became the basis of learning in the Christian Middle Ages, when books were scarce. They were taken for granted, regarded as essential, and developed further by such giants of learning as St Thomas Aquinas, the angelic Doctor of the Catholic Church who has been called the patron saint of memory systems, and who made the unforgettable remark: 'Man cannot understand without images.'

In England in the seventeenth century, the Puritan/Protestant ascendancy of the Civil War made a serious bid to eradicate imagery from all aspects of life – methodically destroying the religious imagery of churches and forbidding the imaginative play of drama. The same spirit also banished from the schools the old-established memory techniques that used 'imagery' and officially replaced them with 'learning by rote'. The discarded methods, dimly associated with paganism and Catholicism, were soon forgotten. If any attempt was made to reintroduce them, they were dismissed as 'tricks' and 'cheating'. 'Learning by rote' became the norm.

ACKNOWLEDGEMENTS

We wish to thank our editor, Christopher Reid; also Anthony Smith, President of Magdalen College, Oxford, for his hospitality.

S.H., T.H.

The editors and publishers gratefully acknowledge permission to reprint copyright material in this book as follows.

W. H. AUDEN: Faber & Faber Ltd for 'Law Like Love' from *Collected Poems* (1976). GEORGE BARKER: Faber & Faber Ltd for 'A Sparrow's Feather' from *Collected Poems* (1962). SAMUEL BECKETT: to Calder Educational Trust for 'What Is The Word', included in *Collected Poems 1930–1989* by Samuel Beckett, *As the Story Was Told* (late prose and other work) by Samuel Beckett. PATRICIA BEER: Carcanet Press Ltd for 'The Postilion has been Struck by Lightning' from *Collected Poems* (1988). JOHN BERRYMAN: Faber & Faber Ltd for Songs 4, 14, 63, 67, 75 from *The Dream Songs*. JOHN BETJEMAN: John Murray (Publishers) Ltd for 'Ireland's Own or, The Burial of Thomas Moore' from *Collected Poems* (1979). ELIZABETH BISHOP: Farrar, Straus & Giroux Inc for 'At the Fishhouses' from *The Complete Poems 1927–1979* by Elizabeth Bishop, copyright © 1979, 1983 by Alice Helen Methfessel. LOUISE BOGAN: Farrar, Straus & Giroux Inc for 'Question in a Field' from *The Blue Estuaries* by Louise Bogan, copyright © 1968 by Louise Bogan. GEORGE MACKAY BROWN: John Murray (Publishers) Ltd for 'The Stone Cross' and 'Deor' from *Selected Poems*. BASIL BUNTING: Oxford University Press for extract from 'Briggflatts' from *The Complete Poems of Basil Bunting*, edited by Richard Caddel (1994). JAMES CARNEY (translator): Colin Smythe Ltd, publishers, for 'Adze-Head' from *Medieval Irish Lyrics* (Dolmen Press, 1967). CHARLES CAUSLEY: David Higham Associates Ltd for 'Eden Rock' from *Collected Poems* (Macmillan, 1992). JOHN CLARE: Curtis Brown Group Ltd, London, for 'The Badger' from *Selected Poems and Prose of John Clare*, edited by Eric Robinson and Geoffrey Summerfield (Oxford University Press, 1967), copyright © Eric Robinson, 1967. AUSTIN CLARKE: R. Dardis Clarke (21 Pleasants Street, Dublin 8, Republic of Ireland) for 'The Straying Student' from *Collected Poems* (Dolmen Press/Oxford University Press, 1974). HART CRANE: Liveright Publishing Corporation for 'Repose of Rivers' from *Complete Poems of Hart Crane*, edited by Marc Simon, copyright 1933, © 1958, 1966 by Liveright Publishing Corporation, copyright © 1986 by Marc Simon. IAIN CRICHTON SMITH (translator): Carcanet Press Ltd for extract from 'Clanranald's Galley' from *The Poetry of Scotland*, edited by Roderick Watson (Edinburgh University Press,

JONES: Faber & Faber Ltd for extract from *In Parenthesis* (1937). GWYN JONES (translator) for extract from 'Hateful Old Age' (first published in 'The Angry Old Men', *Scandinavian Studies*, Seattle, Washington, 1965). PATRICK KAVANAGH: the Trustees of the Estate of Patrick Kavanagh, c/o Peter Fallon, Literary Agent, Loughcrew, Oldcastle, Co. Meath, Ireland, for extracts from 'The Great Hunger' from *Collected Poems* (1964). WELDON KEES: Faber & Faber Ltd for 'The Umbrella' from *Collected Poems*. SIDNEY KEYES: Routledge Ltd for 'The Walking Woman' from *Collected Poems*, edited by Michael Meyer (1945). THOMAS KINSELLA (translator): for 'The rath in front of the oakwood' (Anon) from *The New Oxford Book of Irish Verse* (1986). AEMILIA LANYER: Oxford University Press Inc for extract from 'Salve Deus Rex Judaorum' from *The Poems of Aemilia Lanyer*, edited by Susanne Woods (1993). PHILIP LARKIN: The Marvell Press, England and Australia, for 'Wedding-Wind' from *The Less Deceived*. D. H. LAWRENCE: Laurence Pollinger Ltd and the Estate of Frieda Lawrence Ravagli for 'Bavarian Gentians' from *The Complete Poems of D. H. Lawrence*. IRVING LAYTON: McClelland & Stewart Inc, Toronto, for 'Cat Dying in Autumn' from *Collected Poems of Irving Layton*. ROBERT LOWELL: Faber & Faber Ltd for 'Waking Early Sunday Morning' from *Near the Ocean* (1967). NORMAN MACCAIG: Random House UK Ltd for 'Summer Farm' from *Collected Poems* (Chatto & Windus, 1990). HUGH MACDIARMID: Carcanet Press Ltd for 'The Bonnie Broukit Bairn' from *Complete Poems*. CLAUDE MCKAY: The Archives of Claude McKay, Carl Cowl, Administrator, for 'The Harlem Dancer' from *Selected Poems* (Twayne Publishers, 1953). SORLEY MACLEAN: Carcanet Press Ltd for 'Hallaig' from *Collected Poems* (1989). LOUIS MACNEICE: David Higham Associates Ltd for 'Meeting Point' from *Collected Poems* (Faber, 1966). JOHN MASEFIELD: The Society of Authors as the literary representative of the Estate of John Masefield for 'Cargoes' from *Selected Poems* (Heinemann, 1978). EDNA ST VINCENT MILLAY: Elizabeth Barnett, literary executor, for 'The Princess Recalls Her One Adventure' from *Collected Poems* (Harper Collins), copyright © 1939, 1967 by Edna St Vincent Millay and Norma Millay Ellis. MARIANNE MOORE: Faber & Faber Ltd for 'A Grave' from *The Complete Poems* (1984). EDWIN MORGAN: Carcanet Press Ltd for 'The Unspoken' from *Poems of Thirty Years* (1982). HOWARD NEMEROV: Margaret Nemerov for 'I Only am Escaped Alone to Tell Thee' from *The Collected Poems of Howard Nemerov* (University of Chicago Press, 1977). NORMAN NICHOLSON: David Higham Associates Ltd for 'The Tame Hare' from *Collected Poems* (Faber, 1994). FRANK O'HARA: Carcanet Press Ltd for 'A Step Away from Them' from *Collected Poems* (1991). P. K. PAGE: to the author for 'Photos of a Salt Mine' (first published in *Contemporary Verse*, 1951). EZRA POUND: Faber & Faber Ltd for 'The Seafarer' (Anon), translated by Ezra Pound, from *Collected Shorter Poems*, and 'Canto I' from *The Cantos* (1954). BURTON RAFFEL (translator): Yale University Press for 'The

Dream of the Rood' from *Poems and Prose from the Old English* (forthcoming). DUDLEY RANDALL: to the author for 'Booker T. and W.E.B.' from *Poem and Counterpoint* (Broadside Press), copyright © 1966 Margaret Danner and Dudley Randall. JOHN CROWE RANSOM: Carcanet Press Ltd for 'Captain Carpenter' from *Selected Poems* (1970). HENRY REED: Oxford University Press for 'Naming of Parts' from *Collected Poems*, edited by Jon Stallworthy (1991). LAURA RIDING: Board of Literary Management of the late Laura (Riding) Jackson for 'The Wind Suffers' from *The Poems of Laura Riding* (Manchester: Carcanet; New York: Persea, 1980). EDWIN ARLINGTON ROBINSON: Simon & Schuster Inc for 'Miniver Cheevy' from *Collected Poems of Edwin Arlington Robinson* (New York: Macmillan, 1937). LOUIS J. RODRIGUES (translator): for 'Widsith' from *Anglo-Saxon Verse Charms, Maxims & Heroic Legends* (Anglo-Saxon Books), copyright © Louis J. Rodrigues, 1993. THEODORE ROETHKE: Faber & Faber Ltd for 'The Waking' from *The Collected Poems of Theodore Roethke*. STEVIE SMITH: James MacGibbon for 'The River God' from *The Collected Poems of Stevie Smith* (Penguin Twentieth Century Classics). BERNARD SPENCER: Oxford University Press for 'Behaviour of Money' from *Collected Poems*, edited by Roger Bowen (1981). STEPHEN SPENDER: Faber & Faber Ltd for 'The Truly Great' from *Collected Poems 1928–1985* (1985). JAMES STEPHENS: The Society of Authors as the Literary Representative of the Estate of James Stephens for 'A Glass of Beer' (David O'Bruadair) from *James Stephens: A Selection* (Macmillan, 1982). WALLACE STEVENS: Faber & Faber Ltd for 'The World as Meditation' from *The Collected Poems of Wallace Stevens* (1984). ALLEN TATE: Farrar, Straus & Giroux Inc for 'The Swimmers' from *Collected Poems 1919–1976* by Allen Tate, copyright © 1977 by Allen Tate. DYLAN THOMAS: David Higham Associates Ltd for 'Fern Hill' from *The Poems* (Dent, 1971). R. S. THOMAS: The Orion Publishing Group Ltd for 'Here' from *Collected Poems 1945–1990* (Dent, 1993). DERICK THOMSON and WILLIAM NEIL (translators): for 'O rosary that recalled my tear' (Aithbhreac Inghean Corcadil), and 'Song to the Foxes' (Duncan Ban Macintyre) from *The Poetry of Scotland*, edited by Roderick Watson (Edinburgh University Press, 1995). ROBERT PENN WARREN: William Morris Agency Inc for 'Tell Me a Story' from *New and Selected Poems 1923–1985* (Random House Inc., 1985). RICHARD WILBUR: Faber & Faber Ltd for 'Piazza di Spagna, Early Morning' from *New and Collected Poems*. SIR IFOR WILLIAMS (translator): The Governing Board of the School of Celtic Studies of the Dublin Institute for Advanced Studies for 'I am Taliesin. I sing perfect metre' from *The Poems of Taliesin*. WILLIAM CARLOS WILLIAMS: Carcanet Press Ltd for 'Pictures from Breughel' from *Collected Poems*. W. B. YEATS: A. P. Watt Ltd on behalf of Michael Yeats for 'Long-legged Fly' from *Collected Poems* (Macmillan, 1981). ANDREW YOUNG: The Andrew Young Estate for 'A Dead Mole' from *The Poetical Works of Andrew Young* (Secker & Warburg, 1985).

574

INDEX OF POETS

The badger grunting on his woodland track 423
The batalis and the man I will discrive 458
The city squats on my back 94
The curfew tolls the knell of parting day 403
The darkness crumbles away 222
The Day's grown old, the fainting Sun 116
The King sits in Dunfermline toun 37
The lanky hank of a she in the inn over there 266
The men of my tribe would treat him as game 451
The moon rolls over the roof and falls behind 323
The old farmer, nearing death, asked 88
The old woman sits on a bench before the door and
    quarrels 148
The Owl and the Pussy-cat went to sea 101
The *rath* in front of the oak wood 547
The sea is calm to-night 4
The son of the king of Moy in midsummer 125
The stranger came from Narromine and made his little
    joke 246
The thirsty Earth soaks up the Rain 367
The time is not remote, when I 370
The wave, over the wave, a weird thing I saw 119
The willows carried a slow sound 40
The wind blew all my wedding-day 449
'The wind doth blow today, my love' 532
The wind suffers of blowing 533
The window is nailed and boarded 285
Then he spurred Gringolet, and took up the trail 485
Then, on the headland, the Geats prepared a mighty
    pyre 482
There was a man of double deed 304
There was a roaring in the wind all night 46
There was a sound of revelry by night 465
There was a valley thicke 155
There was this empty birdcage in the garden 234
There's a hard wind yet and a sad road 451
They are all gone into the world of light! 519
They are waiting for me somewhere beyond Eden
    Rock 298
They flee from me, that sometime did me seek 522
They tell me Seven Sisters in New Orleans, that can really
    fix a man up right 348

589